TRANSPORTATION, ENERGY, AND POWER TECHNOLOGY

TRANSPORTATION, ENERGY, AND POWER TECHNOLOGY

ANTHONY E. SCHWALLER

 DELMAR PUBLISHERS INC.®

DELMAR TECHNOLOGY SERIES

NOTICE TO THE READER

Publisher does not warrant or guarantee any of the products described herein or perform any independent analysis in connection with any of the product information contained herein. Publisher does not assume, and expressly disclaims, any obligation to obtain and include information other than that provided to it by the manufacturer.

The reader is expressly warned to consider and adopt all safety precautions that might be indicated by the activities described herein and to avoid all potential hazards. By following the instructions contained herein, the reader willingly assumes all risks in connection with such instructions.

The publisher makes no representation or warranties of any kind, including but not limited to, the warranties of fitness for particular purpose or merchantability, nor are any such representations implied with respect to the material set forth herein, and the publisher takes no responsibility with respect to such material. The publisher shall not be liable for any special, consequential or exemplary damages resulting, in whole or in part, from the readers' use of, or reliance upon, this material.

DEDICATION

The author would like to dedicate this book to his sons, Matthew and Joshua, for their continued support and understanding during the writing of this textbook.

COVER CREDITS

GM Sunraycer photo: *Courtesy of General Motors Corporation*
Gas pipeline photo: *Courtesy of CSX Corporation*
"Aerospace Plane" by Stan H. Stokes: *Courtesy of NASA*
Engine photo: *Courtesy of Chevrolet Motor Division, General Motors Corporation*

DELMAR STAFF
Executive Editor: Wes Coulter
Associate Editor: Cynthia Haller
Project Editor: Eleanor Isenhart
Design Coordinator: Susan C. Mathews
Production Coordinator: Linda Helfrich

For information, address Delmar Publishers Inc.,
2 Computer Drive West, Box 15-015
Albany, New York 12212

COPYRIGHT © 1989
BY DELMAR PUBLISHERS INC.

CONTENTS CREDITS

Section One Photo:	*Courtesy of Grumman Corporation, 1988*
Section Two Photo:	*Courtesy of Bombardier, Inc. Mass Transit Division, Quebec, Canada*
Section Three Photo:	*Courtesy of New York Power Authority*
Section Four Photo:	*Courtesy of Rob Van Stone for Volvo*
Section Five Photo:	*Courtesy of General Motors*

Printed in the United States of America
Published simultaneously in Canada
by Nelson Canada
A Division of International Thomson Limited

10 9 8 7 6 5 4 3 2 1

Library of Congress Cataloging-in-Publication Data

Schwaller, Anthony E.
  Transportation, energy, and power technology /
Anthony E. Schwaller.
    p.   cm.
  Includes index.
  ISBN 0-8273-3227-0.   ISBN 0-8273-3228-9. (Instructor's guide)
  1. Transportation engineering.   2. Power resources.
  3. Mechanical engineering.   I. Title
  TA1145.S36 1989   88-25599
  629.04--dc 19   CIP

CONTENTS

SECTION THREE
ENERGY TECHNOLOGY   149

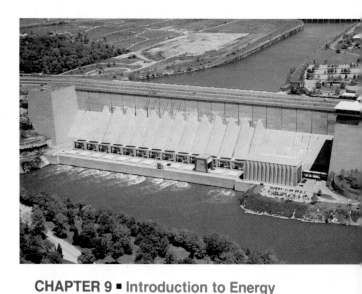

SECTION FOUR
POWER TECHNOLOGY   279

SECTION FIVE
THE FUTURE 379

PREFACE

THE IMPORTANCE OF TRANSPORTATION IN OUR SOCIETY

We live in a society that is reliant upon many forms of technology. These technologies give citizens choices for improving their lives. Transportation is one of the most important of these technologies. Transportation technology has become integrated into every part of our lives on a daily basis. Because of this, most citizens today take transportation technology for granted. Due to the increased ease of moving people and products, our society has changed considerably. We are a much more mobile and transient society. Today, millions of people, products, and goods are transported continuously to keep our economy and society running efficiently.

Energy and power technology play an important part in keeping our transportation systems operating smoothly. Various forms of energy are needed to produce the correct type of power required to move people and products within our society. In addition, energy technology has taken on an increased importance within our society. Energy is not only used in transportation technology, but is also part of all other technological systems. Since the oil embargo of 1973, our society has become keenly aware of the need to develop more efficient and economical energy systems in all aspects of our lives.

SCOPE OF THE TEXT

Transportation technology is a composite of many other technologies. These technologies are all integrated and interrelate with one another. To study the total picture of transportation technology, both energy and power technology must also be studied.

Transportation, Energy, and Power Technology is a text designed for students to learn the basic concepts and principles of transportation, energy, and power. It is designed to introduce all of the major scientific and mathematical concepts supporting transportation, energy, and power. In each chapter, various scientific and mathematical principles are presented along with the technological content.

The content of this textbook is subdivided into five major sections with 20 chapters. These sections include:

Section One   Introduction to Transportation, Energy, and Power (Chapter 1)
Section Two   Transportation Technology (Chapters 2-8)
Section Three   Energy Technology (Chapters 9-14)
Section Four   Power Technology (Chapters 15-19)
Section Five   The Future (Chapter 20)

SPECIAL FEATURES

This text has been developed to include a number of learning aides to help the student study transportation, energy, and power technology. Special features include:

- **Safety Guidelines.** Highlight general safety rules and procedures required in any transportation, energy, and power technology laboratory.
- **Objectives.** Show the expected learning that will take place as a result of studying the chapter.
- **Key Terms.** Highlight important vocabulary to be learned. Definitions are provided in the Glossary at the back of the textbook for all key terms.

- **Chapter Introductions.** Provide statements of the intent and overall content of each chapter.
- **Colorful Art Program.** Illustrates concepts and shows current technologies, components, and systems.
- **Chapter Summaries.** Highlight the important concepts covered in each chapter.
- **Review.** Reinforces and tests readers' comprehension of content.
- **Boxed Articles.** Cover interesting topics drawn from the transportation, energy, and power industries. Each boxed article includes one or more photographs and descriptions of the topic.
- **Techlinks.** Show how transportation, energy, and power content correlates to math and science principles and to other areas of technology.
- **Chapter Activities.** Reinforce the technological concepts presented in a hands-on laboratory setting.
- **Glossary.** Provides definitions of all terms introduced in the chapters.
- **Mathematical Appendix.** Highlights all of the mathematical formulas discussed throughout the textbook.

ACKNOWLEDGMENTS

The author would like to thank several people who contributed to the completion of this textbook. Thanks should go to the staff at Delmar for their continued help, support, and encouragement during the writing of the manuscript. Special thanks should also go to Patricia Zak, who helped in preparation of the manuscript. In addition, the following individuals reviewed the prospectus and offered suggestions for improvement. Their assistance is appreciated.

Dr. Jane Smink, Chief Consultant
Industrial Arts/Technology Education
North Carolina Dept. of Public Instruction
Raleigh, NC

Allen Strouphauer
Teacher—Power & Transportation Computer
    Literacy
Joseph Stilwell Junior High
Jacksonville, FL

Bruce Barnes
Olson Junior High School
Bloomington, MN

Dennis Christensen, Curriculum Supervisor
The School Board of Broward County, Florida
Fort Lauderdale, FL

William E. Dugger, Jr.
Professor and Program Area Leader
    Technology Education
Virginia Polytechnic Institute and
    State University
Blacksburg, VA

M. James Bensen, Dean
School of Industry and Technology
University of Wisconsin Stout
Menomonie, WI

Tom Ryerson
Industry and Technology Education Supervisor
Dept. of Education
St. Paul, MN

Elazer Barnette
Dept. of Public Instruction
Raleigh, NC

Dr. Donald Lauda
Dean, School of Applied Arts & Sciences
California State University — Long Beach
Long Beach, CA

James R. Lees
Associate Professor
Kent State University
Kent, OH

Jerry Balistreri
Industrial Arts Supervisor
State Office of Education
Salt Lake City, UT

Paul Post
Ohio State University
Columbus, OH

John Hemmerly
Pickerington Middle School
Pickerington, OH

James J. Kirkwood, Ph.D.
Professor of Industry and Technology
Ball State University
Muncie, IN

Bill Wargo
Florida Dept. of Education
Tallahassee, FL

John Medlock
Florida Dept. of Education
Orlando, FL

Dr. W.A. Mayfield
Dept. of Technology
University of Texas
Tyler, TX

Myron Bender
Professor and Chairman
University of North Dakota
Dept. of Industrial Tech.
Grand Forks, ND

Dr. Richard Peterson
Dept. of Occupational Education
North Carolina State University
Raleigh, NC

Joe Logsdon, Consultant
Industrial Technology Education
Dept. of Education
Columbus, OH

A number of reviewers assisted by offering support and suggestions based upon an in-depth review of the manuscript. The author would like to extend his thanks to the following individuals for their excellent advice and help in shaping the final text.

Dennis Gallo
O'Fallon Township High School
O'Fallon, IL

Fred Posthuma
Westfield High School
Westfield, WI

Bob D'Agostino
Denbigh High School
Newport News, VA

Gary Shelhamer
Dryden Jr./Sr. High School
Dryden, NY

Charles Sweeting
State University College
Oswego, NY

Dave Pullias
Richardson Independent School District
Richardson, TX

ABOUT THE AUTHOR

Anthony E. Schwaller has been involved with transportation, energy, and power technology for many years, beginning as an automotive technician. He also worked as a technical trainer for General Motors in Detroit, Michigan. After leaving Detroit, he taught energy and power technology at Eastern Illinois University, Charleston, Illinois, and at St. Cloud State University, St. Cloud, Minnesota. He is currently serving both as a professor and administrator within the Department of Industrial Studies at St. Cloud State University.

The author received his B.S. and M.S. degrees from the University of Wisconsin-Stout, and his Ph.D. from Indiana State University. He is the author of three other textbooks, as well as more than 35 articles, and has presented some 40 papers and addresses at various conferences in the field of transportation, energy, and power technology.

SAFETY GUIDELINES

SAFETY GUIDELINES FOR THE TRANSPORTATION, ENERGY, AND POWER LABORATORY

Many safety rules and guidelines must be followed when working in any technology laboratory. Accidents often happen because laboratory rules are not followed. Common laboratory rules to follow in any transportation, energy, and power laboratory are:

1. Always wear safety glasses in and around the laboratory. Make sure the glasses fit comfortably and have side shields.
2. Make sure you know the location and operation of all fire extinguishers. Also, check them occasionally to make sure they have been inspected and are filled correctly.
3. Keep all flammable materials in nonflammable, explosion proof cabinets and containers.
4. Always wear protective gloves when working with cleaning chemicals, when grinding, and when working with hot metals.
5. Make sure you know the location of the first-aid kits in the laboratory. Also, check the contents occasionally to make sure there are sufficient first-aid materials available.
6. Always wear sound protection devices for your ears when working in areas where engines are operating.
7. Make sure you use proper lifting and carrying procedures for heavy parts. When lifting, get as close to the object as possible and keep your back straight. Remember to lift with your legs, not your back.
8. Good housekeeping is important to a safe laboratory. Always put all tools away, keep floor surfaces clean from grease, and keep all tools and equipment in proper working order.
9. When running engines in the laboratory, always remember to run the exhaust outside. Carbon monoxide could build-up and cause headaches, nausea, ringing in the ears, tired-

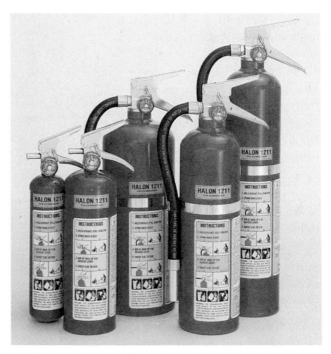

Courtesy of The General Fire Extinguisher Corporation

ness, and a fluttering heartbeat.
10. Always use proper clothing when working in any transportation, energy, and power laboratory.
11. When working with batteries, always guard against acid spills and splashes. Always have baking soda on hand to neutralize acid burns. Make sure there is an eyewash area in the lab to rinse and wash eyes.
12. Always use the proper tools for the job. If you are unsure of the correct and proper use of the tool, always check with your instructor first.
13. Many operations in a transportation, energy, and power laboratory have a *correct procedure list*. Always follow this list exactly to complete the job safely and correctly.
14. In most cases, parts should never be forced together. Parts are usually designed so that they assembly easily and without force.
15. Always remove all metal jewelry (rings, watches, and so on) when working with moving parts and electrical and mechanical components.

SPECIFIC SAFETY RULES

Many situations call for more specific safety rules, such as the following:

1. Always tighten all bolts and nuts with a torque wrench to the correct specifications.
2. Never use an air gun with high pressure to dry or spin roller bearings or ball bearings.
3. Many engine, transmission, and energy components have sharp metal corners. Always be careful not to cut your hands when lifting or moving these parts.
4. Many engine, transmission, and energy components are very heavy. Always use the proper lifting tools when moving these parts. Jack stands, block and tackles, hydraulic lifts, and so forth should be used as necessary to lift these parts.
5. Often, parts that are under tension need to be removed. Always be careful to account for this tension when removing parts and other objects from transportation components.
6. Certain transportation and energy components contain fluids that are under

pressure. Always be sure to release this pressure correctly before working on these components.

7. Gasoline and other fuels are very toxic when inhaled, and also dangerous to the skin and eyes. Be careful not to inhale these fumes, and always protect your skin from these fuels by washing with warm water to flush away the fuel. Also, never work on any electrical components when fuel has been spilled nearby. An explosion and/or fire may result.
8. Many transportation, energy, and power components have spinning parts, such as fans, motors and blades. Always be careful to protect your hands from these spinning objects.
9. Many components on transportation, energy, and power devices are very hot. Always be careful not to touch hot parts to prevent burning your hands and skin.
10. When batteries are charged and discharged, a hydrogen gas is often produced. Any small electrical arc could cause this gas to explode violently. Never disconnect any electrical wire near a charging or discharging battery.

Courtesy of Eagle Manufacturing Co. and Sellstrom Manufacturing Co.

Courtesy of Western Drinking Fountains, Emergency Equipment Division

INTRODUCTION TO TRANSPORTATION, ENERGY, AND POWER TECHNOLOGY

This section addresses transportation, energy, and power technology. Transportation is supported by energy systems and energy systems are further supported by power technology. Other technologies such as production and communications also require energy technology. The text is organized so that transportation (a major system of technology) is presented first. Then energy is addressed, followed by power technology. A systems model can be used to study all three of these technologies. As shown, the systems model includes input, process (including resources needed), output and impact, and feedback elements.

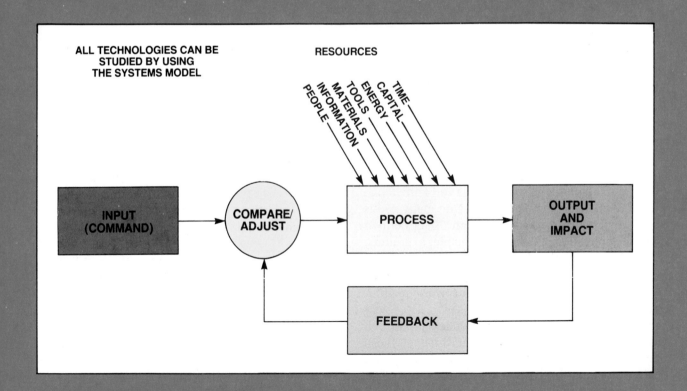

ALL TECHNOLOGIES CAN BE
STUDIED BY USING
THE SYSTEMS MODEL

RESOURCES

TIME
CAPITAL
ENERGY
TOOLS
MATERIALS
INFORMATION
PEOPLE

INPUT (COMMAND) → COMPARE/ADJUST → PROCESS → OUTPUT AND IMPACT → FEEDBACK

CHAPTER 1 ■ Transportation, Energy, and Power Technology

CHAPTER 1

Transportation, Energy, and Power Technology

OBJECTIVES

After reading this chapter, you will be able to:

■ Define *transportation, energy,* and *power,* and tell how they are interrelated.

■ Describe the systems approach to studying technology.

■ Explain how to make logical and sound decisions about technology.

■ Identify potential careers in transportation and power technology.

KEY TERMS

Technostructure	Process	Feedback Loop
Input	Output	Technological Impact

Introduction

Our society is made up of many systems of technology. *Technology* is defined as the knowledge used to change various resources into many goods and services used by a society. It can also be defined as the application of scientific principles to produce products needed by a particular society.

Many technological systems work together to form a total technostructure. The word *technostructure* means that technologies within a society are highly interrelated and dependent upon one another. This textbook is about three of these systems of technology: transportation, energy, and power technology.

Transportation over the past years has become an ever-increasing part of our lives. The transporta-tion revolution has taken place in the past 150 years or so. Transportation systems and networks help all of society to improve the quality of life. Generally, the more choices one has regarding transportation, the higher the quality of life that exists within that society.

Energy is also very important within our society. Energy is the fuel for all of our transportation systems. Without energy, our transportation systems would not function efficiently.

Power, the third area, is also very important. The power section in this textbook is designed to show how energy is converted into useful forms to be used in transportation and other forms of technology. This chapter introduces transportation, energy, and power.

Transportation, Energy, and Power Technology

Many technological systems are used within a society. The most common technological systems include communication, production and transportation. This book is about transportation technology, and the necessary support needed from energy and power technology.

Transportation

Transportation is defined as any technology that is used to move people and products (goods) within a society. Figure 1-1 shows several forms of transportation. In order for our technological society to function, many things must be transported. People are transported by automobiles, buses, trains, ships, aircraft, bicycles, and so forth. Goods, such as food,

(A)

(C)

(B)

(D)

FIGURE 1-1 These technologies are all considered forms of transportation. *Courtesy of (A) Freightliner Inc., (B) British Airways, (C) Sante Fe Southern Pacific Corporation, and (D) Texaco Inc.*

Gantry Robot

Robots are also considered a form of transportation within industry. In any industrial process various parts must be moved from one point to another. In addition, robots perform a variety of tasks during manufacturing. Robots are used to do particular processes such as drilling, welding, etc. Moving on a 50-foot long gantry, two feet above the work surface, this robot drills and deburrs holes in the 47-foot long floor panels for an aircraft. Because of their efficiency, accuracy and cost, robots are fast being integrated in all manufacturing and industrial processes. *Courtesy of Lockheed Corporation, Dick Luria, photographer*

merchandise, and such fuels as natural gas and coal are transported in several ways, including trains, trucks, buses, aircraft, ships, pipelines and conveyers.

In today's advanced technological society, information, as a product, must also be transported. Information can be transported by electrical means and satellite technology, and through glass fibers built into a single cable. Figure 1-2 shows glass fibers that have been installed to link several communication centers together. This technology is one of the fastest and most powerful means available to transport (send and receive) information.

When looking at the total scope of transportation in a society, one finds a variety of modes used to satisfy transportation needs. Some of the many modes of transportation technologies include:

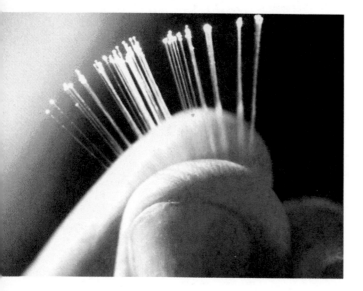

FIGURE 1-2 Information can be transported by using glass fiber technology. Information can be sent and received at an extremely rapid rate. *Courtesy of United Telecom*

Automobiles	Spacecraft	Lift Trucks
Buses	Motorcycles	Hovercraft
Aircraft	Snowmobiles	Rafts
Bicycles	Ships and Boats	Monorails
Conveyers	Skis	Trains and
Elevators	Pipelines	Subways
Escalators	Farm Tractors	Moving
Trucks	Cable Cars	Sidewalks

Energy

Energy is defined as the ability to do work. Energy is usually associated with fuels and other resources. These resources may include coal, oil, natural gas, nuclear, wind, solar and hydroelectric, among others.

Figure 1-3 shows several forms of energy. The resources shown are all considered energy, waiting to be used in a power source. Usually, however, the energy must be converted into the correct form before being used.

(A) COAL

(B) NUCLEAR

(C) SOLAR

(D) WIND

FIGURE 1-3 All of these examples are considered forms of energy. *Courtesy of (A) Gulf Oil Company, (B) Bechtel Group Inc., (C) Standard Oil Co., (D) Southern California Edison Company*

Hot-air Balloons

These hot-air balloons are one form of transportation. However, they are also used for recreational purposes. The use of hot-air balloons has increased in the past few years. In fact, many cities now have hot-air balloon contests for accuracy and distance of flight. The technology is now more affordable and can be learned easily.

Hot air is lighter than cold air. To enable the vehicle to rise, hot air is put into the balloon from the exhaust of large propane burners. Technologically, a hydrocarbon fuel is converted by combustion into thermal energy. Once the balloon is aloft, the thermal energy inside is lost to the outside. As this happens, the balloon slowly descends. Control of the position and height of the balloon is determined by turning on the propane burners for a certain length of time. Usually, someone tracks the balloon over the land to act as support when it lands.

Power

Power technology is the study of ways used to convert the energy or resource into useful power forms needed for the application. For example, a train may need diesel fuel (oil) to be converted into mechanical energy for movement. *Power* is defined as the measure of work that has been done. Power technology includes mechanical power such as an engine, as shown in Figure 1-4, fluid power, and electrical power. Power and energy technology help to operate transportation (and other systems as well). Figure 1-5 shows such a relationship.

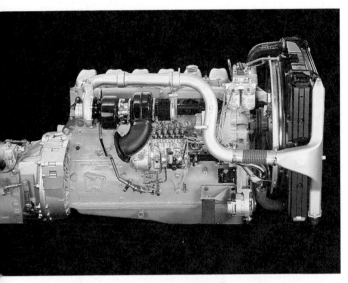

FIGURE 1-4 The engine is considered a form of power technology. It is used to convert an energy resource (oil) into mechanical power. *Courtesy of AB Volvo*

Systems of Technology

The various systems of technology can be very complex and are often interrelated. Just as with production and communications technologies, transportation technology can be studied by looking at a systems approach. Transportation is such a large part of society, it is difficult to study and see all of the parts. A systems approach helps to organize, use and evaluate a specific technology.

All technologies have a similar system which includes five components: input, process, output, feedback loop, and impact. Figure 1-6 illustrates this system.

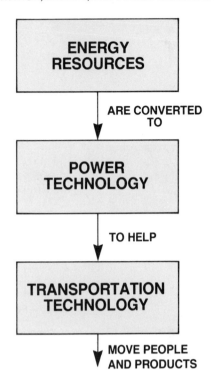

FIGURE 1-5 The relationship among transportation, energy, and power is shown.

Input

The input can also be called the command or objective. The *input* is defined as the objective or that which needs to be accomplished in the transportation system. The input must help accomplish and complete the desired result or output. The input can also be considered a statement of the problem. In order to understand the input, use the following problem as an example:

> Statement of the Problem: to transport 230 people from Chicago to New York. This is called the input, the command or the objective.

Process

The *process* is defined as the technical concept or principle used to accomplish the desired result or output. The process requires many resources for correct operation, including one or more of the following:

People	Tools	Capital
Information	Energy	Time
Materials		

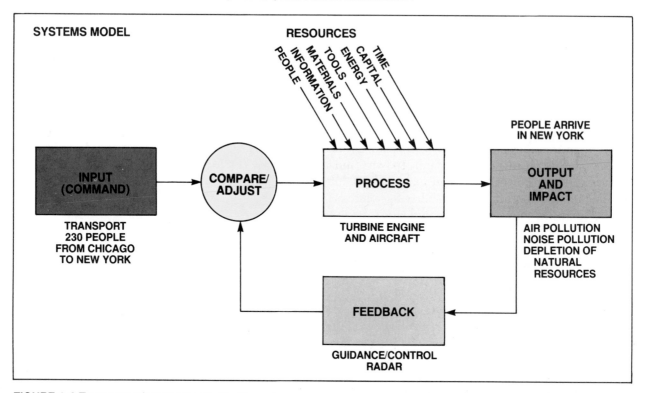

FIGURE 1-6 Transportation can be studied by using the systems approach. It includes an input, a process, an output and impact, and a feedback.

A turbine engine is a technology used to process fuels (a resource) into motion (output). The turbine engine causes a certain process to occur in order to accomplish the desired output. This is one resource put into the process. Figure 1-7 shows a turbine engine in an aircraft.

Typically, in the transportation system, the processes are mostly related to such areas as

- the engine or propulsion system,
- shocks and suspension, and
- materials or structure technology.

The following example shows how the processes achieve the desired result.

In the first example stated, the process is accomplished by placing the people on an aircraft, converting fuel to thrust in the engine, and moving the vehicle to the destination city of New York. The technical processes include propulsion, suspension, support, and structure technology.

FIGURE 1-7 A turbine engine is considered a technology used to process fuel into power to transport objects. *Courtesy of Rob Van Stone for Volvo*

Output

The *output* is considered the actual or final result of the process. The output is often called the industrial application.

> In the previous example, the output is to have the people arrive in New York safely and on time.

Impact

As technology is being studied, more and more importance is being placed on the *technological impact* of using a technology. Every technology always has some form of negative and/or positive impact on people and society. These impacts must be studied to get a complete picture of the technological system. *Impacts* quite often deal with social, environmental, economic and individual consequences of technology.

> Concluding the previous example, the environmental impact of flying 230 people from Chicago to New York may include noise and air pollution from the engine, depletion of natural resources (consuming fuels), and the use of land space for the airport. Social impacts may include the safety of passengers should an accident occur, the way in which people work on their jobs, (Chicago executives traveling to New York causing lifestyles to change), careers that rely upon airports, and cost to consumers, to name a few.

The systems approach of input, process, output, feedback, and impact works throughout all of transportation. Although the example given is of a very broad nature, the systems model can also be applied to more specific technologies, such as energy and power technology.

Feedback

Each technological systems model also needs feedback. *Feedback* is a monitoring system; it is also considered a control system. It takes the form of a loop. The feedback loop exists so that the question can be asked: "Was the result correct and accurately accomplished?" In the given example, the control or feedback includes guidance and control systems, radar, and so forth, to keep the plane on the correct path and at the correct speed. These technologies help to monitor the system so the desired result (output) can be obtained.

During the feedback portion of the loop, the actual result (output) is *compared* to the desired result (input). Sometimes the actual result does not match the desired result. The process must then be *adjusted* to achieve the desired result.

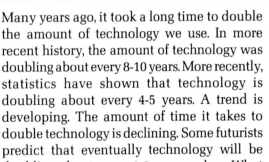

Many years ago, it took a long time to double the amount of technology we use. In more recent history, the amount of technology was doubling about every 8-10 years. More recently, statistics have shown that technology is doubling about every 4-5 years. A trend is developing. The amount of time it takes to double technology is declining. Some futurists predict that eventually technology will be doubling about every 1-2 years or less. What will life be like if this happens? The need for technological literacy increases as the rate of technological change grows greater. This is especially true in the area of transportation, energy, and power.

Making Decisions About Technology

In today's society, people are constantly making decisions about technology and its use. This is also true for transportation, energy, and power technology. For example, logical decisions must continually be made about new and emerging transportation forms. The use of energy resources and their impacts on technology must also be evaluated. How does one make sound decisions about all of these technologies? A person who can make sound decisions about technology is called *technologically literate.*

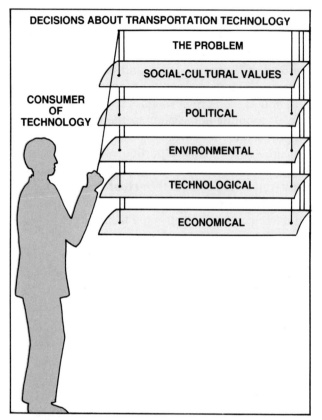

FIGURE 1-8 Decisions about transportation must consider these five areas so that sound and logical information can be obtained.

One decision-making method used is shown in Figure 1-8. Again, transportation is used as an example. Any decision about transportation must be viewed by considering several aspects. These include social-cultural values, and political, environmental, technological, and economical influences. The more these factors are considered, the more the "blinds open," and the more the problem can be observed. If we, as the decision makers, view transportation and consider all of these components, the decision will be clearer, and more practical and justifiable.

Social-cultural Values

Technology today is closely tied to the social-cultural values of society. These are values people believe in. Some new automobiles never became successful because their design didn't meet or match the social-cultural values of their time. The Studebaker, a car built some time ago, was many years ahead in its design. People socially and culturally didn't accept its style. Note that social

and cultural values are tied to the "impact" in the systems model.

Political Influences

The political influences on transportation include any decision that is controlled or decided with rules, regulations, policies, governments (city/state/national), and so on. For example, the decision to build a mass transportation system in a particular city may be decided by the political rules that are in effect in that city or state. Further, the zoning ordinances may restrict the exact location and route of the mass transportation system. Recall that political influence on transportation is also considered a resource to the "process" in the systems model.

Environmental Influences

The environmental impacts of transportation are great. Any decision about the use or development of new or existing transportation technology must consider the environmental impact. For example, if an airport is to be built near a city or subdivision, will too much noise be created in that area? Also, how unsightly will the airport be in the geographical area? Note that these environmental aspects are closely tied to the "impact" in the systems model.

Technological Influences

When making decisions about transportation, the technological aspect must be considered. Ask the question, "Can the technology accomplish what is needed?" "Is the technology available?" Note that the technology is part of the "process" in the systems model.

Economic Influences

In the United States, society is based upon supply and demand and capitalism, among other economic factors. Many decisions are made about transportation based upon the dollar. Questions like "Is this a good investment?," or "Will I spend less money on this mode?" all play an important part in transportation decisions. Note that economic influences are resources that feed into the "processes" in the systems model.

Tying these influences together helps to make complex decisions much easier with transportation technology. All five parts must be considered if the decision is to be sound and justifiable. To help see how these interrelate to one another, consider the following problem:

> **Should the battery-powered car be promoted and developed further within our society?** Using the five parts, the following questions could be asked in each of the areas to help make the best decision. Obviously, both yes and no answers help to make the decision.

Social-cultural. Will society generally accept the battery-powered vehicle? Will people object to having a battery charge rather than a fill-up? Will people mind having more charges than fill-ups? Will people accept less speed and power during acceleration?

Political. Will an insurance company insure the vehicle? Are the passengers covered by insurance if they are in an accident and suffer acid burns? Are the speed limits too high for this vehicle? Will the limits need to be changed?

Environmental. Is the vehicle as safe as other cars in crash tests? Is there less pollution of carbon monoxide, nitrogen oxide, and so forth? What environmental damage will acid spills cause on road surfaces?

Technological. Can an efficient battery-powered car be technologically produced? Can it be designed to last as long as a gasoline-powered car? Can it be designed to pull a boat or trailer, for instance?

Economical. Will driving a battery-powered car be less costly than driving a gasoline vehicle? Will the insurance be more or less? Will the company who manufactures the vehicle make a profit?

Obviously, more questions could be asked. However, as these questions are answered, the decisions then become more clearly defined as to the success or failure of the technology.

Careers In Transportation, Energy, and Power

Choosing a Career

The field of transportation, energy, and power is very broad; consequently, many careers are available. It is an exciting and challenging field to work in. When choosing a career, it is important to know your abilities and skills. Answers to many questions will be important. Such questions may include:

1. Are you a people person?
2. Do you like technical things?
3. What are your interests?
4. Are you mechanically inclined?
5. Do you like to work with the theories and/or the practical applications? For example, do you enjoy working with your hands? Do you enjoy solving complex mathematical and scientific problems?
6. What level of education would you like to achieve?

In the transportation field, careers are open for all of these abilities and interests. Not only are there specific technical areas to work in, but there are also many levels within each area as well. Knowing yourself, your abilities, and your level of education will help you to better decide on a career or occupation in transportation, energy, and power.

Resources for Careers and Occupations

When deciding on a career or occupation, it is important to know what is available. Several resources can help. Your school provides a great deal of information on how to get a job and as to what jobs are available. Summer jobs and part-time work while in school will also help to determine your abilities and interests. Many later career areas were chosen by people because of their part-time jobs while in high school.

The library also has several books about careers. Popular resource titles include:

- *Occupational Outlook Handbook*
- *Dictionary of Occupational Titles (DOT)*
- *Career Guide: Dun's Employment Opportunities Directory*
- *Peterson's Business and Management Jobs*
- *Encyclopedia of Careers and Vocational Guidance*

These resources help to determine the general technical area, and the level of occupation in the industry.

Career/Occupational Areas

Careers in transportation, energy, and power technology can be found in a number of occupational areas, including:

1. Professional
2. Technical
3. Managerial
4. Clerical
5. Sales
6. Service
7. Processing
8. Structural
9. Manufacturing
10. Testing and Repair
11. Customer Relations

Many more occupational areas may be added. However, most of the careers in this field will probably fit into one or more of the areas listed. When deciding what type of career you are interested in, first look closely at the occupational areas, then select a career within the area.

Industry Types

When one chooses to work in transportation, energy, and power, certain types of industries, businesses, and companies typically hire such a person. A small sample of some of these industries include:

1. Trucking
2. Automotive
3. Railroading
4. Coal Mining
5. Petroleum Exploring
6. Petroleum Refining
7. Local and Regional Bus Companies
8. City Transportation Planning
9. Power Plants
10. Road Construction
11. Harbor and Marine
12. Flight and Navigational
13. Airports
14. Pipelines
15. Manufacturing for Transportation
16. Airlines
17. Engine Companies
18. Parts Companies
19. Leisure Boating
20. Recreational Products
21. Alternative Energy Companies
22. Defense Industries (Development of Military Transportation Systems)

Many other companies, industries, and businesses have occupations and careers in transportation, energy and power. Literally thousands of careers are available in this broad field. Figures 1-9 through 1-16 illustrate examples of typical careers and occupations in the area of transportation, energy, and power.

FIGURE 1-9 These technicians have a career in the electric power industry. *Courtesy of Philadelphia Electric Co.*

FIGURE 1-10 These people, called troubleshooters, work for an electric company. Other job titles in this company include customer representatives, distribution technicians and crews, meter readers, and service dispatchers. *Courtesy of Southern California Edison*

FIGURE 1-11 These customer travel representatives help make travel easier. *Courtesy of Delta Air Lines*

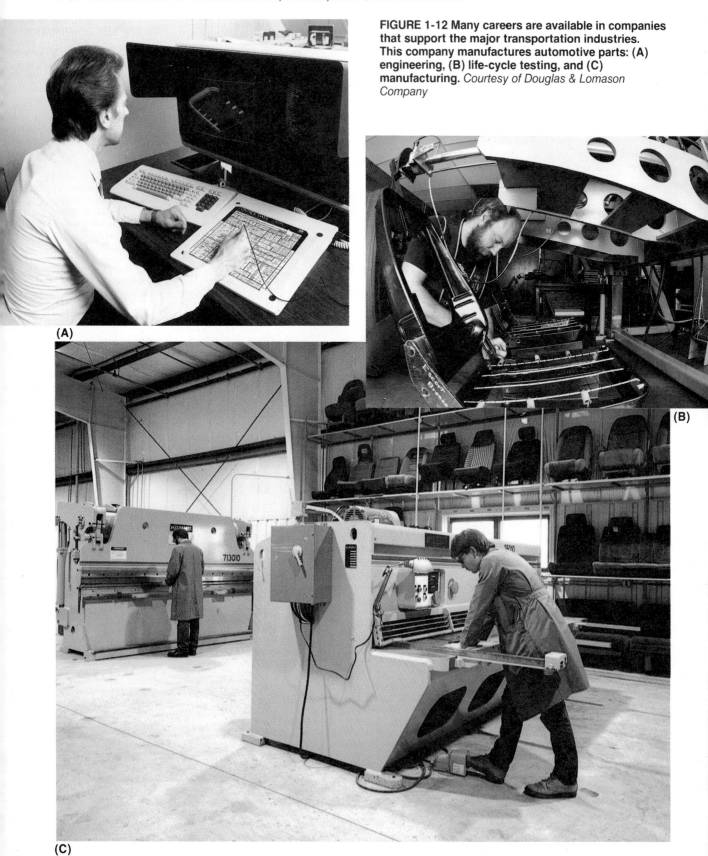

FIGURE 1-12 Many careers are available in companies that support the major transportation industries. This company manufactures automotive parts: (A) engineering, (B) life-cycle testing, and (C) manufacturing. *Courtesy of Douglas & Lomason Company*

(A)

(B)

(C)

FIGURE 1-13 There are many supporting careers in the area of transportation, energy, and power technology. Here technicians use helicopters to work on high voltage transmission lines. *Courtesy of Niagara Mohawk Power Corporation*

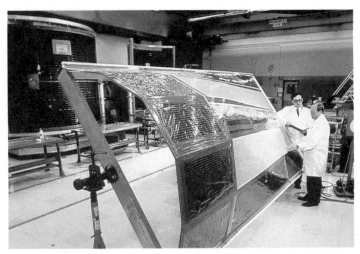

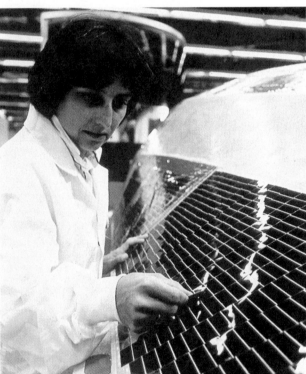

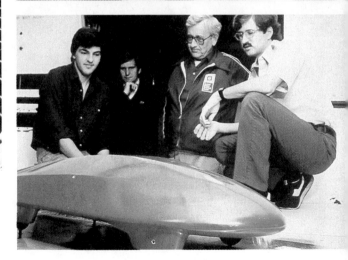

FIGURE 1-14 Research is a very important area in transportation, energy, and power technology. The need for research supports many careers in these areas. These research specialists are testing various parts of a solar powered vehicle recently developed and tested in **Australia.** *Courtesy of General Motors*

FIGURE 1-15 CADD (Computer Aided Drafting/Design) has become an important career area for design and development of transportation vehicles. *Courtesy of General Motors*

FIGURE 1-16 Technicians help to troubleshoot and service various components and systems on transportation vehicles. *Courtesy of Midas International Corporation*

Summary

The purpose of this chapter is to introduce transportation, energy and power technology.

- *Transportation technology* is defined as any technology used to transport people and products within a society.
- *Energy* is defined as the ability to do work. Resources such as coal, oil, natural gas, nuclear and solar, and the like, are part of energy technology.
- *Power* is defined as a measure of work being done. Power technology is the study of the systems that are used to convert energy resources into mechanical, fluid, and electrical power.
- Many types of vehicles are used in transportation, including automobiles, buses, aircraft, elevators, motorcycles, as well as others.
- To help understand how technologies function, a systems approach can be used. The systems approach suggests there is an input (a command or objective), a process (changing the input), an output (the result), a feedback (loop control) and technological impact (effects of technology).
- Many decisions are constantly being made within the field of technology. A technologically literate person asks many questions before making decisions. Five areas should be considered when making any technological decision about technology. These areas include political, environmental, social-cultural values, technological, and economical.
- Many careers and occupations are available in the area of transportation, energy, and power. Typical areas include service, sales, technical support, management, and customer relations, as well as others.
- Careers are decided by the interest and abilities of the person.
- The *Directory of Occupational Titles* will help to determine many of the occupations in this field.

REVIEW

1. Transportation is defined as technology used to transport people and _____ .
2. Energy is defined as the _____ to do work.
3. The systems approach to studying technology includes input, _____ , output, _____ and impact.
4. When making decisions about the use of technology always consider political, environmental, social-cultural, _____ , and economical factors.
5. What is the purpose of using a systems approach when studying transportation technology?
6. What are the five parts of the systems approach to studying transportation?
7. What parts should be considered when making a decision about transportation?
8. What resources are used within a systems model?
9. Select a typical career in the transportation, energy, or power industry. Then identify the type of abilities and skills you think are necessary for the career.

CHAPTER ACTIVITIES

 ## THE SYSTEMS APPROACH

INTRODUCTION

Most technology can be studied by using the systems approach. The parts that are studied include the input, process, output, impact, and feedback loop. This activity will aid the student to better understand and use the systems approach.

TECHNOLOGICAL LITERACY SKILLS

Creativity, group analysis, flowcharting.

OBJECTIVES

After completing this activity, you will be able to:
1. List the components used in the systems approach when studying technology.
2. Analyze a system in each of the areas of transportation, energy, and power technology.
3. Illustrate graphically technological systems through a flowchart.

MATERIALS

1. Pencil
2. Paper
3. Research materials (library)
4. Poster board
5. Markers and/or paint
6. Old magazines
7. Scissors
8. Glue
9. Color ink pens

PROCEDURE

1. As a class, discuss the systems approach, its advantages, and how the approach relates to transportation, energy, and power technology.
2. Divide the class into small groups of three students.
3. Select a particular technology in the area of transportation and develop a flowchart for that technology using the systems approach. Some examples might include a bicycle, automobile, airplane, bus, passenger train, etc.
4. Research magazines for pictures that will identify the flowchart information.
5. On a piece of paper, make a flowchart of the systems approach for your type of technology. Remember to include as many items as possible in each area. This will be a rough or first copy.
6. When all ideas and suggestions have been included, transfer the information to the large poster board. Use color pens, magazine photos, etc. to enhance your flowchart. Remember, this is the final copy and it will be judged along with all the other groups.
7. Each group will present its flowchart to the rest of the class. Each presentation is limited to the maximum of 10 minutes.
8. The class will now judge the best and most complete flowchart and presentation.
9. The top three flowcharts should be posted in the hallways of the school as examples of proper applications for the systems model.

REVIEW QUESTIONS

1. Can your group think of a type of technology in the area of transportation, energy, or power technology where the systems approach cannot be used?
2. Why is it important to include the impact part of the systems approach?
3. What is the importance of studying technology from a systems approach?
4. Can the systems approach also be applied to communications, manufacturing, and construction technology?

 **CAREER RESEARCH**

INTRODUCTION

The area of transportation, energy, and power provides many careers for people. This activity will help you to develop a method you can use to identify careers.

TECHNOLOGICAL LITERACY SKILLS

Research, group work, data analysis, brainstorming.

OBJECTIVES

After completing this activity, you will be able to:
1. Use the *Directory of Occupational Titles (DOT)*.
2. Determine your interest areas in transportation, energy, and power.
3. Write a short one-page research report on at least one occupational area in transportation, energy, or power.

MATERIALS

1. Multiple copies of the current *Directory of Occupational Titles*.

2. Annual reports and other company literature for various transportation, energy, and power companies.
3. Handout from your teacher (one per student), entitled "Occupational Research Report."
4. Pencil

PROCEDURE

1. Divide the class into groups of three students.
2. In this group, for a 10-minute period, brainstorm as many careers and occupations as possible in the area of transportation, energy, and power technology.
3. Now have each group get a copy of the DOT.
4. Using the DOT, select three occupations; one in transportation, one in energy, and one in power.
5. Have each student in the group analyze one of the three occupations. Place this information on the report sheet provided by the instructor.
6. Hand in each sheet to the instructor for evaluation.
7. Based upon this report, list five things that you think are important when selecting a career in transportation, energy, and power.

REVIEW QUESTIONS

1. What do you think are the advantages for having a career in transportation, energy, and power technology?
2. Explain what coal miners, steel workers, and city bus drivers all have in common.
3. Can you identify how many relatives in your family work or have occupations in the area of transportation, energy, and power technology?

SECTION TWO

TRANSPORTATION TECHNOLOGY

Transportation has become a very significant part of our everyday lives. People rely on many transportation systems. All transportation systems have inputs, processes, outputs and impacts, and feedback systems.

1. The input is the objective to move goods and people from one point to another.
2. The processes may include land, marine, air, or space transportation technology.
3. The output is the act of people or goods arriving at the destination. Impacts usually include depletion of natural resources, pollution, lifestyle change, etc.
4. Feedback usually includes some form of technology to control the system.

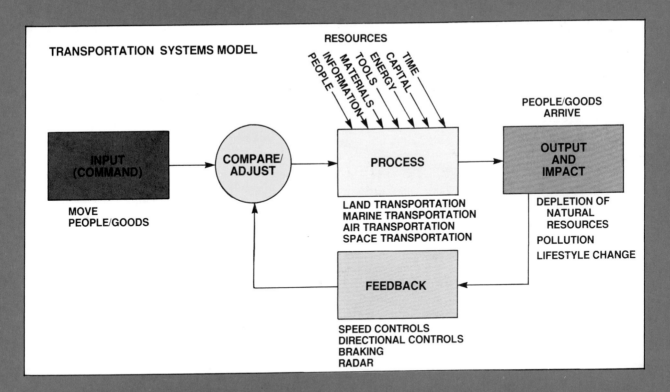

TRANSPORTATION SYSTEMS MODEL

RESOURCES

TIME
CAPITAL
ENERGY
TOOLS
MATERIALS
INFORMATION
PEOPLE

INPUT (COMMAND)

MOVE PEOPLE/GOODS

COMPARE/ ADJUST

PROCESS

LAND TRANSPORTATION
MARINE TRANSPORTATION
AIR TRANSPORTATION
SPACE TRANSPORTATION

PEOPLE/GOODS ARRIVE

OUTPUT AND IMPACT

DEPLETION OF NATURAL RESOURCES
POLLUTION
LIFESTYLE CHANGE

FEEDBACK

SPEED CONTROLS
DIRECTIONAL CONTROLS
BRAKING
RADAR

CHAPTER 2

Introduction to Transportation Technology

OBJECTIVES

After reading this chapter, you will be able to:

- Define *transportation technology.*
- Identify the four major categories of transportation technology.
- Compare the six technologies that are part of transportation technology.
- State the importance of using transportation within our society.

KEY TERMS

Transportation Technology
Terrestrial
Modes
Dirigibles

Propulsion
Suspension
Guidance
Support Technology

Ton Miles
Passenger Miles
Intercity Bus

Introduction

Transportation is one of the more important systems of technology. Transportation is used to move people and products throughout our society. This chapter is about transportation, its categories/divisions, and technological systems.

FIGURE 2-1 People usually associate transportation with the automobile. *Courtesy of Ford Motor Company*

Transportation Technology

Transportation technology can be defined in many ways. Most people immediately associate transportation with the automobile, Figure 2-1. However, transportation is much broader than just the automobile. *Transportation technology* is defined as any technology that is used to transport people and/or products within a society. In some societies, transportation technology is very simple. However, in advanced technological societies, transportation can become a highly interrelated and complex system, as shown in Figure 2-2.

Categories of Transportation

Because transportation is such a large and interrelated industry, it helps to classify it into several groups. These groups can be called *environmental divisions*. All transportation can be subdivided into

FIGURE 2-2 Transportation is a very important part of our lives. Without the many transportation modes our lives would change drastically. *Courtesy of San Francisco Bay Area Rapid Transit*

four divisions, depending upon the environment in which they are used, Figure 2-3. These include land (terrestrial), marine (water), atmospheric (air), and space transportation.

Land Transportation. *Land transportation* is defined as any transportation that is used on or under land to transport people and products or goods. This group includes the automobiles, buses, railroads, escalators, conveyers, and pipelines, to name a few.

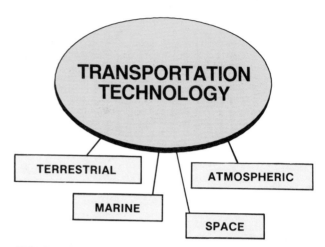

FIGURE 2-3 Transportation can be divided into four divisions. These include land, marine, atmospheric, and space.

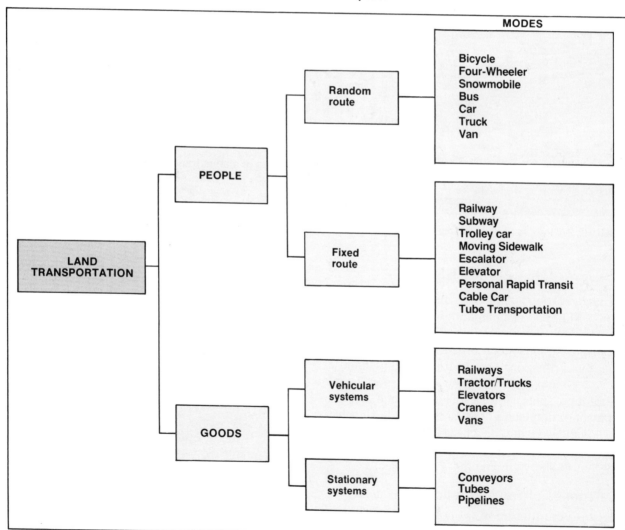

FIGURE 2-4 Land (terrestrial) transportation is subdivided into movement of people and goods. Each is further divided showing many means of terrestrial transportation.

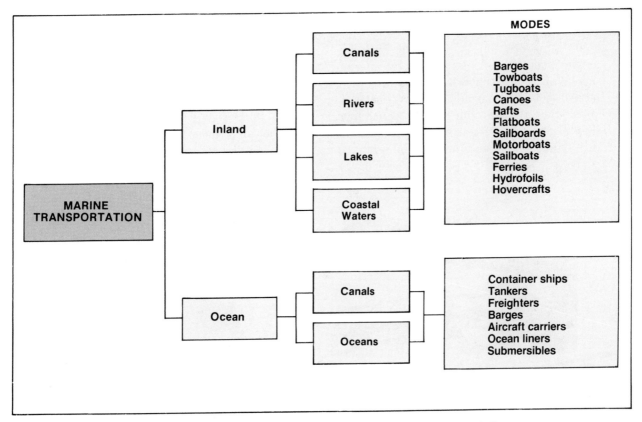

FIGURE 2-5 Marine transportation subdivisions and the many modes of marine transportation.

A complete categorical layout of land transportation, also called *terrestrial transportation*, is shown in Figure 2-4.

Land modes of transportation are subdivided into the movement of both people and goods. People modes are subdivided into both random and fixed routes. Random modes of transportation are routes that are not fixed to one path. A bicycle is a random form of transportation. Fixed routes are those that are set to one path. A conveyor system is a fixed route. The movement of goods also is divided into vehicular systems and stationary systems. Each of these categories then includes different forms and modes of transportation technologies.

Marine Transportation. *Marine transportation* is transportation by water. Today, the following five regions carry most of the marine transportation within the United States.

1. Great Lakes System and St. Lawrence Seaway
2. Mississippi River System
3. Pacific Coast Waterways
4. Gulf Coast Waterways
5. Atlantic Coast Waterways

As with land or terrestrial transportation, marine transportation is also divided into different modes and forms, Figure 2-5. Marine transportation is subdivided into inland waterways and transoceanic maritime travel. Inland waterways include canals, rivers, domestic lakes, and coastal waters. Transoceanic maritime travel takes place in large lakes, inland lakes, oceans, and seas. Each division is again subdivided within the specific types or modes of transportation technologies shown.

Atmospheric Transportation. *Atmospheric or air transportation* is concerned with vehicles that

Roller Coaster

Land transportation is used not only for moving people, goods, and so forth, but also for recreation. The transportation mode shown here is a roller coaster. A roller coaster is considered a fixed-route type of transportation. Today's roller coasters provide a great deal of excitement and thrill for the user.

Although used for recreation, a great deal of technology is designed into these systems. Concepts of load, speed, centrifugal forces, and stresses on structures all play an important part in the design of such systems. Combined together all of these technologies are used to keep the roller coaster on track for maximum safety. The system uses propulsion, guidance, control, support, suspension and materials technology for optimum performance and safety.

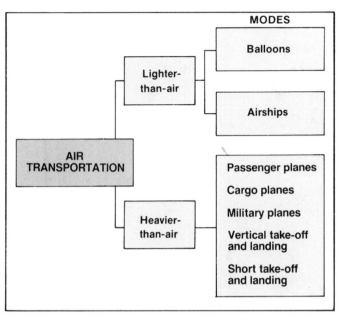

FIGURE 2-6 Atmospheric transportation is divided into lighter-than-air and heavier-than-air forms. Each category includes various modes of transportation.

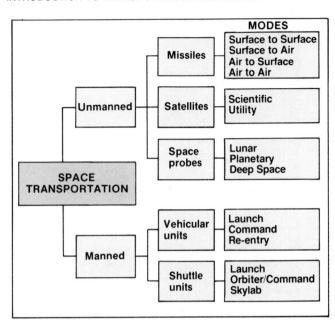

FIGURE 2-7 Space transportation is divided into both unmanned and manned systems. Note the many modes of transportation for space travel.

operate primarily in the earth's atmosphere. Figure 2-6 shows the breakdown and subdivision of atmospheric transportation.

Both lighter-than-air and heavier-than-air vehicles are used. Balloons typically have a light, nonporous bag shape. Airships, also called *dirigibles*, are always steerable, under power and control by the pilot. The figure shows other types of vehicles and the modes of transportation for each category.

Space transportation. *Space transportation* is defined as any form of transportation that reaches beyond the atmosphere surrounding the earth. Today, there are many unmanned and manned modes of transportation. Figure 2-7 shows the breakdown of space transportation.

Technological Systems in Transportation

All modes of transportation have certain types of technology that apply to each. These are called *technological systems.* The technological systems in transportation are shown in Figure 2-8 and include the following technologies:

1. Propulsion   3. Guidance   5. Support
2. Suspension   4. Control   6. Structure

Each of these technologies is needed for any type of transportation required. However, the method or type of technology by which each is accomplished or developed may differ greatly.

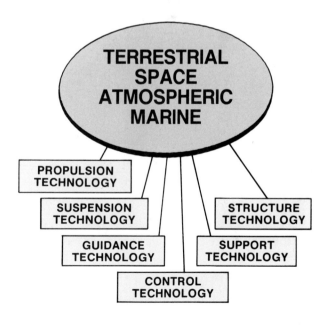

FIGURE 2-8 All transportation modes have certain technologies that are needed for operation.

FIGURE 2-9 These engines are considered forms of propulsion for automobiles. *Courtesy of Ford Motor Company*

Propulsion Technology

All vehicles used for transportation must have some form of *propulsion* technology. For example, automobiles use gasoline or diesel engines, Figure 2-9. Trucks use diesel engines, aircraft use piston and jet engines, ships use both steam and diesel engines, and space transportation uses rocket engines.

The type of propulsion used depends upon the vehicle function, speed, acceleration, distance required, and so forth. Certain other concepts also come into play, including frictional losses, efficiency and type of fuel, among others. Such concepts and their associated technology are discussed further in a later chapter.

Suspension Technology

No matter what type of transportation mode, the vehicle weight must be supported. Therefore, *suspension* technologies are also part of transportation systems. For example three types of suspension technologies include mechanical, fluid, and magnetic. One of the underlying concepts of fluid suspension technology includes hull design for marine applications (buoyancy), Figure 2-10. Other forms of suspension include tires, shock absorbers, air-suspension systems for terrestrial vehicles and wing design on aircraft, to name a few.

Guidance Technology

All vehicles require some form of *guidance* to be operated correctly and safely. This means that information must be given as to the vehicle's direction. For example, on such terrestrial vehicles as trains, the guidance may be the rails. In addition,

many transportation vehicles use electronic guidance systems. For example, boats have a complex navigational guidance system necessary to cross large bodies of water. Devices for guidance may include tachometers, airspeed indicators, inertial sensors, radar, and others. Figure 2-11 shows the various gages used on a car as guidance technology.

Control Technology

The elements of *control technology* on vehicles include both total traffic and vehicle control. Traffic

FIGURE 2-11 The tachometer and other gages on a vehicle are considered guidance technology. *Courtesy of Chevrolet Motor Division, General Motors Corporation*

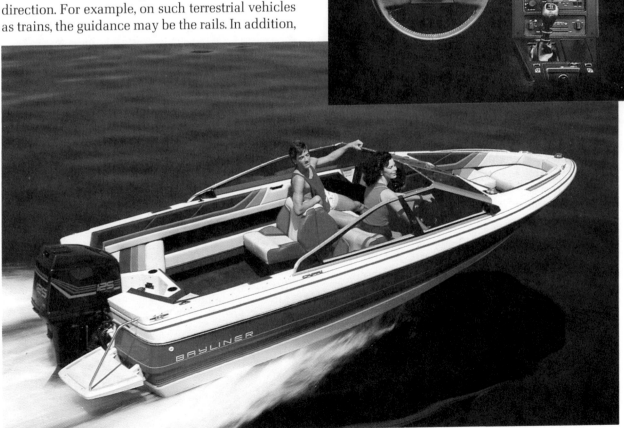

FIGURE 2-10 The hull design of this boat is considered part of the suspension technology. *Courtesy of Bayliner Marine Corporation/Bruce Carron Photography*

FIGURE 2-12 A launch pad is considered a support technology for space travel. *Courtesy of NASA*

control includes such elements as traffic lights, airport control towers, and railroad control centers, among others. Vehicle control may include a force of some kind to change, alter or regulate the speed, direction and attitude of the vehicle. Simple systems include brakes, cruise controls, and computer controls for automobiles. More complex controls include complete guidance systems for large boats, aircraft, and space vehicles.

Support Technology

All vehicles need some form of support technology. *Support technology* is defined as systems of technology used for processing the vehicle, moving passengers to and from the vehicle, and bringing freight to and from the vehicle. Support technologies may include such examples as airports, marinas, launch pads (Figure 2-12), harbors, gasoline stations, parts dealers, and service shops. None of the transportation modes can operate without support technologies. In fact, one reason it is difficult to incorporate new transportation technologies is because the support systems are not yet in place. Take for example the battery-powered car. Although it was a good technology, there were never any support systems such as battery-charging stations and service shops to support its growth.

FIGURE 2-13 These engineers are experimenting with lightweight composite cones for space structures. *Courtesy of NASA*

Structure Technology

In today's advanced society, many new materials and structures are being used to build transportation components and systems, Figure 2-13. The most recent goal is to design lighter structures with stronger characteristics. Structure technology, for instance, is used to make vehicles lighter, stronger, and more heat resistant. For example, the materials used in an engine (propulsion technology) are being made lighter and stronger so that efficiency can be improved and temperatures increased. Automobile manufacturers, for example, are now designing engines made of synthetic materials rather than cast iron. Synthetic engines are able to withstand higher internal temperatures; this translates to more fuel economy and improved efficiency.

Systems Model and Transportation

The systems model of technology described earlier also applies to these six areas just mentioned, Figure 2-14. To begin, the input of any transportation mode is the objective of "What needs to be moved?" The process of moving incorporates propulsion technology, suspension technology, support technology, and structure technology. The guidance and control technologies are part of the feedback loop shown in the systems model.

Need for Transportation in Society

The type of transportation available in a society may determine the technological potential and growth of a society. Transportation has advanced rapidly throughout the years. The time it took to travel across the country by various means illustrates the speed of this advancement. The following list illustrates how the time to go from coast to coast has become shortened over the past 150 years.

1849—166 days by covered wagon
1860—60 days by stagecoach
1870—11 days by train
1923—26 1/2 hours by propeller aircraft
1938—17 1/2 hours by DC-3 piston-engine airplane
1975—5 hours by 747 jet-engine airplane
1981—8 minutes by space shuttle

In the United States, the transportation systems are so integrated and complex that they are interrelated and dependent upon many other technologies. For example, transportation systems cannot exist today without a solid connection to the communications industries, production industries, and energy industries. Can you imagine the flight of a commercial jet aircraft without effective communication between it and the control tower?

It has often been said that transportation and the development of a civilization go hand in hand. As a civilized society develops, its transportation systems, and certainly the materialism (need for more possessions) of a society, has been affected. In

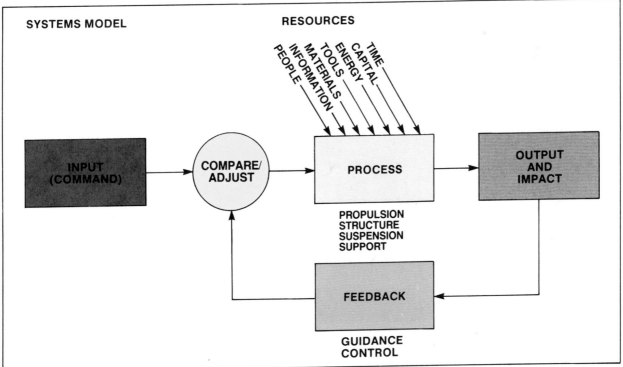

FIGURE 2-14 The systems model can also be applied to the six types of transportation technology.

(A)

(B)

FIGURE 2-15 The quality of life can be improved with **(C)**
the use of more sophisticated transportation forms.
Courtesy (A) British Airways, (B) Ford Motor Company, and (C) Hatteras Yachts

fact, the development of transportation within our society has made specific changes in the way in which people live. As newer, better and more efficient transportation systems are developed, society continues to change and promises to improve.

It is only when people can move freely and safely that an increase in interchange of ideas is possible. As this interchange of ideas develops, it takes on the snowball effect: as more is learned, more technology can be developed.

Why Is Transportation So Important?

Transportation is extremely important within our society for five major reasons.

1. Transportation is a major technology within society. Its growth and development are directly tied to many careers. For example, approximately 25% of all jobs within the United States are connected in some way with the automobile.

2. Transportation is interrelated to communications, production, and energy utilization. All of these technologies must function together in relation to one another. If one technology were missing, the total technological structure would not work.

3. Transportation systems help to improve the quality of life within a society, Figure 2-15. Today, people are extremely mobile. We are able to travel large distances easily, economically, and safely. This has a tendency to increase the number of choices people have within a society. More choices means there is a greater potential to improve the quality of life if used correctly.

4. Transportation is directly related to human needs. People need many things in a technological society. Stress factors have increased the need for leisure. Transportation plays a very important part in our leisure activities. From vacations, to boating, to sightseeing, transportation is tied directly to our basic human needs.

5. Transportation systems help us make economic and time decisions. We are constantly making economic decisions about where to go and how much it will cost. Economic decisions are connected to time decisions about transportation. For example, we ask

Forward-swept Wings on Aircraft

This airplane is called the X-29. It is an experimental aircraft with more than 130 flights to its credit. The purpose of this aircraft is to prove the concept of forward-swept wings. As aircraft technology becomes more advanced, control and lift will constantly be improving. This type of wing is designed to improve the lift and control of the aircraft throughout all types of operation. In addition, advanced aerodynamic, structural, and avionic technologies are being tested. Many of the advanced technologies tested in this type of aircraft will eventually find their way into commercial aircraft use. The goal is to improve control, safety, efficiency, and comfort in aircraft of the future. *Courtesy of Grumman Corporation, 1988*

the question, How much time will it take for transporting people and products? In addition, the types and modes of transportation selected by manufacturers to transport goods also are tied to time and cost.

History of Transportation

The need to transport people and products has been around for a long time. Many years ago, the need for transportation, although evident, wasn't as great as in later years. Then, people needed to move only within a small area. For example, cattle helped to move goods from one point to another. Most activity remained on or near the farming community. People typically moved by horse and carriage or by small boats in rivers and waterways. However, as other technologies increased, the need to move with more frequency and greater distances increased. It is out of the question to think that people today will want to remain only within a small area. Transportation technology has not only expanded our reach, but also our wants and needs as well.

The history of transportation development can be traced by the following four methods of power:

1. Animal Power
2. Wind and Water Power
3. Engine Power
4. Rocket Power

Animal power was one of the first ways used to transport people and products. However, as technology started to expand, eventually wind and water power became important to the development of transportation, Figure 2-16. Rivers became useful for the transportation of many goods while expanding society's horizons. As technology developed, eventually the engine became extremely important for improving transportation. After that, rocket power led humans to the exploration of space. Of course, the progression of these power sources was directly tied to the development of other technologies as well.

A number of major innovations that helped spur the development of transportation include:

1. Steam engine (steamboats).

FIGURE 2-16 Wind power has been around for many years. Its development was a link to our transportation systems of today. *Courtesy of U.S. Coast Guard Recruiting Office, Albany, NY*

2. Horse harness.
3. Canals.
4. Advances in shipbuilding.
5. The development of steel products.
6. Communications technology.
7. Engine designs, such as gasoline, diesel and turbine engines.

Transportation Statistics

To help identify the size and complexity of our transportation systems, several statistics have been compiled. By looking at these statistics one can easily see the interrelatedness, size, and types of industries that exist because of transportation.

The following statistics are given for the United States:

1. In one year, $87.2 billion were spent on the purchase of goods and services for the automobile.
2. In one year, $91.9 billion were spent on gasoline and oil for the automobile.
3. In one year, 2,414 billion ton miles of freight were moved.
4. In one year, 1,812 billion passenger miles were transported by automobiles, airways, buses, and railroads.

TECH L I N K

A ton mile is the movement of 1 ton (2,000 lb) of freight for the distance of 1 mile.

A passenger mile is the movement of 1 passenger for the distance of 1 mile.

---

5. In one year, there were 18,000,000 automobile accidents, 1,700,000 injuries, and 43,800 deaths.
6. In one year, there were 8,002,000 factory sales of automobiles, and 3,357,000 factory sales of trucks and buses.
7. In one year, there were sales of 233,500 motorized homes, 82,900 travel trailers, 35,900 folding camping trailers, and 6,900 truck campers.

8. In one year, there were more than 1,500 operating intercity bus companies, 20,100 buses, 1,022,000 bus miles driven, and 206,000,000 charter and tour passengers served.
9. In one year, 82,500,000 ton miles were transported through the Great Lakes system, and 234,600,000 ton miles transported in the Mississippi River System.

By observing these statistics a clearer picture of the size, types of industries, volume of traffic, types of employment, and the needs of transportation and interrelated industries can be seen.

Summary

The purpose of this chapter is to define transportation technology, review its technological systems, and to see its importance in society today.

▪ *Transportation technology* is defined as any technology used to transport people and/or products within a society.

▪ All types of transportation can be divided into four main environmental types: land or terrestrial, marine, atmospheric or air, and space transportation.

▪ All four divisions of transportation technology also can be subdivided into technologies that are needed for operation. These technologies include, propulsion systems (power source), suspension technology (physical support of the vehicle), guidance (giving direction), control technology (regulation of speed), support technology (needed to keep vehicles operating), and structure (materials).

▪ Our society has a great need for transportation. The amount and degree of transportation technology is closely related to the amount of choices we have as individuals. More choices if correctly used usually improve the quality of life for people in a particular society.

▪ Transportation technology has always existed. Years ago, animal power helped to move people and products. Then, as wind and water power developed, transportation technology expanded. Today, steam, gasoline, diesel, turbine, and rocket engines help to move many of our vehicles.

REVIEW

1. Land transportation is also referred to as _____ transportation.
2. Gasoline stations, airports, and train stations are called _____ technology.
3. How many ton miles were transported if a vehicle moved 52 tons a distance of 243 miles?
4. Why has transportation become so important within our society?
5. What are the four types of environmental divisions for transportation technology? Give examples of transportation technology for each division.
6. Analyze the forms and types of transportation that you might use when traveling to another city, excluding the automobile.
7. Using the train as a total transportation system, identify the type of propulsion, guidance, support, control, suspension and structure technology being used.
8. What is the relationship between transportation technology and the quality of life? Explain.

CHAPTER ACTIVITIES

MOUSETRAP VEHICLE

INTRODUCTION

Many vehicles are designed to get the maximum amount of power for the lowest cost. This activity will help you to design an efficient and simple car.

TECHNOLOGICAL LITERACY SKILLS

Problem solving, creativity, design, research, data analysis.

OBJECTIVES

After completing this activity, you will be able to:
1. Construct a mousetrap vehicle.
2. Test a mousetrap vehicle.
3. Define the importance of efficiency and cost of transportation vehicles.

MATERIALS

1. Mousetraps
2. Wheels
3. Axles (dowel rods)
4. Bearings
5. Ruler
6. Paper money (Monopoly)
7. Instructor's handout
8. Extra wood if needed
9. General tools

Other material available from the instructor includes rubber bands, clothespins, nails, coat hangers, glue, straws, and other items as needed.

PROCEDURE

1. The instructor should divide your class into groups of two. Each group will be designing a vehicle for the competition.
2. In your group, make sure each member knows the definition of *efficiency*. Make sure each group has read the instructor's handout.
3. Each group now is given $100.00 of Monopoly money to buy materials to design and build a mousetrap vehicle.
4. Your group will buy materials from the instructor to build the mousetrap vehicle. Keep an account of all money spent.
5. Now brainstorm ideas on how to design the vehicle. Considerations include:
   a. How to extract the power.
   b. How to improve the distance traveled.
   c. How to keep the cost to a minimum
   d. How to get the vehicle started.
6. When your group needs to buy more materials, ask the instructor and purchase what is needed.
7. After the vehicle has been designed, build a prototype test vehicle.

▶ **CAUTION:** Remember to always check with the instructor for safety procedures before using laboratory tools and equipment. Also, make sure you are wearing safety glasses.

8. This vehicle will be tested for distance traveled in inches.
9. Reevaluate your design and try to make the vehicle more efficient. Do you need to buy everything you originally suggested?
10. At this point, the class will have a competition to reveal its "effective design number." This is determined as shown on the instructor's handout.
11. The group with the highest "effective design number" wins the competition.

REVIEW QUESTIONS

1. Why is efficiency an important factor in designing a land transportation vehicle?
2. How does brainstorming help to solve design problems?
3. Did most students design the same type of vehicle?
4. Explain the relationship between efficiency and cost of construction.
5. How would you redesign the mousetrap vehicle to make it more efficient next time? What other materials might be needed?

 INFLUENCES FROM AUTOMOBILES

INTRODUCTION

Transportation vehicles have had a very significant impact on many aspects of our lives. This activity is designed to identify many of the industries that exist because of the use of a land type of transportation.

TECHNOLOGICAL LITERACY SKILLS

Creativity, brainstorming, group analysis.

OBJECTIVES

At the completion of this activity, you will be able to:
1. Identify the effects of brainstorming.
2. Describe first-, second-, third-, and fourth-level industries that feed the automotive industry.
3. Draw an interrelationship diagram.
4. Gain insight on the impact that one technology, the automobile, has on a society.
5. Identify service, manufacturing, communications, construction, and energy industries.

MATERIALS

1. Color ink pens
2. Rulers
3. Large sheets of paper (2 ft x 3 ft or larger)
4. Large tables to work on
5. Template

PROCEDURE

1. Divide the class into groups of three students each.
2. Each group should obtain several large sheets of paper and the necessary pens, rulers, and so forth.
3. Draw a three-inch diameter circle in the center of a large piece of paper.
4. In the center of the circle write the words, "automotive industry." This is called a first-level industry. Use red ink.
5. Now draw five circles in green ink, two inches in diameter, around the center circle. Draw a line from the center circle to each outer circle.
6. Have your group identify five major industries that exist because of the automobile industry. For example, the road construction industry exists because cars need roads. Cars also require steel and other products. These major industries are called second-level industries. Place each major industry identified in the two-inch circles.
7. Now look at each of the second-level industries. Have your group identify at least five third-level industries that support the second-level industries stated in the two-inch circles. Each industry that is identified should be placed in a one-inch circle around the major industry. Use blue ink. Draw lines to connect the circles again.
8. Select at least five third-level industries. From these, using brown ink, identify as many fourth-level industries as time permits. Use a 1-inch circle.
9. Looking over the entire diagram, can your group identify the manufacturing, service, communications, construction, and energy industries? Label them accordingly.

REVIEW QUESTIONS

1. How many industries might be affected if there were a gasoline shortage?
2. Could a similar diagram be developed for the airplane industry?
3. Can you list additional major (second-level) industries that are supported by the use of automobiles?

CHAPTER 3

Introduction to Land Transportation

OBJECTIVES

After reading this chapter, you will be able to:

- Define land or terrestrial transportation systems.
- Explain the need for land transportation systems.
- Analyze the mass and rapid transit systems.
- Compare support systems for land transportation.

KEY TERMS

Terrestrial	Mass Transportation	Btu
Passenger Miles/Gallon	Pollution	Subway
Efficient	VMT	Transbay
Calories	Miles/Gallon/Person	UMTA
	Ridership	

Introduction

Land transportation (terrestrial) is one of the four major types of transportation systems. Most movement of goods, freight and products, and much of passenger transportation takes place on land. This chapter looks at land transportation used within our society. This includes such areas as the need for land transportation, mass transportation, rapid transit systems, and support systems for land transportation.

FIGURE 3-1 Land or terrestrial transportation has become an important part of everyday life. *Courtesy of Bombardier, Inc. Mass Transit Division, Quebec, Canada*

Land Transportation Technology

Land transportation is one of the most popular types of transportation in the United States, Figure 3-1. In much of the literature, land transportation is also called *terrestrial* (belonging to the land) transportation. Land transportation is critical to our society because it is directly related to our lifestyles.

Deciding the Type of Transportation

Land transportation has developed over the years into a complex network of buses, trains, automobiles, elevators, and so forth. This network has been developed based upon the needs of humans within our society. The greatest motivating factor that helps decide what form of land transportation to use ties directly to the convenience of the customer.

Referring back to Chapter 1, decisions about transportation are based upon five factors: political, social-cultural values, technological, environmental and economical. Convenience to the customer is

tied directly to the social-cultural values of the person. For example, the development of the automobile in the past 80 years occurred because people liked several of its convenient characteristics. These include: 1) the car can be scheduled around the person, 2) the quality of transportation could be determined by the person, and 3) the cost was (and still is) very competitive compared to other forms of transportation. Of course this depends upon insurance and parking costs, length of travel, number of trips, etc.

This caused the automobile manufacturers to continue developing the automobile to meet customer demands. In fact, it is not uncommon for the majority of families to have more than one car. Figure 3-2 shows the average number of vehicles per household in the United States. However, this may not be true in other countries.

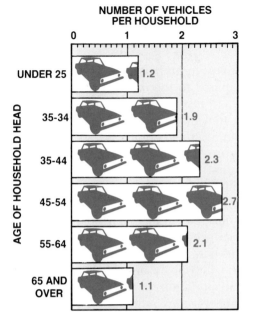

FIGURE 3-2 The United States has more cars per family than other countries; on the average, 2.3 vehicles per family.

In Europe, the average number of cars per family in recent years was approximately 1.0. Part of the reason for this difference may be due to the price of gasoline. Figure 3-3 shows the average price of a gallon of gasoline in a number of countries around the world. Although these prices will vary, the information does suggest that gasoline prices in the United States are still much lower than they are in the rest of the world.

Comparing Transportation Forms for Moving People

In the past, forms of land transportation other than automobiles were not as successful for moving people within the United States. However, because of the price of fuels increasing over the past few years transportation modes have changed slightly. Figure 3-4 shows how three types of transportation compare: the automobile, the train, and the bus. Two numbers are also shown: the percentage of the share of transportation and the miles/gallon/person. The percentage of the share of transportation is a measure as to the number of trips taken by each form of transportation. The *miles/gallon/person*, also called *passenger miles/gallon*, is a measure of the vehicle's average miles per gallon times the average ridership of the vehicle.

For example, the average miles per gallon (mpg) on the automobile is 25 mpg. The average *ridership* is 1.2 persons per vehicle. Therefore, the miles per gallon is shown as 30 (25 × 1.2). In comparison to

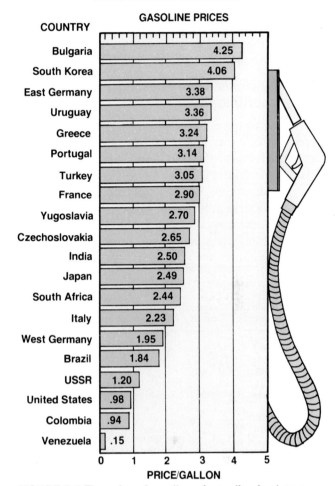

FIGURE 3-3 The price of a gallon of gasoline is shown in selected countries. The United States is still much lower than the others, resulting in the increased use of cars in this country.

SHARE OF TRANSPORTATION

	PERCENTAGE	MILES/GALLON PER PERSON
AUTOMOBILE	80-83%	20-35
TRAIN	4-5%	38-50
BUS	2-5%	113 at 45% CAPACITY
OTHER	7-14%	

FIGURE 3-4 Although the automobile takes on about an 83% share of transportation, it gets only 20-35 miles/gallon/person. The bus, which is much more efficient in terms of energy, has only 2-5% of the share.

other forms of people transportation, the train is much more efficient. As shown, the bus is the most efficient. However, it seems that the more efficient forms of transportation systems are the ones least used. Obviously, this is because of the convenience of the automobile.

Energy versus Land Passenger Transportation

Various forms of land transportation are available for people today. Figure 3-5 shows a comparison of several forms of transportation. Several comparisons are made. These include:

1. Maximum ridership or number of passengers
2. Vehicle mileage per gallon
3. Passenger miles per gallon
4. Energy consumption in Btu/passenger mile

Mode of Transport	Maximum Capacity	Vehicle Mileage	Passenger Miles/ Gallon	Energy Consumption Btu/Pass./ Mile
Bicycle	1	1,560	1,560	80
Walking	1	470	470	260
Intercity bus	45	5	225	550
Subway train (10 cars)	600	0.2	120	1,400
Automobile	4	20	100	1,500
Motorcycle	1	60	60	2,060
Snowmobile	1	20	20	5,000

FIGURE 3-5 Forms of transportation can be compared by capacity, mileage, passenger miles/gallon, and energy consumption. Note that even though a motorcycle gets 60 miles per gallon, it gets only 60 passenger miles/gallon. This is because only 1 person usually rides a motorcycle.

TECH LINK

One Btu (British thermal unit) is the amount of thermal energy needed to raise one pound of water one degree Fahrenheit. One calorie is the amount of thermal energy required to raise one gram of water one degree Celsius.

All energy forms have been put in the same unit and compared to the number of Btu needed. For example, it takes a certain amount of energy, *calories*, to walk a mile. These calories have been converted to Btu so comparisons can be made to other forms of transportation.

The chart in Figure 3-5 gives valuable information about how we transport people throughout the United States. Keep in mind these figures are all based upon maximum ridership, not the average number of people in a vehicle. Some conclusions about this data are:

1. The bicycle is one of the best modes of transportation that can be selected in terms of energy requirements.
2. The automobile is actually more efficient than a motorcycle if there are at least four people in the vehicle. If there were fewer people, however, the automobile could easily become the least efficient.
3. Even though the subway train gets only 0.2 miles/passenger/gallon, it is still somewhat efficient when the vehicle is used at its maximum ridership.

Based upon these statistics, it is seen that Americans again put convenience before efficiency and energy when deciding what mode of transportation to use. Within our society, it can easily be seen that transportation technology does have a direct influence on the choices and the quality of life chosen by people today.

Mass Transportation

Mass Transportation is defined as any technology that is used to transport large numbers or groups of people from one point to another, Figure 3-6. Typically, the system is designed to serve a specific purpose. Several examples of mass transportation systems include buses, subways, and commuter trains, among others.

One of the more innovative systems is the Bay Area Rapid Transit (BART) system of San Francisco, Figure 3-7. The system includes a total of 71.5 miles. BART has 19 subway and tunnel miles, 23 aerial (elevated railway) miles, 25 surface miles, and nearly four miles in the transbay tube, Figure 3-8. The transbay tubes (underwater sections) are huge tubes, 24 feet high and 48 feet wide, connected together under the water. Trackways are located in

FIGURE 3-6 Mass transit systems are used to transport large numbers of people from one point to another.
Courtesy of Bombardier, Inc. Mass Transit Division, Quebec, Canada

each bore to carry trains in each direction. They are separated by an enclosed central corridor for pedestrian access, ventilation and utilities.

FIGURE 3-7 The Bay Area Rapid Transit System (BART) serves as a mass transportation system in the San Francisco area. *Courtesy of San Francisco Bay Area Rapid Transit*

FIGURE 3-8 BART has been designed to travel under water efficiently. An artist's drawing shows the tubes under the bay. *Courtesy of San Francisco Bay Area Rapid Transit*

The need for more mass transportation has grown out of several factors. These factors include: 1) parking in congested areas is becoming more difficult, 2) the cost of driving a personal car is increasing, 3) the costs of using mass transportation systems are being reduced, 4) the environmental impact of mass transportation is less than it is for using automobiles, and 5) the population centers of large cities are changing, creating different transportation needs of people.

Systems Approach to Land Transportation

As stated in Chapter 1, land transportation should be studied from a systems approach. The systems approach views transportation by using input, process, output, feedback and impact, as shown in Figure 3-9. Each area is reviewed briefly by using an example that deals with buses.

Input. The input, command or objective of a bus system is to transport passengers from point A to point B.

Processes. The processes used to transport people on buses are many. First, many resources are needed to feed into the processes. The resources to a bus system or network may include:

1. The people that manage and plan bus routes.
2. The energy used to operate the vehicles.
3. Service and maintenance operations.
4. Engineers needed to design new technology into bus systems' products.
5. The capital needed to run and operate a bus system.
6. Time schedules used for operation.
7. Materials used to manufacture buses.
8. Information needed to operate a bus system, such as ticketing, sales literature, and route layouts.

An example of other processes in a bus system include, but are not limited to, the following:

1. The bus technology is designed as a process for moving people.
2. The process of planning bus routes according to social and regional needs.
3. The process of controlling the position, location and time schedules of buses.

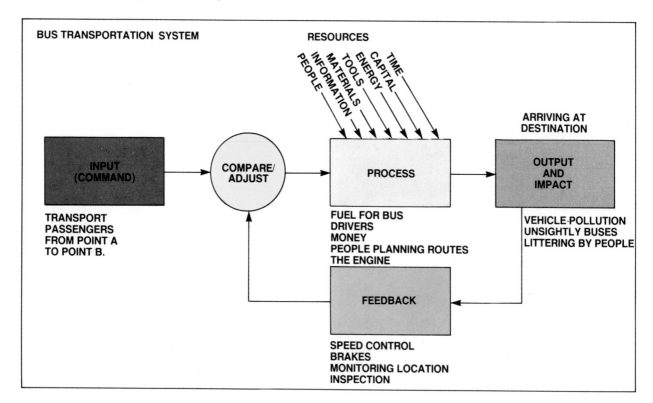

FIGURE 3-9 All land transportation can be studied by viewing the input systems, processes, outputs, feedbacks, and impacts. This example deals with buses.

4. The process of converting the input fuels to power in the engine for propulsion.
5. The process of transmitting energy from the engine to the rear of the vehicle for power.
6. The bus driver driving the vehicle.

Outputs. The outputs in this system include:

1. The action of the people arriving at their destination.
2. The action of people arriving on time.

Feedback. The feedback loop helps to observe the results. The feedback systems within a bus transportation system might include:

1. The controls used to keep the bus at the right speed, braking, and so forth.
2. The monitoring and scheduling of the bus company to make sure the bus arrives at the right time in the right place.
3. Inspecting and checking the operation of the bus, making sure it is operating correctly and safely.
4. Checking road conditions to make sure they are clear and free from hazards for safe travel.

Impacts. Some impacts of using a bus system include:

1. Pollution from the vehicle.
2. Unsightly buses.
3. The pollution produced during manufacturing of the buses.
4. The roads needed for buses take up space and damage the natural environment.
5. The litter that people leave on the bus or at the bus stop.
6. Energy is being conserved because of people using buses.
7. Fewer parking areas in a downtown area may be needed.
8. The cost to the consumer may be less than owning and driving a car.
9. The comfort and efficiency of traveling by bus.

Specialized Land Transportation Networks and Needs

Land transportation systems used within the United States and other countries are directly related to the needs of that society. In the United States, we have a

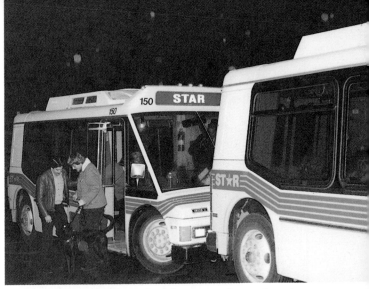

FIGURE 3-10 Medium-sized buses can be equipped with retractable steps for the handicapped. *Courtesy of CDTA*

tremendous need for convenience. This has led to the development and extensive use of the automobile. In addition, because our society is based upon capitalism and industrial growth, we also have a need to purchase many products. These include food, recreational equipment, and clothing, to name a few. Again, transportation systems must be developed to move these goods throughout our society.

However, many other needs are also evident. Special needs of citizens help to develop special transportation networks. For example, broad groups of travelers — the poor, the handicapped, the elderly, the young — often have varying transportation needs. In addition, high density home-to-work travel may create special needs for certain people. This section discusses some of the systems developed because of the different human needs for transportation. These systems were developed in conjunction with UMTA (Urban Mass Transportation Administration).

The Portland Specialized Dial-a-Ride Service

This system is a specialized service developed in the late 1970s for the benefit of the elderly and handicapped persons. These people were unable to use the fixed route service in Portland, Oregon. They were offered the option of taking "The Lift," a door-to-door service provided by the public transit authority. It included 15 medium-sized buses, each equipped with retractable lower steps and wheelchair lifts, Figure 3-10. Service was available from 7 a.m. to 7 p.m. Users were required to request service 48 hours in advance. The fare was 50 cents per trip.

Sears Tower

Usually, when a transportation need arises, a specific type of transportation system is developed. This is true of the Sears Tower in Chicago, Illinois. It is the world's tallest building, 110 stories high. Because of its complex design, a rather extensive transportation system was developed to move goods and people from floor to floor. This is done by an elaborate elevator system.

The Tower is divided into three zones, with elevators in each zone. The building's 104-cab elevator system includes 16 double-decker elevators. In addition, a special high-speed elevator is used to transport people to the Skydeck Observatory. Special elevators are also used to accommodate strollers and wheelchairs. The elevator systems are complete technologies within themselves. For example, the elevator systems use propulsion, guidance, control, suspension, materials, and support technology to operate efficiently and safely. *Courtesy of Sears, Roebuck and Co.*

Milwaukee's User-Side Subsidy Program for the Handicapped

This system provides door-to-door service for the blind, persons confined to wheelchairs, and those using walkers and crutches. Eligible users can travel on any participating taxicab or chaircar company within the county. The minimum fee per trip is $1.50. A voucher system is used to validate and control the operation. After two years, 7,000 persons had enrolled. This represented about 60% of the eligible population. It was found that the primary reasons for this type of travel included such purposes as medical, recreation, work, and personal travel.

The El Segundo Bus Express Employee Program (BEEP)

The El Segundo Employment Center contains a cluster of five large aerospace companies with total employment of more than 18,000 workers. The companies developed a commuter bus service for transporting workers to and from work. Several features of the system include:

1. Schedules matched to working hours.
2. Routes and stops revised to meet changing commuter needs.
3. Ticket books and distance-based fares.
4. New 51-seat buses.
5. Route lengths that vary from about 6 to 21 miles.

BEEP is an express service with limited residential stops. After gasoline prices increased, ridership grew to more than 900 boardings per day. The VMT (vehicle miles of travel) was reduced about 5,300 miles per day. This means that 5,300 fewer miles were driven because of the service. This resulted in approximately 300 fewer vehicles on the road, reducing both peak-hour congestion and the demand for parking spaces.

The Minneapolis Ridesharing Program

This program in the downtown area of Minneapolis and St. Paul involved 11 multiemployer sites employing about 70,000 people. The purpose of the program was to increase the occupancy of vehicles driving to work, using carpools and vanpools. After about two years of operation, the program placed about 1,200 employees into carpools and vanpools. The overall impacts of the ridesharing program were significant. About 28,000 fewer miles per day were traveled. Also, about 890 fewer automobiles were used for commuting.

Many other programs have been tried and tested to help reduce congestion and the cost of transportation, as well as to provide special transportation needs for citizens. The decisions are still based upon political, environmental, social-cultural values, technology availability, and economic implications.

Support Technology for Land Transportation

As mentioned earlier, *support technology* is defined as those systems that are needed for the vehicle to operate effectively. Several support technologies for land transportation include:

1. Fuel stations — Without fuel stations, cars and trucks would be unable to run.
2. Bridges (Figure 3-11A) — Bridges make it possible for various highways to be connected over water, roads, and other features.
3. Highways (Figure 3-11B) — Highways give the passenger in the automobile ease of driving, especially on interstate systems.
4. Harbor-land connections (Figure 3-11C) — Trains bring freight to boats and tankers.

(A)

(B)

(C)

FIGURE 3-11 Each of these examples is a technology that supports the existence of land transportation. Without such support systems as bridges, highways and harbors, the land transportation systems we have today would not be possible. *Courtesy of (A) Morrison Knudson Corporation*

5. Highway construction systems — Many companies build highways. These companies are part of the support systems for land transportation.

6. Bus stops — Without bus stops as a support system, bus passengers would not be able to get on and off the bus.

7. Control centers — Control centers are used as a support system to aid in maintaining speeds, controlling input and output of trucks, and maintaining the position of vehicles with respect to one another. In addition, control centers are used to help control pipeline products. Figure 3-12 shows two types of control rooms for support technology. Figure 3-12A shows a computerized control room for pumping natural gas. Figure 3-12B shows a control room for monitoring a crude-oil pipeline.

8. Parts distribution centers — All transportation forms need maintenance and repair of parts to keep operating and running efficiently.

9. Switching centers — Switching centers are used to switch directions of trains, and to put them on the correct track to their destination.

Without these systems of support our transportation networks on land would not be usable today.

Summary

Land transportation has become a very important part of the total transportation network within the United States and other countries. This chapter presents an introduction to land transportation and its associated technologies.

■ Human needs help to decide the exact type of transportation used within a society.

■ The automobile is a significant part of transportation because of the convenience it affords passengers.

■ Transportation modes can be compared by calculating miles/gallon/person.

■ Average ridership in an automobile is 1.2 people per car.

■ Mass transportation is used to move great numbers of passengers from one point to another.

■ Land transportation can be studied by looking at the input, process, output, feedback, and impact.

■ Specialized transportation systems have been developed for the handicapped, aged, and for people who have special home-to-work transportation needs.

■ Land transportation also requires such support systems as bridges, gasoline stations, highways, control centers, parts distribution centers, and others.

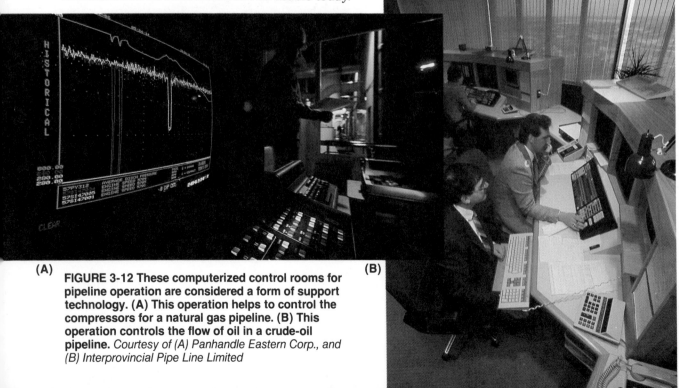

(A)   **(B)**

FIGURE 3-12 These computerized control rooms for pipeline operation are considered a form of support technology. (A) This operation helps to control the compressors for a natural gas pipeline. (B) This operation controls the flow of oil in a crude-oil pipeline. *Courtesy of (A) Panhandle Eastern Corp., and (B) Interprovincial Pipe Line Limited*

REVIEW

1. A person drives a car 8,000 miles to and from work each year (250 round trips). The car gets 17.5 miles to the gallon on this route. Gasoline prices are $1.07 per gallon. How much per year does gasoline cost this driver?

2. This same person can also take a rapid transit system to and from work. The cost per round trip is $1.80. If the person were to use the rapid transit, how much would it cost per year to get to and from work?

3. Based upon the answers to questions 1 and 2, which mode of transportation is less expensive? (Consider only the cost of gasoline versus the cost of the rapid transit fare.)

4. What two other cost items from the previous problems need to be considered when making the decision about which of the modes of transportation is less expensive?

5. Using the bicycle as transportation, state what the input, process, output, feedback, and impacts might be.

6. What is the real underlying reason why our society is so reliant upon the automobile?

7. Describe one specialized system of bus transportation.

8. List at least four support systems used for the automobile.

CHAPTER ACTIVITIES

 DREAM MACHINE

INTRODUCTION

This activity will help you to identify characteristics of a car that are important to you. Also you will be able to determine if these characteristics are realistic.

TECHNOLOGICAL LITERACY SKILLS

Analytical thinking, creativity, brainstorming.

OBJECTIVES

At the completion of this activity, you will be able to:

1. Define the characteristics of a car that you consider important.
2. Select a vehicle and analyze its strengths and weaknesses.
3. Redesign a vehicle to fit your expectations.
4. Analyze the value of your dream machine.

MATERIALS

1. Pencil
2. Current car magazines
3. Handout from instructor

PROCEDURE

1. Divide your class into groups of three students each.
2. As a group, brainstorm a list of car characteristics that would be necessary to buy or build your dream car.
3. Each student now completes the "Dream Machine" handout given by the instructor.
4. Each student will present a description of his or her dream machine to the rest of the class. Remember to justify why your characteristics are important.

REVIEW QUESTIONS

1. What do you think is the primary goal of car manufacturers when they build a car?
2. What is the definition of *planned obsolescence*?
3. Why have imported cars become so popular in America?
4. How have imported cars affected people and the economy in the United States?

 MONITORING TRANSPORTATION

INTRODUCTION

Transportation is a very important part of everyone's life. This activity is an exercise in monitoring your transportation modes.

TECHNOLOGICAL LITERACY SKILLS

Data collection, data analysis, predicting.

OBJECTIVES

At the completion of this activity, you will be able to:

1. Predict transportation modes, times, cost and distance.
2. Monitor transportation modes for one week.
3. Analyze the transportation data collected.
4. Calculate the amount of time spent on transportation in one week.

MATERIALS

1. Handouts from the instructor:
   a. Transportation Data handout
   b. Analysis of Data handout

PROCEDURE

1. As a class, brainstorm as many different modes of transportation as you might use in a week.
2. Obtain the two handouts from the instructor.
3. Answer questions 1 through 4 by making your predictions.
4. Complete the remainder of the "Transportation Data" handout. This will take one week's time. It is important to be as specific and exact as possible. It is best to start on Monday morning and continue through Sunday night. Include all modes of transportation used to get from one building to another (do not include transportation within a building).
5. At the end of the week, complete the "Data Analysis" sheet.

REVIEW QUESTIONS

1. Why is it difficult to make accurate predictions?
2. How would the acceptability and public support be increased if a new mass transit system were to be built in your city?
3. How could you decrease your weekly transportation cost?
4. Are the public transportation systems in your town used widely? If not, why not?

 # AIR CUSHION TRANSPORTER

INTRODUCTION

Most vehicles today are supported by a set of wheels. Other methods are also possible. For example, an air cushion can also be used to transport objects. This lab activity will demonstrate how objects can be transported on a thin film or cushion of air.

TECHNOLOGICAL LITERACY SKILLS

Problem solving, research, design, experimentation, analysis.

OBJECTIVES

At the completion of this activity, you will be able to:

1. Design and build a simple air cushion transporter.
2. Test the air cushion transporter for operational characteristics.
3. Modify the air cushion transporter to improve its performance.

MATERIALS

1. Various sized drills and drill press
2. Heavy-duty shop vacuum, plus extra hose connections
3. General woodworking tools and materials
4. Wood, 4 × 4 sheet of plywood one-half inch thick
5. Disc or belt sander
6. Scale for measuring pounds
7. Books used for weight

PROCEDURE

1. The object of this activity is to design and build an air cushion transporter.
2. Divide the class into groups of two or three students. Each group will design and build an air cushion transporter.
3. The transporter works similar to the design shown in Figure 3-13.
   a. Two round wooden discs are cut from plywood.
   b. The top disc has a connection for the shop vacuum, pressure side.

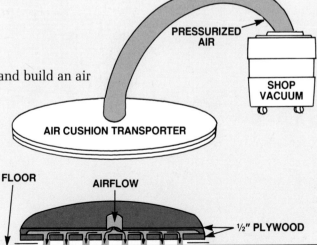

FIGURE 3-13 An air transporter can be built by forcing air into the disc, through holes and to the floor.

c. The top inside disc needs to be sanded to produce a concave surface for the air to flow through.

d. The bottom disc must have holes drilled into it to allow the air to escape; a ⅛-inch drill bit should be used.

e. When the two discs are attached (glued) together, air pressure from the shop vacuum causes the disc to lift and ride on a cushion of air.

4. Several variations will change the air cushion transporter characteristics. These include:

a. Disc diameter

b. Air pressure

c. Number of holes and their size in the bottom disc

d. Amount of space in between the two discs

5. After the air cushion transporter has been designed, build a prototype of the transporter.

6. When built, see how much weight can be placed on the transporter for a prescribed air pressure.

7. After analyzing its operational characteristics, rebuild the air cushion transporter to make it more efficient and able to hold more weight.

8. If time permits, have a contest with other groups to see which air cushion transporter can carry the most weight.

REVIEW QUESTIONS

1. If an air cushion vehicle were to be built for large applications, where would the air pressure come from?

2. What one variable, stated in step 4 of the procedures, improved operational characteristics the most?

3. What effect would an irregular floor surface have on the air cushion transporter?

CHAPTER 4

Modes of Land Transportation

OBJECTIVES

After reading this chapter, you will be able to:

- Identify bus transportation systems.

- Examine the need and operation of trucking systems.

- Describe uses of the automobile.

- Compare the systems used in pipeline transportation.

- Identify rail as a mode of land transportation.

- Examine recreational transportation modes.

KEY TERMS

Fixed Route	Electronic Fuel Injection	Viscosity
BRT	Node	Intercity
Frictional Horsepower	Coefficient of Drag	LPG
Turbocharger	Synthetic	Intermodal
	Btu/ton mile	

Introduction

There are many modes of land transportation. Each type has its own technology, types of propulsion, support, and control. In our daily lives, we rely on all of these modes for transporting passengers and goods, and for recreation. This chapter looks at several modes of land transportation used within our society. These include such areas as rail transportation, trucking systems, buses, automobiles, and others.

Bus Transportation Systems

Introduction to Bus Transportation

Buses are used for much of the transportation needs of people throughout the United States and other countries. Bus transportation makes up about 15% of all passenger miles transported within the United States, Figure 4-1. Bus transportation is considered a form of mass transportation. Bus networks operate both within cities as well as between cities.

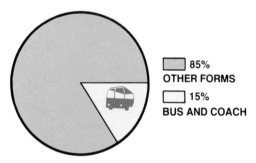

PASSENGER MILES/MODE
MODE OF TRANSPORTATION

85%
OTHER FORMS

15%
BUS AND COACH

FIGURE 4-1 Buses and coach transportation make up about 15% of all passenger miles traveled today.

Since the passage of the Urban Mass Transportation Act (UMTA) of 1964, there has been an increase in federal dollars to renew bus fleets. In the past few years, bus ridership has increased more than 25%. Figure 4-2 illustrates a graph showing the increase in trips per year. The data are projected through 1996. It is anticipated that this trend will continue.

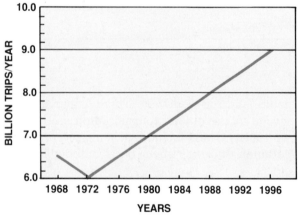

BUS TRANSIT RIDERSHIP

FIGURE 4-2 Bus ridership has been increasing steadily for the past 20 years. This growth is expected to continue.

Many predictions show that gasoline prices will continue to increase in the future. In addition, automobile parking is becoming more of a concern in larger cities. Because of these types of changes, more and more passengers will choose buses for their transportation needs. This, in turn, will prompt bus companies to offer more routes and more frequent schedules for customers.

Advantages of Bus Transportation. There are several advantages to using bus transportation. These include good miles/gallon/person ratings. This means that buses are an efficient means of transporting many people. In addition, buses today are becoming more comfortable and pleasant for riders, as shown in Figure 4-3. This is especially true of highway and charter buses. Bus transportation is also considered a very safe mode of transportation.

FIGURE 4-3 Bus ridership is increasing because buses are being designed for greater comfort. *Courtesy of CDTA*

Disadvantages of Bus Transportation. The disadvantages of using buses primarily are tied to convenience. Typically, customers must adjust their schedules to fit the bus schedule. In addition, buses make many stops, increasing driving time as compared to other forms of transportation for people. However, systems have been planned to eliminate stops by giving buses special lanes on the expressways. For example, the Shirley Highway in Northern Virginia utilizes two median lanes. These are used in one direction in the morning and in the opposite direction in the afternoon.

This type of system can be developed by studying traffic patterns. Figure 4-4 shows the daily home-to-work trips during well-traveled rush hours. Thus, at certain times of the day, different lanes can and should be used more effectively. Commuters who patronize busways such as this find a savings in time and fuel, as well as reduced stress caused by driving a car. An increasing number of other systems such as this are being tested. These systems however, require an analysis of the input, process, output, feedback, and impact before they are tested and developed.

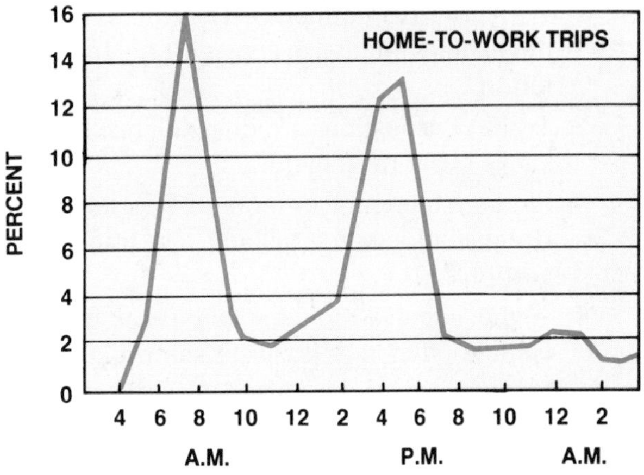

Bus Rapid Transit Systems

Ridership declines and operating losses have troubled conventional bus systems for many years. One suggested system to overcome some of these problems is called the BRT (Bus Rapid Transit). This

system is considered to have solutions to the following problems:

1. Average bus speeds during peak times are limited by traffic congestion on shared streets.
2. Frequent stops to take on or discharge passengers also contribute to low average speeds.
3. The flow of other vehicles is disrupted by buses frequently entering or leaving the traffic system.
4. A large portion of a bus operating cycle consists of acceleration or braking — increasing mechanical wear and driver fatigue as compared to steady operation.

Referring to Figure 4-5, a typical BRT system includes buses that interface with park-and-ride lots and feeder systems. These buses operate on short collection routes in the vicinity of each bus access node (express lane entry). The buses then enter the access node and have nonstop priority on the expressway to a major activity center. The buses travel on special lanes during this time. Here passengers are distributed efficiently at specific spots within the activity center.

PERCENT OF PERSON HOME-TO-WORK TRIPS

FIGURE 4-4 This graph shows when the most home-to-work trips are taken throughout the day. Based upon these statistics, special bus routes can be developed at certain times of the day to eliminate frequent stopping.

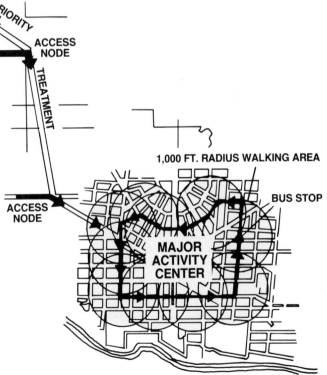

FIGURE 4-5 The Bus Rapid Transit System picks up passengers at various park-and-ride lots, then goes directly to the major activity center via nonstop express lanes.

The advantages to this or similar systems include:

1. With priority treatment, BRT vehicles shorten travel times relative to conventional transportation.
2. Traffic congestion is reduced. This, in turn, keeps buses on schedule.
3. Riders experience a more comfortable trip because of fewer stops and less traffic congestion.
4. Higher average vehicle speeds result in better vehicle efficiency (fuel consumption, maintenance, emissions, noise) and utilization.
5. Higher average speeds also improve driver efficiency.

Bus Schedules

Many forms of bus schedules have been developed by bus companies to communicate with their customers. This information must be made available to the consumer so that customer satisfaction, and thus increased ridership, will result. Bus schedules fit into the "process" part of the systems approach to bus transportation.

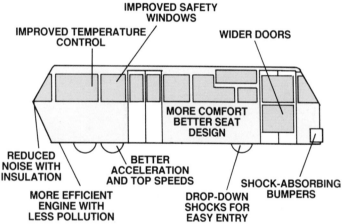

FIGURE 4-6 Buses today are updating many of their designs and safety features.

Buses and Associated Technology

As with any form of land transportation, technology is an integral part of a total system. Buses have improved in several areas of technology, as shown in Figure 4-6. These include:

1. Reducing noise by using baffles and insulation around the engine.
2. More efficient engines that are electronically

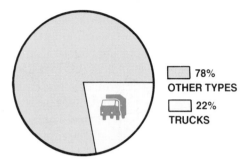

FIGURE 4-7 Trucks use about 22% of the energy within the total transportation sector.

controlled and produce less pollution.
3. Better acceleration and higher top speeds.
4. More comfort for passengers by improvements in seat design and bus layout.
5. Improved safety features including windows and seat design.
6. Wider doors and improved entrance characteristics.
7. Drop-down shocks for ease of boarding the vehicle.
8. Shock-absorbing bumpers.
9. Improved temperature control inside the vehicle.

FIGURE 4-8 Trucks are used to haul gravel and other products. *Courtesy of Freightliner*

Trucking Transportation

A large system of trucks is used to transport many goods within our society. Referring to Figure 4-7, trucks today use about 22% of all the energy consumed within the transportation sector. This means that our society significantly relies on trucks for many of its transportation needs. Trucks are used for a variety of purposes, including:

1. Making all food deliveries.
2. Delivering people engaged in service and maintenance.
3. Carrying merchandise to retail stores.
4. Hauling steel structures for buildings and bridges.
5. Moving gravel and other products from mine site to plant, Figure 4-8.
6. Hauling mail to and from cities.

Without the massive truck networks that are now available, much of the goods consumed by people would not be available. For example, referring to Figure 4-9, more than 1,000 tons of freight are loaded daily at this Memphis terminal. This terminal, in turn, serves 56 other terminals with direct runs. A computer loading system, which is part of the "process" helps to direct the trailers to the correct bays. This helps to minimize the distance employees must travel to unload and reload goods.

Associated Technology for Trucks

Although trucks have essentially been designed and built in the same way over the past years, certain innovative technologies have been developed. These technologies are associated with the

FIGURE 4-9 This trucking company loads more than 1000 tons of freight each day. *Courtesy of Union Pacific Corporation*

propulsion, suspension, guidance and control, and structure systems.

1. Frictional horsepower losses are being reduced by improving tire design, reducing the coefficient of drag from wind resistance, designing more efficient gearing, and reducing the size and weight of the engine (as shown in Figure 4-10).

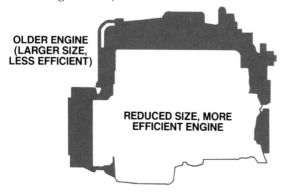

FIGURE 4-10 Truck engines are being designed smaller and more powerful, saving both weight and fuel.

2. Engine design is becoming more efficient. Diesel engines are being designed for better performance and fuel economy. For example, electronic controls are now being incorporated into the fuel injection system for more precise control of air and fuel ratios. Fuel injection systems are also being changed to produce better atomization of fuel with the air. Turbochargers are also being used more extensively for performance and efficiency. Turbochargers use the heat of exhaust to turn a compressor and increase airflow into the engine.

3. More lightweight materials are being used. Lightweight materials result in a greater power-to-weight ratio. The result is that the truck can now haul a greater load with the same amount of power. This, in turn, improves fuel economy per weight and increases a company's profits.

The Systems Approach to Trucking Transportation

As with all forms of transportation the trucking industry can also be studied from the systems approach, Figure 4-11.

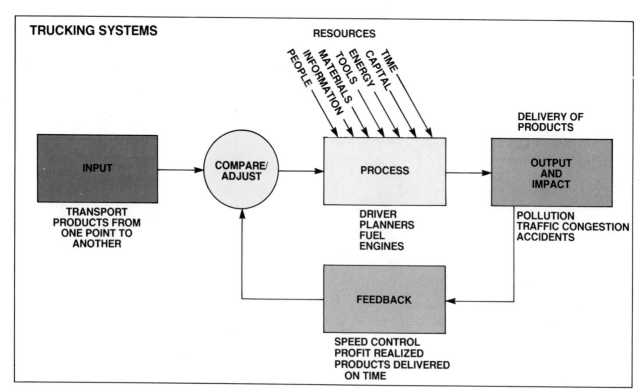

FIGURE 4-11 This systems approach shows the input, process, output, feedback, and impact of trucking operations.

Inputs. The input in a trucking operation includes the command or objective to transport products from one point to another.

Process. The process includes the actual movement of goods from one point to another by the truck. Many resources are needed to aid the process. These include the drivers, the people who plan the routes, the management systems, and the energy resources needed for operation. In addition, the technology for processing the command includes diesel or gasoline engines, the transmission, differential, tires, and so forth.

Output. The output is the final delivery of the product to a store or other destination.

Feedback. The feedback system includes communications to the planning group that evaluates if the products were delivered on time, if the speed and time were within regulations, if a profit was made, and speed controls, among other factors.

Impact. The impact of using trucks includes pollution from the diesel engines; the traffic congestion trucks cause; the dangers of truck accidents, such as spilled fuels or chemicals; and the damage to roads caused by trucks.

Automobiles for Transportation

The automobile has become one of the most significant and important parts of our society. It is used as a primary means of personal transportation. A cut-away view of an automobile is shown in Figure 4-12. The automotive sector accounts for

approximately 22% of all jobs within the United States. These jobs are in the areas of manufacturing, parts distribution, insurance, road construction and sales, among others.

The automobile consumes about 52% of all energy used within the transportation sector, Figure 4-13. However, the number of automobiles in use today has resulted in many negative environmental impacts. These include unsightly salvage yards, tire disposal problems, pollution from vehicles, and excessive use of fuel as a natural resources.

ENERGY USE TYPE

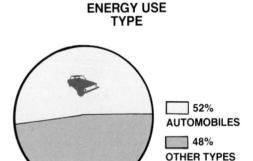

52% AUTOMOBILES

48% OTHER TYPES

FIGURE 4-13 The automobile consumes about 52% of the total energy in the transportation sector.

Even though there was a gasoline shortage several years ago, and gasoline prices rose, Americans preferred to drive alone to work. Figure 4-14 is a chart showing how Americans get to work. At least 64% of all people going to work still preferred to drive alone. The reason for this is tied directly to the convenience the automobile provides.

GETTING TO WORK

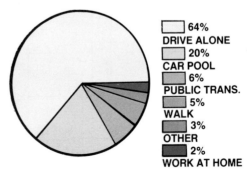

64% DRIVE ALONE

20% CAR POOL

6% PUBLIC TRANS.

5% WALK

3% OTHER

2% WORK AT HOME

FIGURE 4-14 Americans still prefer to drive to work alone rather than using public or other forms of transportation.

FIGURE 4-12 The automobile is one of the most significant parts of our transportation network. A cut-away view of an automobile is shown. *Courtesy of Saab*

World Automobile Use

The United States is not the only country to use the automobile extensively. The chart in Figure 4-15 shows that world auto use has continued to increase over the years.

WORLD AUTOMOBILES IN USE

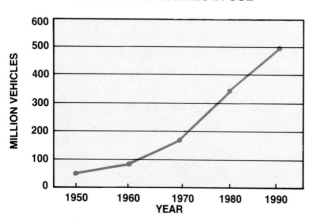

FIGURE 4-15 World automobile use throughout the years continues to increase.

Several factors dictate how much the automobile is put to use. These include the cost of fuel, the economic stability of a country, and the geographical location of people and their workplaces. One way to measure the significance of the automobile within a country is to look at the number of people per car within a country. For example, referring to Figure 4-16, the U.S. has approximately one car for every two people within the country. Many foreign countries are close with 3 to 6 people per car. However, imagine living in a country that has 20 people or more per car. With the standard of living established in the U.S., there would be a major crisis as to "who gets the car."

A second method used to measure the impact of cars within a society is by looking at the "Car Share of Transport." In the U.S., 89% of all passenger miles was driven in an automobile, Figure 4-17. In contrast, Asia has only a 10% share of all passenger transportation by car. The remaining transportation shares are by bus, train, and/or bicycle. This gives an indication of the degree of automobile use in the United States.

CAR SHARE OF TRANSPORT

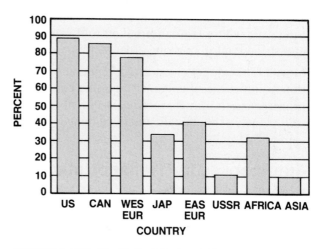

FIGURE 4-17 In the United States, 89% of all passenger miles were driven in an automobile. Other countries use the automobile significantly less.

WORLD CAR POPULATION

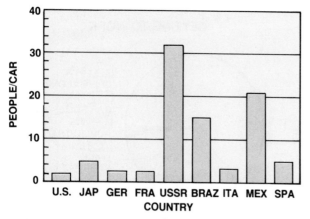

FIGURE 4-16 The United States has about two people for every car in the country. The USSR has approximately 32 people per car.

Statistics and the Automobile

Many interesting statistics give the reader a clear view of how our lives are integrated and related to the automobile.

1. On the average, 63% of all automobile drivers put more than 20,000 miles on their cars each year.
2. Approximately 28% of all cars purchased today were manufactured by foreign companies.
3. Americans spend 15% of their personal income on automobile transportation.

Safety Air Bags

Vehicle safety is becoming more and more important in any transportation system. This is particularly true in automobile transportation. Because the automobile is used extensively in our society, (89% of all transportation takes place by automobile in the U.S.) safety technology is increasing steadily.

One area of major concern has been to provide protection for riders during head-on collisions of passenger cars. To this end, engineers are designing safety systems, such as this inflatable air bag being tested. When an automobile is in a front-end collision, this bag automatically inflates to protect passengers from injury. Problems in the design have centered around noise during inflation, inflating at the wrong time, and not inflating rapidly enough to provide protection. This type of safety protection may be installed as standard equipment on some cars. *Courtesy of TRW Inc.*

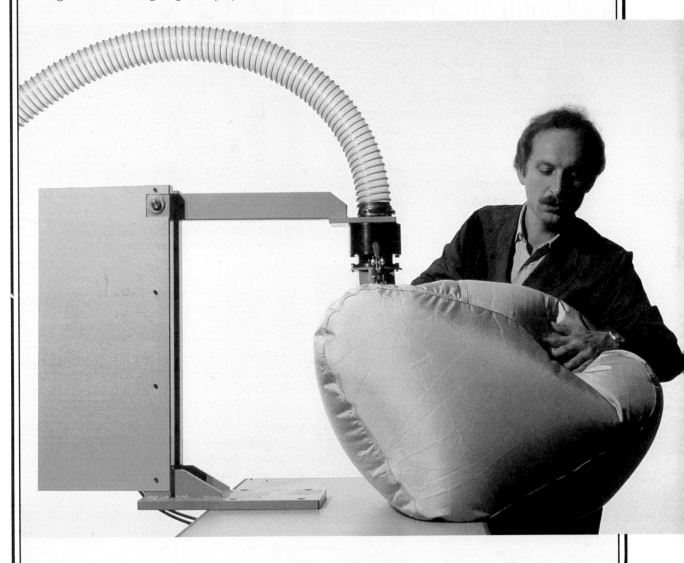

4. World automobile use is projected to increase at about 3% per year. This means that the total number of vehicles in the world will double every 23.3 years.

5. In the late 1980s, the average automobile miles per gallon rose to approximately 29 mpg.

6. In the U.S. as a whole, approximately 80% of automobile trips are shorter than 15 miles.

7. Cars are being made lighter in weight. On the average, for every 400 pounds of weight, the gasoline mileage drops by 1 mile per gallon.

8. At 55 miles per hour, more than half of the fuel is used to overcome wind resistance.

New Automotive Technology

Many factors influence the design of automobiles. In the past 20 years, both an energy shortage and a concentrated effort to reduce pollution have resulted. Because of the widespread impact of these issues, the automobile is constantly being redesigned. The following is a brief view of several important changes in automotive technology.

Vehicle Weight. The car has been reduced in weight by changing the materials used. Engine parts are being manufactured with lighter, synthetic materials. The synthetic-type engine is already being tested for possible use in cars today.

Aerodynamic Shape. The shape of the vehicle can have a significant effect on the fuel mileage. The *coefficient of drag* is a measure of how easily the vehicle cuts or slices through the air, Figure 4-18. These coefficient of drag numbers are being reduced each year, which results in improved fuel mileage.

Electronic Controls. Engines are now using computers to monitor and control the amount of fuel added to the air intake of the engine. Figure 4-19 shows an example of a computer placed in a vehicle. Many factors affect the air-to-fuel ratio.

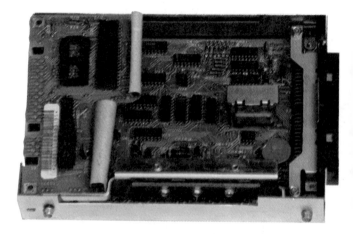

FIGURE 4-19 This computer helps to control the air-to-fuel ratio to a precise and accurate 14.7:1.

FIGURE 4-18 The coefficient of drag on a vehicle is a measure of how easily the car cuts through the air. The lower the coefficient of drag, the better the fuel mileage. *Courtesy of Volkswagon of America*

TECH L I N K

Most engines require a certain air-to-fuel ratio to operate correctly. The air-to-fuel ratio is a measure of the weight of air in relation to the weight of fuel. The best air-to-fuel ratio is 14.7 parts of air to 1 part of fuel. A *rich mixture* means there is too much fuel and not enough air. A *lean mixture* means there is too much air and not enough fuel.

Factors that affect the air-to-fuel ratio are inputs to the computer. These inputs may include load, altitude, vehicle speed, air temperature, ignition timing, cooling temperature and engine speed, among others. Based upon these electronic signals,

Computer-aided Dispatching

Transportation systems are being controlled more and more by computers. In addition to computers controlling engine performance (air-to-fuel ratio) they are also being used to help various service industries with their orders. Here a computer-aided centralized natural-gas service dispatching center is being tested. In operation, service orders are automatically transmitted to 700 vehicles and 100 portable terminals.

This computer network will improve communications between the central office and the many individual service vehicles. This type of network could also be used by other industries that require close contact between the central office and the dispatch vehicle. The goal of this system is to improve response time and enhance overall customer satisfaction. *Courtesy of PSE & G*

the computer tells the injector to inject the exact amount of fuel to each cylinder. Electronic fuel injection improves fuel economy, and at the same time reduces emissions.

Antiskid Braking. With a computer aboard, the vehicle can incorporate equal braking on each wheel. This reduces the chances of skidding, possibly causing an accident. A sensor on each wheel tells the exact r/min (revolutions per minute) to the computer. During braking, when one wheel begins to skid, the computer senses this and immediately releases the brake on that wheel. This causes all wheels to brake evenly, reducing skids.

Automatic Leveling. When the vehicle is braking or accelerating, both front-end alignment and braking are affected. With the computer aboard the vehicle, sensors tell the computer which part of the vehicle is tilting to the front or back. Based upon this input, the computer immediately pumps up load-leveling shock absorbers to keep the vehicle level.

Pipeline Transportation

Certain products used within our society are best transported by pipeline. In fact, if more products could be transported by pipeline a great deal of energy would be saved. Figure 4-20 shows the comparison of the energy in Btu needed to transport a certain weight for a mile (Btu/ton mile). Contrasted to other forms of transportation, the pipeline is the most energy efficient.

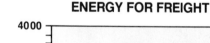

ENERGY FOR FREIGHT

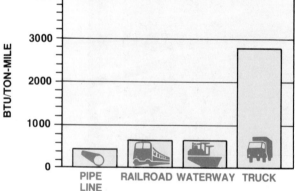

FIGURE 4-20 This chart shows the amount of energy needed to transport a ton of freight a distance of 1 mile. The unit is measured in Btu/ton mile. Pipeline is the most energy-efficient way of transporting a product.

Transportation of freight can be measured in Btu/ton mile. The unit is a measure of the Btu needed to transport a ton of freight a distance of one mile. For example, it takes 450 Btu to transport one ton of oil one mile.

Freight Shipped by Pipeline

Only certain types of products can be shipped by pipeline. Typically, products must be in a liquid or gaseous state. Examples of products that can be transported by pipeline include:

- Crude Oil
- Natural Gas
- Water
- Gasoline
- Diesel Fuels
- Coal Slurry
- Liquid Plastics
- Milk
- CO_2
- Liquid Petroleum Gas (LPG)
- Human Waste Products
- Steam
- Compressed Air

Trans-Alaska Pipeline

The Trans-Alaska Pipeline was one of the largest and most technologically difficult pipeline projects. The Trans-Alaska Pipeline Act of 1973 authorized the construction of a pipeline from Prudhoe Bay on the north slope of Alaska to Valdez. The pipeline today carries crude oil from the north slope of Alaska to Valdez. From Valdez, supertankers transport the crude oil to the northwestern parts of the United States for further distribution.

This pipeline presented several unique design construction problems. Oil has a tendency to change its *viscosity* or thickness with temperature. From the sun, the temperature of the crude oil in this pipeline can be as high as 135°F. At other times the pipeline is underground, causing the oil temperature to fall below freezing. Special insulation was used at these cold spots, whereas refrigeration units were used at the warm spots. Special provisions were incorporated to provide access for wildlife to cross the pipeline. In addition, various designs were incorporated to allow for seismic faults that were encountered and needed to be crossed during construction.

DOMESTIC PIPELINES

FIGURE 4-21 One company's pipeline routes show where each pipeline is located. *Courtesy of Chevron Corporation*

Pipeline Routes

Many pipeline routes are placed within the boundaries of the United States. One company's pipeline routes are shown in Figure 4-21. Four types of products are being transported. These include carbon dioxide, crude oil, natural gas, and LPG (Liquid Petroleum Gas) products.

Pipeline Technologies

Pipeline systems generally consist of pipelines that are 12 to 42 inches in diameter. Typically, a series of compressor or pumping stations are needed to push the fluid or gas through the pipeline. The compressors and pumps are typically run from diesel engines or electrical motors. Some compressor-pumping stations use 2,500 to 20,000 or more horsepower to produce the pressure needed for moving the products. For example, natural gas compressor stations are located between 50 and 100 miles apart. Compression pressures vary for the product being transported. For example, natural gas pipelines have pressures as high as 1,000 pounds per square inch ($1,000 \ lb/in^2$).

Valves, called section valves, are located within longer pipelines systems. These valves make it possible for a section to be shut off for maintenance and repair. Metering and regulating stations are also placed at intervals where products are delivered or further distributed from the pipeline. Depending upon the product that is being transported, various corrosion-protection chemicals and coatings are put on the pipes for protection. Typically, the pipelines are welded pieces of pipe laid in trenches, Figure 4-22.

FIGURE 4-22 Pipelines are constructed by welding pieces of pipe together and then laying them in trenches. *Courtesy of Morrison Knudson Corporation*

Offshore Pipelines

Offshore pipelines are difficult to lay because the pipe must be lowered to the ocean floor from a barge. After being laid, the pipe is usually buried by barges. These barges use high-pressure water jets to dig a trench under the pipe. The pipe must be inspected carefully before it is laid; this is because of the expense and difficulty of repairing an offshore pipeline.

Rail Transportation

Rail transportation, as shown in Figure 4-23, is considered a fixed form of transportation. It is a highly significant form of transportation within our society. Rail transportation is used mostly for transporting goods within the United States. These goods include almost any product from automobile parts, steel, bridge beams, and so forth, to grain and food products. Figure 4-24 shows a unit train carrying coal. A *unit train* means that each unit or car has the same contents.

FIGURE 4-23 Rail transportation has become a significant means of transporting goods, freight and products within our society. *Courtesy of Sante Fe Southern Pacific Corporation*

FIGURE 4-24 Rail transportation is used to haul coal from the mine to the power-plant site. *Courtesy of American Petroleum Institute*

Rail transportation is also used for passenger transportation in the U.S. European countries, however, utilize rail transport more efficiently for passengers than is common in the United States. Rail transportation is one of the easiest and most convenient means for transporting people in Europe. Rail transport is more popular in Europe because of several reasons. These include the closeness of large population centers, the increased cost for gasoline, and a well-developed rail system.

Rail Transportation Networks

As with other forms, rail transportation is dependent upon economic, political, and other considerations. The degree to which passengers use rail transportation is related to the cost of travel and convenience. Although not as complete as other systems, passenger rail transportation is available. Figure 4-25 shows an intercity rail passenger route system. There is a total of more than 26,000 miles of rail within the United States.

INTERCITY RAIL PASSENGER ROUTES

FIGURE 4-25 Intercity rail passenger routes to designated points. *Courtesy of Amtrak*

Freight transportation has more rail routes available. This is because the cost of shipping freight by rail is considerably less than it is with other forms of transport. This lower cost has a tendency to generate many more rail transportation operations and routes.

Rail Transportation Control

As with other forms of transportation, a significant amount of control is needed. Figure 4-26 shows a

FIGURE 4-26 This computerized train control room is able to monitor the movements of 50 trains per day. *Courtesy of Union Pacific Corporation*

panoramic screen that displays train movements through a typical system. This center controls more than 50 trains per day. It has a computerized auto-routing system which is used to automatically prioritize trains and then route them accordingly.

Intermodal Freight

Rail freight transportation is now using *intermodal* systems. This means that the freight is placed in a container. The container can then be transported

(A)

(B)

FIGURE 4-27 This intermodal container facility is used to stack containers on top of one another on the train. *Courtesy of (A) Southern Pacific Transportation Company, and (B) Sante Fe Southern Pacific Corporation*

either by truck or rail. Figure 4-27 shows an intermodal container transfer facility. It is able to handle 360,000 containers per year. The stacking of containers on the train is also shown.

The use of this facility and associated technology has added greatly to train efficiency.

Recreational Transportation

Many forms of land transportation are being used for recreational activities. Figure 4-28 shows an example of recreational vehicles. Other forms of recreational transportation include motor homes, bicycles, sport automobiles, four wheelers, motorcycles, and others. When studying each of these modes of transportation, again there is an input, process, output, feedback, and impact part to the total system.

FIGURE 4-28 Recreational vehicles are also part of the land transportation system. *Courtesy of Polaris Industries*

Summary

Land transportation has become a very important part of the total transportation network within the United States and other countries. This chapter presents data on several of the modes and forms of land transportation.

- Bus transportation is an efficient means of transporting many people.
- Special bus lanes and rapid transit systems are being used with buses.
- Buses are improving their technology with reduced noise, more efficient engines, improved safety features, and drop-down shocks for boarding.
- Trucking systems deliver much of the goods and products purchased each day.
- Trucks are becoming more efficient by using turbochargers, improving aerodynamic design, and by improving fuel injection.
- Automobiles consume about 52% of all energy in the transportation sector.
- World automobile use is steadily increasing.
- About 25% of all people are employed because of the automobile.
- New automotive technology includes lighter vehicles, aerodynamic shaping, electronic controls, antiskid braking, and automatic leveling.
- The pipeline is the most efficient means of transporting many forms of freight.
- The Trans-Alaska Pipeline carries oil from Prudhoe Bay to Valdez.
- Rail transportation has realized improved efficiency by using container trains.
- Recreational transportation includes such transportation modes as motorcycles, four wheelers, snowmobiles, motor homes, and others.

REVIEW

1. One reason that bus transportation is becoming more attractive is because of increasing _____ .
2. When a vehicle is sleek and offers little wind resistance, the _____ is very low.
3. _____ . _____ uses the automobile more than other countries.
4. On the average, there are _____ people for every car in the United States.
5. For every _____ pounds, gasoline mileage on a car goes down by one mile per gallon.
6. A _____ train carries the same contents in each car.
7. What percentage of people use car pooling if a total of 122,000 people must go to work and only 12,130 people are car pooling? (See Mathematical Appendix) _____
8. What are some of the impacts, both positive and negative, of using bus transportation?
9. State some advantages and disadvantages of building the Trans-Alaska Pipeline.
10. Why is rail transportation not used as much for passenger transportation as it is for freight?
11. Define the term *intermodal freight systems*.
12. Using a trucking system as your model, identify the input, process (resources), output, feedback and impact used for operation.

CHAPTER ACTIVITIES

 ## TRANSPORTING GRAPEFRUIT

INTRODUCTION

All goods, such as the food we eat, must be transported from one point to another. This activity will help you to identify the many modes of transportation used to move food from producers to the home.

TECHNOLOGICAL LITERACY SKILLS

Analysis, creativity, group analysis, brainstorming, evaluation.

OBJECTIVES

After completion of this activity, you will be able to:
1. Identify all modes of transportation used to move a particular food product.
2. Analyze the requirements for transporting goods.
3. Evaluate the cost of transportation.

MATERIALS

1. Ink pens
2. Ruler
3. Large pieces of paper (paper rolls work well)
4. Large table

PROCEDURE

1. The object of this activity is to identify all modes of transportation used to transport a grapefruit from a tree in Florida to a kitchen table in Iowa.
2. Divide your class into groups of two or three.

3. Each group should have plenty of paper, rulers, pens, and other equipment.
4. Each group now must list *every* mode of transportation required to transport the grapefruit from Florida to Iowa.
5. Each group will develop a diagram to show each mode of transportation. Include the following for each mode on the diagram:
   a. Type of transportation
   b. Length of time for each
   c. Direction of movement
   d. Amount of energy required (1 low, 10 high)
   e. Identify points of storage (when no travel occurs)
   f. Identify points where extra transportation requirements are needed, such as refrigeration, careful handling, heating, and others.
6. When finished, present your transportation diagram to the class.

REVIEW QUESTIONS

1. Can you identify any transportation modes that were not included?
2. What would happen if there was not enough fuel for the high-energy level transportation modes?
3. Could you redesign the transportation system developed to make it more efficient and less expensive to the customer? What would you change?

 # SAVING WITH MASS TRANSPORTATION

INTRODUCTION

Quite often, mass transportation is more efficient than using a car. This activity is a sequential math problem. It is designed to show how much energy and cost could be saved by using mass transportation for a certain number of trips.

TECHNOLOGICAL LITERACY SKILLS

Problem solving, math analysis, data analysis, drawing conclusions.

OBJECTIVES

At the completion of this activity, you will be able to:
1. Determine energy usage for different modes of transportation.
2. Calculate the amount of energy used by different modes of transportation.
3. Calculate how much energy and cost can be saved by using mass transportation.

MATERIALS

1. Pencil and paper
2. Statistical data
3. Pocket calculator

PROCEDURE

1. The problem statement is as follows:
   a. Statistics show that about 80% of all automobile trips are less than 15 miles in length. How much energy in Btu, gallons of fuel, and dollars, could be saved per person, if half of the trips taken were on a local bus rather than in an automobile?

2. Statistical Data:
   a. An automobile requires 2,580 Btu/passenger mile.
   b. A local bus requires 1,180 Btu/passenger mile.
   c. Total distance a person drives in the city per year = 5,000 miles.
   d. There are 5,200,000 Btu in a barrel of gasoline, also equal to 42 gallons.
   e. Price per gallon of fuel = $1.10.
3. Remember to keep track of all units at each step in the calculation.
4. If half of the trips will be on a local bus, calculate the savings. Work with 2,500 miles of savings on a local bus compared to a car.
5. Multiply 2,500 miles × 2,580 Btu to get energy required for automobile.
6. Multiply 2,500 miles × 1,180 Btu to get energy required for local bus.
7. Subtract the two to get the savings in Btu if half the trips are on the local bus.
8. Convert the savings in Btu into barrels of gasoline saved by dividing the savings by 5,200,000 Btu per barrel.
9. If calculated correctly, the result will be less than a barrel of gasoline saved.
10. If there are 42 gallons in a barrel of gasoline, how many gallons will be saved? This is found by dividing the barrels saved into 42 gallons.
11. Now multiply the gallons saved by the cost of gasoline per gallon. The answer will show how much is saved per person if half of all city trips were on a local bus rather than in a car.

REVIEW QUESTIONS

1. What are the advantages of taking a bus rather than a car?
2. Do you think it is worth it to use a bus rather than a car for transportation?
3. Why would a person not want to take a bus rather than a car for the short, less than 15-mile trips?

 # PLANNING A TRIP

INTRODUCTION

This activity will help to investigate different modes of transportation when planning a trip.

TECHNOLOGICAL LITERACY SKILLS

Creativity, problem solving, data collection, research, brainstorming.

OBJECTIVES

At the completion of this activity, you will be able to:
1. Identify different modes of transportation.
2. List advantages and disadvantages of different modes of transportation.
3. Choose different modes of transportation when planning a trip.
4. Calculate the cost of transportation for a vacation.

MATERIALS

1. Telephone and telephone book
2. Handouts:
   a. Destinations handout

   b. Plan-a-trip Criteria handout
   c. Plan-a-trip handout
3. Maps and/or globe

PROCEDURE

1. In a total class setting, brainstorm how the following will affect the planning of a trip.
   a. money
   b. own a car or not
   c. condition of car
   d. distance of trip
   e. time allowed
   f. number of people
   g. children and age
   h. climate
   i. luggage amount
2. On the board, list as many modes of transportation as possible that people might use on a trip.
3. Randomly distribute trip destinations to each student.
4. Randomly distribute trip criteria to each student.
5. Locate your destination on a map or globe.
6. Obtain the Plan-a-trip handout from the instructor. Complete this handout.

REVIEW QUESTIONS

1. How did your individual criteria influence which mode of transportation you selected?
2. What mode of transportation do you enjoy the most when going on a vacation?
3. Do you feel that our transportation systems are fair and equal to all people?
4. How do seasons and holidays affect the public transportation systems?

 CO$_2$ RACE CAR

INTRODUCTION

The CO$_2$ race car is a popular activity in which students participate in the building and testing of a small carbon dioxide-powered vehicle. In addition, a final competition takes place in class, school, school district, state and/or national level.

TECHNOLOGICAL LITERACY SKILLS

Problem solving, creativity, research, data analysis, data collection.

OBJECTIVES

At the completion of this activity, you will be able to:
1. Research aerodynamic principles that are applied to a CO$_2$ race car.
2. Generate sketches that illustrate possible race car designs.
3. Incorporate given design specifications into the race car.
4. Choose your best design for a race car.
5. Construct a CO$_2$ race car.
6. Participate in a race car competition.

MATERIALS

1. Paper for sketching.
2. One block of pine, balsa or basswood, (1⅝″ × 2¾″ × 12″).
3. Two ⅛″ rod axles.

4. Finishing materials (paint, etc.).
5. Various grades of sandpaper.
6. Plastic straw or brass axle bearings.
7. Four washers and four wheels.
8. Two screw eyelets.
9. At least two CO_2 cartridges per student.
10. General woodworking laboratory tools and machines.
11. Race car specifications manual.

PROCEDURE

1. Research and discuss aerodynamic theory as a total class. The goal is to make the race car as aerodynamically efficient as possible.
2. Sketch possible body designs for your vehicle.
3. Choose your best design and incorporate the specifications supplied by your teacher. These specifications are standard throughout the competition and must be followed carefully.
4. Draw to scale the side and top views of your design and cut patterns.
5. Trace your patterns onto the block of wood.
6. Mark axle locations and cartridge holes.
7. Drill necessary holes in the race car body.
8. Rough cut the outline of your race car on the bandsaw.
9. Further shape your vehicle to the exact design using files and rasps.
10. Sand your vehicle with the appropriate sandpaper.
11. Paint your race car and apply any decals if desired.
12. Assemble the remaining parts of your race car, including the axles, bearings, wheels, and screw eyelets. (The screw eyelets are to guide the race car along a tightly strung wire). Again, make sure the race car is exactly to the specifications given to you by the instructor.
13. You are now ready to participate in the CO_2 competition.

REVIEW QUESTIONS

1. How could your car be improved aerodynamically?
2. Describe the characteristics of the fastest car in your class competition.
3. Describe the following systems as they are used in your race car:
   a. Guidance and control system
   b. Support
   c. Propulsion system

CHAPTER 5

Introduction to Marine Transportation

OBJECTIVES

After reading this chapter, you will be able to:

■ Identify the cost and need for marine transportation systems, and their role in our society.

■ State the definition of such marine terms as *yaw, roll, prop pitch, intercoastal, hull, bilge, aft, port,* and others as given.

■ Identify the important waterways used for marine transportation in the U.S.

KEY TERMS

Navigational	Nautical	Chine
Vessel	Ton mile/gallon	Taconite
Buoyed	Breadth	Gypsum
Displacement	Propeller	Locks
Conical	Sequential	

Introduction

Marine transportation technology is one of the four major forms of transportation in our society. In fact, marine transportation has become a major technology in other countries as well. This is especially true in countries that have major population centers near or around islands or oceans. For example, many of the Scandinavian countries in Europe, such as Denmark, Norway, Sweden and Finland,

have a highly developed marine passenger transportation system. Copenhagen, Denmark, is located on an island. Marine transportation must be able to transport cars, trains, goods, products, and other articles from one land mass to another. The United States uses a significant amount of marine transportation. This chapter is about marine transportation, its related terms, and various marine waterways.

FIGURE 5-1 Americans have long had a "romance" with marine technology. This ship is the U.S. Coast Guard Cutter *Eagle*. *Courtesy of U.S. Coast Guard*

Marine Transportation

The Need for Marine Transportation

Marine transportation played a significant role in the past. Even before the engine was developed, marine transportation has had an impact on the way in which people live. Most of the transportation of goods or products in the 1800s was by marine forms of transportation. Americans have had a long standing "romance" with the marine industry. Figure 5-1 shows the U.S. Coast Guard Cutter *Eagle*. The vessel was built in Hamburg, West Germany, in 1936. She was one of the lead ships during the 1986 July Fourth celebration in New York City. The gathering of tall ships was part of the celebration for the refurbished Statue of Liberty's 100th birthday.

Throughout the years, marine transportation has filtered down to many aspects of our lives. Many of the goods used within society today are transported by marine vessels. In fact, more than 18% of all U.S. goods is carried by water freight, not including the Great Lakes Waterways. Some of the

FIGURE 5-2 Many of the products we use each day are brought to us by marine transportation. Here coal is being transported by a barge. *Courtesy of General Dynamics Corporation*

products include coal, as shown in Figure 5-2, oil, stone, trucks, construction equipment, rail cars, grain, iron ore, waste products and food products, among others.

Role of Shipping

The role that marine transportation fills in our society is recognized by the increasing attention being given to this form of transportation today. The ships of today are among the most striking products of science and technology. Improvements in hull design, navigational systems, and propulsion systems are being tested and designed by high-speed computers. At the same time, ships are being built in longer lengths to hold more cargo. Older ships are even being cut in half and extended; this is done by adding cargo compartments. Ships that are 1,000 to 1,600 feet in length are not uncommon in the marine transportation networks, Figure 5-3.

FIGURE 5-3 Ships today are being built to greater lengths to hold more cargo. *Courtesy of U.S. Army Corps of Engineers*

Fuel consumption, computed on a ton-mile/gallon basis			
	Water	Rail	Truck
Ton-miles per gallon of fuel	500	200	60
Fuel consumption for transporting 15 million tons of iron ore from Duluth, Minnesota to Chicago, Illinois	24 million gallons	35 million gallons	123 million gallons

Most Efficient — Least Efficient

FIGURE 5-4 This chart shows a comparison of fuel needed to ship a certain weight of iron ore by water, rail, and truck. As indicated, water transportation is generally much less expensive than the other forms.

Accelerating research into new forms of marine transportation suggests the probability that there will be many new types of ships in the future as well.

Cost of Marine Transportation

Marine transportation is significantly less expensive than transportation of goods by trucks or trains, for example. Figure 5-4 shows a simple comparison of three different forms of transportation: water, rail, and truck.

Recreational Boat

Marine transportation affects many parts of our lives. In addition to using marine transportation to transport people and goods throughout society, boats are also used for recreational use. This boat is used for leisure sport. It is designed with style and comfort in mind, as well as for high performance and power. The boat is more than 35 feet in length; weighs approximately 9,000 pounds; and has over a 200 gallon fuel capacity. It uses two engines for power (propulsion). The draft is 24 inches (suspension). The fin on the back is said to produce stability at high speeds, although, in reality, it is used more to improve style rather than performance. The hull is designed to displace minimum water during operation. Although out of the price range now for many sports boaters, many of the new designs on this boat will probably find their way into smaller and more affordable recreational boating technology. *Courtesy of Wellcraft Marine*

The comparison is made on a ton mile/gallon basis. This unit of measure shows the amount of energy in gallons, to move freight in tons, transported a certain distance in miles. For example, the chart shows the comparative fuel utilization to transport 15 million tons of iron ore from Duluth, Minnesota to Chicago, Illinois. To deliver this amount of iron ore, it takes 123 million gallons of oil in a truck, 35 million by rail, and only 24 million by water. This translates into a saving of about 100 million gallons of fuel if shipped by water rather than by trucks on the highway.

Marine Transportation and the Systems Approach

As with other forms, marine transportation can also be studied through the systems approach. Refer to Figure 5-5 to study the systems approach. Use a small, six-person, 65-hp recreational boat in the example to travel across a lake from point A to point B.

Input. The input or command to the system is to transport six passengers from point A to point B.

Processes. The processes required in this example include boat technology (hull design, steering, and so forth), and propulsion technology. Several resources are required to aid the process. These include the fuel used to operate the motor, the money needed to buy the boat, the fuel to manufacture the boat and accessories, the navigational information needed to operate the boat properly, the operator, and the materials needed to build the boat, among others.

Outputs. The output includes the boat arriving with the people at its destination.

Impacts. The impacts include pollution from the motor, the environmental drawbacks from refining, and the depletion of natural resources in wood, plastics (petroleum), and metals.

Feedback. The feedback systems include the navigational aids to direct and control the boat's direction, the use of the speed controls, and the use of the steering systems. All of these technologies are related to feedback systems.

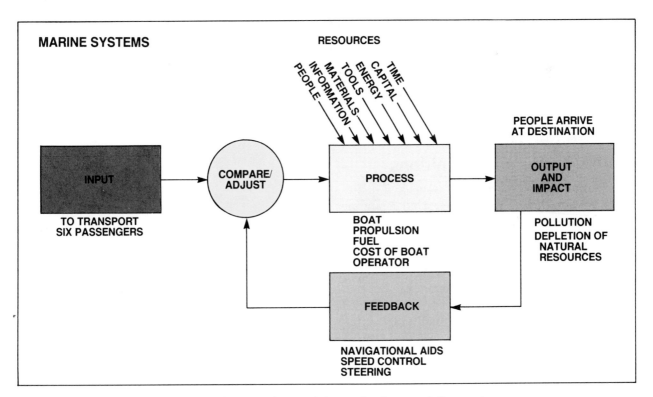

FIGURE 5-5 The systems approach helps to understand the marine transportation system.

FIGURE 5-6 This photo illustrates the definition of the term beam. The *beam* is the breadth of the vessel at its widest point. *Courtesy of Niagara Mohawk Power Corp.*

Marine Terms and Definitions

The marine industry uses many terms and definitions to describe its operations. Understanding these terms will help to make the reader more technologically literate in the area of marine technology. This section looks at many of the terms that are used in the marine industry today. The terms "she" and "her" are used with reference to boats in several of the definitions. These terms are still used because of their historical and traditional significance.

Aft — The aft is defined as the rear area of a ship

Beam — The beam is the breadth of a vessel at its widest point, Figure 5-6.

Bilge — The bilge is the lower part of a boat or ship below the floor, near the center. It is the point on the bottom of the ship or boat upon which she will rest when on ground. It is also where any internal water will collect inside the hull.

Bulkhead — The bulkhead is defined as the vertical wall dividing the hull into separate compartments.

Buoyancy — A body partially or completely immersed in water is said to be buoyed up or in a state of buoyancy. It is sustained by a force equal to the weight of the fluid displaced. Cork and wood float because they are lighter than water. Metal, however, is denser. A one-pound chunk of metal will sink to the bottom of the water. However, if shaped into a thin, shallow bowl, it will float. It is now presenting a larger surface area to the water. When placed on the water, it will displace more water, in this case, a pound of water. A force equal to the weight of the displaced water is buoying up the metal bowl.

Figure 5-7 shows the relationship between buoyancy and gravity. These two forces act against each other. The water pushes up all around on the submerged hull. The total push acts as a single upward buoyant force shown as B (buoyancy). The downward force of gravity is equal to the weight of the ship and everything in it. The total force G (gravity) is exerted at approximately the center of the ship. These two forces and their position help to make the vessel either stable or unstable. A stable ship is able to return to the upright position after being tilted on its side. An unstable ship will not be able to return as easily to the upright position. Quite often, the position of the load in a boat can cause it to be unstable.

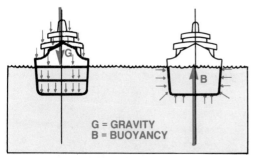

G = GRAVITY
B = BUOYANCY

FIGURE 5-7 The forces of buoyancy and gravity work against each other to stabilize the ship or craft.

Boat propellers or props can be damaged by a process called cavitation. A partial vacuum can be produced in water near a propeller. As the propeller blades cut through the water, vacuum bubbles are formed on the back edge of the blades. As these bubbles implode, they have a tendency to eat away at the nearby metal, causing damage to the metal. This is called *cavitation*. In some cases, the metal looks like it has been attacked by acid. However, the cavitation process has simply eaten away the metal.

Bow — The bow of a boat is considered the front of the craft.

Cuddy — A cabin in the ship or boat is called a cuddy. On newer sports boats, the cuddy is in the front of the vessel, usually in the bow. On older ships, the cuddy was referred to as the cabin under the poop deck.

Dock — The area of water in a port or harbor totally enclosed by piers is known as the dock.

Draft — The vertical distance from the waterline to the keel is called the ship's draft. The draft is an indication of the amount of water that is displaced by a hull. A heavier boat has a greater draft than a lighter boat. Obviously, the greater the draft the more energy required to move the vehicle. Draft marks are placed on large ocean-going vessels to measure the depth during loading, Figure 5-8.

Dry Bulk — Freight that is usually dry, such as grain, salt, gypsum, coal, and others is referred to as dry bulk. Many freighters and cargo ships are able to transport several types of dry bulk as opposed to liquid products.

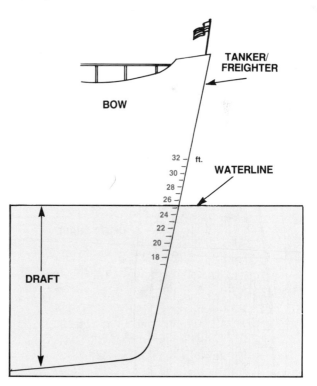

TANKER/
FREIGHTER

BOW

WATERLINE

DRAFT

FIGURE 5-8 The draft of a vessel is a term used to indicate how deep the vessel sits in the water. The front of large tankers and other freight ships display numbers on the bow to indicate the draft.

Fore — Typically referenced as the front of the ship. Fore is also used to define certain sails on the boat; for example, the *fore* or *aft* sail.

Gunwale — The gunwale is the top of any rail of a boat or vessel.

Hull — The hull is usually referred to as the main body of a vessel, not including the upper parts, such as the masts, and so forth. The hull is considered the sides and bottom of a ship or boat. Typically, there are two types of hulls: the displacement hull and the planing hull. *Displacement hulls* are designed to carry heavy loads. *Planing hulls* are designed to ride on top of the water. A planing hull is much like a stone skipping across the water. Today, many manufacturers are designing hulls to plane more efficiently at all speeds. For example, some manu-

facturers use a sequential lift hull. A *sequential lift hull* is designed to redistribute lifting forces with each change in hull speed. The result is less wetted surface and less drag. This, in turn, produces greater engine efficiency.

An example of the design of a planing hull is shown in Figure 5-9. The delta shape of the hull provides stability and makes it easier to plane the boat. The conical contour of the hull provides clean cutting through the water for optimum waterflow with minimum drag. The chine improves ride during roll and reduces splashing over the bow.

Intercoastal — Intercoastal shipping is marine transportation that takes place between coastal regions.

Intracoastal — Intracoastal shipping is marine transportation that takes place within a specific coastal region or area.

Intermodal — Intermodal refers to that of using more than one form of transportation mode to move freight or products. For example, in Figure 5-10, freight is transported to the harbor by rail. It is then transported by boat to another destination.

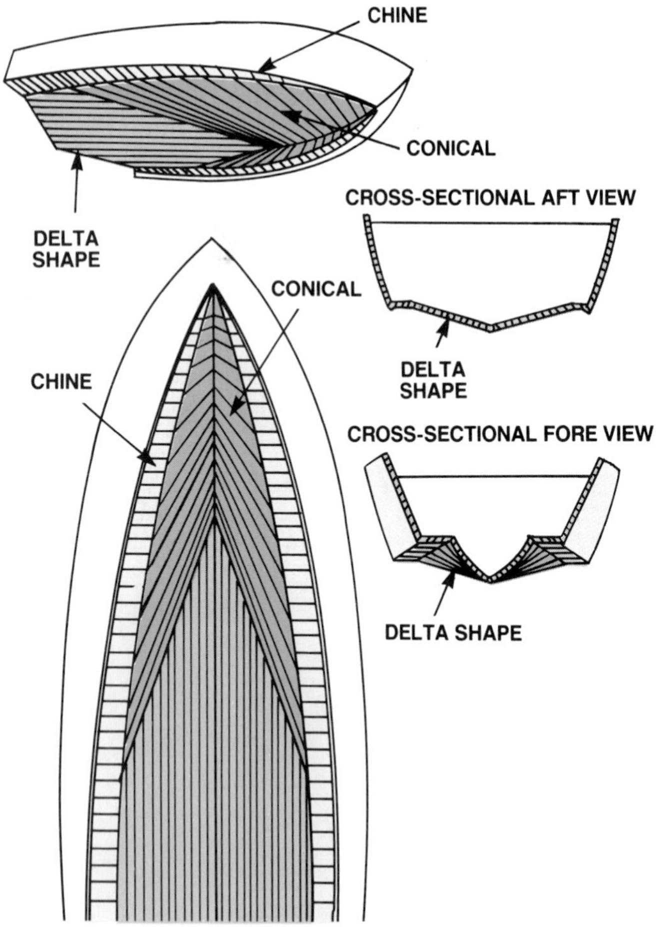

CHINE

CONICAL

DELTA SHAPE

CROSS-SECTIONAL AFT VIEW

DELTA SHAPE

CONICAL

CHINE

CROSS-SECTIONAL FORE VIEW

DELTA SHAPE

FIGURE 5-9 Hulls are designed to reduce drag and improve ride and safety. This hull uses a delta shape near the stern, a conical shape near the front, and a chine to reduce rolling and splashing.

FIGURE 5-10 Intermodal transportation uses more than one form of transportation mode. This harbor scene shows that freight can be transported by several modes, both land and marine. *Courtesy of Penzoil Company*

Keel — The lowest continuous line on the bottom of the ship or boat is called the keel. Typically, the keel is made of a metal or timber form (runner) extending along the centerline of the bottom of the vessel.

Moor — The condition of a boat when she lies in a harbor, or when she is anchored using two anchors.

Pitch — The term pitch is used to indicate the angle of the ship when a wave lifts the bow and then, after passing under the boat, lifts her stern.

The pitch is also a term used to indicate the angle of the blades on the propeller. The pitch is a measure of the distance the propeller moves forward during each revolution, Figure 5-11. For example, a pitch of 17 means that the propeller, and thus the boat, will move 17 inches forward for each revolution of the propeller. This assumes that there is no slip between the propeller blades and the water. In comparison, a pitch of 19 usually produces a higher top speed; a pitch of 15 will produce a lower speed. The lower the pitch, the more pulling power, but the less top speed. The greater the pitch, the higher the top speed, but the lower pulling power.

Knot — A nautical measure of speed. Ships and boats typically measure speed in knots rather than in miles per hour.

TECH L I N K

> One knot is equal to the speed of 6,080 feet per hour or about 1.15 miles per hour. For example, if a boat is going 30 knots, it is going about 34.5 miles per hour. Or, if a boat is going 35 miles per hour, it is going about 30.1 knots.

Poop deck — A term used to describe any raised deck near the aft or stern of the boat.

Port — The name for the left-hand side of the ship as viewed from the rear, stern or aft of the vessel.

Quarterdeck — The part of the upper aft or stern deck on a boat that is usually reserved for the captain. Also, the part of a deck from which the ship is commanded.

Roll — A term used to indicate the oscillation motion of a vessel from side to side.

Rudder — A device on a ship or vessel to steer or control the direction while under way. The rudder usually resembles a large blade placed in the stern of the vessel. As the rudder is turned, the boat turns accordingly. Figure 5-12 shows the position of a typical rudder.

Starboard — The right-hand side of the vessel as viewed from the aft or stern section.

Stern — The stern is the term used to describe the rear of the vessel.

Tramp — Tramp refers to a type of cargo-carrying vessel that does not work on a regular route. It is available to carry general cargo to any destination, as required.

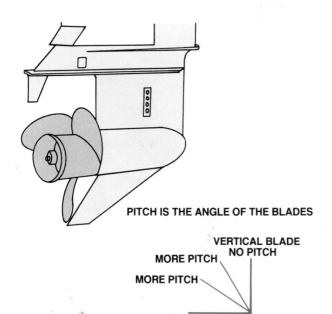

PITCH IS THE ANGLE OF THE BLADES

VERTICAL BLADE
NO PITCH
MORE PITCH
MORE PITCH
CENTER OF DRIVESHAFT

FIGURE 5-11 Pitch is defined as the angle of the blades on the propeller.

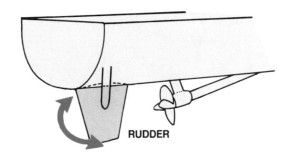

RUDDER

FIGURE 5-12 The rudder is used to control the direction of a vessel or ship.

Yaw — Ships at times do not hold a steady course. This may be caused by wind or water currents. The ship then yaws away or deviates from the original path. A trained captain can usually anticipate when a boat is likely to yaw. Thus, a compensation can be made to keep the vessel on course.

These are just a few of the many terms used throughout the marine industry. Many other terms are used as well. However, these terms, as defined, will help the reader to better understand the boating and marine industry.

Marine Waterways

St. Lawrence Seaway

The St. Lawrence Seaway System is an international waterway extending from the Atlantic Ocean to Duluth, Minnesota. More than 50 nations utilize this waterway system for freight shipping. Its total distance represents 2,342 miles, or about eight days of travel time. From Duluth, Minnesota, to the Atlantic Ocean, the water level drops 602 feet. Locks are used to aid in this process.

TECH LINK

A lock is an enclosure, usually in a canal, with gates at each end used to raise or lower boats in the water as they pass from one level to another.

A more detailed description of locks is given in Chapter 6.

Figure 5-13 shows the entire St. Lawrence Seaway System. Each of the cities listed is a port for loading and unloading freight and cargo. The St. Lawrence Seaway is used to transport many such products as grain, gypsum, coal, iron ore, and others for a large portion of the United States. Figure 5-14 shows the areas and states served by the waterway.

Inland and Coastal Waterways

The United States has another 25,380 miles of navigable inland and coastal channels in addition to the St. Lawrence Seaway. Statistics show that at

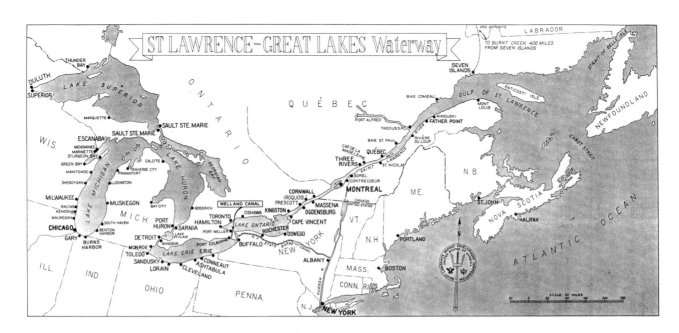

FIGURE 5-13 This map shows the complete St. Lawrence Seaway transportation system. Each city listed is a port where freight is loaded and unloaded. *Courtesy of Detroit District U.S. Army Corps of Engineers*

ST. LAWRENCE SEAWAY SERVICE AREA

FIGURE 5-14 The St. Lawrence Seaway transports products for a large portion of the United States.

least 38 states can be serviced by marine transportation. Most of these waterways were designed and operated as federal projects in past years. Figure 5-15 shows some of the major commercial inland waterways within the United States.

International Waterways

International waterways are another form of marine transportation. Many routes are used for international shipping. Major routes exist among the United States, South America, Africa, Europe and other countries as well. Because these routes are very exact, the vessels must follow a predetermined shipping lane or route for safety purposes.

FIGURE 5-15 Shown are the major inland and intracoastal waterways used for marine transportation in the United States. *Courtesy of U.S. Army Corps of Engineers*

Summary

■ Marine transportation systems are an integral part of the economy in the United States.

■ The cost of shipping a product by waterway is generally less expensive than by truck or rail transportation.

■ Many terms are used in the marine industry. Some of the terms used most include aft, bulkhead, bilge, buoyancy, bow, cuddy, draft, fore, gunwale, hull, moor, keel, pitch, knot, roll, rudder, stern, and yaw. These and other terms are defined.

■ The St. Lawrence Seaway is one of the most popular and busiest inland waterways in the United States.

■ Several other inland waters support marine transportation, especially near inland rivers.

REVIEW

1. The rear area of a ship is called the _____ .
2. The vertical distance from the water line to the keel is called the _____ .
3. The angle of the blades of a propeller is called the _____ .
4. If a boat is moving 32 miles per hour, its speed in knots is _____ knots.
5. When a ship will not hold a steady course, it has a tendency to _____ away from the original course.
6. A recreational boat using an outboard engine has the propeller turning at 4,200 revolutions per minute (rpm). The boat is moving 71,400 inches per minute. What is the pitch of the propeller? _____
7. Discuss the importance of marine transportation in the United States.
8. Using the systems approach, discuss the input, processes, outputs, impacts, and feedback systems of a sailboat.
9. Define the term buoyancy and state how it relates to boats.
10. State the terms used for the front, back, sides, and bottom of a vessel.
11. What is the difference between inter and intracoastal waterways?

CHAPTER ACTIVITIES

 BUOYANCY

INTRODUCTION

This activity is designed to show you how buoyancy can be produced and changed in a piece of material.

TECHNOLOGICAL LITERACY SKILLS

Problem solving, research, data analysis, experimentation, predicting.

OBJECTIVES

At the completion of this activity, you will be able to:

1. Identify how materials can be shaped to produce buoyancy.
2. Shape a material to produce the best buoyancy.
3. Test the material for weight and stability.
4. Reshape the material to improve buoyancy.

MATERIALS

1. Ballpeen hammer
2. Pieces of malleable metal to form into different shapes
3. Weights for testing buoyancy
4. Water bin for testing purposes
5. Metal band saw
6. Buoyancy handout

PROCEDURE

1. This activity is done by each student.

   ▶ **CAUTION:** Always wear safety glasses when working with tools in the laboratory. Also, make sure you know how to use the tools in the laboratory correctly. If you're not sure, check with your instructor.

2. Each student obtains a piece of malleable metal, preferably a flat 10″ × 10″ piece of aluminum.
3. Cut the metal into a 10-inch diameter circle.
4. Try to get the metal disc to float. Notice that it cannot be done in its present flat shape.
5. Now shape the piece of metal into a small bowl about ½ inch in depth.
6. Try floating the piece of metal as it is now shaped.
7. Add weights to the bowl until it sinks and record the maximum weight on the instructor's handout.
8. Now shape the piece of metal to produce a deeper bowl, about 1 inch in depth.
9. Try floating the bowl again in the water and adding weight until it sinks. Record the weight again on the handout.
10. Again, reshape the bowl to have a depth of about 1½ inches. Add weights, and record on the handout.
11. Complete the remaining parts of the Buoyancy handout.

REVIEW QUESTIONS

1. What happens to the buoyancy as the bowl sinks deeper?
2. What in the experiment has the greatest effect on buoyancy?
3. How would the buoyancy be affected by using different materials, such as wood or plastic, for example?

CHAPTER 6

Marine Transportation Technology

OBJECTIVES

After reading this chapter, you will be able to:

■ Analyze several support systems used for marine transportation, including harbors, docks, marinas, locks, and others.

■ Compare the different types of vessels, craft, and boats used for marine transportation.

■ Explain the need for certain associated technology in marine transportation.

KEY TERMS

Hydrofoil	Horsepower	Jib
Tacking	Four Cycle	Thrust
Sonar	Aerodynamics	Two Cycle

Introduction

A great deal of technology is tied to marine transportation. For example, many types of vessels are used for a variety of purposes. These may include, freighters, hydrofoils, and sailboats, among others.

Support facilities are also needed for marine transportation. This chapter is about the various technologies and support facilities used in marine transportation.

FIGURE 6-1 A harbor is considered a support facility for marine transportation. This is an aerial view of the Duluth/Superior Harbor in Minnesota and Wisconsin. *Courtesy of Detroit District U.S. Army Corps of Engineers*

Support Facilities

Support and control facilities are designed to aid or help marine vehicles operate. Some of the most common facilities include harbors, docks, and locks. This chapter looks at each of these support and control facilities.

Harbors and Ports

Ports and harbors are support facilities for marine transportation systems. Ports and harbors help to dispatch and receive goods involved with trade. Their main purpose is to provide a rapid, safe and economic link between marine transport and other forms of transport such as rail and truck.

Figure 6-1 shows a typical harbor used for shipping. This harbor in Duluth, Minnesota, is part of the St. Lawrence-Great Lakes waterways. This harbor is used to load and unload several primary products, such as coal, grain, and iron ore. Ships from both the United States and foreign countries arrive and depart each day. Some of the foreign countries served include Belgium, France, Greece, India, Italy, Liberia, Norway, Panama, United Kingdom, Russia, West Germany, and Yugoslavia.

MINNESOTA POINT
SUPERIOR BAY
ST. LOUIS RIVER
1
2
3
4
5
6
7
8

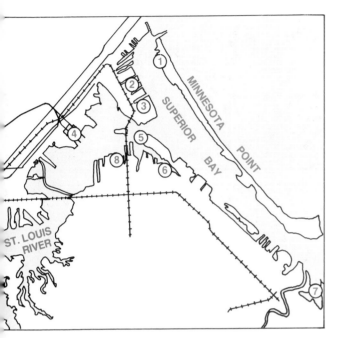

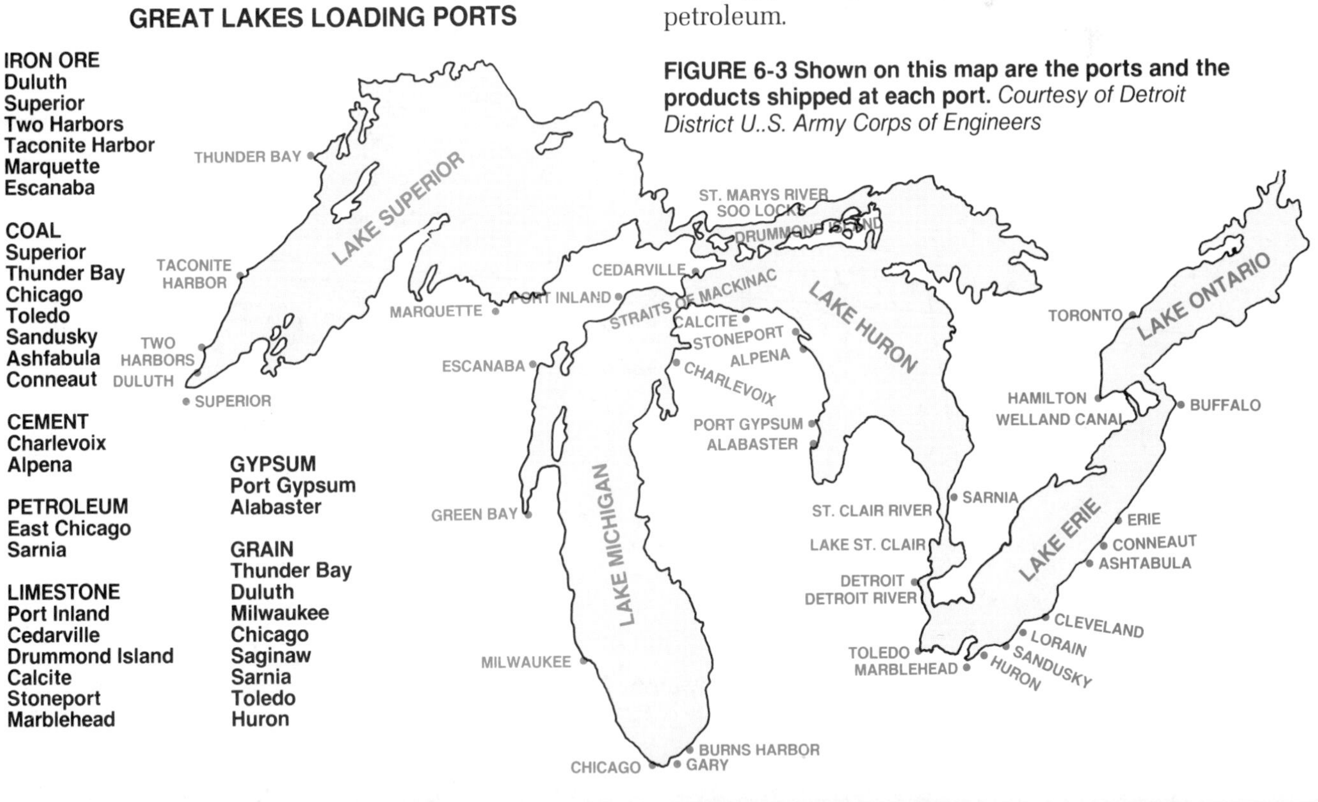

FIGURE 6-2 This map shows a typical harbor and the many ports that are needed for support operations. *Courtesy of Detroit District U.S. Army Corps of Engineers*

A more detailed layout of the harbor and port is shown in Figure 6-2. Referring to this map will help you understand the support systems needed for shipping. Several points are described on the map.

Point 1 is the government docks used primarily for the U.S. Army Corps of Engineers. Point 2 is a series of grain elevators. More than 100 ships load and unload grain each year at this point. Point 3 is the general cargo loading and unloading area. This area includes cranes, holding berths, tank-farms, warehouses and a Free Trade Zone area.

Point 4 includes the iron ore and taconite (low-grade iron ore) docks. This area is used by several hundred lake freighters each year. It has open storage for 300 million tons of taconite. Point 5 is one of the world's largest and busiest grain elevators. Point 6 is a 65-acre plant for building and repairing ships. Point 7 serves as ore docks, using conveyor-type shiploaders. Point 8 is an efficient coal dock, able to handle 6 million tons of Montana coal annually. Although most ports have similar technology for support systems, they may be laid out differently. The reason for different layouts is primarily because of the original geographical structure of the shoreline.

Great Lakes Loading Ports

Figure 6-3 shows the ports developed on the Great Lakes waterways. There are 35 ports involved in this inland water transportation system. The primary products transported by these ports include limestone, gypsum, grain, iron ore, coal, cement, and petroleum.

GREAT LAKES LOADING PORTS
IRON ORE
Duluth
Superior
Two Harbors
Taconite Harbor
Marquette
Escanaba
COAL
Superior
Thunder Bay
Chicago
Toledo
Sandusky
Ashfabula
Conneaut
CEMENT
Charlevoix
Alpena
PETROLEUM
East Chicago
Sarnia
LIMESTONE
Port Inland
Cedarville
Drummond Island
Calcite
Stoneport
Marblehead
GYPSUM
Port Gypsum
Alabaster
GRAIN
Thunder Bay
Duluth
Milwaukee
Chicago
Saginaw
Sarnia
Toledo
Huron
THUNDER BAY
LAKE SUPERIOR
TACONITE HARBOR
TWO HARBORS
DULUTH
SUPERIOR
MARQUETTE
PORT INLAND
CEDARVILLE
ST. MARYS RIVER
SOO LOCKS
STRAITS OF MACKINAC
CALCITE
STONEPORT
ALPENA
CHARLEVOIX
ESCANABA
LAKE HURON
PORT GYPSUM
ALABASTER
GREEN BAY
LAKE MICHIGAN
MILWAUKEE
CHICAGO
BURNS HARBOR
GARY
ST. CLAIR RIVER
SARNIA
LAKE ST. CLAIR
DETROIT
DETROIT RIVER
TOLEDO
MARBLEHEAD
HURON
SANDUSKY
LORAIN
CLEVELAND
LAKE ERIE
ASHTABULA
CONNEAUT
ERIE
HAMILTON
WELLAND CANAL
BUFFALO
TORONTO
LAKE ONTARIO

FIGURE 6-3 Shown on this map are the ports and the products shipped at each port. *Courtesy of Detroit District U..S. Army Corps of Engineers*

Self-Unloading

With the efficiency required of today's shipping fleets, it is most important to be able to unload and load the freight quickly. Because of this need, most vessels built since 1970 use a self-unloading system.

As shown in Figure 6-4, this self-unloader uses several conveyor belts to bring the product from the cargo holds, up to a loop conveyor belt to the unloading boom. The dry bulk cargo is held (squeezed) between two belts as it flows from the lower belt to the boom. The unloading boom then is able to swing sideways to the shore and unload the freight. Using this system, it takes only about eight hours to unload 70,000 tons of pelletized iron ore from a 1,000-foot vessel.

As with any technology, a self-unloading system can be related to the systems approach. The process of self-unloading has an input, process, output, feedback loop and impact. For example, the input would be the command to unload a certain cargo. Materials, people, tools, energy, and so forth are all used to carry out the process. The output is the completed cargo being unloaded. The feedback systems are those that control the direction, location, and speed of the self-unloader. Impacts would include less cost economically and quicker unloading, thus improving efficiency and reducing pollution as compared to other forms of unloading.

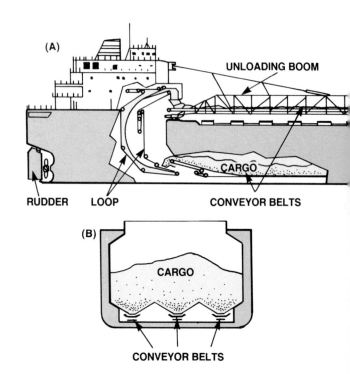

FIGURE 6-4 Today, most modern cargo ships have a self-unloader conveyer belt system to unload the product. In (A) the lower cargo is transferred to the unloading boom by a series of loop belts. (B) shows a view of the conveyor belts under the cargo.

Locks

Locks are used in many of the inland waterways to move vessels, ships and small craft from a lower to a

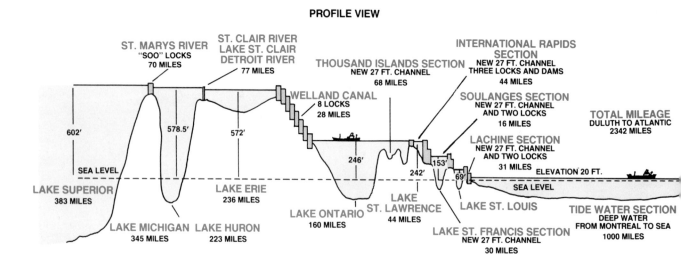

FIGURE 6-5 The St. Lawrence-Great Lakes waterway drops 602 feet to the Atlantic Ocean. Locks are used to move boats and ships from level to level. *Courtesy of Detroit District U.S. Army Corps of Engineers*

higher body of water, or vice versa. For example, referring to Figure 6-5, the St. Lawrence-Great Lakes waterway is shown. When a cargo ship goes from Lake Superior to the Atlantic Ocean, the vessel must drop approximately 602 feet. Locks are used to accomplish this. Figure 6-6 shows a view of boats going into a lock.

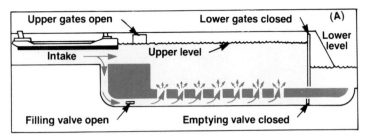

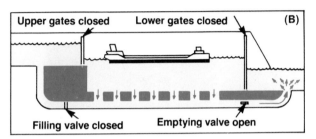

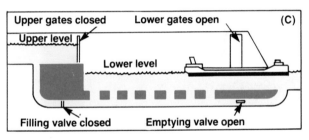

FIGURE 6-7 (A) Locks operate by filling the lock chamber to the higher level of water. **(B)** The ship enters the lock. **(C)** The water is released to the lower level and the ship moves out of the lock on the lower level. *Courtesy of Detroit District U.S. Army Corps of Engineers*

FIGURE 6-6 This is a view of a set of locks used to lower or raise boats. *Courtesy of State of NY DOT*

The St. Lawrence-Great Lakes waterway has many locks to accommodate ships that must go through. Typically, locks are able to lift or drop a ship between 20 and 35 feet. The level depends upon the amount of drop or rise necessary at each particular point. Locks can be 80 to 110 feet wide and 1,350 feet or more in length. Locks carry many types of vessels, from small passenger craft to large ships. Ships carrying more than 68,000 tons of freight in a single cargo are not uncommon. About 13,000 vessels may pass through any one lock in a year. Ships with drafts of up to 26 feet are able to pass through the locks.

Lock Operation. Figure 6-7 shows how a ship is lowered in a lock. Figure 6-7A shows the lower gates closed. The emptying valve is also closed and the filling valve is open. The lock chamber has been filled with water to the upper level. With the upper gates opened, the ship enters the lock chamber.

Figure 6-7B now shows the ship in the lock chamber. The upper and lower gates and the filling valve are closed. The emptying valve has been opened to allow water to flow from the lock chamber to the lower level.

Figure 6-7C shows the water level in the lock chamber down to the lower level. The lower gates have been opened, and the ship is able to leave the lock chamber. The lock is now ready for an up-bound ship or vessel to enter for lifting. The chamber may be filled and lowered again for the reverse passage of a down-bound ship as well.

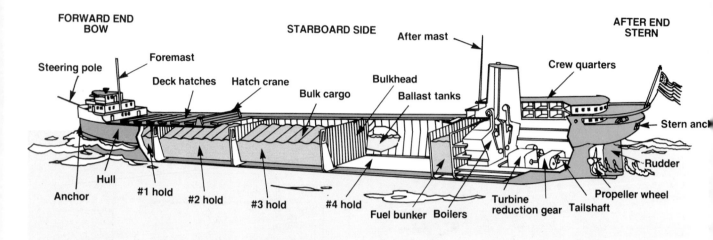

FIGURE 6-8 This ship is a bulk-cargo freighter. It is capable of transporting such dry bulk cargo as grain and cement. *Courtesy of Detroit District U.S. Army Corps of Engineers*

Types of Vessels, Boats, and Other Craft

Marine transportation uses many forms of vessels, boats, and other craft for both freight and passenger transportation. This section describes some of these forms used today for passenger, freight and recreational purposes.

Bulk-Cargo Freighter

Figure 6-8 is a cut-away view of a bulk-cargo freighter. These ships are designed for the transportation of coal, grain, gypsum, or iron ore. The largest ships are 1,000 feet-plus (average 600 feet) carrying about 60,000 tons. Both diesel- and turbine-powered propulsion systems are used. These freighters have engines that produce about 5,000 horsepower, travel at 16 knots and carry a crew of 35. Approximately 300 bulk-cargo freighters operate in the Great Lakes waterways today.

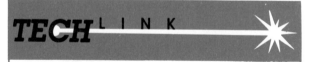

Bulk-cargo freighters are very large. An average-sized bulk freighter is able to carry about the same amount of cargo as a 115-car railtrain. Some even larger bulk freighters are equivalent in cargo capacity to that carried in a 923-car rail train.

Tanker

Tankers are designed to carry liquids, most often oil. Small tankers carry about 50,000 barrels of liquid. The average length of the tanker for inland tranportation is about 450 feet long traveling at a rate of approximately 10 knots.

Large tankers are used for ocean transportation. An oceangoing oil tanker is shown in Figure 6-9. Smaller vessels are able to hold nearly 500,000 barrels of oil, whereas larger ships are able to hold up to 2 million barrels.

Oceangoing General Cargo Vessel

Oceangoing general cargo vessels are identified by the derricks and booms on board. These booms enable the ships to load and unload various packaged cargos, such as cars, construction equipment, and so forth. These ships are usually 550 to 600 feet in length. They are able to carry up to 12,000 tons, at speeds of up to 20 knots, with a crew of 40. Figure 6-10 shows a typical cargo ship.

Air Cushion Vehicle

The air cushion vehicle (ACV) is also being developed as a possible marine transportation mode. Figure 6-11 shows such a vehicle. This craft hovers (maintains altitude) just a few feet above the surface of the water. The craft uses large fans that force air downward through the hull. An air cushion is

FIGURE 6-9 Large oceangoing tankers can hold up to 2 million barrels of oil. *Courtesy of American Petroleum*

FIGURE 6-10 This is an oceangoing general cargo vessel, capable of loading and unloading various sizes of cargo. *Courtesy of National Steel and Shipbuilding*

FIGURE 6-11 This air cushion vehicle is able to hover several feet above the surface of the water. Propellers on the top of the craft propel the vehicle forward. *Courtesy of Textron*

developed between the craft and the water. The vehicle is then propelled forward by stern-mounted propellers.

Figure 6-12 shows how the cushion is developed. Air is drawn in through an intake and then compressed. It is then forced down both sides of the ship and directed inward under the hull. This creates a cushion of air that causes the vehicle to lift off the water. The cushion is maintained by a continuous airflow.

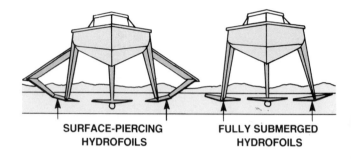

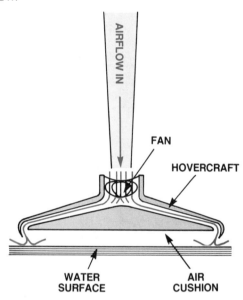

FIGURE 6-12 On this vehicle an air cushion is developed below the craft by using large motors and fans. The compressed air is sent down and inward to create a cushion to ride on.

In the past, several ACVs have been used to ferry passengers short distances across small bodies of water. Although these craft have been tested and used, work still needs to be done before they can be used significantly in marine transportation.

Hydrofoil

Hydrofoils operate on much the same principle as airplanes. Hydrofoils have struts attached to the vessel on the outside of the hull. Figure 6-13 shows examples of the two types commonly used. These are the surface-piercing and the fully submerged types. The surface-piercing type is primarily used on calm waters. The fully submerged type is somewhat more stable and can handle rougher waters. These foils generate lift when water flows around them.

FIGURE 6-13 Hydrofoils are used to lift the vessel up and out of the water. This action produces less drag and allows the vessel to travel much faster. *Courtesy of Boeing*

The design of a hydrofoil eliminates a great deal of hull friction in the water. The result is that the hydrofoil can travel at up to 40 knots without the effect caused by waves on the craft. Typically, hydrofoils can travel about 60% to 70% faster than conventional craft of similar size. Several companies have developed and are now selling hydrofoils. At present, hydrofoils are used in European countries and the Soviet Union. The United States has several in use; however, more testing is still needed.

Vacation Cruises

Marine transportation takes on many forms and types. Cruise ships such as this are able to hold 960 passengers, and move at a speed of 19 knots. Vessels of this size weigh approximately 24,500 tons.

This type of vessel utilizes the six basic technologies of all transportation forms: propulsion, guidance, control, suspension, support, and materials technologies. Steam turbines are used for the propulsion system. Guidance and control through elaborate radar systems help to control the direction and speed of the boat. The hull shape and design are part of the suspension technology. Support technology includes the docking facilities, crew and captain, fueling operations, and others. A wide variety of materials are used including steel, wood, carpet, concrete, glass, plastic, composite materials and synthetics. *Courtesy of Regency Cruises, Inc.*

Towboat and Tugboat

Towboats and tugboats form an important team in marine transportation. These boats are used to help move larger vessels in and out of ports. Their push-towing or pulling operations are used on most of the inland systems. Figure 6-14 shows a typical example of a tugboat, although a wide variety of types is used.

FIGURE 6-14 This is a typical example of a tugboat. *Courtesy of U.S. Coast Guard*

The following statistics give an idea of the size of these boats.
- They are designed with single- to four-propeller propulsion systems.
- They range in size from 36 feet long, 12 feet wide, with a 6-foot draft, to 170 feet long, 58 feet wide, with a draft of 11 feet.
- Their diesel engines range from 100 horsepower to more than 9,000 horsepower.

Sailboats

Sailboats have been used for as long as marine transportation has been around. Today, sailboats are primarily used for recreation and leisure, Figure 6-15. Depending upon the interest of the consumer and the available money, sailboats range in price from $500 up to well above $60,000. The following terms help to describe the sailing process.

FIGURE 6-15 Sailboats are used primarily for recreation, racing, and leisure in the United States today. *Courtesy of Detroit District U.S. Army Corps of Engineers*

Aerodynamics of Sailing. *Aerodynamics* plays an important part when sailing a boat. When the sailboat travels in the same direction as the wind, usually there is no problem. However, when the boat must travel against the wind, certain aerodynamics come into play.

The top drawing in Figure 6-16A shows the boat going in almost the same direction as the wind. The wind is moving from top to bottom. With the sail in this position, the boat has little problem moving. The three numbers on the drawing indicate forces and direction. Their lengths indicate the amount of force. The longer the line, the greater the force.

The number 1 indicates the direction and speed of the boat, based upon the position of the sail. The number 3 indicates the forces created on the hull in the water. The number 2 represents the force of the wind on the boat. The number 2 force is divided into the motion of the boat number 1 and the force on the hull number 3. Note that as the boat turns into the wind, (turns left) the forward force of the boat number 1 is becoming less (shorter line). Also, more energy is being forced against the hull number 3, indicated by a longer line.

(A)

1 = DIRECTION AND SPEED OF BOAT
2 = FORCE OF WIND ON BOAT
3 = FORCE ON THE HULL

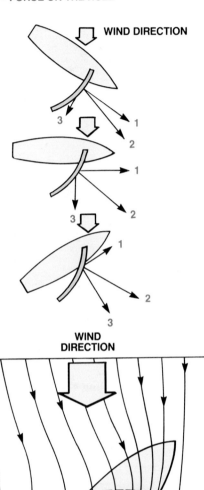

(B)

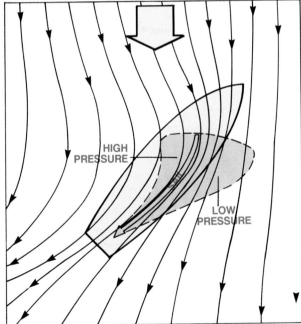

FIGURE 6-16 The aerodynamics of sailing is illustrated.

Figure 6-16B shows how airflow and pressure are created to push the boat against the wind. The sail develops a lift or push much the same as an

aircraft. Air flowing past the outside of the sail's winglike curve has farther to travel. This causes the air to speed up. The result is a lower air pressure in the right side of the sail. The air is also compressed on the left or inside of the sail. The difference in air pressure results in a force that moves the boat forward somewhat against the wind.

The sail on a sailboat acts much like an airfoil. Air flowing over the sail (airfoil) of a sailboat causes the boat to move according to Bernoulli's Theorem. *Bernoulli's Theorem* states that when a fluid flows through a restriction, its speed will increase and the pressure will decrease. It is the pressure differences across a sail that causes a sailboat to move in a certain direction.

Sails. Several types of sails are used on sailboats today. The *mainsail* is usually centered in the boat and is used to capture the majority of the wind. A *jib* is a triangular sail set forward of the mainsail. A *spinnaker* is a large, triangular sail. It is made of lightweight material having a wide spread at the bottom. The spinnaker is placed opposite or alongside the mainsail.

Tack. *Tacking* is a process in sailing a ship wherein the vessel heads perpendicularly and slightly into the wind. The sailboat then comes about (turns around) and heads back into the wind in the opposite direction. This process is continued back and forth. The net gain is that the craft moves into the wind in a zig-zag fashion.

Catamaran. A *catamaran* is a raft consisting of two hulls. The twin hulls are connected together by a deck that holds the remaining parts of the vessel. In todays terms, the catamaran is usually referred to as a sailing rig for racing. A *trimaran* is a similar-type craft having three hulls side by side.

FIGURE 6-17 A jet ski is also a form of marine transportation, usually used for recreational and leisure activities.
Courtesy of Kawasaki

Jet Ski

A recreational sport that is becoming popular is called jet biking or jet skiing. Figure 6-17 shows an example of a jet ski. This craft has a small, two-cycle engine that draws in water. The water is then pressurized and shot out of the rear of the craft. This action propels the jet ski forward. The operator normally stands up or kneels with both hands on the handlebars.

Associated Technology

Sonar

Sonar is used today by many water craft for determining the depth of a body of water. Although used for years on all commercial vessels, it is only in the past 15 to 20 years that sonar has been economically available for smaller craft. The word *sonar* is an acronym of the initial letters of the words sound, navigation, and ranging. Sonar was developed as a means of tracking enemy submarines during World War II.

Describing sonar in its simplest terms, an electrical impulse is converted into a sound wave and transmitted into the water. This wave rebounds when it strikes an obstacle, such as the bottom of the lake or body of water, Figure 6-18. Since the speed of sound in water is known, the time between the transmitted signal and the received echo can be measured. This then gives the distance to the obstacle. Electronic sonar units can both send and receive sound waves, measuring and recording them as a certain depth.

Sonar is a way of measuring distances in water by sending sound waves through water. Sound, when transmitted through water, travels at approximately 4,800 feet per second. Sound when transmitted through air, travels about 1,100 feet per second.

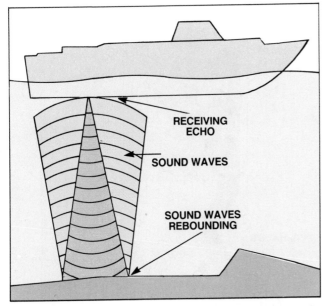

FIGURE 6-18 Sonar is used to determine the depth of water. A sound wave is sent downward, hits the bottom, and rebounds upward. The echo is then picked up and electronically translated into a depth.

Bow Thrusters

Vessels that are very long, in the range of 1,000 feet or longer, are difficult to turn. The longer the vessel, the more difficult it is to turn. In harbors for example, it may be necessary for a ship to turn completely around in a small space. In this case, bow thrusters are used, Figure 6-19.

A 500 to 700 horsepower engine is used to turn a four-blade propeller in a tunnel through the front of the hull. Depending upon the direction needed, the propeller pushes the front of the vessel to the left or right. In operation, to move the bow to the left, the propeller pulls water into the left side of the thruster tube; it then forces the water out the right side. The thrust from the jet of water being ejected to the right pushes the bow to the left.

Propulsion Systems

Marine transportation uses many types of propulsion systems. Propulsion systems are related to the processes in the systems approach. Propulsion systems process the energy of fossil fuels into mechanical power.

The type and style of propulsion used depends upon the weight, hull design and type of cargo, among others. For larger freighters and oceangoing vessels, diesel, turbine and steam boilers, and nuclear systems are used.

Figure 6-20 shows a schematic of a nuclear power system. The reactor holds the nuclear fuel. As the fuel is consumed, it produces steam. The steam and energy are transferred through the steam generator. The steam is then used to turn a turbine. The turbine then turns the propeller. A condenser is used to cool down the steam to begin the cycle over again.

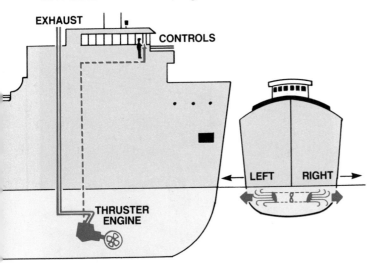

FIGURE 6-19 Bow thrusters are used to move the front of long ships with greater ease. An engine is used to turn a center propeller. Water is then drawn into one side and forced out the other. This force causes the bow to move sideways.

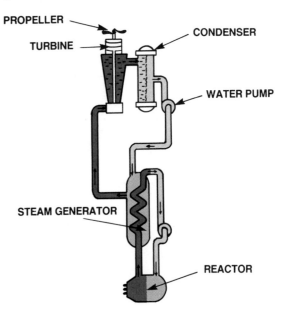

FIGURE 6-20 A nuclear power reactor is used as a propulsion system on some larger military vessels.

Note that when relating nuclear energy to the systems approach, there are significant environmental impacts (radiation) when using nuclear energy for such a purpose. These are covered in a later chapter.

For smaller craft, several methods are used for propulsion systems. These include the outboard, inboard/outboard (I/O), inboard, and jet-drive systems.

The outboard engine is the most common propulsion system used today on small craft. These engines range from 3 to 4 horsepower to more than 265 horsepower, depending upon the manufacturer. These engines are typically of a two-cycle design, as illustrated in Figure 6-21. Their characteristics include quick response and ease of maintenance. Propeller pitch is sized according to the horsepower of the engine and style of boat. Steering is accomplished by turning the engine, lower unit, and propeller. The entire lower unit acts as the rudder.

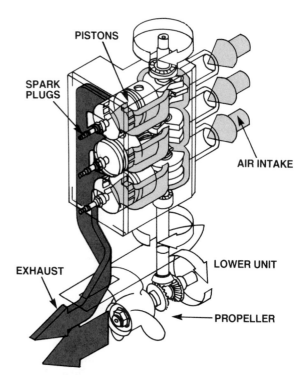

FIGURE 6-21 The two-cycle engine has very quick response and is simple to service and maintain.

FIGURE 6-22 The inboard/outboard (I/O) is a very popular type of propulsion system on smaller leisure craft.
Courtesy of Outboard Marine Corporation

The inboard/outboard (I/O) propulsion system uses four-cycle engines, typically greater than 120 horsepower, Figure 6-22. These engines are located inside the aft or stern of the vessel. The power is then sent out a stern drive. The stern drive unit is placed on the outside of the boat. This unit is the mechanical linkage between the output of the engine and the propeller. Steering is accomplished by turning the stern drive and propeller unit.

The inboard propulsion system typically uses a four-cycle engine placed inside the boat near the center. Power ranges are usually greater than 175 horsepower. The output of the engine turns a shaft and propeller directly below the keel. The shaft and propeller are not capable of turning sideways. Steering is accomplished by using a rudder.

The jet-drive system uses a four-cycle engine placed in the rear or stern of the boat. The engine, usually higher than 200 horsepower, is used to turn a water pump. Referring to Figure 6-23, water is drawn into the lower unit. After being pressurized by the power of the engine, the water is shot out at high speeds from the rear of the boat. This action produces thrust to move the vehicle forward. Steering is accomplished by turning the direction of the jet spray coming from the jet nozzle. The advantage to this drive is that the boat can operate in very shallow waters. However, the maneuverability of the craft is somewhat reduced.

Summary

This chapter is about marine transportation technology. Several technologies are studied, including support systems, types of vessels, and their associated technologies.

- Harbors and ports are part of a massive support system needed for marine transportation.
- Self-unloading freighters are now being built for efficiency of unloading dry bulk.
- Locks are used to raise and lower ships, craft, and boats on inland waterway systems.
- Many types of ships are used on waterways today. Some of the more important ones include the bulk-cargo freighter, tanker, and general cargo vessel.
- Other forms of marine transportation are also in use, including the air cushion vehicle and the hydrofoil.
- Sailing is becoming more popular today because of improved technology.
- A significant amount of aerodynamics is at work when operating a sailboat.
- The jet ski is a recreational craft that uses a small, two-cycle engine to produce a jet of water for propulsion.
- Sonar is an important part of any boat. It is used to measure depth of water and distance to submerged objects.
- Bow thrusters are used to move the front of long ships to the left or right in a harbor.
- Several types of propulsion systems are used on marine craft. Large ships use diesels, steam boilers and turbines, or nuclear reactors.
- Smaller craft use several types of propulsion systems. These include the outboard, inboard/outboard (I/O), inboard, and jet-drive systems.

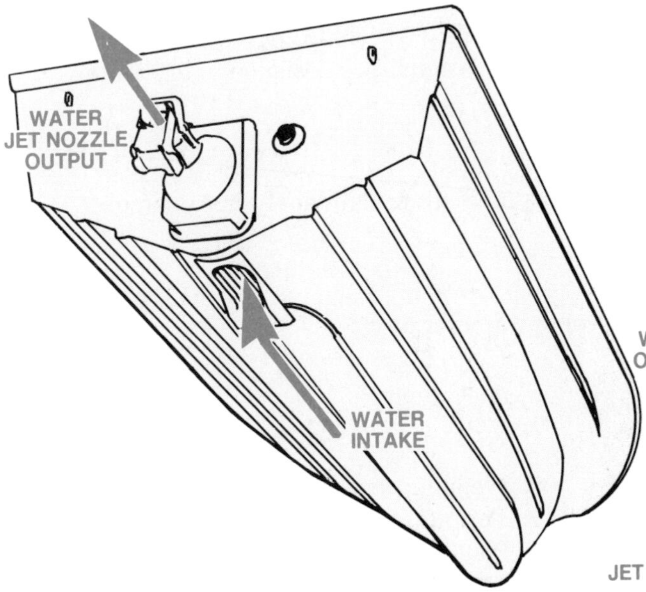

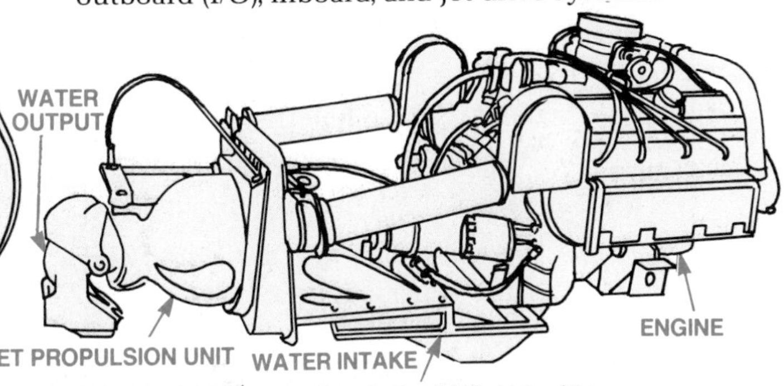

FIGURE 6-23 The jet propulsion system draws in water, compresses it, and shoots it out at a high speed to produce forward thrust.

REVIEW

1. Ports and harbors are considered part of the _____ technology for marine transportation.
2. To move a ship or boat from one level of water to another, _____ are used.
3. The _____ in the marine industry uses the same principles as the airplane does in the aviation industry.
4. When a sailboat goes back and forth against the wind it is said to be _____ .
5. A boat that has twin hulls is called a _____ .
6. Define the term *sonar*.
7. Discuss the reasons why the St. Lawrence Seaway is so important to marine transportation.
8. Explain the complete operation of a lock.
9. List three types of vessels used to ship or transport goods today.
10. Explain how a boat can go against the wind aerodynamically.
11. What are two differences between an inboard/outboard (I/O) and an inboard propulsion system?

CHAPTER ACTIVITIES

 ## BOAT HULL DESIGN

INTRODUCTION

Boat hulls are designed to do many things. For example, boats must travel through water with ease. They must do this whether they are empty or fully loaded. This activity is designed to test various boat hull designs for ease of traveling through the water.

TECHNOLOGICAL LITERACY SKILLS

Problem solving, creativity, data analysis, experimentation, predicting, math analysis, research.

OBJECTIVES

At the completion of this activity, you will be able to:

1. Design a boat hull to carry weight and to travel in water rapidly.
2. Build the boat hull design.
3. Test the boat hull design in a test tank.

MATERIALS

1. One piece of 2″ × 4″ × 8″ pine wood
2. Scrap paper and pencil
3. Ruler
4. General woodworking tools in a laboratory
5. Eye screws
6. Weighing scales to determine weight
7. Various grades of sandpaper
8. Plate washers for weight or load
9. Stop watch
10. Test tank provided by instructor

PROCEDURE

1. The object of this activity is to design the most efficient hull for speed and weight. Break into small groups of two or three students.
2. Sketch on paper the various hull designs your group might use.
3. Choose the best hull design, the one that will carry the most weight at a high speed.
4. Mark your design onto the piece of wood given to your group.
5. Using the general woodworking tools in the laboratory, build the boat hull. Remove wood from the upper interior of the hull to hold weights. The more wood removed the more weights that can be added.

   ▶ **CAUTION:** Always wear safety glasses when working with tools in the laboratory. Also, make sure you know the correct operation of all tools used in the laboratory. If not, check with your instructor.

6. Sand and finish the boat to smooth the bottom and sides of the hull.
7. Pretest the boat in the testing tank. See Figure 6-24 for an example of how the boat is tested.

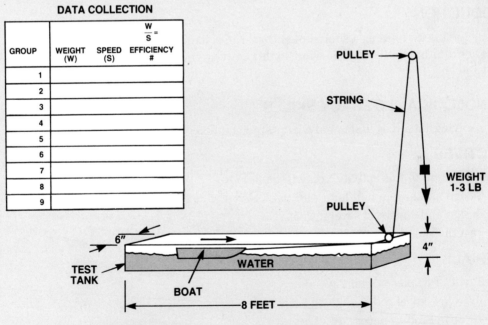

DATA COLLECTION

GROUP	WEIGHT (W)	SPEED (S)	$\frac{W}{S} =$ EFFICIENCY #
1			
2			
3			
4			
5			
6			
7			
8			
9			

FIGURE 6-24 As the weight drops, the boat is pulled forward. Variables include both the speed and the weight carried.

a. Weigh the boat out of the water.
b. Place your boat in the test tank and add weights (washers) until it sinks.
c. Test the boat for speed without using any weights by using the pulling mechanism on the test tank.
d. Now test the boat to see how long it takes to go from one end of the tank to the other in seconds with as much weight as possible. The most efficient hull design is calculated by dividing the weight of the washers by the time in seconds. The higher the number, the better the design. The object is to get the highest number possible.

8. Now work with your group to improve your design. Think about what can be done to carry more weight and to make the boat go faster.
9. After the design has been changed test the boat again for weight and speed.
10. The final phase of this activity is to test your boat in a competition with the other groups. The group with the highest number is the winner and the best boat hull designers.

REVIEW QUESTIONS

1. What type of hull design characteristics improved the weight-carrying capacity the best?
2. What type of hull design characteristics improved the speed the most?
3. After seeing the other groups' designs, how would you improve your boat hull design?

 # SAILBOAT DESIGN

INTRODUCTION

Wind has long been used as a source of energy. Kites, hang-gliding, and wind surfing are popular hobbies and sports, all utilizing the wind. In this activity you will design and build a wind-powered sailing vehicle.

TECHNOLOGICAL LITERACY SKILLS

Problem solving, creativity, data analysis, interpersonal skills, and design.

OBJECTIVES

At the completion of this activity, you will be able to:
1. Design and form a hull for a sailboat.
2. Design and construct several sails.
3. Test the sails to determine the most efficient design.

MATERIALS

1. 2″ × 4″ × 8″ piece of pine wood
2. 15″ × ¼″ dowel rod
3. ⅛″ dowel rod as necessary
4. General woodworking tools and finishes
5. Scissors
6. Twine
7. Miscellaneous parts such as paper clips, wire, small screws, tissue paper, glue
8. Testing tank
9. Variable-speed fan
10. Sailboat testing handout
11. Tape measure and stop watch
12. Sail design handout

PROCEDURE

1. At the end of this activity, you will test your sailboat in competition with the other sailboats built.
2. Divide the class into groups of two or three students each.
3. Brainstorm possible hull designs for your sailboats. Each boat must be not more than 8 inches in length. Draw the hull design on paper. Include the approximate dimensions.
4. Using the woodworking tools, construct the hull and apply a coating of polyurethane finish.

▶ **CAUTION:** Always wear safety glasses when working with tools in the laboratory. Also, make sure you know the correct operation of all tools used in the laboratory. If not, check with your instructor.

FIGURE 6-25 Use a variation of these sail designs on your sailboat project. *Courtesy of Bruce Barnes*

5. After the hull design has been established, design three types of sails. Figure 6-25 illustrates several types that may be used. Use the Sail Design handout to help design your sails.
6. Cut the sail designs from tissue paper.
7. Cut a "boom" from the ⅛" dowel rod and attach to bottom of the sails.
8. Attach the sail to the boat by placing the dowel rod into a hole in the body of the boat.

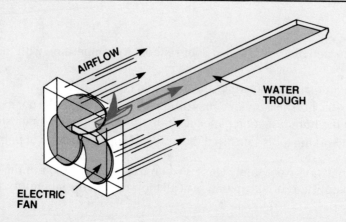

FIGURE 6-26 Sailboats can be tested using a fan and a water trough. Make sure each boat is tested by using the same method, fan speed, etc.

9. Now test the boat as indicated on the Sailboat Testing handout. You will be testing all three sails. Figure 6-26 shows how your sail will be tested.

REVIEW QUESTIONS

1. What are the characteristics of your most successful sail?
2. How would you redesign your sails to get increased speed?
3. What effect does the hull design have on the sailboat's performance?

CHAPTER 7

Air Transportation

OBJECTIVES

After reading this chapter, you will be able to:

■ State the economic and social impact of air transportation.

■ Define the aviation industry, including the agencies and companies that are used.

■ Examine several aviation principles dealing with aerodynamics.

■ Identify important parts of an aircraft.

■ Describe several types of support technologies in the aviation industry.

KEY TERMS

Air Routes	Aircraft	Axis
Airfoil	Airspeed	Gyroscope
Airport	Aerial	Pitot tube
Altimeter	Controls	Rudder
Department of	Pitch	Thrust
Transportation	Propeller	Wing
Federal Aviation	Stall	
Administration	Vortices	

Introduction

Air transportation systems have been in use for both freight and passenger transportation for many years. Today, however, air transportation systems have become a major way in which people transport themselves. In the past few years, the price and availability of flights for both business and pleasure have all become more attractive to the consumer. This chapter is about the need for air transportation, aviation principles, aircraft systems and various support technologies.

Air Transportation

During the past 80 years, the aviation industry has gone from only a few test flights to a complex and integrated system within our technological society. Today, air transportation has taken on a significant share of both passenger transportation, Figure 7-1, and freight transportation.

Air Transportation Industry Defined

The air transportation industry includes all civil flying that is performed by air carriers and general aviation. These include such companies as commercial airlines, cargo airlines, and business airlines, Figure 7-2. The key to defining this industry is that most aviation in this sector is done for hire.

FIGURE 7-1 The Boeing 737 is used for passenger transportation within our society. *Courtesy of U.S. Air Corporate Communication Department*

FIGURE 7-2 This Learjet is one type of airplane used by many business groups for transportation to and from meetings. *Courtesy of Gates Learjet*

Economic Impact of Air Transportation

Air transportation fits easily into the systems model of technology. For example, air transportation has many impacts. Air transportation has generated a great deal of economic development within the United States. The following statements illustrate the impact that air transportation has on the economy in a given year.

1. Airline companies employ more than 330,000 people.
2. More than 293 million passengers travel an average of 833 miles each per year.
3. Approximately 6.9 billion ton miles of freight and mail are carried per year. See Figure 7-3.

4. Upwards of $9.7 billion is spent on fuel in one year.
5. More than $1 billion is spent on passenger meals in one year.
6. Maintenance materials and other costs account for $7.1 billion in one year.
7. Approximately $731 billion is spent on advertising in one year.
8. About $1.4 billion is spent on interest payments.
9. More than $1 billion is spent on new equipment and facilities.

These statistics, although changing each year, give an indication of the impact that air transportation has on the economic development of our country.

FIGURE 7-3 Air freight is a major part of the aviation industry. (A) Here freight is identified by zip code. (B) A computer then automatically sorts the package into spiral chutes. (C) Personnel then pack it into a container for air travel to another city. *Courtesy of Emery Air Freight Corp.*

(A)

(B)

(C)

Social Impacts of Air Transportation

The development of the air transportation industry has produced other impacts as well. These include:

1. Business and industries have realized improved efficiency. Air transportation has a tendency to expand a company's geographical area, thus improving personal contacts and communications. Air transportation also expands an individual's scope for travel, work and leisure.
2. Enhancing lifestyles. Because of air transportation, more opportunities are available for vacations, educational travel, and family visits. International travel is becoming more accessible through improved airline routes. Figure 7-4 shows an international airliner in flight.

FIGURE 7-4 Airlines offer more choices and opportunities for international business and vacation travel. *Courtesy of United Airlines Inc.*

3. Improved communications due to the rapid delivery of products, letters, and other mail.
4. Support of travel-related industries. Because of air transportation, such industries as hotels, rental cars, and travel agencies are possible. In addition, air transportation has helped the economic development of entire areas, such as Florida, Hawaii, and others.

History of Air Transportation

Air transportation and its development can be divided into several periods. The formative period took place from 1918 to 1938. During this time period, air-mail service was started. In addition, air routes and companies were being established. Also, the type of aircraft and associated technology was developed. The growth years were between 1938 and 1958. During this time, various governmental agencies were formed and the technology of the aircraft continued to develop. Speed, comfort and safety improved. The jet era started in 1958. This was when jet engines were developed and used on aircraft. This development improved speed as well as fuel efficiency.

Today, many new and innovative technologies are used in aircraft. The industry continues to grow and expand faster than other transportation industries. For example, between the years 1939 and 1982, the U.S. population grew by 75%. However, during that same period, travel on commercial airlines increased by 626%. Neither land nor marine transportation has increased at this rate.

Regulations, Agencies, and Associations

Because of the scope of the air transportation industry, several agencies have been developed. These organizations help to regulate the industry for proper operation.

1. DOT or the Department of Transportation —primarily put in place to help the development and improvement of a coordinated transportation service, including air transportation. The DOT is an agency used to make sure the objectives of any transportation system, including air transportation, are in line with federal objectives. The following are some of the many agencies that are part of the DOT:
   a. Federal Highway Administration (Land Transportation)
   b. Maritime Administration (Marine Transportation)
   c. St. Lawrence Seaway (Marine Transportation)
   d. Urban Mass Transportation Administration (Land Transportation)
   e. United States Coast Guard (Marine Transportation)
   f. National Highway Traffic Safety Administration (Land Transportation)
   g. Federal Railroad Administration (Land Transportation)

Inflatable Evacuation Slides on Aircraft

Safety is a critical concern for all commercial aircraft copanies. The Federal Aviation Administration works with many technologies used to improve safety for passengers. Evacuation systems are one such area.

An evacuation system such as this is used on aircraft around the world. Shown is a lightweight, inflatable structure that enables passenger and crew members to exit an aircraft rapidly during emergency conditions. It is filled with a pressurized gas that inflates the structure rapidly. Passengers then slide down the chute to exit the aircraft. *Courtesy of United Airlines*

h. Federal Aviation Administration (Air Transportation)

2. FAA or the Federal Aviation Administration — used to promote aviation safety while ensuring efficient use of the navigable airspace. The FAA is part of the DOT.

3. NTSB or the National Transportation Safety Board — primarily responsible for determining the cause of transportation accidents, in this case, civil aviation accidents. The NTSB is also responsible for investigation of highway, train, marine, and pipeline accidents.

4. CAB or the Civil Aeronautics Board — primarily responsible for regulating the aviation industry.

Many other aviation associations have been formed for various purposes. Some of the more common of these include:

1. Air Transportation Association of America (ATA)
2. Regional Airline Association (RAA)
3. Aircraft-manufacturing Association (AMA)
4. Aviation Distributors and Manufacturers Association (ADMA)
5. National Business Aircraft Association (NBAA)

Although there are many others, those mentioned give an idea as to the degree of involvement and control that federal agencies and associations have within the air transportation industry.

Types of Air Transportation Industries/Companies

Many companies make up the air transportation industries. Some industries are categorized as part of the General Aviation Industry. These industries often provide a service to other companies or agencies. These include:

1. Air taxi/commuter industries, Figure 7-5

FIGURE 7-5 **Many airline commuter companies provide flights for commuters during daily working hours. This company has more than 125 departures per day.** *Courtesy of Pan Am Corporation*

2. Rental industries
3. Aerial application, observation, and other:
   a. Applications of agricultural chemicals
   b. Aerial advertising
   c. Aerial photography
   d. Fire fighting
   e. Fish and wildlife conservation
   f. Insect control
   g. Traffic control
   h. Pipeline and power-line construction/surveillance
   i. Transportation between ships and land, Figure 7-6
   j. Weather research, modification and monitoring
4. Air cargo industries, Figure 7-7

In addition, commercial airline companies comprise another category of aviation industries. Their purpose is primarily to transport people from one point to another. This airline industry includes companies such as American Airlines, Pan American World Airways, Delta Airlines, Piedmont Airlines, Eastern Airlines, Northwest Airlines, Republic Air-

FIGURE 7-6 **This helicopter is used for transportation between ships and land.** *Courtesy of U.S. Coast Guard*

FIGURE 7-7 **This airplane is used for air cargo operations.** *Courtesy of Burlington Air Express*

lines, and many others. These companies have large planes that hold usually fewer than 500 passengers.

Figure 7-8 shows an example of the family of airplanes one such company uses. Note the length, wingspan, number of passengers and range of travel for comparison.

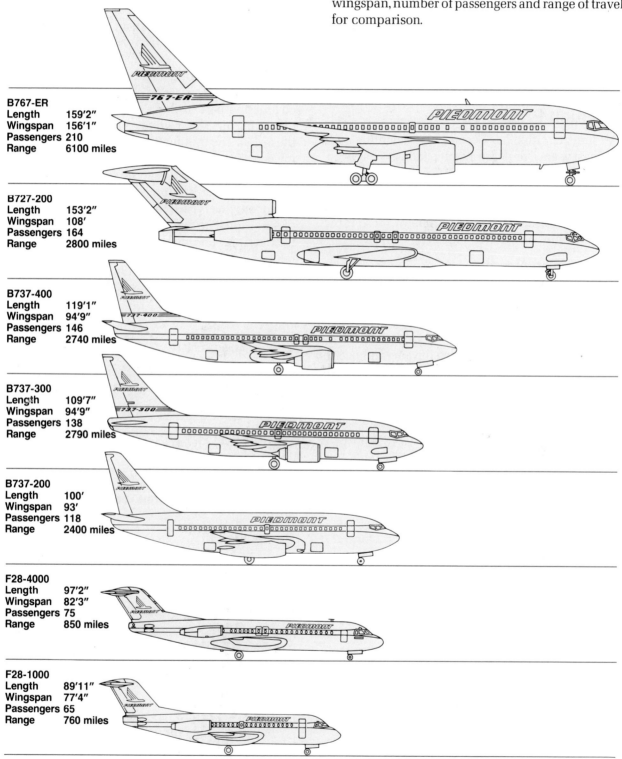

FIGURE 7-8 An airline company for passenger transportation may have many sizes of aircraft. *Courtesy of Piedmont Aviation, Inc.*

Included in this category also are many commuter airlines, called *regionals*. Some regional companies include Air Midwest, Pacific East, Southern Air, Air Wisconsin, and others. These companies and their routes are designed to serve a smaller regional area for passenger or cargo transportation. Typically, these aircraft hold fewer than 70 passengers or less than 18,000 pounds of cargo.

Aviation Principles

Air transportation has become very scientific over the past years. The entire aviation industry has been built upon many aerodynamic principles and concepts. These concepts are used to aid in the design and safe operation of air transportation vehicles today. This section discusses some of these principles within the aviation industry.

Forces on an Aircraft

Typically, four forces act on an airplane in flight: lift, gravity, thrust, and drag. These forces are shown in Figure 7-9. *Lift* is the upward acting force that causes the plane to rise. *Gravity* or weight is the downward acting force drawing the aircraft toward the earth. *Thrust* is a force that causes the craft to move forward from propulsion. *Drag* is the backward or retarding force holding the plane back. These forces in reaction to one another cause the craft to move upward, downward, or forward.

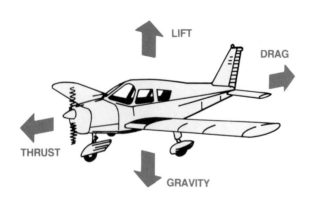

FIGURE 7-9 Any aircraft in flight has four forces acting on it: lift, gravity, thrust, and drag.

Airfoils

Once the aircraft leaves the ground, it is supported in the air by the aerodynamic force of lift. Lift is produced by a device called an *airfoil*. The aircraft *wing* is the primary type of airfoil used to produce lift.

Figure 7-10 shows a cut-away view of an airfoil or wing and the associated terminology. The *leading edge* is the part of the airfoil that first meets the oncoming air. The *trailing edge* is the aft or rear of the airfoil. The trailing edge is where the upper and lower airflow meet each other after passing over the wing. The *chord line* is an imaginary straight line drawn from the leading edge to the trailing edge. The chord line is used to identify the angle of attack of the airfoil. The *angle of attack* is an angle formed between the chord line and the direction of the relative wind. The *camber* of an airfoil is the curvature of its upper and lower surfaces. The *relative wind* is the wind moving past the airfoil.

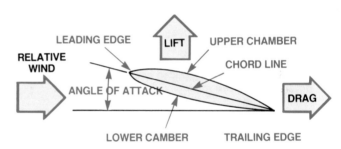

FIGURE 7-10 An airfoil is used to produce lift for the airplane. The parts and terms used to describe it are shown.

Producing Lift

Lift is produced on an airfoil or wing because of a difference in pressure between its upper and lower surfaces.

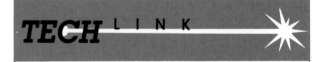

TECH LINK

Lift on an aircraft can be explained by using Bernoulli's Principle. This principle states that with any airflow, as the speed of the air increases (velocity increases) pressure decreases. Bernoulli's Principle is applicable to airfoils, to produce pressure differences for lift.

Referring to Figure 7-11, note that the upper camber is greater, whereas the lower camber is lesser. The camber causes the airflow across the upper wing surfaces to increase in speed. However, because the upper camber is greater, the velocity on the top of the wing is greater. This means that there is less pressure on top of the airfoil compared to the bottom. This difference in pressure causes the wing or airfoil to lift. Note also that the greater the speed of the aircraft, the greater is the difference between the two pressures. Therefore, lift can then be increased by increasing the speed.

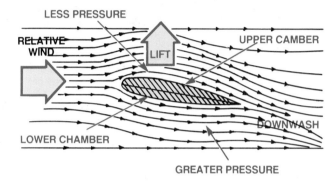

FIGURE 7-11 Lift is produced because of the pressure differences on the wing.

Angle of Attack

A second way to increase lift is by changing the angle of attack. If the angle of attack is increased, as shown in Figure 7-12, there is a greater force against the lower surface of the wing. This increased force aids in producing lift. However, most lift, about 75%, comes from the difference in pressure between the upper and lower surfaces of the wing. Lift can thus be increased in two ways. One is by increasing the forward speed of the aircraft. A second way is to increase the angle of attack.

Stall

Quite often one hears about the term stall within the aviation industry. *Stall* is defined as a condition in which there is no more lift on an airfoil. Stall can be produced by continually increasing the angle of attack on the airfoil. As the angle of attack increases, eventually air on the top may start to separate from the wing. When this occurs, a burbling or turbulent pattern is produced near the trailing edge of the

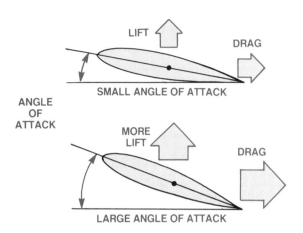

FIGURE 7-12 One way to increase lift is by increasing the angle of attack.

airfoil. As the angle of attack continues to increase, this turbulence progresses forward. Eventually, all lift is removed from the airfoil, thereby producing a stall. Figure 7-13 shows the effect of increasing the angle of attack from 4° to about 20°.

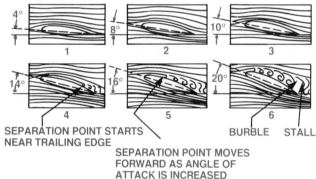

FIGURE 7-13 As the angle of attack increases on an airfoil or wing, air starts to separate from the surface. Eventually there is all turbulence and no lift on the wing. This is the point at which the aircraft stalls.

Frost, Snow and Ice

Even a light accumulation of frost, snow, or ice on the wings can increase the chances for an aircraft to stall. For example, any ice accumulation may disrupt the smooth flow of air over the wing. This, in turn, may decrease the lift on the wing or airfoil, increasing the chance for producing a stall. With frost, snow and ice on the wing, the aircraft must fly much faster in order to eliminate the possibility of a stall. Aircraft are sprayed with ethylene glycol (an antifreeze) to eliminate ice, frost, and snow build-up.

Wing Shapes

The shape of the wing on an aircraft is also very important for correct operation. The wing shape is determined by the type of aircraft and its use. For example, if the aircraft is designed for slow speeds, a thick airfoil is used. An aircraft designed for high speed uses a thin airfoil. Wings are designed differently by changing their shape as viewed from the top.

Two terms help to define the shape or contour of the wing. When the wing shape is viewed from the top it is called the *planform*. The relationship between the length (span) and the width (chord) of a wing is called its *aspect ratio*. It is calculated by dividing the span or distance from wingtip to wingtip by the average chord of the wing. In general, the higher the aspect ratio, the more efficient the wing. Figure 7-14 shows several wing shapes, their dimensions and aspect ratios.

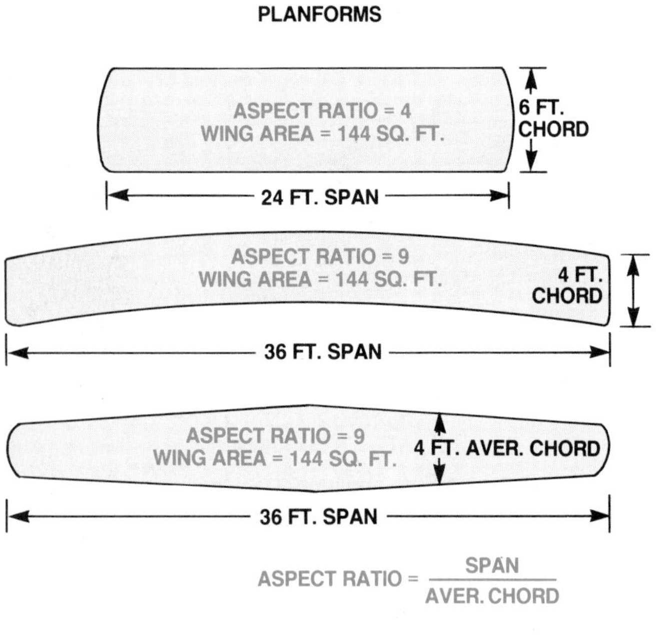

PLANFORMS

ASPECT RATIO = 4
WING AREA = 144 SQ. FT.
6 FT. CHORD
24 FT. SPAN

ASPECT RATIO = 9
WING AREA = 144 SQ. FT.
4 FT. CHORD
36 FT. SPAN

ASPECT RATIO = 9
WING AREA = 144 SQ. FT.
4 FT. AVER. CHORD
36 FT. SPAN

$$\text{ASPECT RATIO} = \frac{\text{SPAN}}{\text{AVER. CHORD}}$$

FIGURE 7-14 Wings are designed differently by changing the chord, or width, and the span.

Several years ago, the Voyager flew around the world without refueling. To do this, the plane's wings had to be specially built with a very large aspect ratio. Figure 7-15 shows the Voyager. Its wingspan is 110.8 feet; the wing aspect ratio is 33:8. Note also the use of the winglets on the tips of each wing.

FIGURE 7-15 The Voyager, which flew around the world without refueling, has a wing aspect ratio of 33:8. The wingspan is more than 110 feet. *Courtesy of Goodyear Tire and Rubber Company*

Types of Wings

There are several types of wings:

1. The *straight wing* has excellent stall characteristics. It is very economical to build. However, it is very inefficient from a structural weight and drag standpoint.
2. The *tapered wing* is more efficient from structural, weight and drag standpoints. Stall characteristics are not as good as a straight wing.
3. The *elliptical wing* is the most efficient from structural, weight, and drag standpoints. Stall characteristics are not as good as straight wings. However, this wing is more expensive to build than the tapered wing.
4. The *sweptback* and *delta wings* shown in Figure 7-16 are efficient at higher speeds, near the speed of sound. These wings, however are less efficient at the approaching and landing speeds.

Wing Tip Vortex

Considerable wake turbulence is generated behind the wings when an aircraft is in flight. This is shown in Figure 7-17. This is caused by a pressure differential between the top and the bottom of the wing

FIGURE 7-16 These Air Force planes have a delta wing shape. *Courtesy of General Dynamics Inc.*

during flight. The high pressures on the bottom of the wing have a tendency to slide outward and curl around the wing tips. The wing tip vortex that is produced may have serious effects. For example the vortices can be very dangerous to smaller aircraft flying behind larger aircraft. These vortices may last for as long as five minutes in the air after the aircraft has gone by.

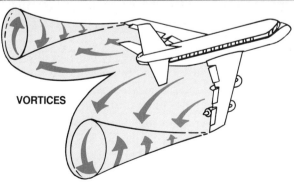

VORTICES

FIGURE 7-17 Wake turbulence (vortices) is generated behind the wings of an aircraft in flight.

One design being incorporated today to help reduce wing tip vortex uses winglets. These are shown in Figure 7-18. These winglets reduce the vortex that is normally produced, and also increase the amount of lift on the aircraft.

FIGURE 7-18 Winglets on these aircraft help reduce the wing tip vortex. *Courtesy of Raytheon*

Wing Flaps

Wing flaps, also called elevators, are used most often to aid the aircraft during takeoff and landing or during flight maneuvers. Wing flaps are used to change the lift on the wing at different times during flight. This is done by changing the camber on the wing. Four types of wing flaps generally are found on aircraft: plain, slotted, split, and fowler flaps, Figure 7-19.

FLAPS

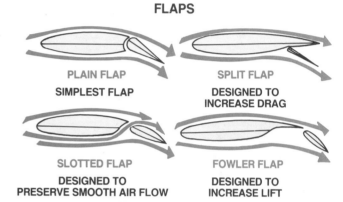

PLAIN FLAP
SIMPLEST FLAP

SPLIT FLAP
DESIGNED TO INCREASE DRAG

SLOTTED FLAP
DESIGNED TO PRESERVE SMOOTH AIR FLOW

FOWLER FLAP
DESIGNED TO INCREASE LIFT

FIGURE 7-19 There are four major types of wing flaps found on airplanes. Each is shown for reference.

Scale Model Airplane Testing

Testing of products by manufacturers is becoming more and more important. This is especially true in the aviation industry. Wing shapes, sizes, styles, and other features must all be tested before the manufacture and construction of the airplane begins. To aid in this testing, some companies build scale models of their product to be tested. The advantage of using a scale model is that the cost is reduced while the data generated by the test increases accuracy.

This is a scale model of the F-15 aircraft. It is being tested in a 16-foot wind tunnel. The test is to determine whether the aerodynamic characteristics of the airplane are affected by the presence or absence of *tail feathers* or external nozzle flaps on the wings. Many industries refer to these tests as *simulations*. *Courtesy of USAF/AEDC*

The plain flap is the simplest type and is used to produce lift. The slotted flap is used to keep a smooth airflow behind the wing, also producing increased lift. The split flap is used to increase the drag, thus slowing the plane down. The fowler flap is used to increase the wing area, also producing more lift.

Aircraft Control, Parts, Systems, and Design

Controlling the Aircraft in Flight

Controls on an aircraft are part of the feedback loop in the systems approach. These systems are used on an airplane to help control its speed and direction.

As an aircraft is flying through the air it can be viewed as being on three axes: the lateral axis, the vertical axis, and the longitudinal axis, Figure 7-20. All of these axes pass through the plane's center of gravity. Airplane controls are designed to cause the plane to rotate on these three axes.

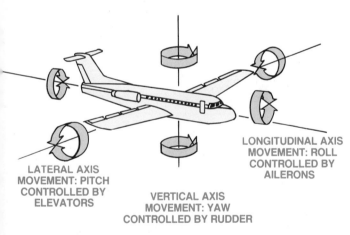

FIGURE 7-20 Controls of any aircraft are designed around the airplane's three axes: vertical, lateral, and longitudinal axes.

Major Parts of an Airplane

An aircraft has many parts. Most of these parts are used to control the aircraft on its three axes, as well as to aid in takeoff and landing. Figure 7-21 shows the major parts of a typical aircraft.

Ailerons. Ailerons are located on the airplane's wings. They are used to control the pitch (upward or downward motion) of the aircraft on the lateral axis.

PARTS OF AIRCRAFT

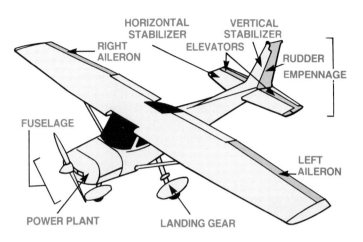

FIGURE 7-21 The major parts of an airplane are shown.

Stabilizer. The stabilizer is usually a fixed airfoil on the airplane used to increase stability. It is usually located near the aft or rear of the craft. Typically, a stabilizer is either horizontal or vertical. The horizontal stabilizer helps to control the lateral axis. The vertical stabilizer helps to control the vertical axis.

Elevators. Elevators are located on the rear horizontal stabilizer. They are used to increase the control of the aircraft's lateral axis.

Rudder. The rudder is used to increase control of the vertical axis on the aircraft. The rudder is located on the rear vertical stabilizer.

Empennage. The empennage is defined as the combination of rear or aft parts, including the stabilizers, rudders, and elevators.

Power plant. The power plant includes the components that produce the necessary forward thrust for the vehicle. The power plant can be either a piston engine with a propeller, or a jet (or reaction) engine.

Landing Gear. The landing gear is designed to support the aircraft on the ground as well as to absorb the landing load.

Fuselage. The fuselage is considered the main body of the aircraft. The fuselage supports the wings, empennage, landing gear, and the power plant.

Military Aircraft

This F-14A+ military aircraft is being flight tested. The aircraft has more powerful turbofan engines, and will have digital avionics and improved radar. Avionics is a term used to describe various electronic guidance control systems used on aircraft. These technologies are part of the guidance and control systems on the aircraft. The aircraft is designed to produce very high speeds with improved lift capabilities. In addition, newer aircraft such as this are being designed and tested to produce minimum frictional losses produced from air drag. Technologies being tested in this military aircraft will eventually find their way into the commercial aviation industry. *Courtesy of Grumman Corporation, 1988*

Propulsion System

The propulsion system in an aircraft is designed to produce the forward thrust on the plane. Typically, a piston-type engine is used on smaller and slower aircraft. Turbine engines are used on larger, higher-speed aircraft. However, with newer developments in engine design, turbines are being used on smaller aircraft today.

The thrust can be developed in one of two ways. Propellers can be attached to the rotating engine or power plant, Figure 7-22. A propeller is simply a special airfoil that rotates roughly 90° to the flight path. As propellers rotate, they bite into the air, causing acceleration and thrust. The second method is by using a jet (or reaction) engine that produces thrust. Figure 7-23 shows a typical jet engine.

FIGURE 7-22 Propellers are often used to produce the necessary thrust to move the vehicle forward. *Courtesy of American Eagle*

(A)

FIGURE 7-23 (A) A jet engine, also called a reaction engine, produces the necessary thrust to propel the aircraft forward. (B) A cut-away view of this engine is also shown. *Courtesy of Pratt & Whitney*

(B)

TECH L I N K

Thrust is explained by using Newton's Third Law of motion. This law states that for every action there is an equal and opposite reaction. As hot gasses escape the rear of a jet engine (the action), a reaction is produced in the opposite direction. This reaction is called *thrust*. Thrust is used to push the aircraft forward.

A newer propulsion design is being tested and used on some aircraft. Figure 7-24 shows this system, called the prop-fan or UDF (Unducted Fan) system. This engine utilizes a set of special propellers placed on the turbine engine. The prop-fans, which turn in opposite directions, are connected directly to the turbine shafts. They are made of lightweight composite materials that provide stiffness and strength to the blades. This propulsion system is presently used in short-to-medium-range aircraft. The aircraft can operate at jet speeds, yet save 30% or more in fuel consumption.

FIGURE 7-24 This prop-fan system uses lightweight materials to produce stiffness and strength on the blades. The blades turn directly from the turbine shafts, producing a 30% savings in fuel. *Courtesy of Pratt & Whitney*

FIGURE 7-25 A modern cockpit design for flight controls and instruments. *Courtesy of Gates Learjet*

Flight Instruments

Many flight instruments are used to monitor and control aircraft. Figure 7-25 shows a modern cockpit design with many electronic controls. Some of the more important instruments used on aircraft today include:

- A compass, used to determine the direction of flight.
- An outside air-temperature gage, used to determine the outside air temperature.
- A pitot tube, used to measure airspeed. The pitot tube is usually located on the leading edge of the wing. It supplies pressure (ram air) to help operate the air speed gage.
- An altimeter, used to measure how high the aircraft is flying.
- A vertical airspeed indicator, used to measure the rate of climb and rate of descent of the aircraft.
- Gyro instruments. These systems use a gyroscope to help monitor the flight. Gyro instruments are used for instrument flying rather than for visual flights. Gyro instruments monitor the altitude of the aircraft, including rate of climb or descent, glide, left and right bank, and flight level.

TECH LINK

An aircraft is a highly complex and integrated system of many technologies. To build a medium sized commercial aircraft, it takes more than:

- 700,000 aluminum rivets.
- 580,000 fasteners.
- 1 mile of hydraulic hoses.
- 14,000 companies in 45 states that supply parts.
- 50 miles of wire.

In addition, the electricity required is enough to supply more than 170 single-family homes.

Airports

The airport is a major support system in aircraft operation. With the increased amount of flying today, airports play a highly important role in the safety and operation of aviation. A typical airport provides:

1. Weather conditions for aircraft.
2. Fuel and maintenance for aircraft.
3. A place for passengers to board or leave the aircraft.

4. A place for freight to be transferred to and from the airplane.

5. Navigational support.

6. Air-traffic control for takeoff and landing and inflight operations.

7. Training for pilots and other personnel.

8. Medical and emergency support.

Summary

- Aviation and air transportation has increased in use more than other sectors within our society.

- Because of its size and complexity, the air transportation industry has a very significant impact on the economy.

- Air transportation also has a social impact. Aviation has made businesses more efficient, enhanced lifestyles, and improved communications by speeding letters, packages and industrial products to their destination.

- Aviation has had a long history, beginning with the formative years from 1918 to 1938.

- Aviation and air transportation agencies used for control include DOT, FAA, NTSB, and CAB.

- Air transportation is used for air taxi industries, commuter industries, rental, aerial applications, and air cargo, as well as commercial passenger transportation.

- Airfoils are designed to cause lift for the aircraft.

- Lift is produced by the action of different pressures on the top and bottom of the wing.

- Stall is produced when lift is removed from the airfoil for whatever reason.

- Many wing shapes are designed to produce different load and speed capabilities.

- A wing tip vortex is produced at the end of the wing. These vortices can be dangerous to other aircraft, and can also reduce the lift. Winglets reduce the vortex, and increase the amount of lift.

- Wing flaps are used to aid in the takeoff and landing of the aircraft.

- Some of the main parts of the aircraft include the ailerons, stabilizers, elevators, rudder, power plant, landing gear, fuselage and empennage.

- The propulsion system uses either a piston or jet engine to produce thrust. Propellers are also used on both types of engines to produce thrust.

- Flight instruments help to monitor and control the aircraft, during both visual and instrument flying.

- The airport is considered a major support technology for air transportation.

REVIEW

1. The _____ has a primary goal of coordinating all transportation services in the United States.
2. The force that causes an aircraft to move forward is called _____ .
3. An imaginary straight line drawn from the leading edge to the trailing edge of a wing is called the _____ .
4. Lift on an aircraft wing can be increased by _____ .
5. It is very dangerous to fly directly behind another large plane because of _____ produced behind the large plane.
6. Thrust on a aircraft can be produced from _____ .
7. What are some of the economic impacts of the aviation industry?
8. State the types of social impacts produced by the air transportation and aviation industry.
9. List three agencies that help control air transportation, and include their purpose.
10. Describe the terminology of an airfoil and indicate how lift is produced.
11. What is stall, how is it produced, and what can be done to reduce the chances of stall?
12. Define the angle of attack.
13. What is being done to reduce wing tip vortex?
14. What are wing flaps used for?
15. List the major parts of an aircraft and state the purpose of each.
16. State the purpose of three flight instruments.

CHAPTER ACTIVITIES

 GLIDER

INTRODUCTION

This activity will help the student explore different designs using a glider.

TECHNOLOGICAL LITERACY SKILLS

Problem solving, creativity, data analysis, experimentation, and predicting.

OBJECTIVES

At the completion of this activity, you will be able to:

1. Identify the aerodynamic design and forces that act on an aircraft.
2. Design a model glider.
3. Construct a glider.
4. Test the glider and record flight data.
5. Redesign the glider based upon flight data.

MATERIALS

1. Scrap paper
2. Pencils
3. Basic drafting equipment
4. 1/16″ and 1/8″ thick balsa wood
5. X-acto® knives

6. White glue
7. Other connection devices
8. Paint, markers, pins, etc.
9. Flight Data Analysis Handout from instructor

PROCEDURE

1. Review the parts of a glider in Figure 7-26.

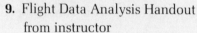

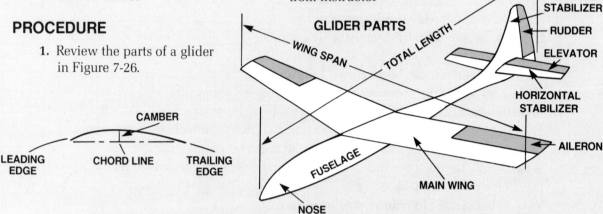

GLIDER PARTS

VERTICAL STABILIZER
RUDDER
ELEVATOR
HORIZONTAL STABILIZER
AILERON
WING SPAN
TOTAL LENGTH
FUSELAGE
MAIN WING
NOSE
CAMBER
LEADING EDGE
CHORD LINE
TRAILING EDGE

FIGURE 7-26 The parts of a glider are shown for reference when designing your airplane pattern.

2. On a sheet of blank paper, sketch various possible glider designs considering the shape of the wing, its weight and thickness, and so forth. Using scrap paper and appropriate drafting tools, draw a pattern for each part of the glider.
3. Carefully cut out the patterns with an X-acto® knife. These patterns should include wings, body (fuselage), and tail (vertical and horizontal stabilizers), as well as the rudders, ailerons and elevators.

▶**CAUTION:** X-acto® knives are surgically sharp. Be very careful not to cut yourself.

4. Mark construction slits for connecting parts (which when slid together act to fasten them) and the location of the fasteners.
5. Trace the patterns onto the balsa wood pieces. Lay them out to produce the least waste.
6. Using the X-acto® knife, carefully cut out the parts.
7. Assemble the glider.
8. Test the aircraft according to the criteria listed on the Flight Data Analysis handout provided by the instructor.
9. After testing the glider, redesign, retest, and record data again. Needed changes may include:
   a. Changing wing dimensions
   b. Adding weights (nose, wings, etc.)
   c. Reshaping parts
   d. Increasing/decreasing camber
   e. Changing shape of fuselage
10. Have a class flying competition to select the most efficient glider.

REVIEW QUESTIONS

1. What are some designs that cause the glider to fly the farthest?
2. What causes a glider to loop or to nose dive?
3. How did the performance change after the first design change?

CHAPTER 8

Space Transportation Systems

KEY TERMS

Mission	Stratosphere	Rocket
Manned space flight	Mesosphere	Propellant
Reentry	Thermosphere	Orbit
Astronauts	Exosphere	Elliptical
Module	Radiation	Perigee
Satellites	Weightlessness	Apogee
Troposphere	Newtons	

Introduction

As our society progresses toward the future, we are relying more on space transportation. Space transportation is relatively new as compared to other forms. However, as technological benefits come from space research and experimentation, the need for more space technology also increases. This chapter looks at the need for space transportation, space environments, and several technological fundamentals to support space transportation.

FIGURE 8-1 The Space Shuttle is designed as a Space Transportation System (STS). *Courtesy of NASA*

FIGURE 8-2 The purpose of the Apollo program was to land a person on the moon. *Courtesy of NASA*

The Need for Space Transportation

Space Programs

The National Aeronautics and Space Administration (NASA) has been the primary organization within the United States involved with space travel. However, numerous private companies are also involved with the manufacturing of space components. Figure 8-1 shows an example of the Space Shuttle, a true space transportation technology. The major goal for NASA is to seek greater knowledge of space travel, and expand this information into benefits and practical applications for our society.

The space program has been in existence for a number of years. It is generally accepted that the space age began in the early 1960s. However, space technology has been studied as far back as the 1940s. Initial research has been credited to Doctor Wernher von Braun. The following programs illustrate the commitment and research to space transportation.

Project Mercury. One of the first major manned space programs undertaken by the United States was the Project Mercury, organized in 1958. Six missions were flown. One purpose of this project was to investigate human ability to survive and perform in a space environment. A second purpose was to develop the basic space technology and hardware of manned space flight programs in the future. This was a one-manned space flight program.

Project Gemini. A second major project was the Gemini spacecraft. This program had a total of 12 missions. This spacecraft consisted of a two-manned space flight. The vehicle consisted of a reentry and an adapter module.

Project Apollo. The next major program was a three-manned flight called Apollo. The purpose of this program was to land a person on the moon. Apollo completed 17 successful missions. Figure 8-2 shows an example of one Apollo mission that landed astronauts on the moon.

Skylab. The Skylab program was designed to orbit a space laboratory, occupied by astronauts, for conducting scientific studies. The Skylab space station was used in four missions, and remained in space for about six years.

Apollo-Soyuz Test Project. This was the first international space program designed to link two spacecraft (U.S. and U.S.S.R.) together for experiments. The successful mission not only produced spacecraft docking technology, but also achieved a full array of scientific results as well. In addition, there was a strong political impact of having two countries work together toward a comon goal.

Other programs followed, including unmanned probes reaching distant planets. These expeditions were:

- Mariner 10 — Explored Venus and Mercury
- Pioneer 10 and 11 — Explored Jupiter and Mars
- Voyagers 1 and 2 — Explored the outer planets

The Shuttle Program

The Shuttle program is probably the best example of space transportation. The Shuttle program is designed to be a Space Transportation System (STS). The Shuttle has a large cargo bay area, Figure 8-3. This large cargo area carries satellites and other equipment into space.

The Shuttle is designed as both a sophisticated airplane and spacecraft. Its purpose is to transport payloads between earth and space on a continuous basis. The previous space programs were more for exploratory purposes. The Shuttle, however, was designed for practical use. It has carried satellites into space, helped to retrieve and repair satellites, and developed improved technology for space walks, Figure 8-4. It has also given researchers a place to experiment in many areas previously not available.

The year 1986 inevitably will be remembered as the year of the Challenger tragedy. Looking back, this tragedy caused a temporary disruption of America's launch and space capability. However, many flights took place prior to the Challenger tragedy. For example, the Columbia Space Shuttle operated seven flights from 1981 through 1986. The Challenger had 10 flights between 1983 and 1985.

FIGURE 8-3 The Shuttle (Columbia) has a large cargo bay area to transport satellites and other equipment to and from orbit. *Courtesy of Lockheed Corporation*

FIGURE 8-4 The Shuttle missions helped to improve technology for space walks for service and repair of satellites. *Courtesy of NASA*

Shuttle Transportation (747)

Many times different forms of transportation are interrelated. Sometimes entire transportation systems must be designed to support other transportation systems. To move the Space Shuttle from one location to another, a 747 aircraft was modified to support the shuttle. The shuttle is placed on the top of the aircraft in a piggyback fashion. The shuttle can then be transported easily from its landing site to the launch site. This technology is considered part of the "support" systems for space transportation.

A great deal of research and design was completed before this appraoch could be carried out. For example, it was important to see if the aircraft still produced the necessary lift for takeoff and landing. The propulsion systems were also tested to determine power and thrust requirements with the shuttle on top of the aircraft. Once these calculations proved useful, the 747 was refitted to allow the shuttle to be attached to the top of its body. *Courtesy of NASA*

SPACELAB

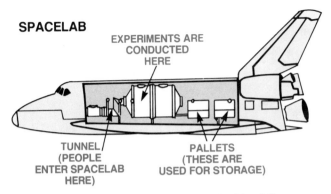

EXPERIMENTS ARE CONDUCTED HERE

TUNNEL
(PEOPLE ENTER SPACELAB HERE)

PALLETS
(THESE ARE USED FOR STORAGE)

FIGURE 8-5 Spacelabs were installed inside of the cargo bay on several Shuttle flights to conduct research and experiments.

Spacelab. Some shuttle missions carried a Space-lab. Figure 8-5 shows that the entire Spacelab fits into the cargo bay of the Space Shuttle, along with two pallets. *Pallets* are used for housing outside equipment, such as satellites for repair. The entire Spacelab module is then returned to earth. Data is collected and the module is refitted for another mission. The Spacelab is used by scientists from countries around the world. Its use is open to research institutes, scientific laboratories, industrial companies, governmental agencies, and individuals.

Long Duration Exposure Facility (LDEF). The LDEF was placed in orbit by the Shuttle program. The LDEF is a free-flying, cylindrical structure used for experiments. This facility, shown in Figure 8-6, was placed in orbit from the shuttle's cargo bay area.

FIGURE 8-6 This Long Duration Exposure Facility (LDEF) is used for scientific research over long periods of time. It was placed in orbit by the shuttle program. *Courtesy of NASA*

After an extended period of time in orbit, the LDEF is retrieved. Experiments are being done in four categories. These include:

1. Materials coatings
2. Power and propulsion
3. Science
4. Electronics and optics

Satellites

It is important for many reasons to continue a viable and technologically superior space program. One of the most important reasons is to develop satellites for weather monitoring, for communications, and for navigational aid.

Weathersats. Weather Satellites (Weathersats) enable the National Weather Service to view almost our whole planet at one time. Figure 8-7 shows a weather satellite called TIROS (Television Infrared Observation Satellite) for monitoring weather. Specific weather patterns can also be tracked, Figure 8-8. Movement of large air masses can be detected and analyzed. Today's weathersats carry advanced photographic and measuring equipment to help monitor and detect weather patterns.

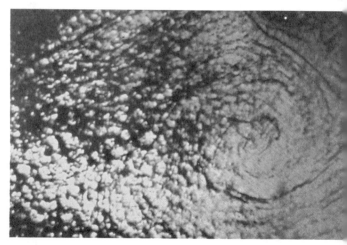

FIGURE 8-8 Weather satellites enable the National Weather Service to monitor and track storms such as this hurricane. *Courtesy of NASA*

Landsat. For more than 10 years, NASA Landsat satellites have been recording photographs of the Earth's surface. This type of satellite, shown in Figure 8-9, literally changed the way in which we look at our planet.

FIGURE 8-7 This TIROS (Television Infrared Observation Satellite) is used as a weather satellite. *Courtesy of NASA*

FIGURE 8-9 A Landsat satellite is used to take photos of the earth's surface. *Courtesy of NASA*

 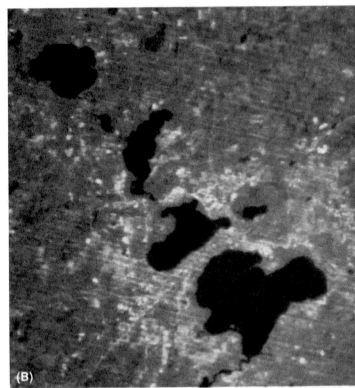

FIGURE 8-10 These are Landsat images showing urban areas (blue), vegetation (red), water (dark blue), and polluted water (lighter blue). *Courtesy of NASA*

Through a complex optical system, the Earth's surface is broken into narrow slices or scan lines. The data collected from the satellite is then sent through a computer and color enhanced. To make just one colored view of land, more than six million pieces of Landsat data had to be assembled by the computer.

Figure 8-10 shows two examples of a false color photo of cities near water. Vegetation appears red, suburban areas appear a dark pink, and urban areas appear blue because of the high percentage of buildings. Water appears dark blue, and polluted water appears a lighter blue.

An example of some of the benefits from Landsat include research about:

1. Traffic patterns
2. Pollution patterns (both water and air)
3. Weather patterns
4. Diseases in trees and crops
5. Water erosion
6. Fault-line shifting
7. Population patterns

Spinoffs from Space Research

Spinoffs from the space program are part of the impacts section in the systems model. Without the research and development done in space, our lives would be drastically different. Each year, NASA publishes a book called *Spinoff*. This book describes some of the many innovations derived from the space program. Keep in mind that there are literally thousands of spinoffs each year. This section looks at a selected number of benefits that have resulted from space transportation and exploration.

Space Technology Transfer

Some of the many areas of technology that benefit from space travel include:

1. Manufacturing of Consumer Products
2. Electrical Utilities
3. Environmental Quality
4. Food Production and Processing
5. Petroleum and Gas Production
6. Construction
7. Law Enforcement

8. Highway Transportation
9. Rail Transportation
10. Air Transportation
11. Communications
12. Water and Marine Transportation
13. Health Services

Computer Software. In the course of its varied activities, NASA has developed and makes extensive use of computers and software. Approximately

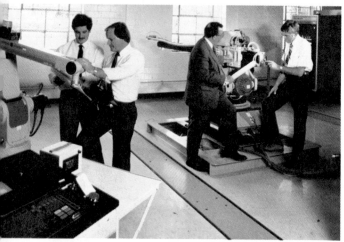

FIGURE 8-11 The development of automated manufacturing systems grew out of the space program. *Courtesy of NASA*

1,400 programs are available at the Computer Software Management and Information Center. These provide data on structural analysis, design of fluid systems, electronic circuit design, chemical analysis, and energy requirements in buildings, among many others.

Citrus Inventory. An aerial color infrared mapping system developed by NASA has been adopted by companies in Florida for an inventory of citrus trees.

Manufacturing Systems. Because of NASA's research and development in manufacturing systems, companies are now able to develop advanced manufacturing systems, Figure 8-11. These systems improve the productivity of manufacturing and lower production costs.

Anti-corrosion Coating. NASA has done considerable research in corrosion protection for spacecraft. The by-products of this research have been applied to public utilities. Corrosion protection is needed for the scrubbers and emission controls systems in coal-fired power plants.

Robotic Hand. NASA has been doing research in robotic hand dexterity for space use, as shown in Figure 8-12. This has led several robot manufacturers to utilize this research for improved robot manipulative capability.

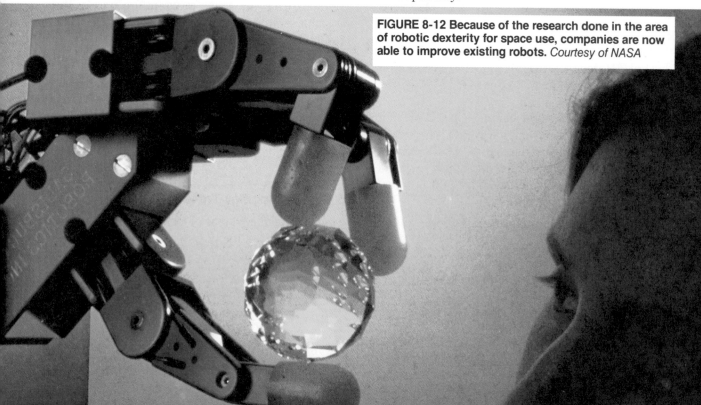

FIGURE 8-12 Because of the research done in the area of robotic dexterity for space use, companies are now able to improve existing robots. *Courtesy of NASA*

Composites for Lighter Structures. NASA has been doing a great deal of research in materials technology. There is a never-ending quest for materials having reduced weight and improved strength characteristics for use in all types of space vehicles. This research has been transferred to hundreds of products from jet engines, aircraft parts and tires, to tennis rackets, running shoes, and snow skis.

The list of transfer technology is too lengthy to mention. However, the list shown in Figure 8-13 helps to give a view of the many benefits from space transportation.

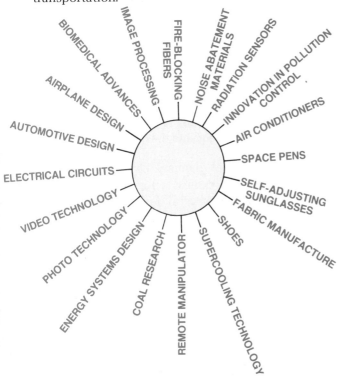

FIGURE 8-13 This list shows some of the many areas and products that have benefited from the research and development in space.

Space Environment

The Atmosphere

Knowing what constitutes the atmosphere is an important part of space transportation. The Earth's atmosphere is composed of several regions. Depending upon the mission objectives and goals, the spacecraft may operate in one or all of the regions shown in Figure 8-14. Because of this, certain technological changes must be made in transportation systems.

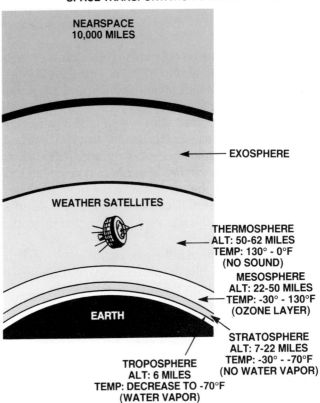

FIGURE 8-14 This chart shows the different regions of atmosphere around the Earth. Temperature changes are also shown for reference. Near space is defined generally as a distance about 10,000 miles from the Earth's surface.

The *troposphere* is the lowest region of the atmosphere. It extends upward to an average height of about six to seven miles from the surface of the earth. Most clouds and weather occur in this region. The temperature typically drops to about -70°F at the top of the troposphere. In addition, the farther from the surface of the earth, the lower the pressure.

The next region outward is called the stratosphere. The *stratosphere* is the area ranging from seven miles to about 22 miles above the surface of the earth. The temperature in this region is between -70°F and -30°F. There is an absence of water vapor and clouds in this region.

The *mesosphere* extends to about 50 miles from the surface of the earth. This region contains an ozone layer. *Ozone* is a form of oxygen that has three atoms per molecule instead of the usual two. Because of the ozone, a large part of the sun's ultraviolet radiation is absorbed. This region helps to shield the earth from cosmic radiation. At the outer part of this region, the temperature drops to about -135°F.

The next region outward is called the *thermosphere*. It starts about 50 miles from the Earth's surface and extends to between 200 and 300 miles. In this region, the atmosphere is so thin that no sound is transmitted. This region is also called the *ionosphere* because of its intense electrical activity. At about 75 miles from the surface of the earth, radio communications are able to bounce back to the surface of the earth. Many satellites are in an orbit in this region. Because of the lack of molecules in this region, there is very little friction upon the satellite vehicle.

The *exosphere* is the next region outward. This region actually blends into outer space at about 500 to 1,000 miles from the surface of the earth.

Near Space

The region beyond the atmosphere is called *near space*. An arbitrary limit of near space is about 10,000 miles from earth.

Space Characteristics

Several important characteristics of the space environment have affected the development of technology for spacecraft. One of the most predominant characteristics is vacuum, and thus no sound.

A second characteristic is the wide variation between intense heat and extreme cold. Once a spacecraft is out of the mesosphere, there is very little protection from the sun's radiation. In addition, molecules of any surface material of a spacecraft vibrate easily. Temperature is a measure of how rapidly these molecules vibrate. A surface subjected to the sun becomes very hot, whereas a surface not subjected to the sun becomes very cold. These factors cause certain stresses in the materials used on spacecraft.

Radiation is also a concern for manned space flights. Radiation can severely disrupt the chemical process within living cells. Normally, at altitudes below 250 miles this is not of concern. However, special radiation protection is required at altitudes above 250 miles.

Weightlessness is a condition caused by a balance between forces acting on a body. For example, when a person bounces on a trampoline, weightlessness occurs at the height of the bounce. A person in orbit experiences the same effect, as shown in Figure 8-15. Gravitational forces draw the body toward the earth. Centrifugal forces pull the body outward. When these two forces are in balance, weightlessness occurs. These points are shown as dots forming an orbit.

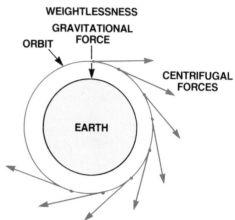

FIGURE 8-15 Weightlessness occurs when the centrifugal forces are equal to the gravitational forces.

Certain physical dangers can develop from being in a weightlessness condition for a long period of time. After several days, a person's heart has a tendency to become lazy. The heart does not have to pump against the pull of gravity. When reentry occurs, initially there were problems with the blood pooling in the legs. To overcome this problem, a special exercise program was developed for use while in weightlessness conditions.

Technological Fundamentals

Space technology can also be related to the systems model. For example, many of the topics presented here are part of the process. Tools, energy, money, information, people and materials are all resources into the process of launching and flying a spacecraft. This section looks at some of the principles related to the "process" of flying a space craft.

Thrust Defined

All of the motion produced on a spacecraft is a result of thrust. *Thrust* is defined as any force tending to produce a motion in a body or alter the motion of that body. In a rocket engine, thrust is the force that pushes the engine forward. Thrust is measured in pounds or newtons. For example, the liftoff thrust generated by the shuttle (Figure 8-16) is about 28,650,000 newtons or 6,400,000 pounds.

FIGURE 8-16 Thrust is created to cause the shuttle to lift off and be put into orbit. *Courtesy of NASA*

Action/Reaction

Thrust is created by a reaction. Rocket engines use a reaction to produce the necessary thrust. Reaction forces to produce thrust are based upon Newton's first, second, and third laws of motion.

Newton's First Law. The first law states that a body or mass in a state of rest tends to remain at rest. A body or mass in motion tends to remain in motion, unless acted upon by another force. For example, once a satellite is put into orbit, it will continue at that speed, unless acted upon by another force. The other force may be gravity, friction or more thrust.

Newton's Second Law. The second law says that an unbalance of force on a body tends to produce an acceleration in the direction of the force.

Newton's Third Law. The third law states that for every acting force there is an equal and opposite reacting force.

A pressure is created inside the rocket. The pressure is created by the burning of fuel. A hot-air balloon can be used as an example to illustrate the pressure. Figure 8-17A shows pressure in the balloon. The pressure is felt in all directions. Thus, there is no unbalance of forces. However, if the end of the balloon is opened, as shown in Figure 8-17B, an unequal pressure condition is created. This causes the balloon to move upward, producing thrust.

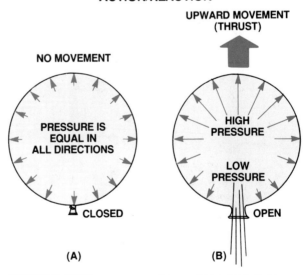

ACTION/REACTION

FIGURE 8-17 When pressure is equal in a rocket as shown in the balloon example, there is no movement. When there is an unequal pressure inside, the balloon moves upward due to the reaction.

TECH L I N K

When measuring thrust, either newtons or pounds can be used:

To convert thrust in pounds of force to newtons: One pound of force = 4.448 newtons

To convert thrust in newtons to pounds of force: One newton = .224 pounds of force

FIGURE 8-18 This rocket engine uses liquid fuel and a liquid oxidizer to operate. *Courtesy of Rockwell International*

Rocket Engine Thrust

The same internal forces are applied to the inside of a rocket engine. As heat is created inside the engine from burning of fuel, pressure increases. If there is a pressure differential (exhausted on one side) then the rocket will move forward or upward. Rockets have an advantage over other forms of engine propulsion systems: they are able to operate in the vacuum of space. Note that the reaction causes this upward motion. Upward thrust is not created by the force of the exhaust against the atmosphere.

Solid- and Liquid-fueled Rockets

Typically, two types of rockets are used today in the space transportation program: the solid-fueled and the liquid-fueled rocket. The liquid-fueled rocket uses a type of liquid fuel (*propellant*) mixed along with an oxidizer (oxygen for burning). The fuel and the oxidizer are in a liquid form. Figure 8-18 shows an example of a liquid-fueled engine. These engines have several advantages, including variable thrust, intermittent combustion, and they are reusable.

The solid-fueled rocket uses a fuel and oxidizer in a solid, powdery or rubbery mixture known as the *grain* or *charge*. Once a solid-fueled rocket is ignited, it usually burns completely. There is little variation and control of thrust. Solid fueled rockets consist of a solid fuel and oxidizer compound with the following hardware:

- Case — high-pressure gas container which encloses the propellant.
- Nozzle — gas expansion device through which the rocket exhaust flows.
- Insulation — protection from hot gases for the case and nozzle.
- Igniter — device to start the combustion of the propellants.
- Stabilizers — directional control system during flight.

Grain Design. The thrust produced by the propellants is determined by the combustive nature of the chemicals used, and by the shape of their exposed burning surfaces. The greater the exposed propellant surface area that is burning, the greater the thrust. A solid propellant will burn at any point that is exposed to heat or hot gases at the right temperature. The propellant is thus designed and shaped (grain design) to maximize the thrust.

Figure 8-19 shows three types of grain design. End-burning burns the slowest. It produces the least amount of thrust but prolongs the thrust over a longer period of time. The internal-burning design produces a greater thrust. However, the burning time is reduced. The star-shaped, internal-burning design produces the greatest amount of thrust for the least amount of time. It should be noted that the Shuttle booster rockets are of a solid propellant, star-shaped, internal-burning design.

GRAIN DESIGN

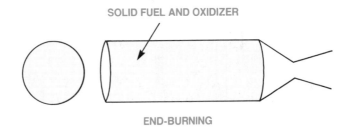

END-BURNING

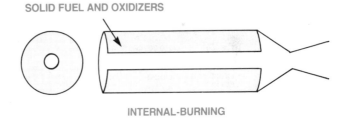

INTERNAL-BURNING

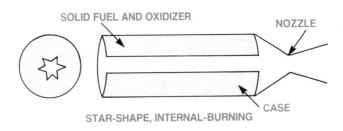

STAR-SHAPE, INTERNAL-BURNING

FIGURE 8-19 Solid fueled rockets are designed with different grain designs. The one most used is the star-shaped, internal-burning grain design.

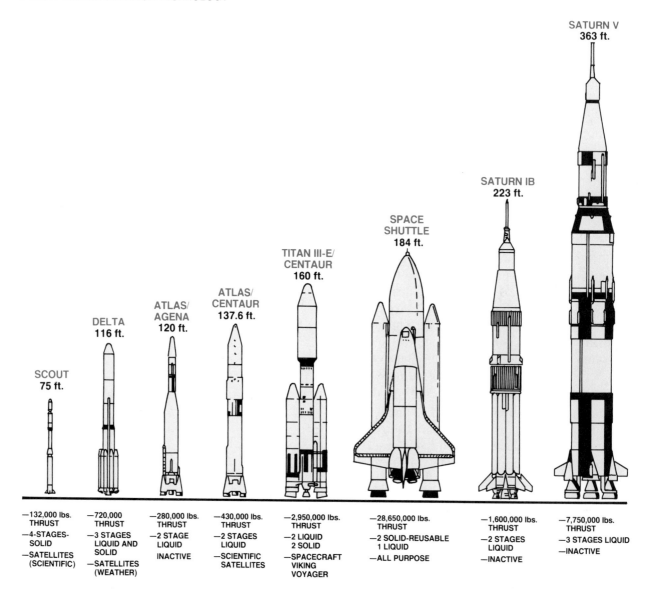

SATURN V
363 ft.

SATURN IB
223 ft.

SPACE
SHUTTLE
184 ft.

TITAN III-E/
CENTAUR
160 ft.

ATLAS/
CENTAUR
137.6 ft.

ATLAS/
AGENA
120 ft.

DELTA
116 ft.

SCOUT
75 ft.

—132,000 lbs.
THRUST

—4-STAGES-
SOLID

—SATELLITES
(SCIENTIFIC)

—720,000
THRUST

—3 STAGES
LIQUID AND
SOLID

—SATELLITES
(WEATHER)

—280,000 lbs.
THRUST

—2 STAGE
LIQUID

INACTIVE

—430,000 lbs.
THRUST

—2 STAGES
LIQUID

—SCIENTIFIC
SATELLITES

—2,950,000 lbs.
THRUST

—2 LIQUID
2 SOLID

—SPACECRAFT
VIKING
VOYAGER

—28,650,000 lbs.
THRUST

—2 SOLID-REUSABLE
1 LIQUID

—ALL PURPOSE

—1,600,000 lbs.
THRUST

—2 STAGES
LIQUID

—INACTIVE

—7,750,000 lbs.
THRUST

—3 STAGES LIQUID

—INACTIVE

FIGURE 8-20 Typical launch vehicles, among many, that have been used in space transportation.

Launch Vehicles

Figure 8-20 shows examples of various launch vehicles powered by rocket engines. Several statistics are compared, including the name, shape, thrust in pounds, type of fuel, and use. Figure 8-21 shows the launch of an Atlas/Centaur rocket for putting a communications satellite into orbit.

Achieving Orbit

Several forces work together to achieve orbit for a space vehicle. When a rocket is forced upward above the atmosphere, gravitational forces cause it to fall back to earth. When the vehicle is moving at

the correct speed parallel to the Earth's surface, it will break away from the Earth's gravity because of centrifugal forces. The typical speed at which this occurs is about 17,500 miles per hour. A vehicle is said to be in orbit when the gravitational forces are equal to and opposite the centrifugal forces. As long as the correct speed is maintained to cause the correct centrifugal forces, the vehicle will remain in orbit. Referring to Figure 8-22, if greater centrifugal forces are created by increasing the speed, either a higher orbit will result or the vehicle may slingshot out of orbit into space (see gravity assist). If the vehicle slows down, lesser centrifugal forces are created. This will cause the vehicle to go into a lower orbit or back to reenter the Earth's atmosphere.

Orbit Terminology

Several terms are used to describe orbits. Most satellites and spacecraft follow *elliptical* orbits, not circular orbits. The lowest point of the orbit is called the *perigee*. The highest point of the orbit is called the *apogee*. Figure 8-23 shows the apogee and the perigee.

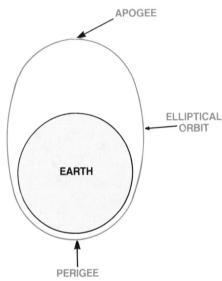

FIGURE 8-23 The *apogee* is the part of the orbit farthest from the surface of the earth. The *perigee* is the part of the orbit closest to the surface of the earth.

Escape Velocity

In order for a spacecraft to travel to other planets for scientific experimentation, it must escape the gravitational pull of the Earth. For example, recent scientific missions, such as the Voyager, Mariner, and Pioneer projects, required the spacecraft to escape the earth's gravitational pull completely. The spacecraft needs to travel at about 25,000 miles per hour to reach escape velocity.

Gravity Assist

Gravity assist is defined as obtaining additional speed of a spacecraft by using a planet's gravitational forces. The spacecraft can even be boosted on to still more distant planets, often with greater velocity. When a spacecraft passes very close to another planet or moon (within its gravitational field), it has a tendency to speed-up. This technique

FIGURE 8-21 This Atlas/Centaur produces 430,000 pounds of thrust during liftoff. *Courtesy of General Dynamics Inc.*

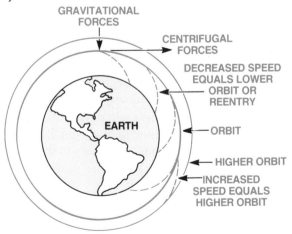

FIGURE 8-22 When the gravitational forces equal the centrifugal forces, the spacecraft will remain in orbit. However, if the speed is increased, a greater centrifugal force is created, producing a higher orbit.

has been called the *slingshot effect* or *gravity assist*. It is an established method used to cut down on travel time between planets without spending additional rocket propellant.

The Voyager mission took advantage of gravity assist. Figure 8-24 shows several planet orbits and the path taken by Voyager. The Voyager path first went around Mars, then Jupiter, then Saturn, then Uranus.

**VOYAGER'S PATH
GRAVITY ASSIST**

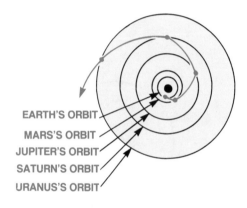

EARTH'S ORBIT
MARS'S ORBIT
JUPITER'S ORBIT
SATURN'S ORBIT
URANUS'S ORBIT

FIGURE 8-24 Voyager's path past several planets was accomplished by gravity assist.

Summary

Space transportation is becoming more and more important in our society. Because of space transportation, many new technologies and innovations are continually being developed. This chapter presents the need for space transportation and environments, and discusses several technological fundamentals.

- The space program began as far back as the 1940s.
- Several projects helped to develop space transportation: Project Mercury, Project Gemini, Project Apollo, Skylab, Apollo-Soyuz, and the Shuttle program, called STS (Space Transportation System).
- The Shuttle program also uses a Spacelab for conducting experiments in space.
- Part of the space transportation program is to provide transportation to space for satellites. These include weather, communications, scientific research, and navigational satellites.
- Landsat is a satellite program designed to take photographs of land masses in order to check for population changes, pollution, diseases, and other factors.
- Space technology has generated many new innovations. Technological developments have occurred in such areas as environmental, construction, communications, biomedical, electrical, and many others.
- Knowing what constitutes the atmosphere is an important part of space travel. The atmosphere is composed of the troposphere, stratosphere, mesosphere, thermosphere, and exosphere.
- Several characteristics of space affect transportation modes. These include weightlessness, radiation, and temperature variation.
- *Thrust* is defined as a force tending to produce a motion in a body.
- Thrust is produced by causing a reaction. A reaction is part of Newton's three laws of motion.
- Two types of rockets are used today in the space transportation program; these include both solid-fueled and liquid-fueled rockets.
- Solid-fueled rockets use a grain design to change thrust.
- Many launch vehicles are used today to put satellites into orbit.
- Achieving orbit occurs when gravitational forces are equal to centrifugal forces of the spacecraft.
- Gravity assist is a process whereby a spacecraft comes very near another planet's gravitational forces. The spacecraft has a tendency to slingshot farther into space by the additional gravitational forces.

REVIEW

1. If a space vehicle produces 25,000,000 newtons of thrust it also produces _____ pounds of thrust.
2. The lowest region of the atmosphere is called the _____ .
3. The characteristics of outer space include _____ and _____ .
4. Which of Newton's laws states that for every force there is an opposite and equal reacting force?
5. The _____ is called the highest point in an orbit.
6. _____ is defined as using additional speed produced by the addition of gravitational forces around a planet.
7. What space projects led up to the Shuttle missions?
8. Describe the Shuttle program and its purpose.
9. What is the purpose of the Spacelab as part of the Shuttle program?
10. Identify several types of satellites and their purposes.
11. List several major benefits derived from the space program.
12. Define the term *near space.*
13. Identify how weightlessness is produced in a spacecraft.
14. List the three laws of motion and state how they relate to producing thrust in a spacecraft.
15. Name the high and low points of an elliptical orbit.
16. Define the term *gravity assist* in terms of space transportation.

CHAPTER ACTIVITIES

 ## ROCKET ENGINE DESIGN AND OPERATION

INTRODUCTION
This activity is designed to learn about launching model rockets and testing their performance.

TECHNOLOGICAL LITERACY SKILLS
Problem solving, data analysis, design, and predicting.

OBJECTIVES
After completing this activity, you will be able to:
1. Construct model rockets.
2. Launch model rockets.
3. Test model rocket performance.
4. Redesign model rockets to improve their performance.

MATERIALS
1. Model rocket launch pad with rocket ignition system.

2. Several model rockets or kits with which to build different shapes and forms of rockets.
3. Several types of rocket engines that produce different thrust.
4. An obstacle-free area for launching rockets.
5. Rocket Engine handouts

PROCEDURE

1. Using a model rocket kit, build a model rocket. During this procedure, research and identify different rocket designs. What design changes could you suggest that would improve the efficiency, speed and thrust of the rocket? Place answers on handout provided.

   ▶ **CAUTION:** Always wear safety glasses when working with tools in the laboratory. Also, make sure you know the correct operation of all tools used in the laboratory. If not, check with your instructor.

2. Study the engine or propellant. What type of engine is used and how is it rated? Place answers on handout.
3. What type of grain design is used on the engine? Place answer on handout.
4. Using the launch pad and igniter, ignite the rocket with the smallest engine available. Retrieve the rocket and prepare for a second launch.

   ▶ **CAUTION:** Always wear safety glasses when launching model rockets. Also, make sure you are safely away from the blast of the rocket engines.

5. Place the next-larger-size engine in the rocket and launch again. What was the difference in the thrust (distance and height) and the length of time of the burn? Place answers on the handout.
6. Continue to increase the engine size in the rocket and launch again. What was the difference in the thrust (distance and height) and the length of time of the burn? Place answers on handout.
7. Look at the design of the rocket and its external shape and weight. Redesign the rocket to make it more efficient. State what you did to make it more efficient. Place answers on handout.
8. Now launch the redesigned rocket and observe its characteristics. Use the same engine size as used in the first launch. Identify the difference in flight and operation of the redesigned rocket.

REVIEW QUESTIONS

1. What changes did you make in the rocket to improve its flight?
2. What causes the forces to propel the vehicle upward?

ADDITIONAL EXPERIMENTS

1. Build a two-stage rocket.
2. Build a rocket that has a cargo bay as in the Shuttle Space Transportation System.
3. Build a device to measure thrust of engines.

 # PLOTTING A JOURNEY TO MARS

INTRODUCTION

This activity will help you determine how to plot a trip to Mars.

TECHNOLOGICAL LITERACY SKILLS

Data analysis, plotting data.

OBJECTIVES

After completing this activity, you will be able to:

1. Plot a path a spacecraft would take to reach the planet Mars.
2. Determine the number of days to travel to Mars.

MATERIALS

1. Pencil
2. 3 × 5 card
3. The Plotting Sheet handout

PROCEDURE

1. Using the Velocity Scale on the Plotting Sheet handout, select a speed for travel to Mars. For example, 8 means the spacecraft will travel at 80,000 miles per hour.
2. Using a 3 × 5 notecard on its long edge, mark a line from the end of the card that represents the velocity selected. For example, if you selected 8 (80,000 mph), then there should be a ½-inch line from the end of the notecard inward on the edge.
3. Now look at the Plotting Sheet handout. Using the edge of the notecard, line up the edge of the card with the dots at Earth's position at launch and Mars's position at launch. Now draw a line between the two dots. This is the distance the spacecraft traveled in 10 days. This distance is also shown on the distance scale. If 8 was selected, then the spacecraft traveled about 20 million miles during the first 10-day period.
4. After 10 days, both the Earth and Mars have also moved to the next dot on the Plotting Sheet handout. Now draw a new line from the dot just made to the next dot directly above Mars.
5. Repeat step 4 until the line segments and dots (path of spacecraft) meet with Mars.
6. Now repeat steps 1 through 5 using two other velocities.

REVIEW QUESTIONS

1. How many days did it take the spacecraft to travel to Mars for each velocity? (Count the dots made with each dot representing 10 days.)
2. How far did the spacecraft travel to get to Mars for each velocity?
3. Which spacecraft will arrive at Mars first?
4. If electronic communications travel at 186,000 miles per second, how long will it take to communicate with the spacecraft for each velocity?

BALLOON-POWERED VEHICLE

INTRODUCTION

Propulsion systems can be produced from many sources. One propulsion system is by reaction, as used in a jet engine. This activity will show how to produce thrust in a vehicle. The object of this activity is to design a method for using a balloon to power a vehicle.

TECHNOLOGICAL LITERACY SKILLS

Data analysis, design, experimentation, problem solving, collection of data.

OBJECTIVES

At the completion of this activity, you will be able to:

1. Design a balloon-powered vehicle.
2. Construct a balloon-powered vehicle.
3. Test a balloon-powered vehicle.

MATERIALS

1. Several sizes of balloons.
2. Small pieces of wood for building a car used to attach the balloon to the vehicle.
3. Woodworking laboratory general tools.
4. Paper and pencil
5. Balloon Vehicle handout.

PROCEDURE

1. The object of this activity is to design a system in which a balloon will propel a vehicle. Divide into small groups of two or three students.
2. Design a land vehicle. The vehicle cannot be more than 8 inches in length.
3. Things to consider in the design include:
   a. Will the balloon be put into the structure of the vehicle?
   b. Can the balloon be blown-up easily?
   c. Will the size of the balloon be matched to the vehicle size?
   d. If the balloon is outside the vehicle, will it produce a wind drag?
   e. Will the vehicle be too light or too heavy?
   f. Will the exhaust of the balloon be restricted?
   g. What frictional losses can be reduced or eliminated?
   h. Can the vehicle be made lighter?
   i. What will be the size of the balloon exhaust area?
4. After designing the balloon vehicle, build a prototype to test its operation and characteristics.

   ▶**CAUTION:** Always wear safety glasses when working with tools in the laboratory. Also, make sure you know the correct operation of all tools used in the laboratory. If not, check with your instructor.

5. When completed, test the vehicle. Measure the distance traveled and record it on the Balloon Vehicle handout provided by the Instructor.
6. Based upon your first test, redesign the vehicle to improve its operation and reduce frictional resistance.
7. Test the vehicle again and record the distance on the handout.
8. Record the increase in distance.
9. Now compare the two tests done by your group to those of the other groups.

REVIEW QUESTIONS

1. What produces the power to propel the vehicle forward?
2. What frictional losses were reduced to improve the design of the vehicle?
3. What was the biggest design change the group made?

ADDITIONAL EXPERIMENTS

1. Try using a balloon to propel a glider, plane, or space vehicle. The vehicle could be placed on a tight wire and propelled across the room.
2. Try using a balloon to propel a boat across water. The vehicle could be placed on a trough of water, such as a rain gutter.

SECTION THREE

ENERGY TECHNOLOGY

This section discusses many of the energy forms used within the transportation systems of society, and other systems of technology as well. Many energy technology systems are studied by using the input, process, output, impact, and feedback loops of the systems model. For example, a solar collection system can be studied as follows by using the systems model:

1. The "input" command or objective would be to change the radiant energy of the sun into thermal energy for use in a residential dwelling.

2. The "processes" include resources such as solar collector materials, people for building the equipment, engineering drawings (information), various tools, money used for purchasing materials, and the time required to construct the solar system.

3. The "output" or result is the actual operation of the solar system. The "impacts" include pollution from the manufacturing processes, the saving of our natural resources by using solar energy, and the economic gain realized when using a solar system.

4. The "feedback" would be the operation of the solar contols used to turn the collector pump on and off, depending upon the intensity of the sun and the time of day.

All of the other technologies discussed in Section Three can be studied in the same way by using the systems model.

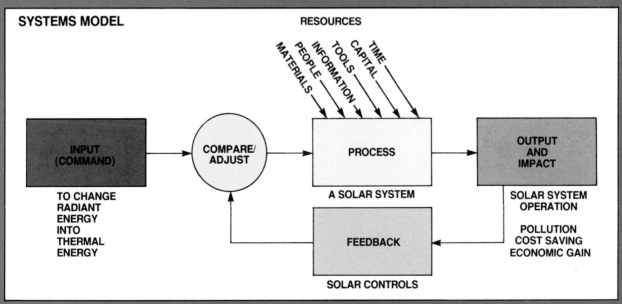

SYSTEMS MODEL

RESOURCES

MATERIALS PEOPLE INFORMATION TOOLS CAPITAL TIME

INPUT (COMMAND)

COMPARE/ADJUST

PROCESS

OUTPUT AND IMPACT

TO CHANGE RADIANT ENERGY INTO THERMAL ENERGY

A SOLAR SYSTEM

SOLAR SYSTEM OPERATION

POLLUTION COST SAVING ECONOMIC GAIN

FEEDBACK

SOLAR CONTROLS

Introduction to Energy Technology

KEY TERMS

Potential	Random Energy	Calorie
Infrared	Nondepletable	Electromagnetic
Fossil	Depletable	Supply
Sea Kelp	Efficiency	Demand
Kinetic	Converter	Doubling Time
Generators	Molecular	Rejected Energy
Entropy	Btu	

Introduction

Energy is a very important part of any transportation system. It is used as one of the "resources" in the process section of the systems model. Energy is used for propulsion systems on all of the transportation modes previously discussed. Energy is also part of other technological systems such as communications and production. This chapter introduces energy, and discusses its forms, associated terminology, and the concept of energy supply and demand.

Energy Technology

Energy Defined

Quite often, the terms energy and power are used interchangeably. However, these terms are different. *Energy* is defined as the ability to do work. This means that any resource that is able to do work, or has the potential to do work, is considered energy. A hydroelectric dam, as shown in Figure 9-1, has the potential to turn a set of turbine blades. It has energy waiting to be used. A gallon of gasoline is also energy. It has the potential to do work. Keep in mind that energy is not work that has been done.

Power is a term used to describe the measure of the work being done.

FIGURE 9-1 A hydroelectric dam has potential energy to do work. *Courtesy of American Petroleum Institute*

Forms of Energy

Energy exists in six forms: radiant, chemical, thermal, mechanical, electrical, and nuclear. No matter for what it is used, energy will always be in one of these six forms.

In addition, all energy on this planet is said to come from the sun. For example, as the sun shines on the earth and its plants, a process called photosynthesis takes place. *Photosynthesis* is the process in plants that takes the sun's energy and converts it to another form of energy in the plant. In our society, we have learned with technology to extract energy from many plants. The sun's energy is said to be limitless. This means that as long as the sun shines on the earth, we will have energy available for our technologies to operate.

Radiant Energy

Radiant energy is defined as an energy form given off by hot objects. Radiant energy is like the rays of light coming from a light bulb. Radiant energy is also that form which comes from the sun. The sun is constantly giving off radiant energy, measured by the frequency of its electromagnetic waves, Figure 9-2. Radio waves, microwaves, visible light, infrared waves, and ultraviolet waves are all forms of radiant energy.

Typically, as any object becomes hotter it emits a higher frequency of radiant energy. The cooler an object becomes, the lower the frequency. In addition, higher frequencies produce more energy, while lower frequencies produce less energy.

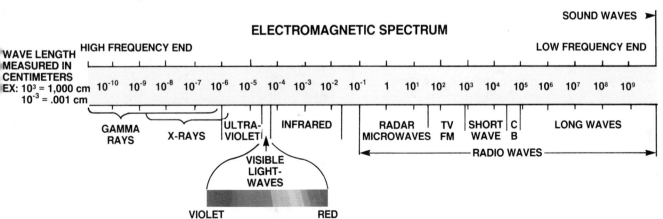

FIGURE 9-2 Radiant energy is transmitted by electromagnetic waves. This chart shows the frequency of many electromagnetic waves.

FIGURE 9-3 Coal is a good example of chemical energy. *Courtesy of Quaker State Oil Ref. Corp.*

Chemical Energy

A good example of chemical energy is coal, as shown in Figure 9-3. Coal is considered a fossil fuel. This means that the sun's energy (radiant) was absorbed by plants many millions of years ago. As the plants absorbed radiant energy, the energy was converted to *chemical energy* in the plant. The plants then either decayed or were eaten by large animals. As these plants and animals died, they eventually turned into fossil fuels. Fossil fuels are also considered a form of chemical energy.

Three types of fossil fuels have been used extensively as energy. As shown in Figure 9-4, these include (A) coal (solid), (B) crude oil (liquid), and (C) natural gas (gaseous). Other forms of chemical energy less frequently used are wood, grain and sea kelp, among others. Figure 9-5 shows examples of some other forms of chemical energy, including (A) corn and (B) shale oil.

FIGURE 9-4 Fossil fuels are considered chemical energy. Fossil fuels include (A) coal, (B) crude oil, and (C) natural gas. *Courtesy of (A) The Standard Oil Co., (B) Chevron Corp, (C) Hamilton Bros. Co.*

Deepwater Port

Crude oil is considered one of the three types of fossil fuels used in our society today. A certain percentage of crude oil is imported into the United States by large oil tankers. As part of the transportation of crude oil, various ports and harbors must be built to load and unload the crude oil. Deepwater ports are used to unload crude oil without going directly into a harbor area. These deepwater ports are considered part of the support technology for moving oil throughout the world.

This photo shows a deepwater port, the 350,000-ton London Trader. It is unloading a million and one-half barrels of crude oil at an offshore oil port in the Gulf of Mexico. The vessel is moored to a single-point buoy system 18 miles off the Louisiana coast. The system's pumping platform is in the background. *Courtesy of Marathon Oil Company*

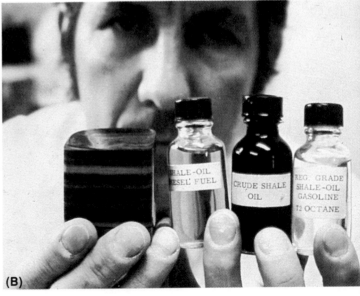

FIGURE 9-5 These examples of (A) corn and (B) shale oil are considered chemical forms of energy. *Courtesy of (A) Texaco, Inc., (B) ERDA (Dept. of Energy)*

Thermal Energy

Thermal energy is defined as heat energy. Thermal energy can be arrived at in several ways. For example, as radiant energy from the sun strikes a solar collector, it is converted to thermal energy. Figure 9-6 shows a solar energy installation used to produce thermal energy for water and space heating.

In addition, as any chemical form of energy is burned during combustion, thermal energy is produced. For example, if a gallon of gasoline (chemical energy) were burned, it would produce a great amount of thermal energy. Typically, thermal energy can be measured by stating the temperature.

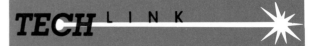

Thermal energy exists in any object having a temperature above -273°C (-460°F). At -460°F, no thermal energy exists. This means that thermal energy still exists in the air even when it is -20°F outside, although our bodies don't feel it. The higher the temperature, the more thermal energy that exists. Many energy technologies are able to extract thermal energy from objects that seem cold to the touch.

FIGURE 9-6 Solar energy is captured and converted to thermal energy in a solar collector. Here the thermal energy is used for water and space heating. *Courtesy of Exxon Enterprises, Inc.*

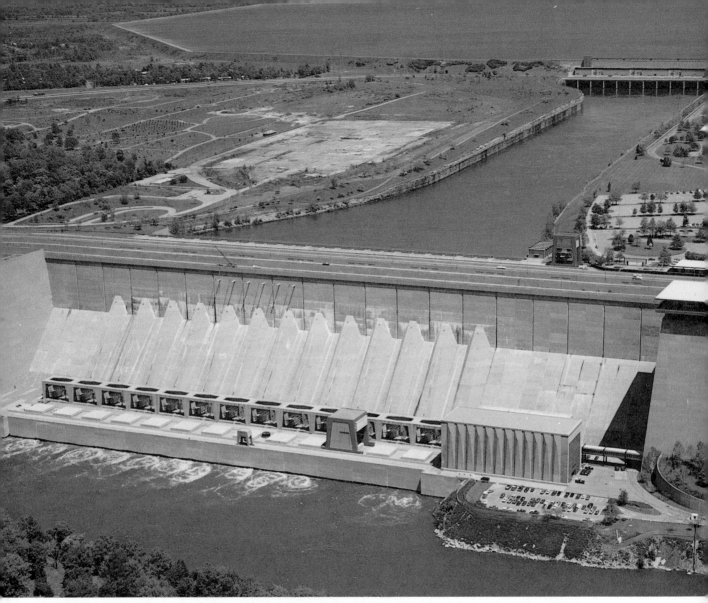

FIGURE 9-7 This hydroelectric dam has a great potential to produce mechanical energy as the water falls to a lower level. *Courtesy of New York Power Authority*

Mechanical Energy

Mechanical energy is energy that is able to move or impart motion. For example, our bodies take in chemical energy in the form of food. Our bodies then take this energy and convert it to mechanical energy, used for walking, running and various sports, for instance.

Another example of mechanical energy is a hydroelectric dam. A dam, holding back water, has a great potential for producing mechanical energy as the water falls to a lower level, Figure 9-7. A spring or rubber band is another example of stored mechanical energy. A spring or rubber band is also said to have potential energy.

Quite often, mechanical energy is also called kinetic energy. *Kinetic* energy is derived from objects in motion.

TECH LINK

Kinetic energy can be calculated by knowing the values of both the mass (m) and speed or velocity (v) of an object. The formula for calculating kinetic energy is:

$$\text{Kinetic energy} = \tfrac{1}{2} \times mv^2$$

Thus, if an object were heavier (more mass) or the object moved faster (velocity), there would be more kinetic energy.

Monitoring Electric Energy

As consumers and industries use electrical appliances, machines, lights, and other products, more electrical energy is demanded from an electric generating power plant. The amount of electrical energy (electrons moving in a wire) used by the consumer is called the *electrical load*. The generator at the power plant must be able to provide the necessary electrical energy demanded to keep the loads operating. The load must be monitored to determine how much energy is being used.

This operator is monitoring an electric system's conditions. The operator can monitor the amount of electricity being demanded by the consumers of the electric utility system. As the electric load is monitored, the total output power is monitored.

The information obtained from these monitoring systems helps operators to make instant decisions about when and if the public will make too many demands on the electrical energy supply. Technology such as this is considered part of the "feedback" loop in the systems model. *Courtesy of Union Electric Company*

Electrical Energy

Electrical energy is defined as energy that causes electrons to move in a wire. Figure 9-8 shows an example of high line wires used for transmission of electrical energy. Electrical energy is also produced from batteries and generators. A *battery* simply converts the chemical energy inside into electrical energy for use in various appliances. A *generator* converts mechanical energy into electrical energy, Figure 9-9.

FIGURE 9-8 These high line wires are used to carry electrical energy from a power plant to residential and commercial buildings. *Courtesy of Niagara Mohawk Power Corp.*

FIGURE 9-9 This generator converts mechanical energy into electrical energy. *Courtesy of Niagara Mohawk Power Corp.*

FIGURE 9-10 These samples of uranium ore, a source of nuclear energy, will eventually be used in a nuclear power plant. *Courtesy of Kerr-McGee Corp.*

Nuclear Energy

Nuclear energy is defined as the energy held within the atoms of certain elements. For example, uranium molecules contain energy. Figure 9-10 shows samples of uranium ore which will eventually be used in a nuclear power plant. If a uranium atom were caused to split in two, great amounts of energy would be released as thermal energy.

Conversion of Energy Forms

Any technology associated with energy usually converts the energy from one of its six forms to another. Conversion of energy is considered part of the "processes" in the systems model. Conversion is needed because quite often energy does not come to us in the form needed. Thus, it must be changed to a form that is usable by the specific technology. For example, consider the energy needed to run a slide projector in a home. A slide projector needs radiant energy to shine through a slide so viewers can see it. Let's follow the series of events and conversions needed to obtain radiant energy for a slide projector.

1. The sun's energy comes to the earth as RADIANT energy.
2. The RADIANT energy is converted to CHEMICAL ENERGY by photosynthesis in a plant.
3. The plant, over millions of years, condenses the CHEMICAL energy into coal.
4. Humans extract CHEMICAL energy as coal from a coal mine and burn it in a power plant to produce THERMAL energy.
5. THERMAL energy causes water to turn to steam in a boiler where it expands and produces MECHANICAL energy.
6. The MECHANICAL energy of steam turns a turbine which turns a generator.
7. The generator converts MECHANICAL energy into ELECTRICAL energy.
8. The ELECTRICAL energy is sent through wires to a home and then to the projector.
9. The bulb in the projector converts ELECTRICAL energy into RADIANT energy to view a slide.
10. The ELECTRICAL energy is also converted to MECHANICAL energy for a fan motor.
11. The fan motor is used to exhaust THERMAL energy produced by the bulb.

The various technologies (turbines, generators, motors, bulbs, and so forth) are all used to convert one form of energy to another.

Defining Energy Technology

Based upon the series of conversions just discussed, we can now define energy technology. *Energy technology* is defined as any technology used to convert one of these six forms of energy to another for use in our lives, Figure 9-11.

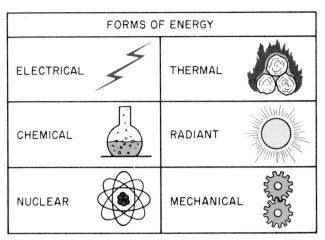

FORMS OF ENERGY	
ELECTRICAL	THERMAL
CHEMICAL	RADIANT
NUCLEAR	MECHANICAL

FIGURE 9-11 Energy technology is any technology used to convert one of these six forms of energy to another. *Courtesy of DCA Educational Products*

Laws of Energy Conservation

Two laws of energy conservation help to understand the conversion from one form of energy to another. One law is called the *First Law of Thermodynamics*. It states that:

> Energy cannot be created or destroyed; it can only be transformed from one form to another. The total energy in any system is considered to be constant.

This law, simply stated, says that energy cannot be destroyed. It will always exist in one form or another.

The second law is called the *Second Law of Thermodynamics*. It states that:

> A natural process always takes place in such a direction as to cause an increase in the randomness (entropy) of the universe.

The key word in this law is entropy. *Entropy*, simply stated, means that things have a tendency to become more random. For an analogy, a bucket of water contains many droplets of water, highly condensed. If the bucket is spilled, the droplets are spread all over and become more random. This analogy suggests that the bucket of water has gone through the process of randomness or entropy.

The same thing happens to energy every time it is converted from one form to another. Figure 9-12 shows two cooling towers in a coal-fired power plant. The thermal energy coming out of the cooling towers is very random. Thus, some of the coal has gone through the process of entropy. Some of the input energy (coal) becomes more random. This process is called entropy.

FIGURE 9-12 Entropy occurs when coal is converted in a power plant to electricity, making some of the energy more random. These cooling towers are giving off this random thermal energy. *Courtesy of Middle South Services, Inc.*

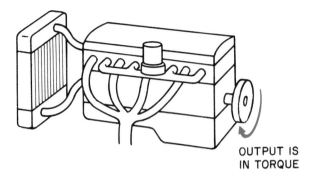

OUTPUT IS
IN TORQUE

FIGURE 9-13 In this gasoline engine, only about 25% of its input energy goes into work. The remaining 75% is lost because of entropy. *Courtesy of DCA Educational Products*

Let's use an automobile propulsion system for another example, Figure 9-13. Gasoline as chemical energy (input) is converted by the engine into mechanical energy (torque/output). To do this, a certain amount of the energy (the exhaust, cooling system heat, and radiant heat) has become more random. Some of the input energy has gone through the process of entropy. This energy, (exhaust/cooling/radiant) is very random and not usable in its present form. In fact, about only 25% of the input energy is actually converted to mechanical output energy. The remaining 75% has been converted to thermal energy in the exhaust and cooling system and given off as radiant energy. No matter what type of conversion occurs, some energy will always become more random. Although the random energy is not destroyed, it is, however, changed into a form not usable by our technology.

It should be noted that any energy lost through entropy can be classified in the systems model as "impacts." Because of the constant increases in thermal energy losses due to entropy, some scientists believe the temperature of the atmosphere is increasing steadily. This could have quite a negative impact on the future of our environment.

Renewable and Nonrenewable Energy

Energy forms can be stated as renewable or nonrenewable. *Renewable* energy forms, also called nondepletable, are those that continue to be renewed for use. Examples of renewable energy forms include solar, wind, hydroelectric dams and wood resources. These forms of energy, for all practical purposes, will never run out. Figure 9-14 shows the renewable energy of the wind.

FIGURE 9-14 Wind is considered a renewable energy resource. *Courtesy of Southern California Edison Co.*

Nonrenewable energy forms, also called depletable, are those resources that are being used up by our society. They will never be totally renewed in our lifetime. Examples of nonrenewable energy forms include coal, oil, natural gas, and nuclear resources. If we keep using these resources as we have in the past, eventually they may become depleted in our lifetime. The problem is that our technology today is designed to run almost totally on nonrenewable resources.

Energy Terminology

Many terms are used to describe energy forms and how energy is used in technology. Understanding these terms will help to identify energy problems now and in the future.

Efficiency

The term *efficiency* is a measure of how well technology converts energy from one form to another. There are many types of efficiency. One type, called the *First Law Efficiency*, compares the input energy to the output energy. Figure 9-15 shows the formula for efficiency. Efficiency is measured as the ratio of output to input energy multiplied by 100. For example, let's say 100 units of chemical energy were put into a propulsion system for an automobile. The mechanical energy output of an automobile engine is only 25 units. This means the engine operates at about a 25% efficiency. This efficiency is sometimes written as .25. Figure 9-16 shows various First Law efficiencies for different converters. Of course, entropy plays an important role in determining efficiency.

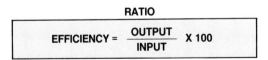

RATIO

$$\text{EFFICIENCY} = \frac{\text{OUTPUT}}{\text{INPUT}} \times 100$$

FIGURE 9-15 Efficiency is a ratio of the input as compared to the output multiplied by 100.

Efficiency of Total Energy Systems

Many energy technologies have more than one converter having a specific efficiency. For example, use the automobile again. The automotive engine has an alternator to convert mechanical energy into electrical energy. In addition, the electrical energy is

also used to crank the starter motor and charge the battery. Each of these converters has its own efficiency. To obtain the total efficiency of an

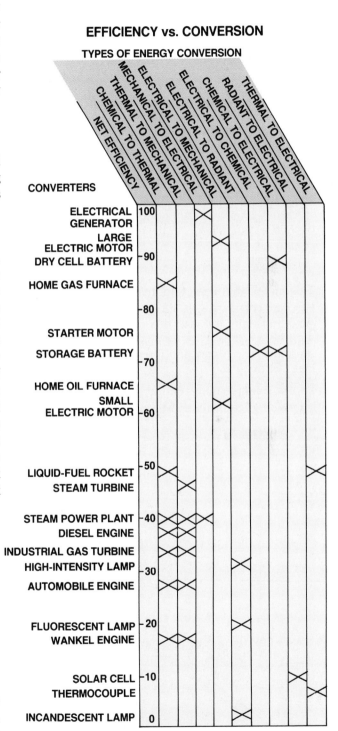

FIGURE 9-16 This chart shows various converters, their efficiency and the type of energy conversion.

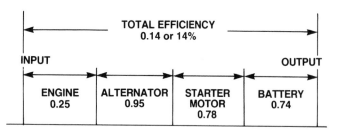

FIGURE 9-17 The total energy efficiency of any system is determined by multiplying together all separate efficiencies. The automobile is used for example here.

automobile, each individual efficiency is multiplied together, Figure 9-17. For example, when the engine efficiency (.25) is multiplied by the alternator efficiency (.95), the starter motor efficiency (.78), and the battery efficiency (.74), the total efficiency of this system is:

$(.25 \times .95 \times .78 \times .74) = .137$ or about 14% efficient

This means that an automotive vehicle has a total efficiency of nearly 14%. About 14 units are used for each 100 units put into the system. The other 86 units have become random because of entropy.

Heat Energy

Thermal energy is also defined as heat energy. Heat is the energy transmitted from a higher-temperature body to a lower-temperature body. Heat is said to always flow from a hotter body to a colder body. Heat energy is developed in a body because the molecules bounce against one another. As more energy is put into the body, more molecules vibrate and bounce into one another, resulting in heat. Heat is always present as long as there is molecular movement in a body. Molecular movement is said to stop at -273°C (-460°F) also called *absolute zero*.

British Thermal Unit

British thermal units (Btu) are used to measure thermal or heat energy. One *Btu* is equal to the amount of energy needed to raise one pound of water one degree Fahrenheit. This is about the same amount of energy needed to burn a wooden match completely, Figure 9-18. Other examples of Btu include:

1. A gallon of gasoline has about 120,000 Btu.
2. A standard home in a northern U.S. climate requires about 20,000 Btu per hour to maintain a temperature of 68°F.
3. A cord of wood contains about 20,000,000 Btu.
4. A cubic foot of natural gas contains about 1,000 Btu.

Figure 9-19 shows several common energy resources and the number of Btu for specific amounts of each.

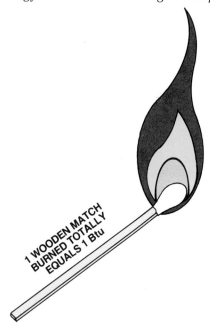

FIGURE 9-18 One Btu is about equal to the energy released when a wooden match is burned completely.

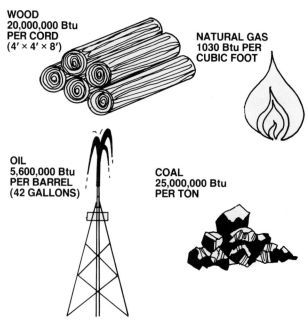

WOOD
20,000,000 Btu
PER CORD
(4' × 4' × 8')

NATURAL GAS
1030 Btu PER
CUBIC FOOT

OIL
5,600,000 Btu
PER BARREL
(42 GALLONS)

COAL
25,000,000 Btu
PER TON

FIGURE 9-19 Several forms of energy are shown with the number of Btu for each amount.

TECH L I N K

The Btu has become a common unit to measure sizes and capacity of many energy products. For example, an air-conditioning system is designed to remove heat from a building. An air conditioner may be rated at 10,000 Btu. This means that the air conditioner is able to transfer 10,000 Btu out of the room every hour. Many air-conditioning systems are also rated in tons. One ton of refrigeration in an air-conditioning system removes 12,000 Btu per hour.

You can also determine how many Btu per hour your house is using by looking at your monthly energy bill. Look for the number of ccf or therms. Multiply that number by 100 to get the number of cubic feet used in a month. Multiply that number by 1,030 to get the number of Btu per month.

Divide the Btu per month by the number of days in that month to get the Btu per day. Divide the number of Btu per day by 24 hours to get the Btu per hour used in your home over a month's period.

Calorie

The term calorie is used in the metric system to measure thermal energy. One *calorie* is the heat required to raise one gram of water one degree Celsius. A calorie is a much smaller unit than a Btu. The calorie is often used to measure the amount of energy in food.

Energy Transfer

Conduction. Energy can be transferred from one body to another in several ways. *Conduction* is the transfer of thermal energy from a solid to another solid. For example, heat or thermal energy conducts from the electric coil on a stove to the metal pan, Figure 9-20.

Convection. A second way heat can be transferred is by convection. *Convection* is defined as the transfer of thermal energy from a solid or a liquid to a liquid or a gas. Convection is most commonly used to move heat around a room. Figure 9-21 shows an electric heater in a room. As the electric coil heats

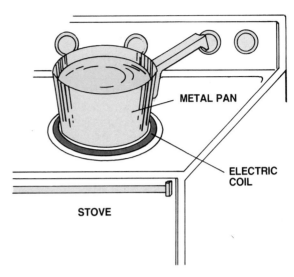

FIGURE 9-20 Heat is transferred by conduction from the hot coil on the stove to the metal pan.

the air, the air becomes less dense and starts to rise. The more dense cold air drops. This action causes a convective loop to develop within the room.

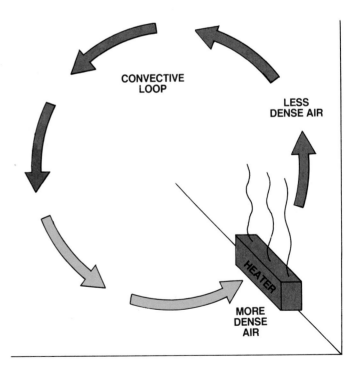

FIGURE 9-21 Convection occurs when a heater warms up the air around it. The warm air becomes less dense and rises. The cool, more dense, air drops. A convective loop is created.

Radiation. The third way heat can be transferred is by radiation. *Radiation* is defined as heat transfer by using electromagnetic waves. The sun's surface transmits radiant energy to the earth via electromagnetic waves. Several things affect the amount of energy being transmitted by radiation. The first is the temperature difference between the source and the collection object. The greater the temperature difference, the more heat that is transferred. It is generally accepted that any object that contains heat gives off radiant energy. The hotter the object, the greater the amount of energy transmitted. Second, the color of the body which receives the energy also affects the amount transferred. Normally, darker colors absorb more energy which causes more radiant transfer.

A good example of transfer of energy by radiation occurs when using a fireplace or woodburning stove, as shown in Figure 9-22. The hot stove and coals radiate energy to a person standing in front of the stove. The front of the person will feel very warm; however, the back of the person will not feel the warmth.

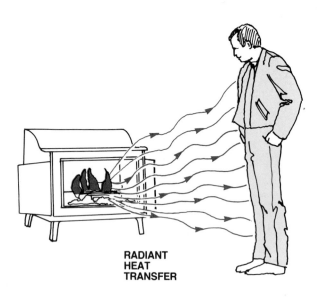

RADIANT
HEAT
TRANSFER

FIGURE 9-22 Radiation can be felt when standing in front of a woodburning stove.

TECH LINK

In your home, always be aware of how energy is moving around. Energy is transferred by conduction, convection, and radiation. Look at how energy is transferred in your home. Can it be improved? Is energy being conducted to places you don't want to heat? Place your hand on different walls. If the wall feels cold, the energy is conducting out of the house. Is there proper convection to move thermal energy from one level to another? Are you making maximum use of any radiant energy transfer? Being aware of simple energy transfer in a home can help to save significant amounts of money over a year's period.

Energy Supply and Demand

Supply versus Demand

In our society, many technological systems are based upon the laws of supply and demand. Supply and demand are considered part of the "impacts" in the systems model when using energy. Typically, the *supply* is the input of the system and *demand* is the output. For example, our society demands a certain amount of energy. This is because of the style of life we have chosen. Thus, energy companies are in business to provide a supply of coal, oil, and natural gas to meet the demand. Obviously, many impacts, both positive and negative, are part of the supply and demand formula.

As long as there is a sufficient and equal (balanced) supply available to meet the demand, few problems exist, Figure 9-23. However, when supply and demand are not equal, certain problems will develop. For example, if a petroleum company has a large supply of oil, it may drop the price to get rid of the excess oil. Or, if the demand is greater than the supply, companies usually increase their prices. When the demand is so great, consumers will pay increased prices to get more. In order to have stable prices for our energy products, careful planning and sound energy policies are necessary to keep supply and demand equal.

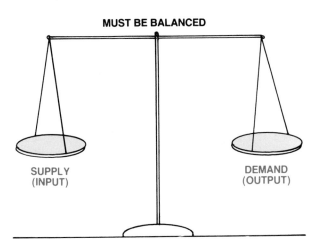

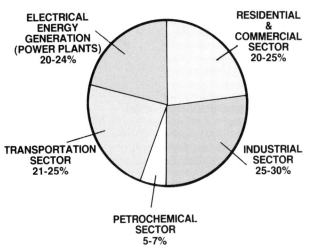

FIGURE 9-23 It is important for the energy supply and demand to be equal, or cost and availability problems will develop.

FIGURE 9-25 This pie diagram shows the percentages of each demand sector that uses energy.

Resources for Supply

Six major resources are used to fuel our technological society: coal, oil, natural gas, nuclear, and hydroelectric plus alternatives. Figure 9-24 shows a diagram of current percentages of each. These percentages continually change from year to year.

Demand Sectors

Five sectors consume energy in our society, as shown in Figure 9-25.

The residential and commercial sector use (demand) energy for:

- space heating
- water heating
- cooking
- clothes drying
- refrigeration
- air conditioning
- appliances (TV, freezers, dishwashers)
- computer operations
- lighting

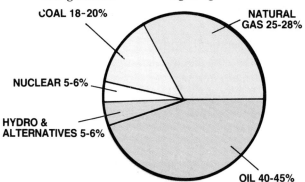

FIGURE 9-24 This pie diagram shows the percentages of each major resource that supplies energy to society.

Such buildings as homes, offices, schools, churches, hotels, and motels make up this sector.

The industrial sector uses energy for producing the goods and products we buy. This sector uses energy to operate machines and drying processes, and for the manufacture of parts and production of foods and chemicals, plus others.

The petrochemical sector has been separated from the industrial sector. This sector uses oil and natural gas to manufacture such products as plastics, alcohol, and polyester. This sector is also called the "nonenergy" sector. The remaining energy goes into electrical generating stations to produce electricity, and into transportation used for moving products and people in society.

Doubling Time

When studying energy, the doubling time is used to show how fast a particular product will double in its demand. *Doubling time* is defined as the time in years it takes for a product to double in size. For example, say a person has $1,000.00 in the bank and it is drawing 7% interest. Each year the money in the bank ($1,000.00 the first year) increases by 7%. After one year, the amount in the bank is $1,070.00 ($1,000.00 × 1.07). After the second year, the amount is $1,144.90 (1,070 × 1.07), and so on. Doubling time is said to be the number of years it will take for the $1,000.00 to double. The approximate doubling time is found by dividing the percentage of increase or growth of any product (7%), into a constant of 71. When 7 is divided into 71, the result is 10.2. Thus, anything that grows at 7% will double in size in 10.2 years.

Energy and Doubling Times

Doubling times are closely related to energy growth and supply and demand. Doubling times have great impacts on the future of energy. Energy demand in the past few years has been increasing. Recently, energy has been increasing between 2% and 3% each year. Energy growth depends upon several factors, including supply available, cost, economic wellbeing of consumers, and so forth. If energy is growing by 3% each year, the doubling time is 23.4 years (71 divided by 3). This means that every 23.4 years, the total amount of energy supplied must be doubled. Figure 9-26 shows the doubling times for various percentages of increase. This concept is also referred to as *exponential growth*.

DOUBLING TIMES

PERCENTAGE INCREASE PER YEAR	DOUBLING TIME IN YEARS	MULTIPLICATION FACTOR
0	Infinite	1.0
1	69.7	1.01
2	35.0	1.02
3	23.4	1.03
4	17.7	1.04
5	14.2	1.05
6	11.9	1.06
7	10.2	1.07
8	9.0	1.08
9	8.0	1.09
10	7.3	1.10
12	6.1	1.12
14	5.3	1.14
16	4.7	1.16
18	4.2	1.18
20	3.8	1.20
25	3.1	1.25
30	2.6	1.30
40	2.1	1.40
50	1.7	1.50
75	1.2	1.75
100	1.0	2.00

FIGURE 9-26 This table shows the doubling times for various percentages of increase. For example, if energy increases by 3% each year, the amount of energy required will double every 23.4 years.

Energy Flow

Figure 9-27 shows a complete energy-flow diagram, including supply, demand, and both useful and rejected energy. *Rejected energy* is a result of all

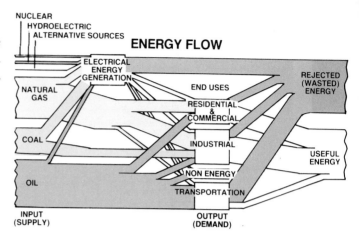

FIGURE 9-27 This is a complete energy-flow diagram. The thickness of the line represents the amount of energy. The energy flows from the supply (left side) to the demand (right side).

entropy processes. The diagram has three major sections.

1. The input (supply) is defined as the resource. Resources include petroleum, coal, natural gas, nuclear, hydroelectric and alternatives.
2. The output (demand) is the application (sector) for which the energy is being used. Sectors include commercial/residential, industrial, petrochemical (nonenergy), transportation, and electrical. Note that many resources of energy must first be converted to electricity at a power plant. This is considered an intermediate step in the energy flow. On the average, power plants are about 33% to 36% efficient.
3. The third section shows the useful energy and the rejected (downgraded) energy in total.

Conclusions about Energy Flow

First let's look at oil. Oil is supplied for use in all sectors of society. Coal is mostly sent to the industrial sector. In addition, a certain amount of coal is sent to the electrical energy generation. From the electrical energy generation, electricity is then sent back for use in the individual sectors. Natural gas is used mostly in the industrial and residential/commercial sector.

By reviewing the energy-flow diagram (Figure 9-27), several conclusions can be made, including:

1. If an oil shortage were to exist, the transportation sector would be most affected.
2. When any energy resource is changed to electricity, the total efficiency is less.

3. If a coal shortage were to exist, all sectors except transportation would be severely affected.

4. On the average, our society is using about 51% of the energy, while 49% is being rejected or downgraded because of entropy.

5. If a natural gas shortage were to exist, both the residential/commercial and industrial sectors would be severely affected.

Summary

- *Energy* is defined as the ability to do work.
- *Power* is defined as the measure of the work being done.
- Six forms of energy are: chemical, radiant, thermal, mechanical, electrical, and nuclear.
- *Energy technology* is defined as any technology used to convert energy from one form to another.
- *Entropy* is a process that results in randomness. Some of the input energy becomes more random when changed from one form to another.
- *Renewable* energy resources are those that will continue to be renewed or will never be depleted. *Nonrenewable* resources will eventually be used up.
- *Efficiency* is a ratio of the input energy compared to the output energy.
- Heat energy, measured in Btu, can be transferred by conduction, convection or radiation.
- A Btu is the amount of heat necessary to raise one pound of water one degree Fahrenheit.
- Ideally, there is a very delicate balance between the supply and demand of energy.
- Energy supplies include coal, oil, natural gas, nuclear, hydroelectric, and alternative resources.
- Energy demand includes the sectors of residential/commercial, industrial, petrochemical, transportation, and electrical power plant.
- Doubling times of any energy growth period can be determined by dividing the growth rate into a constant of 71.
- In total, about 49% of the input energy in our society is rejected because of entropy, and the 51% of energy left is usable for work purposes.

REVIEW

1. If the use of coal as an energy resource is increasing at 5% each year, it will take _____ before coal energy will double.

2. A furnace in a home consumes 50,000 Btu each hour. The furnace actually outputs 42,000 Btu into the home during this condition. The efficiency of the furnace is _____ percent.

3. A battery is an energy conversion technology that changes ____ energy to ____ energy.

4. An alternator on a car is used to convert _____ energy into _____ energy.

5. If the supply of an energy resource is greater than the demand, the cost of the energy resource will typically _____ .

6. When the demand of an energy resource is greater than the supply available, the cost of the resource will typically _____ .

7. Identify how energy is converted from different forms, starting with the sun and finishing with the energy coming from a light bulb.

8. Define the term *entropy* and state how it affects efficiency.

9. Define what happens in a total energy system when each individual converter has its own efficiency.

10. Identify the differences between depletable and renewable energy resources.

11. State how efficiency is measured.

12. What is a Btu?

13. What is a calorie?

14. Compare the three ways in which thermal energy can be converted.

15. Why is it so important to keep the supply and demand of energy equal and in balance.

16. What are the major resources for energy supply and their approximate percentages of the total energy?

17. Identify the sectors that use energy today, including specific uses with each sector.

CHAPTER ACTIVITIES

 ENERGY FLOW

INTRODUCTION

Energy is converted from one form to another in many technological systems. This activity is designed to show how energy is converted to different forms in an automobile.

TECHNOLOGICAL LITERACY SKILLS

Problem solving, flow diagraming, group analysis.

OBJECTIVES

At the completion of this activity, you will be able to:

1. Trace the energy flow in a standard automobile.

2. Identify the forms of energy in an automobile.

3. Identify where energy is stored in an automobile.

MATERIALS

1. Any automobile

2. Energy-flow handout

PROCEDURE

1. Select an automobile and identify the parts that need energy to operate. These should include the power door locks, power seats, power steering, transmission, starter, ignition system, radio and speakers, generator, battery, lights, and spark plugs.

2. Identify what form of energy is used in each of the aforementioned components.

3. Using the symbols and arrows shown on the energy-flow handout, draw a complete energy-flow diagram for the automobile including the previously stated components. Figure 9-28 shows an example of a similar flow-type diagram.

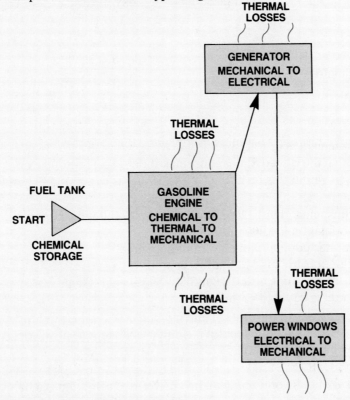

FIGURE 9-28 An example of an energy-flow diagram.

REVIEW QUESTIONS

1. How many forms of energy are used in an automobile?

2. What form of energy is usually lost at each conversion point?

3. How can a converter, such as a transmission, change one type of mechanical energy to another type of mechanical energy?

PERSONAL ENERGY USAGE

INTRODUCTION

This activity is a mathematical sequence problem. It is designed to help the student use statistical data to arrive at an answer about energy. The object of this activity is to determine how much energy each person in the United States uses per day as compared to Africa.

TECHNOLOGICAL LITERACY SKILLS

Problem solving, mathematical analysis, drawing conclusions.

OBJECTIVES

At the completion of this activity, you will be able to:
1. Use statistical data to solve a math problem.
2. Determine how much energy each person uses per day in the United States.
3. Determine how much energy each person uses per day in Africa.

MATERIALS

1. Pencil and Paper
2. Electronic Calculator
3. Statistical Data

PROCEDURE

1. The problem statement is as follows:
   Statistics show that the United States consumes about 1/3 of the total world energy. How much energy per person would this be in the United States as compared to Africa?
2. Statistical Data:
   a. The world consumed about 120 million barrels of oil (equivalent) per day.
   b. The world population is 3,900 million persons.
   c. The United States population is 215 million people
   d. The population in Africa is 412 million people.
   e. People in Africa consume about 2.8 million barrels of oil (equivalent) per day.
   f. One barrel of oil is equal to 42 gallons.
3. Remember to keep track of the units of energy. One unit used is the MB/DOE. This stands for Million Barrels per Day Oil Equivalent. It is a unit used to represent all energy used in barrels of oil for a one-day period.
4. First, calculate the MB/DOE used in the United States. Multiply the total MB/DOE (120) by the number .33 or 1/3 of the world energy. The answer is the amount of energy all people in the United States use per day.
5. Calculate the amount of energy in barrels per day used per person in the United States. This is done by dividing the MB/DOE calculated in step 4, by the number of people in the U.S.
6. Now convert into gallons the number of barrels used per day by each person in the U.S. This is done by multiplying the barrels per day by 42 gallons per barrel. The answer is the amount of energy each person uses each day of the year in the United States.
7. Now calculate the amount of energy (barrels) used each day by people in Africa. This is done by dividing the amount of MB/DOE energy used in Africa (2.8) by the population of Africa.

8. To change the barrels of oil used each day per person in Africa, (calculated in step 7) to gallons, multiply the number of barrels by 42. The final number calculated is the number of gallons each person consumes each day in Africa.

REVIEW QUESTIONS

1. How much more energy in gallons does each person use in the United States as compared to Africa?
2. Why do people use so much more in the United States as compared to Africa?
3. How would your lifestyle change if you had to reduce your energy consumption by ½?

 EXPONENTIAL GROWTH AND DOUBLING TIMES

INTRODUCTION

This is a simple one-day activity that demonstrates the principles of exponential growth and doubling times.

TECHNOLOGICAL LITERACY SKILLS

Prediction, data analysis.

OBJECTIVES

At the completion of this activity, you will be able to:
1. Define exponential growth and doubling times.
2. Make predictions about exponential growth and doubling times.
3. Relate exponential growth and doubling times to energy usage.

MATERIALS

1. A checkerboard
2. A small cup of uncooked rice
3. Exponential Growth/Doubling Times handout

PROCEDURE

1. Divide the class into groups of two.
2. Answer questions 1, 2 and 3 on the handout provided.
3. Looking at the checkerboard, predict how many squares you will be able to fill on the checkerboard, increasing exponentially from one to the other. Enter your prediction on the handout.
4. Using your cup of rice and the checkerboard, fill the first square with one piece of rice, the second square with 2, the third square with 4, the fourth square with 8, the fifth square with 16, and so on. Continue until you are out of rice.
5. Complete the remainder of the handout.

REVIEW QUESTIONS

1. How are exponential growth and doubling times related to energy supply and demand?
2. What factors could eventually limit the exponential growth in this experiment?
3. What is the doubling time for the energy supply if the increase in energy was 4% per year?
4. How can doubling times of energy be increased?

CHAPTER 10

Fossil Fuel Energy Resources

OBJECTIVES

After reading this chapter, you will be able to:

■ Identify coal types and characteristics.

■ State where coal resources are located.

■ Compare the technologies for coal mining.

■ Describe petroleum exploration.

■ State how petroleum is produced.

■ Discuss petroleum characteristics and refining.

■ Compare the transportation modes for petroleum.

■ Identify the characteristics and refining of natural gas.

■ Describe the transportation of natural gas.

KEY TERMS

Political Constraints	Stratum (Strata)	Refinery
Fossil	Overburden	Distillation
Acid Rain	Unit Train	Therm
Alkaline	Scrubber	Associated Well
Btu/pound	Seismograph	

Introduction

Coal, oil (petroleum), and natural gas are considered fossil fuels. They supply approximately 85 to 90% of all energy used within the United States. Each of these resources is also considered a depletable or nonrenewable resource of energy. These resources have many technological aspects. This chapter is about these fossil fuels, their technology, and the systems used to support them.

FIGURE 10-1 Coal, considered a fossil fuel, is used in many power plants to produce electricity. *Courtesy of Oglebay Norton*

Coal Energy Resources

Coal has been used as an energy resource for many years, Figure 10-1. Only recently, has coal usage started to increase. Coal is the most plentiful resource available within the United States. Estimates suggest that coal will be available for approximately 350 to 400 more years at present coal demand rates. However, if more coal is used each year, this time may become less.

Coal usage is anticipated to increase significantly in the next few years. The reason for this is because of the number of political constraints on petroleum and the availability of natural gas resources. Coal is the one resource that is available

Coal Gasification

Because coal is so abundant, much research has been done to find additional ways to use coal. A great deal of research has gone into the process of coal gasification. *Coal gasification* is the process of converting coal into a natural gas form and using the gas to produce energy.

Coal gasification is attractive because coal can then essentially be used in existing natural gas furnaces. This will help to reduce costs of generating electricity by the power company, especially as fuel types change over the years.

This is a diagram of a power generating unit, showing how it produces clean-burning natural gas fuels from coal for the production of electricity. *Courtesy of Texaco, Inc.*

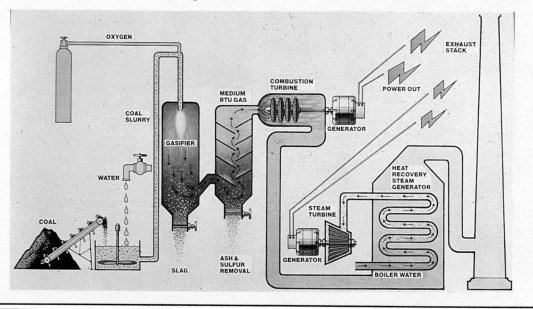

for the future, and is not controlled by foreign suppliers. Coal is primarily used for producing electricity. Figure 10-2 shows coal consumption in the United States by market areas. Note that about 65% of the coal is used for electrical power generation.

Coal Characteristics

Coal is considered a combustible fossil fuel. It is brown to black in color and solid in form. Several characteristics help to identify coal, including carbon content, heating value, and various impurities.

First, let's look at impurities. All coal has impurities in its makeup. The content of these impurities usually includes moisture, ash, and sulfur. When a power company selects the coal to use, these impurities become very important. Moisture has an effect on the burning and combustion quality of coal. A certain amount of ash usually remains after

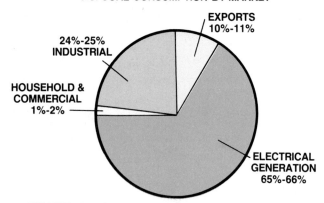

U.S. COAL CONSUMPTION BY MARKET

FIGURE 10-2 Coal is mostly used for the production of electrical energy.

combustion. Ash content is important because the ash is considered a waste product. Sulfur content is critical because of the acid rain problem produced from burning coal within the United States.

Liming Lakes

Because of the increased use of coal in producing electricity, acid rain has become a serious problem. One method used to reduce the amount of acid in the lakes is to neutralize the lakes. This can be done by adding an alkaline solution such as lime to the lake. When lime is added to an acid, the solution becomes neutral. The helicopter shown here is used to lime lakes in the Adirondack Mountains of New York state. Liming lakes by this method is considered by many companies to be a cost-effective means to control the acidic solutions of lakes. The result is increased protection of the fish population. *Courtesy of American Electric Power*

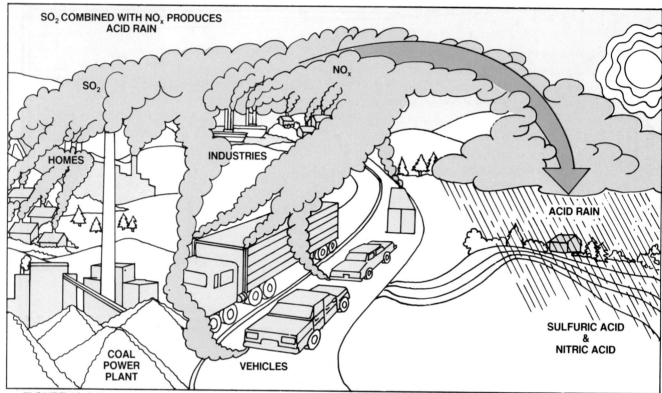

FIGURE 10-3 there are several sources of acid rain. Homes and power plants produce SO_2 and industries and vehicles produce NO_x. These chemicals are then converted into sulfuric and nitric acid. These acids in the atmosphere, when mixed with water, produce acid rain.

Acid Rain

Our society has a problem with acid rain due to the sulfur in coal and other fossil fuels. Acid rain is considered one of the major negative "impacts" as applied to the systems model of technology. As the coal is burned in the power plant, the sulfur is allowed to escape into the atmosphere. When the moisture in the atmosphere mixes with the sulfur, acids are produced. Then when it rains, acidic water falls on the rivers and streams.

Figure 10-3 shows how acid rain is produced. Sulfur dioxide (SO_2) and nitrogen oxides (NO_x) from the combustion of fossil fuels rise into the air. Water is then mixed in to produce sulfuric and nitric acids as acid rain.

Acid Measurement (pH Scale)

Acid can be measured by using the pH scale. When tests are made on lakes, the pH of the solution can be determined. The scale has numbers from 0-14. When the test results are between 0-7, the solution is considered an acid with 7 being the weakest acid. If

the test results show 7-14, the solution is considered alkaline or the opposite of an acid. Figure 10-4 shows an example of the pH scale along with various solutions. Power companies are restricted by law to allow only a certain amount of sulfur into the atmosphere.

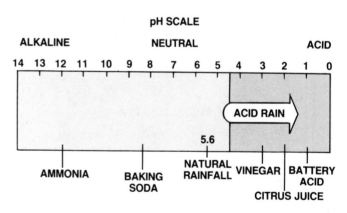

FIGURE 10-4 Acid rain has a very strong level of acid, usually measured at about 4.5 on the pH scale.

Carbon Content

Each type of coal also has a certain carbon content. *Carbon content* is defined as the amount of carbon within the chemical makeup of coal, as determined by the percentage by weight of carbon in the coal. The average carbon content in coal today is about 50%. Typically, as the carbon content of coal increases, the quality of the coal also increases.

Heating Value

The heating value of coal is a measure of how many Btu can be produced per pound. Generally, the higher the carbon content, the higher the heating value of the coal. It should be noted that both heating value and carbon content are directly related to the type and amount of impurities in the coal.

Types of Coal

Four types of coal are normally used in the power plants of the United States:

1. Lignite
2. Subbituminous
3. Bituminous
4. Anthracite

Each type of coal has a different heating value and carbon content. Figure 10-5 shows the four types, and the carbon content of each. Note that lignite has the lowest carbon content, whereas anthracite has the highest.

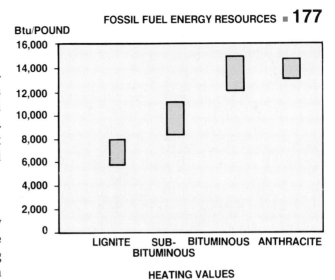

FIGURE 10-6 This chart shows the heating values in Btu per pound for each of the four types of coal.

Each of the four types of coal also has a different heating value. Figure 10-6 shows a chart comparing heating values in Btu per pound of coal. Again, note that lignite has the lowest heating value, whereas anthracite has the highest.

Location of Coal Reserves

Coal is distributed throughout the entire United States. Depending upon its type, coal is found in several major areas, Figure 10-7. There are five types of coal. Bituminous coal is further subdivided into two different levels.

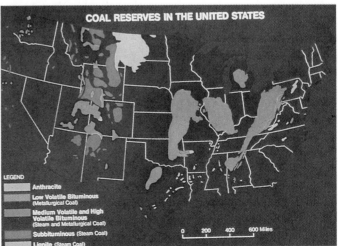

FIGURE 10-7 This map shows the various types of coal used, and where each type is located in the United States. *Courtesy of National Coal Association*

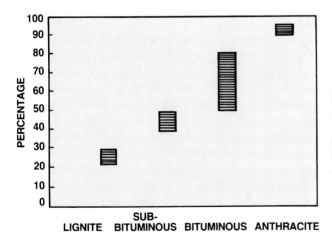

FIGURE 10-5 This chart shows the carbon content percentages for each of the four types of coal.

Mining Coal

Two types of coal mining are presently in operation. They are surface mining and underground mining. The type of mining operation depends upon how deep the coal is embedded in the ground and what type of terrain is above ground. Coal is normally found in a coal seam, also called a stratum (plural strata). Typically, if the coal seam is close to the surface, say 50 to 60 feet, the mining company will surface mine the coal. Figure 10-8 shows coal being removed from a surface mine. If the coal is much deeper in the ground, it is usually mined by underground mining methods.

Surface Mining. Surface mining takes place in many areas and regions throughout the United States. Typically, the coal seam is located close to the surface of the ground. Usually, the seam is between 10 and 40 feet thick. To get at the coal, several stages of mining must first occur. The top layer of soil must first be removed and separated for later use.

Second, the overburden must be removed down to the coal seam. The *overburden* is the material on top of the coal deposit. A dragline is used to remove this material, Figure 10-9. Once the coal seam is uncovered, it is extracted from the seam by large

FIGURE 10-8 Surface mining is often used when the coal seam is near the surface of the earth. Here coal is being removed from a surface mine. *Courtesy of Oglebay Norton*

FIGURE 10-9 A dragline is used to remove the overburden and expose the seam of coal. *Courtesy of American Electric Power*

shovels and cranes and loaded into trucks for removal, Figure 10-10. The coal is then washed, crushed to a certain size (about ½ to ¾ inch in diameter) and sent to the power plant. After the coal is removed, the overburden is restored to the area from which it was taken, and the top layer of soil again placed on the overburden. This process is called *reclamation*.

Underground Mining. When the coal seam is located deep in the ground, underground mining is used. For example, the coal in many parts of Utah and Colorado is taken out by underground mining techniques. Many forms of underground mining have been used throughout the years, although conventional and continuous mining have typically been used. *Conventional underground mining* uses a cutting machine to cut a block of coal. Drilling machines are also used to drill holes for explosives. The coal is blasted into pieces for loading and removal. *Continuous underground mining* cuts the coal from a seam and loads it onto conveyors. Roof supports, called *pillars*, and ventilation operations continually advance ahead of the mining as it progresses. Figure 10-11 shows an example of the pillars used in underground mining. The pillars are used to support the mine's roof.

FIGURE 10-10 This coal shovel extracts coal from the seam and loads it into large trucks for removal from the mine. *Courtesy of Standard Oil*

PILLARS

FIGURE 10-11 Pillars are used to support the roof for continuous mining operations. *Courtesy of Bureau of Mines, United States Department of Interior*

Longwall Mining. Another type of underground mining today is called *longwall mining*. In this process, coal is removed from the seam in one operation. A cutting machine moves back and forth across a wide block of coal. This process shears off coal and carries it away on a conveyor. The machine in this method of mining uses hydraulic jacks to support the roof. As the machine moves farther into the coal seam, the roof collapses behind it. There are efforts to eliminate longwall mining, because some underground shifting occurs when using this method. Relating to the systems model, this technology is considered an "impact."

Transportation and Handling of Coal

Once the coal has been removed from the mine, it must be transported to the coal power plant site. This is done using many forms of transportation. Some of the more common transportation forms include, unit train, barges, and large freighters. Two of these forms of coal transportation are shown in Figure 10-12.

When the coal arrives at the power plant, it must be unloaded. Figure 10-13 shows an example of how the train coal car is unloaded. The car is tilted about 160 degrees without unhooking the car, using a rotary car unloader. Using this special dumping system, workers can unload 35 cars per hour.

After the coal has been unloaded, it is placed on the storage pile, Figure 10-14. Most power plants can store an approximate 60-day coal supply on the plant site. Storage is provided to ensure there is a coal supply, should there be a transportation strike or mine shutdown.

Coal-fired Power Plant Operation

There are many types of coal-fired power plants. However, the basic principles of each are much the same. Coal-fired power plants are rated by the amount of electrical energy created at peak loads. For example, a large power plant may be able to produce 750 to 850 megawatts of electricity.

Figure 10-15 shows a typical, coal-fired power

FIGURE 10-12 Coal can be transported by (A) barge and (B) unit trains. *Courtesy of (A) The British Petroleum Company p.l.c. and (B) American Petroleum Institute*

FIGURE 10-13 This coal car is tilted 160 degrees, and the coal is dumped onto a conveyor belt. *Courtesy of Northern States Power Company*

FIGURE 10-14 Most power plants have on-site facilities to store coal for several months. *Courtesy of Montana Power Company*

plant diagram. The first step in producing electricity from coal is to pulverize the coal to the consistency of flour (1). This helps the coal burn more efficiently. Then, large fans blow the pulverized coal into one of several boilers (2) where it burns in fireballs of intense heat. This 3,000°F heat boils water into steam.

Pipes then carry the steam (3) to a large turbine (4). The turbine has many rows of windmill-like blades rotating on a shaft. The steam expands and hits the blades, thereby spinning the shaft to rotate an electromagnet within a generator (5). As the magnet spins inside the windings of wire, electricity

is produced. The electricity then travels to the transformer (6). From the transformer, electricity is then sent to the different demand sectors of our society (7).

After the turbine has extracted the energy from the steam, the steam is then condensed back to water by cooling it in the condenser (8). The extra thermal energy from the condenser is then sent to the cooling towers (10) to be evaporated into the air. The energy being given up in the cooling towers is a result of entropy. Water is then pumped (11) from a river nearby to replace water lost due to evaporation (9).

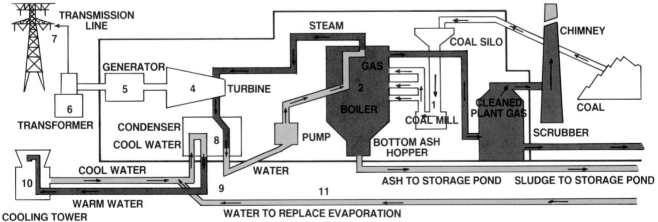

FIGURE 10-15 This power plant schematic shows the main parts of a coal-fired power plant, including the generator and the scrubber.

The exhaust gases from the boiler are then sent out through a scrubber. The scrubber uses lime (an alkaline) to reduce the sulfur in the exhaust. Sludge from the scrubber is then sent to a storage pond.

Petroleum Energy Resources

Petroleum is often referred to as *black gold*. Presently, petroleum supplies approximately 41% of the total energy to our society. This amount is quite often affected by several factors. These include the amount of oil supplied by foreign suppliers, the balance between supply and demand, and the world cost of oil per barrel.

Barrels of Oil

Petroleum is usually measured by the barrel as the standard unit of oil. The standard barrel capacity in the oil industry is 42 gallons. Today, our society consumes between 20 and 25 million barrels of oil per day.

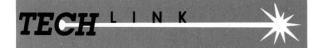

TECH **L I N K**

When comparing oil to other forms of energy, such as coal and natural gas, a common energy unit is needed. Many times the term MB/DOE is used. This unit represents *M*illions of *B*arrels per *D*ay, *O*il *E*quivalent. Coal, oil, and natural gas quantities are all combined together into this unit to indicate a total amount of energy being used by a society.

Oil Exploration

Oil exploration is a complete technology within itself. Its purpose is to locate the oil reserves. Years ago, oil could only be found and extracted when it was no deeper than about 5,000 feet below the surface of the earth. Today, however, with improved exploration technology, oil can be found at depths of 15,000 to 17,000 feet. The most common type of apparatus used in exploration technology is the *seismograph*. Figure 10-16 shows a typical seismograph operation. In this technology, a shock wave is sent into the earth. As the shock wave hits the hard rock cap directly above the oil reserve, it bounces back. Recording sensors then pick up the returned

FIGURE 10-16 Exploring for oil is done by using a seismograph which sends shock waves into the ground to determine rock formations. *Courtesy of Amoco Corp.*

shock waves. The information is then sent to a computer for plotting and determining the exact amount of oil in the reservoir. Core samples are then taken for analysis of rock formations near the oil reservoir, Figure 10-17.

FIGURE 10-17 During oil exploration, core samples of rock are taken and analyzed to determine rock formations, and thus oil location. *Courtesy of Marathon Oil Company*

FIGURE 10-18 This drilling bit (looking up from the bottom of the rig) is used to drill the hole for the oil well. *Courtesy of Huges Tool Co.*

Oil Production

Once the oil is located, it must be taken from the ground so it can be sent to a refinery. This process is called *production*. An oil drill is used to produce a hole down to the oil reservoir. Figure 10-18 shows a typical rotary drill bit used to cut through the rock, sand, and other material. Figure 10-19 shows a schematic of an oil drilling rig, and a photo of an offshore drilling platform. The oil drilling rig uses a rotary table to turn the drill pipe and bit. As the bit is turned and cut into the ground, water is flushed down through the center of the bit. The water helps to wash away the ground that has been cut away. A casing pipe is then placed in the hole to keep the ground from caving in. When the drill bit finally reaches the oil reservoir, the natural oil pressure forces the oil up through the pipe. A blowout valve is used to stop the oil from spilling when it reaches the surface.

CROWN BLOCK

TRAVELING BLOCK
SWIVEL
KELLY

ROTARY TABLE
BLOWOUT VALVES

DRILL PIPE

CASING

BIT
(A)

MUD HOSE

DRAW WORKS
MUD PUMP

PLATFORM

WATER

(B)

FIGURE 10-19 A schematic and photo of a typical oil drilling rig in the ocean, used for offshore drilling operations for oil. *Courtesy of (B) The Standard Oil Co.*

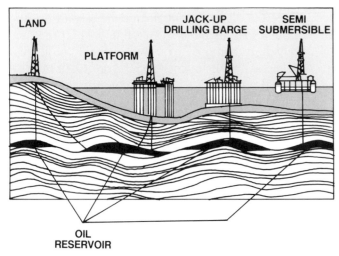

FIGURE 10-20 Several types of oil drilling rigs are used for both land and sea operations.

Oil Rigs

Many types of oil rigs are used both on land and offshore. *Offshore drilling* refers to drilling for oil beyond the shoreline. This can be either in coastal waters or far out in the sea. Figure 10-20 shows several types of oil rigs. The platform and the jack-up types are used in shallow waters. The semisubmersible is used in deeper waters, as deep as 1,000 feet. Figure 10-21 shows three examples of different oil rigs.

FIGURE 10-21 Examples of oil rigs: (A) An offshore production platform in the Gulf of Mexico, (B) building the North Brae platform, and (C) the deepwater or semisubmersible type, used for water depths greater than 1,000 feet. *Courtesy of (A) Standard Oil Co. of California, (B) Marathon Oil Co., and (C) Phillips 66*

Improved Recovery

Improved recovery, also called secondary recovery, is used to force more oil out of the existing oil reservoir. Quite often, the natural pressure in an oil well is not enough to extract all of the oil. With improved or secondary recovery, oil can be removed from an oil well reservoir even if there is low natural pressure. Injector wells are drilled first, as shown in Figure 10-22. These injector wells are used to force water or steam down into the oil reservoir. The heat from the steam or warm water causes the oil to thin out. The pressure from the steam then forces the oil through and out the producing well.

Oil Transportation

Once the oil is removed from the earth, it must be transported to the refinery. This is done by using a variety of methods. The most common method is by super tanker, Figure 10-23A. In addition, oil pipelines are also used. The Trans-Alaska pipeline shown in Figure 10-23B is used to transport crude oil from the northern slopes of Alaska to the Valdez port. Other transportation modes are also used,

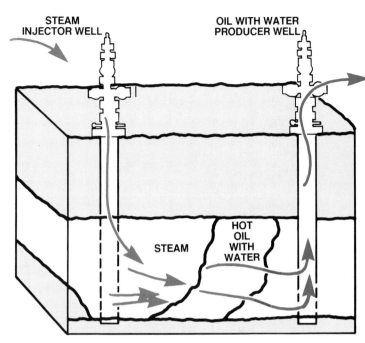

FIGURE 10-22 Secondary or improved recovery is done by sending steam down an injector well. The oil is then thinned and removed through the producer well.

FIGURE 10-23 Oil can be transported by using several methods: (A) a VLCC (*Very Large Crude Carrier*), and (B) the Alaska Pipeline. *Courtesy of American Petroleum Institute*

Petrochemical Industry

The petrochemical industry is an industry that is continually growing. The petrochemical industry converts fossil fuels into products used by consumers. A typical petrochemical plant converts such hydrocarbon fuels as gas and oil into plastic and synthetic materials. This is accomplished as part of the refining process.

The plastic materials are then sent to various manufacturers. The manufacturer then forms the plastics into many products consumers use on a daily basis. These products include, for example, toys, plastic panels, computer cases, plastic potato chip bags and plastic tool cases, among others. *Courtesy of Texaco, Inc.*

including railroad tank cars, barges and, at times, highway trucks.

Products from Oil Refining

The purpose of oil refining is to change the crude oil into chemical products that can be used in a variety of applications. The refining process works well when studied from the systems model. The input or command is to convert crude oil into different chemical products. Various inputs (energy, people, capital, and so on) are used to process the crude oil into different chemicals. The output or application is the actual chemical being produced. The feedback loop includes control of the refining process in terms of flow rates, temperatures and pressures, among others. Impacts include such factors as pollution and depletion of natural resources.

The following list illustrates some of the many products refined from crude oil.

1. Rubber tires, inks and paints
2. Varnish and painters' chemicals
3. Turpentine
4. Lubricating oil
5. Soaps
6. Gasoline
7. Diesel fuels
8. Insecticides and tree sprays
9. Cutting, paper, leather, and textile oils
10. Synthetic lubricants
11. Rubber compounds
12. Salves, creams, ointments, and petroleum jelly
13. Rust preventatives
14. Shingle and paper saturants
15. Fuel and metallurgical coke

Refining Principles

The products listed previously are all called *hydrocarbons*, meaning they are made of different chemical combinations of hydrogen and carbon. In fact, a single drop of crude oil has hundreds of different chemical combinations of hydrocarbons.

Each of these hydrocarbons also has a different boiling point. The point at which a liquid changes to a gas is called the *boiling point*. Some hydrocarbons have very high boiling points (700°F), whereas others have low boiling points (300°F). Once the boiling point has been reached, the hydrocarbons take on the form of a vapor. If the vapor is cooled back down, the hydrocarbon then turns back into a liquid. This process is called *condensation*. Refining is based upon these principles.

TECH LINK

As thermal energy (heat) is added to a liquid, the liquid will eventually turn into a gas or vapor. This is called *evaporation*. Evaporation occurs (say in a pan of water being heated) because the added heat causes the liquid molecules to increase in energy. The higher energy molecules will begin to move, and escape to become a vapor. If enough heat is applied, all of the molecules will be evaporated.

If a vapor is cooled down to below its boiling point, the reverse occurs. The vapor becomes so heavy it turns back into a liquid.

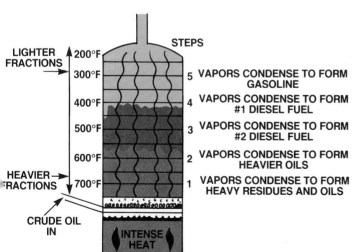

LIGHTER FRACTIONS → 200°F

300°F — 5 VAPORS CONDENSE TO FORM GASOLINE

400°F — 4 VAPORS CONDENSE TO FORM #1 DIESEL FUEL

500°F — 3 VAPORS CONDENSE TO FORM #2 DIESEL FUEL

600°F — 2 VAPORS CONDENSE TO FORM HEAVIER OILS

HEAVIER FRACTIONS → 700°F — 1 VAPORS CONDENSE TO FORM HEAVY RESIDUES AND OILS

STEPS

CRUDE OIL IN

INTENSE HEAT

FIGURE 10-24 This distillation column boils and vaporizes crude oil. Then, as the vapors rise, they cool and condense to form different products.

Refining Process

The refining process is accomplished by putting the crude oil into a distillation column. Referring to Figure 10-24, all of the crude oil in the bottom of the column is boiled to a vapor. As the vapors rise, they cool. As the vapors cool they condense to produce different liquids. For example, on the bottom of the distillation column, all of the hydrocarbons are vaporized by intense heat. As the vapors rise, the highest boiling point products start to cool and condense at step (1). As the remaining vapors continue to rise, they eventually cool at points (2), (3) and so on. Note that the heavier hydrocarbons have higher boiling points, whereas lighter hydrocarbons have lower boiling points. These are called *fractions* in the refining industry. At this point, the products are transported to the various sectors for use in our technological society.

Many other refining processes are used. Hydrocarbons can also be chemically altered to improve their individual characteristics. Some of these processes include:

1. *Cracking* — Breaking the petroleum molecules into smaller sizes. This is done so that more of a specific product, such as gasoline, can be obtained from the barrel of crude oil. Also, cracking improves the antiknock characteristics of gasoline.
2. *Polymerization* — Forcing small petroleum molecules together to produce large molecules.
3. *Alkylation* — Rearranging molecules to form high-octane products.
4. *Treating* — The process of "sweetening" the crude oil to eliminate acids from "sour" crudes.

Natural Gas Energy Resources

As with coal and petroleum, natural gas is considered a hydrocarbon. The difference is that natural gas is in a gaseous form rather than a solid (coal) or liquid (petroleum) form. Natural gas is a fossil fuel, having evolved over millions of years from decaying plant and animal life. Many natural gas wells are

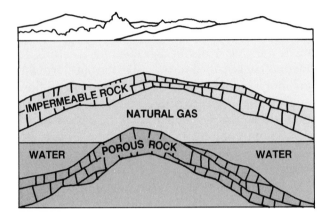

FIGURE 10-25 These rock formations show how natural gas is produced. As natural gas rises, it tends to collect below the impermeable rock, causing a reservoir to develop.

much the same as petroleum reservoirs, Figure 10-25. Quite often, natural gas is found directly above the oil in the ground.

Measuring Natural Gas

Natural gas is measured by the cubic foot. As the gas is taken out of the ground it is processed and sold by the cubic foot. In addition, customers measure the amount of natural gas used in the home by cubic foot or by the therm. One *therm* is equal to 100

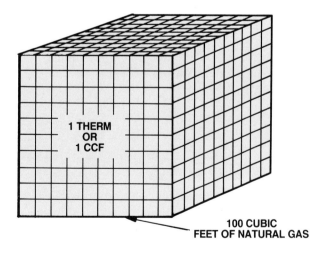

FIGURE 10-26 Natural gas is measured by the therm or ccf. One therm or ccf is equal to 100 cubic feet of natural gas.

cubic feet of natural gas. On a monthly bill, quite often the term ccf is used for measuring amounts of natural gas. One *ccf* is equal to 100 cubic feet. One ccf is also then equal to one therm, Figure 10-26.

Natural Gas Characteristics

When natural gas is taken from the ground, it consists of four primary hydrocarbons: methane, ethane, propane and butane. Each hydrocarbon can be extracted by using a distillation process similar to that of oil. In addition, these hydrocarbons have boiling points below the temperature of the surrounding air. This means that they boil and are in a gaseous form under normal atmospheric conditions.

Methane is primarily used for heating processes both in industry and in residential dwellings. Ethane is used for making certain types of plastic and alcohol products. After propane and butane are extracted, they are placed in pressurized containers. As the propane and butane are pressurized, their boiling points increase. It increases enough to cause them to turn into a liquid under pressure. However, if the pressure is released, they again turn back into a gas. Propane is used for various products such as propane torches and tanks and butane uses are similar.

Each of these hydrocarbons has a different energy content and quantity in each cubic foot that is removed from the ground. For example, methane is the major quantity in a cubic foot of natural gas, with smaller quantities of ethane, propane and butane.

Natural Gas Heating Values

A cubic foot of natural gas is said to have about 1,030 Btu. The exact amount is determined by the location of the resource and the amount of impurities in each cubic foot. Each of the four hydrocarbons in a cubic foot of natural gas also has a different heating value measured in Btu. For example, Figure 10-27 shows a comparison among five different samples of natural gas. Methane, (the greatest quantity) has the least number of Btu. Ethane, propane, and butane have increasingly more Btu per cubic foot, respectively. Note that sample 1 is mostly methane, thus it has a relatively low Btu content. In samples 2, 3, and 4, ethane, propane, and butane have a tendency to increase

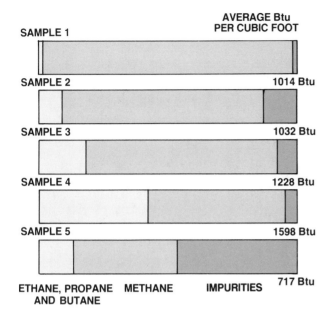

AVERAGE Btu
PER CUBIC FOOT

SAMPLE 1

SAMPLE 2 .... 1014 Btu

SAMPLE 3 .... 1032 Btu

SAMPLE 4 .... 1228 Btu

SAMPLE 5 .... 1598 Btu

ETHANE, PROPANE   METHANE   IMPURITIES   717 Btu
AND BUTANE

FIGURE 10-27 Depending upon location or source, natural gas has a specific heating value. The heating value depends upon the amount of impurities, methane, and remaining ethane, propane and butane. Normally, the more ethane, propane and butane, the higher the heating value in Btu per cubic foot.

some form of underground storage. This may include salt domes, water caverns, coal mines, or depleted oil and/or gas fields.

From storage, natural gas is then transported by pipeline to the main gate at a city or metropolitan area. From the main gate the natural gas is then sent to various subdivisions, industries, businesses, and so forth. Eventually, the natural gas arrives at the home gas meter. The gas meter then measures the amount of natural gas used by the customer.

the Btu per cubic foot. Also note in sample 5, that as the impurities increase, the Btu content of the fuel decreases.

Natural Gas Distribution

Figure 10-28 shows an example of how natural gas is transported from the well (the supply) to the customer (the demand). Most of the transportation is done by underground pipeline. One type of natural gas well is the wet or associated well. This type of well has the natural gas mixed with the oil. The dry well pumps only natural gas. After the natural gas is separated from the oil, it is sent to the processing refinery. This is most often done by using a natural gas pipeline.

From the pipeline, natural gas is sent usually to a processing plant where impurities and certain amounts of ethane, propane and butane are removed. The propane and butane, also called liquid products, are then pressurized and readied for storage. Ethane is sent by pipeline to another refinery to make plastic and other products.

At various points, compressor/pumping stations are installed to help pressurize the gas for transportation. Eventually, the natural gas will be sent to

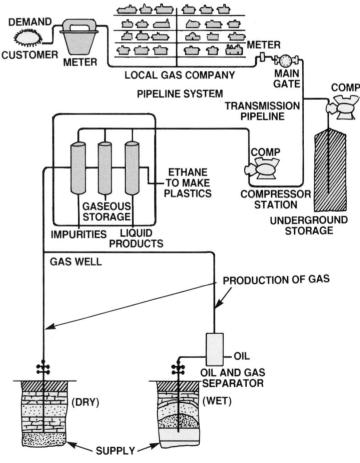

FIGURE 10-28 Natural gas has a complete pipeline transportation system. After the natural gas is taken from the well, it is sent to the processing plant, then to storage, to the city, and finally to the customer.

Offshore Fire

The process of drilling for oil and natural gas has both advantages and disadvantages. One disadvantage is that, occasionally, severe damage to the environment can occur at the drilling site.

This offshore natural gas rig has had a blowout. Because of the blowout, flames engulf this jack-up rig, located in the Gulf of Mexico. A *blowout* occurs when the pressure from the natural gas well is not capped off and gas escapes uncontrolled at the head of the well.

Many safety features have been developed for installation on natural gas and oil rigs to eliminate such danger. One such safety feature is the use of various types of improved blow-out valves which are placed on top of the drilled hole. *Courtesy of PCI Aerographics, Inc.*

Summary

- Coal, oil, and natural gas are all considered hydro-carbons and fossil fuels.
- Coal is the most available fuel in the United States.
- Coal has three impurities: moisture, ash, and sulfur.
- Sulfur in coal is the cause of acid rain.
- The pH scale is used to measure the acidity of a liquid solution.
- The carbon content of coal is about 50%.
- The four most common types of coal are: lignite, subbituminous, bituminous, and anthracite.
- Both surface mining and underground mining are used to extract coal from the ground.
- Coal is transported by unit trains, barges, and large freighters.
- Draglines are used to extract the overburden and coal from the ground.
- The major parts of a coal power plant include the boiler, scrubber, turbine, generator, cooling towers, and ash ponds.
- Oil is measured by barrels of oil and Millions of Barrels per Day Oil Equivalent (MB/DOE).
- The seismograph is used to explore for oil by using shock waves.
- Oil production is the process of drilling and removing the oil from a reservoir.
- The improved recovery process is used to extract as much oil as possible from wells that have lower pressures and quantities of oil.
- Some of the products of oil refining include rubber, gasoline, lubrication oil, insecticides, textile oils, shingle and paper saturants, and rust preventatives.
- The refining process uses a distillation column to extract many products from crude oil.
- Natural gas is found in much the same way as oil exploration.
- Natural gas is measured by the therm and the ccf.
- The four major ingredients in natural gas are: methane, ethane, propane and butane.
- Each of the four types of natural gas has a different heating value.
- Natural gas is transported mostly by pipeline.

REVIEW

1. A solution of water that has a pH reading of 4.5 would be considered _____ .
2. Which type of hydrocarbon in natural gas has the highest Btu content per cubic foot?
3. What percentage of increase (growth rate) in fossil fuels would take place in a one-year period if 20 MB/DOE were used in one year, and the next year 24 MB/DOE were used? Refer to the Mathematical Appendix to calculate percentage of increases or growth rate.
4. How many cubic feet of natural gas were used in a residential dwelling if 72 ccf were used in one month?
5. If 72 ccf were used in one month, how many Btu were used in this dwelling during that same period of time?
6. What would be the effect if all coal energy was eliminated from our supply in a matter of one year?
7. What are the advantages and disadvantages of using a low-value heating coal versus a high-value heating coal?
8. Compare the results of surface mining against underground mining. Consider the environmental and economic impacts as well.
9. What is the purpose of having a 60-day coal shortage supply at a power plant?
10. Describe the process of drilling for oil.
11. List at least 10 products made from crude oil.
12. Describe the process of distillation.
13. Describe the four types of natural gases and compare the heating value of each.
14. Describe the transportation of natural gas from the well to the end user. Include all components such as processing, storage, compressing, and others.

CHAPTER ACTIVITIES

 READING A NATURAL GAS METER

INTRODUCTION

Many instruments are used to measure energy forms today. One such instrument is the natural gas meter. Each home that uses natural gas for heating has such a meter. This activity is designed to teach how to read a natural gas meter on a residential dwelling.

TECHNOLOGICAL LITERACY SKILLS

Data collection, data analysis, using instruments, mathematical calculations.

OBJECTIVES

At the completion of this activity, you will be able to:
1. Read a natural gas meter.

2. Determine the amount of natural gas consumed in a residential building.
3. Identify all natural gas appliances in a residential dwelling.

MATERIALS

1. A residential dwelling that has a natural gas meter
2. Small pocket calculator
3. Natural Gas Meter handout

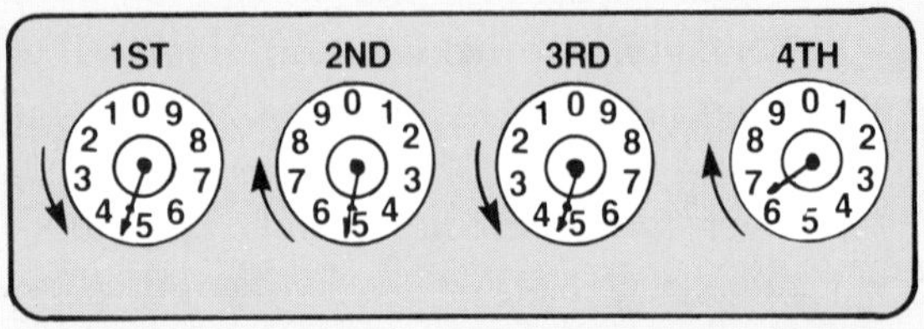

FIGURE 10-29 When reading the natural gas meter, always read from the left to the right, and read the number the pointer has just passed.

PROCEDURE

1. Learn how to read a natural gas meter.
   a. Referring to Figure 10-29, note that there are four dials.
   b. The pointer of the 1st dial rotates counterclockwise (cc). The pointer of the 2nd dial rotates clockwise (c). The pointer of the 3rd dial rotates counterclockwise (cc). The pointer of the 4th dial rotates clockwise (c).
2. To read the meter indicating the amount of natural gas consumed:
   a. Read the number the pointer in the 1st dial just passed (cc).
   b. Read the number the pointer in the 2nd dial just passed (c).
   c. Read the number the pointer in the 3rd dial just passed (cc).
   d. Read the number the pointer in the 4th dial just passed (c).
   e. Add two zeros to the four-digit number obtained.
3. The final number indicates the amount of natural gas used, measured in cubic feet.
4. Read your gas meter over a period of one week and record on the Natural Gas Meter handout.
5. Answer the remaining questions on the handout to complete the activity.

REVIEW QUESTIONS

1. Which appliance is the largest consumer of natural gas in your building?
2. Approximately what percentage of natural gas is being used by the largest appliance?
3. What could you do to reduce the amount of natural gas used in your home?

HEATING WITH COAL

INTRODUCTION

As the price of fuels continues to increase, coal has been considered for heating homes. This is a mathematical problem to analyze the price of burning coal for heating a home.

TECHNOLOGICAL LITERACY SKILLS

Problem solving, data analysis, mathematical analysis, predicting, drawing conclusions.

OBJECTIVES

At the completion of this activity, you will be able to:

1. Calculate the amount of coal needed to heat a standard residential home.
2. Determine the cost of heating with coal.
3. Compare the cost of heating directly with coal to using the coal in a power plant for electricity.

MATERIALS

1. Pencil and paper   **2.** Hand calculator   **3.** Coal Usage handout

STATISTICAL DATA NEEDED

1. Bituminous coal has 4,500 Btu per kilogram.
2. Subbituminous coal has 3,600 Btu per kilogram.
3. The price of coal is $0.0826 per kilogram.
4. The kilowatt-hour cost from the power plant is $0.0528.
5. One kilowatt is equal to 3,413 Btu.
6. The average home consumes 10,000 Btu per hour through the year.
7. A home heating coal burner is 60% efficient.
8. The average number of days in a month is 30.

QUESTIONS TO ANSWER

1. How much coal is needed to heat a standard home per month when heating with bituminous and subbituminous coal?
2. How much would it cost to heat the standard home when bituminous and subbituminous coal is used for a period of a year?
3. If the coal is used in a power plant as a fuel, how much would it cost to heat the same standard home?

PROCEDURE

Note: Use the Coal Usage handout to record each answer.

1. Multiply the home energy requirements per hour times 24 hours, times 30 days. This will give the number of Btu required per month.
2. Multiply the Btu in both coal types times .6 to get the amount of Btu actually available from each coal type.
3. Divide the actual Btu of each type of coal into the monthly energy required. This will give the kilograms of both bituminous and subbituminous coal per month needed to heat the home. Question number 1 has now been answered.
4. Multiply the monthly amount of coal times 12 to find the amount of coal in kilograms needed per year.
5. Multiply the yearly kilograms used for each coal type times the price of coal per kilogram. Question 2 has now been answered.
6. Since 1 kilowatt is equal to 3,413 Btu, divide the amount of energy required each month by 3,413. This will give the average kilowatt-hours per month needed by the standard home.
7. Multiply the monthly kilowatt-hour requirement times 12 to get the amount of kilowatt-hours required yearly.
8. Multiply the yearly kilowatt-hours times the price per kilowatt-hour to get the cost to heat the standard home if the coal is used in a power plant. Question 3 has now been answered.

REVIEW QUESTIONS

1. Why is it more costly to use subbituminous coal?
2. Why is it less costly to run the coal through a power plant rather than burning the coal at home?

CHAPTER 11

Solar Energy Resources

OBJECTIVES

After reading this chapter, you will be able to:

■ Identify several solar principles, including sun angles, radiation, convective loops, and units for measuring solar energy.

■ Define *solar payback*.

■ Compare active and passive solar technology.

■ Examine residential uses of solar energy, including envelope homes and thermal mass designs.

■ Compare different types of concentrating collectors.

■ Examine the Solar Thermal Energy Conversion system.

■ Describe the operation and use of solar photovoltaic cells.

KEY TERMS

Low-grade heat	Azimuth	Sensible Heat
Payback	Zenith	Phase-change
Solar Constant	Thermal Mass	Parabolic
Langley	Hydronic	Trough
Insolation	Latent Heat	

Introduction

Solar energy is one of the more popular types of energy for use in the future. Solar energy is classified as an alternative energy resource. It is also considered a renewable (never used up) energy resource. Advancements in solar technology in the past 10 years have been increasing at a steady and continuous pace. Many companies have developed solar technologies in the past few years. The increase in solar development is tied to the oil embargo of 1973. From that time on, consumers and industries have become more and more interested in solar energy. This chapter looks at the principles, the types, and the uses of solar energy.

Solar Principles

Solar energy has been the source of all the earth's energy since creation. The sun's energy comes to the earth as radiation and is absorbed by plant life. Thus, fossil fuels, such as coal, oil, and natural gas, are created. However, with the use of solar technology, the sun's radiation can be immediately collected and used for residential and commercial building use. Figure 11-1 shows a typical residential solar home using solar collectors.

FIGURE 11-1 This solar home has several collectors on the roof to supply solar energy for space heating.
Courtesy of Kai Dib Films International

TECH LINK

The Department of Energy suggests that the solar energy generated in a two-week period is equivalent to the fossil energy stored in all of the earth's known reserves. In fact, more solar energy is striking the average home each year than is actually needed. Statistics show that 2½ times the amount of energy needed is striking the average home in the United States. However, presently most of this energy is reflected back into the atmosphere.

Solar Cells

Solar cells are continually increasing in use for a variety of applications in the residential, commercial, and industrial sectors of society. Solar cells are also used extensively in the space program. The advantage of using solar cells is that radiant energy can be converted directly into electricity. In addition, solar cells are used when there is difficulty in providing conventional sources of electricity.

These rigid solar cells are used to power a spacecraft. They are two-inch square photovoltaic cells made of silicon with silver. A film on the cell screens out ultraviolet light and gives the cells their blue color. In the future, solar cell technologies are expected to be used in residential, commercial, and industrial applications of society. *Courtesy of Lockheed Corp/Dick Luria photographer*

Solar Energy Use

Solar energy is being considered mostly for use in the residential and commercial sectors of society. This is because these demand sectors are able to use the low-grade heat produced from solar energy. Low-grade heat normally ranges between 80 and 250°F. Applications, such as water heating and space heating, are easily put to use with solar energy. If 300 to 1,000°F are required in an application, then the solar energy must be more concentrated or else fossil fuels must be used. Figure 11-2 shows a residential home that uses solar energy for low-grade heating.

Solar Advantages and Disadvantages

There are both advantages and disadvantages when using solar energy.

Advantages

1. The thermal energy produced is free of cost after the initial investment is paid.
2. Solar energy will never run out, which is not true of fossil fuels.
3. Solar energy can be used with many existing technologies, such as appliances for water heating and space heating.
4. Very little pollution occurs as compared to fossil fuels when using solar energy.

FIGURE 11-2 Solar energy is most often used to provide low-grade heating for residential homes. *Courtesy of Kai Dib Films International*

Disadvantages

1. The first few years of solar energy use will be more expensive than using existing fuels.
2. Solar energy is not always available, especially during bad weather, cloudiness, and at night. This means that solar energy must be stored for later use. Storage technology is still in the developmental stage, and is not economically useful at this time.
3. Solar energy is very diffused and thinly spread out. This means that solar energy must be concentrated for use in high-grade heat applications.

Cost Payback

When developing and using solar energy, cost payback can be determined. *Cost payback* is defined as the length of time it takes for an initial solar investment to be paid off by the savings from the system. For example, a typical hot water solar energy system initially costs $3,000.00. If the yearly savings amounts to $500.00, then the payback time will be six years, ($3,000.00/$500.00 = 6). After six years, the initial cost will be paid back, and the consumer will then begin to save $500.00 per year by using solar energy.

Two important factors affect cost payback. Both are graphically displayed in Figure 11-3. These include:

1. Fossil fuel costs — As the price of fossil fuels increases, the cost payback will decrease, Figure 11-3 (a). As the cost of fossil fuels decreases, the cost payback will increase, Figure 11-3 (b).
2. Amounts used by the consumer — As the amount of solar energy used increases, the cost payback decreases, Figure 11-3 (c). As the amount of solar energy used decreases, the cost payback time increases, Figure 11-3 (d).

Electromagnetic Spectrum

All of the sun's energy comes to the earth in the form of wavelengths of radiant energy. Wavelengths are much like the ripples of water on a pond when a stone is thrown in the center. These radiant energy wavelengths are referred to as *electromagnetic wavelengths*. Included in electromagnetic wavelengths or the electromagnetic spectrum are light waves, sound waves, radio waves, TV waves, micro-

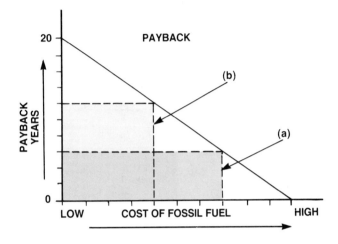

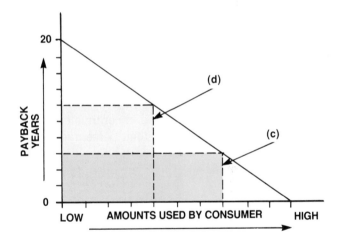

FIGURE 11-3 These charts show the payback effects of the price of existing fuels and the amount of solar energy used.

waves and gamma rays, among others. These radiant wavelengths travel from the sun to the earth at the speed of light, about 186,000 miles per second.

Wavelengths are most often measured by frequencies. Shorter wavelengths produce higher frequencies; longer wavelengths produce lower frequencies. Figure 11-4 shows an example of the total electromagnetic spectrum. Note the area of visible lightwaves.

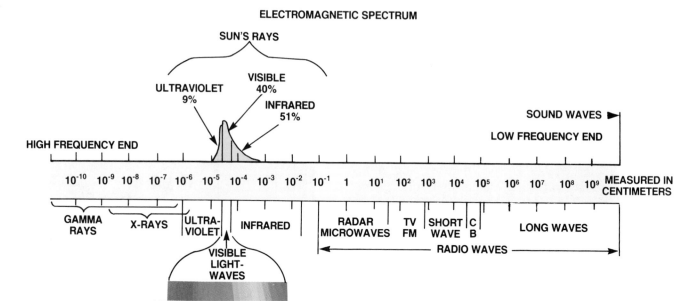

FIGURE 11-4 The electromagnetic spectrum is used to illustrate different frequencies and wavelengths. The sun's rays are shown for comparison.

Frequency of the Sun's Wavelengths

The sun's electromagnetic wavelengths are measured by frequency. *Frequency* is a measure of the length of the waves, measured in centimeters. The three types of sun's rays and their percentages are: ultraviolet (about 9%), visible (about 40%), and infrared (about 51%). These are also shown in Figure 11-4.

Ultraviolet frequencies are defined as invisible light waves. This frequency starts beyond the violet end of the visible frequencies. Any object that is glowing very hot gives off waves in this frequency range. *Visible frequencies* are defined as those that the human eye can see. These include all waves that are normally observable as colors. Each color is seen by the human eye as a different frequency. *Infrared frequencies* are lower as compared to others. An object that is warm but not glowing will emit these frequencies. As an object becomes cooler, the frequency of the emitted waves becomes longer. When manufacturers build solar collectors, they design the materials so that the sun's energy can be collected in all three frequency ranges.

Measuring Solar Energy

Solar Constant. Solar radiant energy can be measured accurately to determine how much is hitting a particular surface. Three units are commonly used: the solar constant, the Langley, and insolation. The *solar constant* is defined as the unit of measure of the amount of radiation at the outer edge of the earth's atmosphere. Common measurements for this unit are about 4,860 Btu/hour/square meter or about 524 Btu/hour/ square foot. This means for every square foot hitting the edge of the earth's atmosphere, about 524 Btu are available. However, this amount of energy is not really available at the surface of the earth. The sun's energy and intensity are reduced as they go through the earth's atmosphere. The location for measuring the solar constant is shown in Figure 11-5.

Insolation. Insolation is the unit used to measure the sun's radiation at the surface of the earth. Insolation comes from the words *Incident Solar radiation*. *Insolation* is defined as the amount of solar radiation striking a flat surface on the earth per area, within one hour. The term normally used to represent insolation is Btu/sq.ft/hour. Insolation can be measured by using an insolation meter, Figure 11-6. The exact amount of insolation can be determined by facing the meter perpendicular to the sun's radiation.

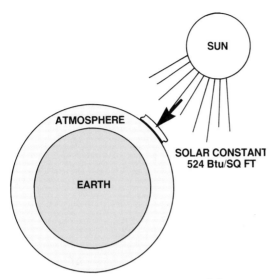

FIGURE 11-5 Solar constant is a measure of the amount of the sun's energy hitting the outer edge of the atmosphere.

FIGURE 11-6 This meter is able to measure insolation in Btu/sq. ft/hour.

TECH L I N K

The sun's energy can be measured by a unit called *insolation*, measured in Btu/sq.ft/hour. The maximum amount of insolation hitting a roof on a sunny day in the center of the United States is between 300 and 350 Btu/sq.ft/hour. The average insolation throughout the year, including nights and days, winter and summer, is between 45 and 90 Btu/sq.ft/hour, depending upon the geographical location.

As a practical example of insolation, if a home has a roof that is 48 feet by 26 feet, the total amount of solar energy available on the roof per hour can be determined.

1. 48 feet × 26 feet = 1,248 square feet in total
2. According to insolation tables, this home has 235 Btu/sq.ft/hour striking when the sun is shining. Therefore:
3. 1,248 × 235 = 293,280 Btu/sq.ft/hour

Most furnaces are able to produce about 100,000 Btu/hour. The availability of the sun in the previous example is nearly three times that amount. Many types of tables are used to determine exactly how much insolation is available at many locations throughout the United States. Figure 11-7 shows

INSOLATION TABLES

SOLAR POSITION AND INSOLATION, 40°N LATITUDE											
							SOUTH FACING SURFACE ANGLE WITH HORIZONTAL				
	AM	PM	ALT	AZM	NORMAL	HORIZONTAL	30	40	50	60	90
MAY 21	5	7	1.9	114.7	1	0	0	0	0	0	0
	6	6	12.7	105.6	144	49	25	15	14	13	9
	7	5	24.0	96.6	216	214	89	76	60	44	13
	8	4	35.4	87.2	250	175	158	144	125	104	25
	9	3	46.8	76.0	267	227	221	206	186	160	60
	10	2	57.5	60.9	277	267	270	255	233	205	89
	11	1	66.2	37.1	283	293	301	287	264	234	108
	12		70.0	0.0	284	301	312	297	274	243	114
SURFACE DAILY TOTALS					3160	2552	2442	2264	2040	1760	724
JUN 21	5	7	4.2	117.3	22	4	3	3	2	2	1
	6	6	14.8	108.4	155	60	30	18	17	16	10
	7	5	26.0	99.7	216	123	92	77	59	41	14
	8	4	37.4	90.7	246	182	159	142	121	97	16
	9	3	48.8	80.2	263	233	219	202	179	151	47
	10	2	59.8	65.8	272	272	266	248	224	194	74
	11	1	69.2	41.9	277	296	296	278	253	221	92
	12		73.5	0.0	279	304	306	289	263	230	98
SURFACE DAILY TOTALS					3180	2648	2434	2224	1974	1670	610

FIGURE 11-7 This table shows the solar positions and insolation values for a certain latitude.

**MEAN DAILY SOLAR RADIATION (Langleys)
JUNE**

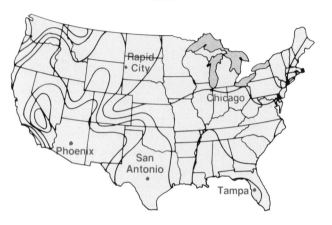

FIGURE 11-8 This type of map is used to show the Langley's at various cities throughout the United States.

one such table. For example, at 40° north latitude, on May 21, at 9 and 3 o'clock, both the sun's zenith (ALT) and azimuth angle are shown. Insolation values are also shown for different angles to the sun.

Langley — Another term that is used quite often at the U.S. Weather Service is called the Langley. The *Langley* is used to measure and indicate solar weather patterns over a period of one year. Langleys are measured again on the surface of the earth. Many types of Langley weather graphs are available, one of which is shown in Figure 11-8. Keep in mind that these weather patterns represent an average throughout the total year. The Langleys for December, January, February, and so forth will be much lower than the average. However, the Langleys for June, July, and August will be much higher.

Solar Orientation

Solar orientation is defined as the position of the sun in relationship to a particular building on the surface of the earth. The solar orientation must be known to determine the exact angle and placement position of various solar technologies. To help determine the position of the sun, two angles are commonly used: the azimuth and the zenith angles.

The *azimuth angle* is defined as the angle to the left or right of due south. For example, if the sun is at the 10:00 A.M. position in Figure 11-9, the azimuth angle is 32° east. If the sun's position is at the 4:00 P.M. position, the azimuth angle is 45° west.

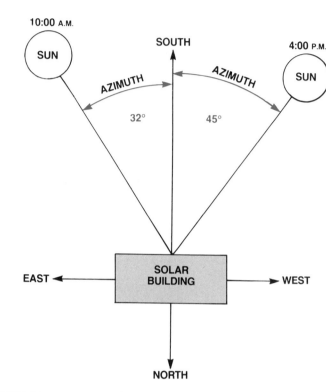

FIGURE 11-9 The azimuth angle is the angle to the left or right of due south. This angle is important when determining solar orientation of a building.

The *zenith angle* is the vertical angle of the sun from the horizon. Figure 11-10 shows examples of the zenith angle.

Both zenith and azimuth angles play an important role in solar orientation. Throughout the year, the positions of the earth and sun change. The azimuth angle changes throughout the day; the zenith angle changes throughout the year. If solar

POSITION OF SUN AT NOON FOR LATITUDE 40° N.

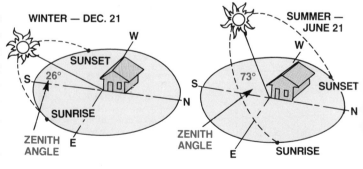

FIGURE 11-10 The zenith angle is the vertical angle of the sun from the horizon.

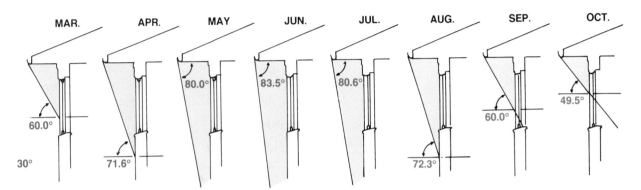

FIGURE 11-11 These angles show the shading produced from the sun at different months of the year. This information is useful in the design of solar homes.

energy is to be used effectively and efficiently, the solar orientation of the building should be considered. When the azimuth and zenith angles are known, homes or buildings that use solar energy can be positioned to gain the maximum amount of solar energy. Usually, windows and collectors are placed due south. Collectors are also positioned to get the maximum sun throughout the day and at specific times of the year.

Shading Profile

Because of the changing position of the sun, the angle of shade upon a solar home also changes. This information can be helpful in the design of the home. For example, the overhang of the roof can be designed to provide shade in the summer (cooling) and sun in the winter (heating).

Figure 11-11 shows different shading profiles on a window from March through October at a latitude of 30°. The exact length of the overhang can be designed to gain maximum solar benefit. Figure 11-12 shows an example of how the position of the

FIGURE 11-12 This building is designed to use the shading produced from overhangs for cooling in the summer. *Courtesy of Kai Dib Films International*

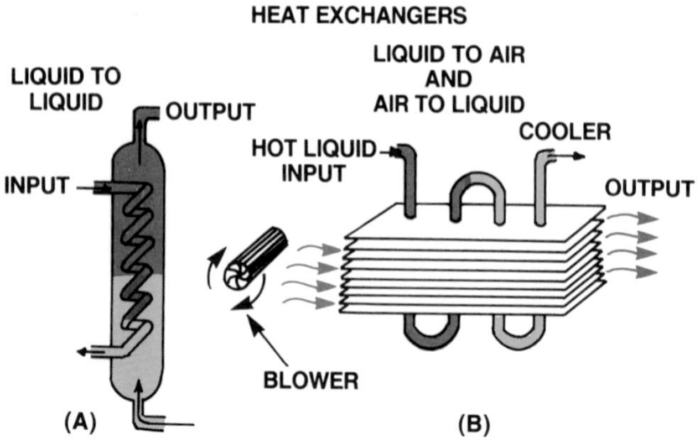

HEAT EXCHANGERS

FIGURE 11-13 Heat exchangers are used to transfer heat from (A) liquid to liquid and, (B) liquid to air.

window and the overhang shades the sunlight. When this information is known, the shape and length of the overhang and the position of the window on the building can be determined.

Heat Exchanging

In many solar systems, it is important to change the thermal energy from one substance to another. This is done by using heat exchangers. Thermal energy can be transferred in the following directions:

■ From air to air
■ From air to liquid
■ From liquid to liquid
■ From liquid to air

Figure 11-13 shows an example of different heat exchangers. Figure 11-13A shows a simple liquid to liquid heat exchanger system. It has both an input and an output. For example, if hot water from a collector were passed through the input tube, it would transfer the thermal heat to the output. Figure 11-13B shows a simple liquid to air system. As the hot fluid moves through the inside tubes, the heat is conducted into the fins. A fan then pumps air through the fins to capture the warm air. This system could be changed to an air to liquid system if the input and output were changed.

Several factors affect the heat being transferred in a heat exchanger. These include:

1. The temperature difference between the input and the output. (Heat always flows from the hotter to the colder fluid.) The greater the temperature difference the greater the heat transfer.

2. The surface area that the fluid is contacting. Normally, the greater the surface area, the more heat transferred.

3. The speed of the fluid moving over the surface. Normally, the faster the fluid moves, the greater the heat transfer.

Thermal Mass

Thermal mass is a term used to describe the amount of mass in a solar home that contains or holds heat. For example, a cubic foot of brick has a high thermal mass. Brick is able to hold large quantities of heat. Air, on the other hand, has a low thermal mass. It is unable to hold much heat per cubic foot. Quite often, solar homes use as much thermal mass as possible for holding heat.

Solar Energy Systems

Solar Technologies

All solar energy systems are designed to incorporate four technologies: 1) collection, 2) storage, 3) control, and 4) distribution.

Collection. All solar energy systems are designed to have some form of collection. Normally, solar collectors are used for this purpose. The number of collectors depends upon how the collected energy is to be used. For example, a simple solar domestic hot water system uses between two and five collectors. The number depends upon the number of people in the home. If the solar energy is to be used for space heating, then the entire roof would be covered with collectors. Figure 11-14 shows a solar home using many collectors on the roof for space heating.

Storage. Once the solar energy is collected, it must be stored. Solar energy can be stored by using several methods. Water is considered a good storage medium for solar energy. Also, concrete can act as a good thermal mass. Many systems use small rocks for storage. Most importantly, the solar storage medium must have a high thermal mass.

Control. Solar systems must also have certain controls. For example, controls are needed to turn off/on pumps, close dampers, and sense temperatures.

Distribution. The final technology in any solar system is distribution. Once the thermal energy is collected, it must be distributed to storage, to the

FIGURE 11-14 This home uses solar collectors for space heating. The collectors cover the entire roof surface.
Courtesy of Kai Dib Films International

Solar Photovoltaic Cells

Solar cells are able to convert the sun's radiant energy directly into electricity. As the sun shines upon the cells, a low voltage and current is generated in the cell. When added together, enough electrical energy can be captured to operate various electrical devices. Solar photovoltaic cells are considered an active system of solar energy. Solar cells need to have various electrical controls for regulating the electrical energy generated.

Solar photovoltaic cells are often used to provide power for remote locations. Cost is one advantage of using photovoltaic cells in such a situation. The cost of solar cells is much less than the cost of running wire from the power source to the remote location. Here, a small photovoltaic array provides power to automatically monitor and control a petroleum company's equipment in a remote location. *Courtesy of AMOCO Corporation*

rooms, or to other heat exchangers. All solar systems must be designed to incorporate distribution of thermal energy.

Active and Passive Systems

Solar energy systems can be divided into two types: active and passive. *Active* solar energy systems are designed to use pumps, fans, and electrical controls to operate. These systems are usually the most costly. *Passive* solar systems operate without using fans, pumps or extra electrical controls.

Active Domestic Hot Water System (DHW)

Figure 11-15 shows a typical active solar domestic hot water (DHW) system. This system is used for heating hot water for dish washing, bathing, cooking, and other purposes in a residential dwelling. Under normal conditions, without a solar system, city water comes into the system at point (a) at about 55°F. The water is then sent to point (b) into the hot water heater. The heater uses natural gas or electricity to heat the water. Enough heat must be added to raise the water temperature from 55 to 120°F at point (c).

When the additional solar heating system is installed, the water entering the water heater is preheated. Following the flow, four collectors are used to heat a mixture of water and antifreeze. The heated antifreeze and water (called a *hydronic system*) flows from the collectors at point (d) through the expansion tank at point (e). From there, the hydronic fluid moves into a liquid to liquid heat exchanger inside the solar storage tank at point (f). Here, the hot hydronic fluid (about 160°F) gives up its heat to the incoming water from the city. The city water then increases in temperature from about 55°F to about 100°F before it enters the water heater.

The control system uses a *proportional controller* for comparing the temperature of the collectors with the temperature inside the storage tank. When the storage tank is at least 3 degrees hotter than the collectors, the pump (point g) is turned on. For example, if the storage tank is at 65°F, the collectors must increase to 68°F before it turns on. Also, if the storage tank is at 100°F, the collectors must be at 103°F before the pump is turned on. Thus, in this system, there is collection, storage, control and distribution. The payback on similar DHW systems ranges between 3 and 6 years, depending upon the existing price of fuel regionally.

The DHW System and the Systems Model

As with other technologies, a solar DHW system can be studied by using the systems model discussed previously. For example, the "input" or objective of this system is to convert the sun's energy to thermal energy to heat water. The resources for the "process" include money (capital investment), people to build the system, materials used in the solar collector system, and others. The "output" is the actual hot water produced in the system. "Feedback" includes the controls used to turn the pump on and off. Examples of "Impacts" include: 1) less fossil fuels used, 2) cost payback for the customer, and 3) pollution produced when manufacturing the solar system parts.

Solar Collectors

Many types of solar collectors are used today. Both hydronic and air collectors are used to capture the heat. Figure 11-16 shows a typical hydronic collector. It has an absorber, pipes for fluid, a glass plate to hold in the heat, and insulation. Heat is collected by the following sequence of events, as shown in Figure 11-17.

DOMESTIC HOT WATER SYSTEM (DHW)

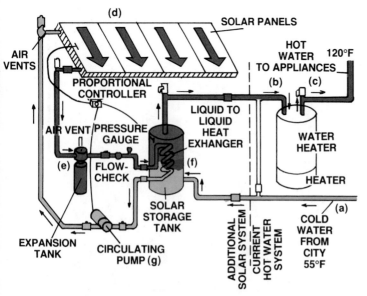

FIGURE 11-15 This shows the operation of a solar domestic hot water (DHW) system for preheating the water entering the water heater.

5. The thermal energy then conducts to the hydronic fluid and is carried to the storage tank.

Passive Solar Energy Systems

Many homes recently have been using passive solar systems to capture the sun's energy. Passive solar energy systems require no motors, fans, or electrical energy. Collection is accomplished by using windows or greenhouses. Storage is provided by using as much thermal mass as possible in the home. Control is by manually opening and closing air vents. Distribution takes place by creating a convective loop in the dwelling. Figure 11-18 shows a typical passive solar home. The home shown was designed to demonstrate passive solar heating and thermal storage principles. The south side of the house has thermal mass walls and triple-glazed windows. Heat from sunlight is trapped by the glass and is absorbed by the thermal mass wall. Heating costs are about one-third those of a similar-sized home.

Normally, passive solar homes have a solar orientation that is due south. The goal is to expose as much open window area as possible. However, windows should be covered during cold nights to eliminate or reduce heat losses.

FIGURE 11-16 The solar collector has a glass plate, absorber, frame, and insulation. *Courtesy of Kai Dib Films International*

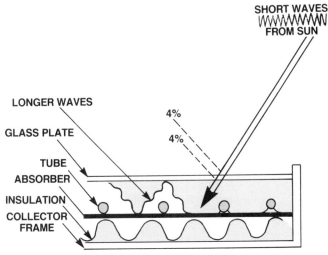

FIGURE 11-17 A typical hydronic collector catches the sun's rays, converting short waves from the sun into long waves inside the collector.

1. The sun's radiation shines on the collector.
2. Some of the sun's radiation is reflected back into the atmosphere by the top and bottom of the glass plate surface.
3. Most of the sun's radiation gets through the glass and is absorbed by the absorber.
4. When the radiation hits the absorber, the frequency is changed into very long waves, most of which are unable to get back through the glass.

FIGURE 11-18 This home is designed with a passive solar system. *Courtesy of Department of Energy*

Solar Greenhouses

Greenhouses are another method used for passive solar homes. Greenhouses normally are placed on the south side of a home. The greenhouse itself acts as the collector. Typically, a brick wall and/or floor tile is placed inside the greenhouse for thermal mass. The distribution of thermal energy is usually accomplished by setting up a convective loop. This is done by opening vents to the main part of the dwelling. Many restaurants use a greenhouse to provide supplementary heat for winter space heating. Figure 11-19 shows an example of a solar greenhouse. Typical paybacks for greenhouses range between 6 and 15 years.

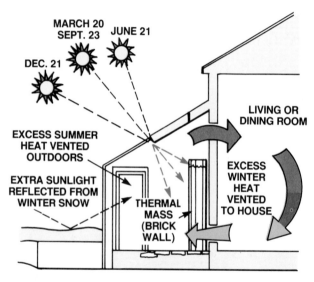

FIGURE 11-19 This greenhouse captures solar energy during the winter. The heat is transferred to the main part of the house by convection.

Envelope Homes

The envelope home has been designed to make use of the convective loop. This design actually has one structure built within another. Figure 11-20 shows an envelope home. This home design uses many south-facing windows to collect the heat. Then, as the heat rises in the front of the house, a convective loop is developed completely around the house. As the thermal energy flows through the rocks below the house, the rocks absorb and store thermal energy. Then, at night, they slowly give up heat that rises into the living areas.

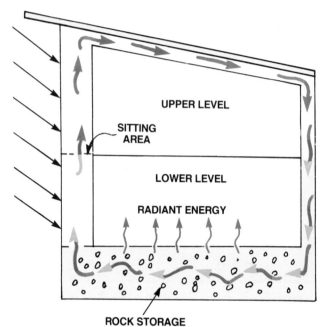

FIGURE 11-20 An envelope home has one structure built within the other. As the front part of the home heats up because of solar energy, a convective loop is created to heat the rock storage and to keep the rest of the dwelling warm.

Eutectic Salts Storage

Eutectic salts storage systems are being considered as an optional form of storage for solar energy homes. *Eutectic salts systems,* also called phase-change or change-of-state storage, use special salts to store thermal energy.

To understand eutectic salts, both latent heat and sensible heat must be defined. *Latent heat* is defined as heat that is present but not visible. It is referred to as "hidden heat." *Sensible heat* is heat that can be observed by noting a termperature rise. Phase-change storage salts use both types of heat.

Eutectic salts have a certain phase-change point. Usually, this point is near 80°F. At this temperature, the solid salts turn into a liquid. This is the same action as an ice cube turning into a liquid at 32°F. The phase-change temperature of water is 32°F.

In operation, as thermal energy is applied to eutectic salts, they absorb heat and thus increase in temperature. This rise in temperature is called sensible heat. Referring to Figure 11-21, this is represented by section (a) on the chart. Once the phase-change temperature is reached, the solid salts start to change to a liquid. As this occurs, a

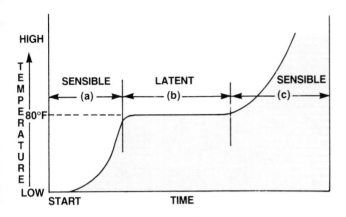

FIGURE 11-21 This chart represents the rise and fall of heat absorption using eutectic salts.

great deal of thermal energy (latent heat) can be continually absorbed. The temperature remains exactly at 80°F, Figure 11-21 (b). In comparison, an ice cube remains at 32°F as long as it is changing into a liquid.

Eventually, enough thermal energy has been added to the salts so the entire substance is now a liquid. At this point, the temperature of the salt continues to rise, shown as point (c). This again is referred to as sensible heat.

Once the thermal energy is removed, the cooling process follows the same line back. This means that the salts will give off thermal energy (about 80°F) for a long period of time. This process then acts as a heater for nightime heating.

Parabolic Collectors

One disadvantage of using solar energy is that the thermal energy is considered low grade: 120 to 160°F. This implies that solar energy can only be used for certain applications, such as residential and commercial buildings. However, if the solar rays were concentrated, a higher grade of heat could be produced. One method used to concentrate solar energy is by using parabolic collectors. A *parabolic collector* uses a reflective surface to concentrate the sun's rays to a focal point.

The parabolic collector must also track the sun so as to be at the best angle. At the focal point, the temperature is increased to above 500°F. Both the parabolic dish and trough-type collectors have been researched. Figure 11-22 shows an example of a dish and a trough collector. On the trough collector, water and antifreeze flow through a tube in the center of the trough at the focal point. As the water/antifreeze solution flows through the tube, it is heated to above 500°F. Figure 11-23 shows an experimental trough collector.

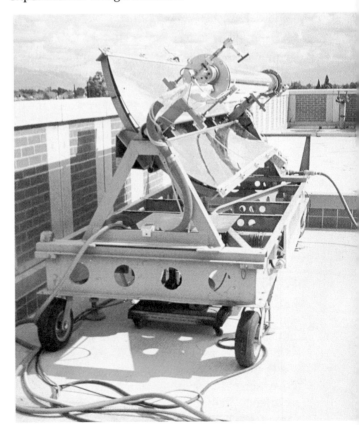

FIGURE 11-23 A trough concentration collector is being tested. *Courtesy of Kai Dib Films International*

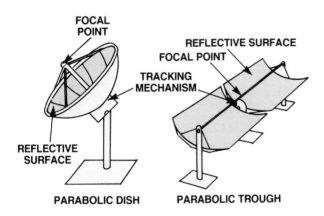

FIGURE 11-22 A parabolic dish and a parabolic trough collector. Both concentrate the sun's energy to a focal point.

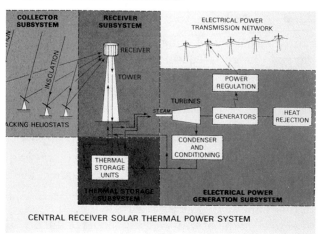

FIGURE 11-24 This schematic shows how a solar thermal energy conversion plant operates. *Courtesy of Department of Energy*

Solar Thermal Energy Conversion (STEC)

In all of the past examples of solar energy, the technology was specifically designed for a home or residential/commercial building. However, if solar energy could be mass produced as electricity, its costs could be reduced. Solar Thermal Energy Conversion (STEC) does just this. Figure 11-24 is a schematic of a typical solar thermal power plant.

Several parts make up the thermal power plant. In the center is a large boiler with water inside. Surrounding the entire area are large mirrors. These mirrors act as a large parabolic collector. These mirrors reflect the sun's radiation to the center boiler. The thermal energy is condensed and focused so that the temperature might reach close to 5,000°F. This intense heat is used to change water into steam. The steam is then used in a steam turbine/generator to produce electricity. The electricity is then distributed to homes and other buildings. The advantage of using this system is that solar energy can be used in more than just the residential and commercial sector. The energy from such a system can now be used for running computers, industrial machines, and various other processes.

Each mirror has a *heliostat*, a device used to position the mirror throughout the day. As the sun moves across the sky, the mirrors must be repositioned to keep the focal point of each mirror exactly correct. Each mirror's position is controlled by a computer network. Figure 11-25 shows two views of a solar thermal energy conversion plant.

FIGURE 11-25 The central receiver on the tower is used as a focal point for the sun's energy. This energy is concentrated enough to produce steam and thus electricity. *Courtesy of Department of Energy*

Solar Photovoltaic Cells

A solar electric (photovoltaic) system converts visible sunlight directly into electricity. This electricity can then be used to meet the requirements of the electrical load. Solar cells are made of semiconductor materials, such as silicon or cadmium sulfide.

The basic principles of solar electric cells are quite simple. Light hitting silicon dislodges electrons. Thus, whenever light hits a solar cell it produces both a positive charge and a negative charge, as shown in Figure 11-26. The cell then acts as a small battery. The solar cells can then be connected

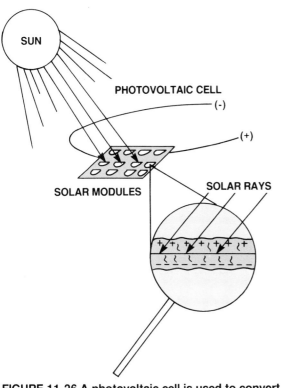

FIGURE 11-26 A photovoltaic cell is used to convert the sun's energy directly into electricity.

(A)

together to produce the correct amount of voltage and current. These combined cells are called *solar modules.* Solar modules are then connected together to form a solar array. Figure 11-27 shows two typical solar array applications. Figure 11-27A is the world's largest photo-voltaic facility, operated by ARCO. Figure 11-27B shows a view of gas pumps and a 72-panel photovoltaic array that provides power to the service station. Approximately 5.2 kilowatts can be produced. Part of the electricity is stored (for about 5 days) while the remaining is used directly.

FIGURE 11-27 Examples of solar cell arrays used for practical applications. (A) The world's largest photovoltaic facility, operated by ARCO. (B) Gas pumps and a 72-panel photovoltaic array that provides power to the service station. *Courtesy of (A) Southern California Edison Co. and (B) Department of Energy*

(B)

Figure 11-28 shows the components of a total solar electric system. The energy from the array is first sent to a regulator. The regulator is used to control the voltage and current output of the solar system. After the regulator, the electrical energy can be transmitted directly to DC (direct-current) loads. The output can also be sent to storage batteries for use at a later time. Some of the electrical energy must also be sent into a power converter. The power converter is used to change the DC voltage into AC (alternating-current) voltage. Almost all of the electrical loads in homes, commercial buildings, and industry require AC-type electricity.

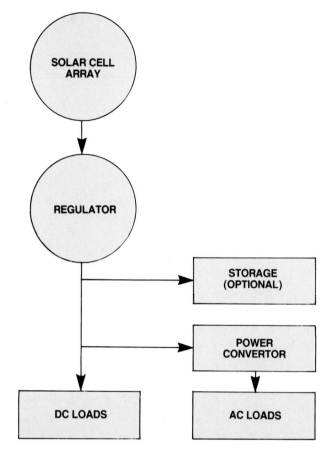

FIGURE 11-28 A solar electric (photovoltaic) system requires several parts for operation. The regulator is used for voltage control. Storage shown must also be made available. The power conditioner is used to convert DC electricity to AC electricity.

Solar-powered Vehicle

Solar photovoltaic cells can also be used in the transportation sector. The sun's radiation can be transformed into electricity and stored in batteries. The batteries can then be used to power electric motors for the propulsion system.

This is a solar-powered vehicle built by General Motors. Recently, many companies competed in a solar-powered vehicle race in Australia. Solar cells are placed on the top of the vehicle to capture the sun's energy. The vehicle is then battery powered. The vehicle is designed to be operated with a minimum of rolling and wind resistance, yet still have sufficient surface for the placement of the solar cells. As battery technology and solar cell technology continue to develop, consumers eventually may see this type of technology in the transportation sector. *Courtesy of General Motors Corporation*

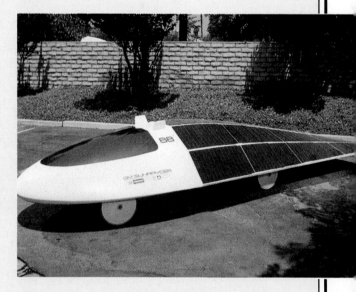

Summary

- An abundant supply of solar energy is available for use in residential dwellings.
- Most of the solar energy projects and technology has been used in the residential and commercial sectors of society.
- One big advantage of using solar energy is that it is basically free of cost after the initial investment in the equipment.
- Cost payback is the time in years it takes to gain back the initial cost of solar equipment.
- The sun's wavelengths as part of the total electromagnetic spectrum, are measured by frequencies and in centimeters of length.
- Solar energy can be measured by the solar constant, Langleys, and by insolation (Btu/ sq.ft/ hour).
- Solar orientation is the placement of a building to maximize the sun's position in the sky through the day and year.
- Shading is used in many solar buildings by designing roof overhangs to match the solar orientation.
- Many solar systems use heat exchangers to transfer the thermal energy from liquid to liquid and from liquid to air and back.
- Thermal mass is used in many solar designs to enhance the storage capabilities of solar energy.
- The four common technologies used in solar energy are collection, storage, control, and distribution.
- The two types of solar systems are based on the passive and active technologies.
- A domestic hot water solar system is an active design, using hydronic fluid (antifreeze and water) to carry the thermal energy to the storage tank. This system is mostly a preheater to the existing hot water system.
- The solar greenhouse is one popular type of passive solar design.
- Envelope homes are designed to allow a large convective loop of warm air to circle around in the entire home.
- Eutectic salts are used to store solar thermal energy. They have a phase-change temperature of nearly 80°F.
- There are several types of concentration collector designs for use in a solar system. The dish type of parabolic collector has one central focal point. The trough collector uses a tube through the center of a trough as the focal point.
- The Solar Thermal Energy Conversion (STEC) system uses large numbers of mirrors to reflect solar energy to a central receiving point. The steam produced from the high temperature is used to operate a turbine and generator system.
- Solar photovoltaic cells are used to convert solar energy directly into electrical energy. The DC electricity must first be changed to AC before it is used in a residential dwelling.
- The solar energy resources discussed in this chapter are considered renewable energy resources.

REVIEW

1. A solar hot water system costs $3,100.00. What is the cost payback in years if $700.00 are saved by using the solar system each year?
   (See Mathematical Appendix.)

2. How many Btu are hitting the roof of a residential dwelling that has a roof size of 28 feet × 41 feet, when the sun is shining, if the insolation is 290?

3. Any solar system uses several types of technology including, collection, storage, _____ and distribution.

4. The type of solar system that uses no fans, motors, or other electrical sources is called a _____ solar system.

5. An envelope home uses a _____ loop to transfer and distribute the solar energy throughout the home.

6. Heat that is not visible but that is present is said to be _____ heat.

7. If one Btu is the amount of energy necessary to raise one pound of water 1°F, how many Btu are needed for a solar system to raise a 55-gallon tank of water from 55°F to 100°F? (One gallon of water weighs approximately 8 pounds)

8. List at least three advantages and disadvantages of using solar energy.

9. What major factors affect the cost payback of solar energy? Identify what the effect is.

10. What is the best method to use to determine how much solar energy is available directly on a roof?

11. What is the difference between the zenith and azimuth angles, and how do these angles change solar orientation?

12. What are the four major technologies used in any solar system?

13. What are the major differences between active and passive solar technologies?

14. Describe how a solar domestic hot water system works.

15. What three major passive solar energy designs are being used?

16. Describe how a solar envelope home is designed.

17. Name several applications using solar photovoltaic cells.

18. What items will make solar photovoltaic cells enter the commercial market sooner?

CHAPTER ACTIVITIES

 ## AZIMUTH AND ZENITH ANGLES

INTRODUCTION

The position of the sun during the day helps engineers to design the most effective systems to capture the sun's energy. This activity will help you to determine the azimuth and zenith angles of the sun for a particular geographical location.

TECHNOLOGICAL LITERACY SKILLS

Mathematical analysis, data analysis, problem solving, data collection.

OBJECTIVES

At the completion of this activity, you will be able to:
1. Calculate the azimuth angle of the sun.
2. Calculate the zenith angle of the sun.
3. Apply azimuth and zenith angles to the use of solar energy.

MATERIALS

1. Compass
2. Paper (8½″ × 11″)
3. Pencil
4. Level
5. Large thread spool
6. Protractor
7. Azimuth and Zenith angle handout .
8. Ruler
9. Trigonometric tables

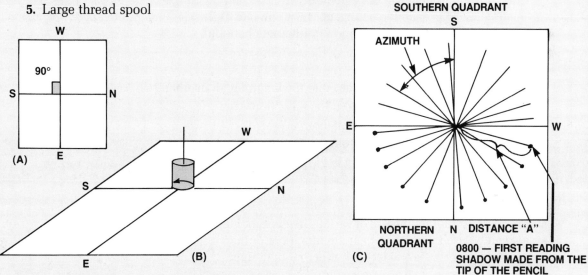

FIGURE 11-29 (A, B, C). These drawings show how to lay out the paper when checking the azimuth and zenith angles of the sun in your laboratory activity.

PROCEDURE

Note: readings will be taken throughout an entire sunny day, from 0800 to 1700 hours (8 A.M. to 5 P.M.).
1. Take a standard piece of paper (8½″ × 11″) and draw two lines crossing in the center of the paper, as shown in Figure 11-29A. Each of the four angles in the center is 90°.
2. Label each line north, south, east and west, as shown in Figure 11-29B.
3. Insert a pencil into the end of a thread spool.
4. Using the compass and level, place the paper on a level surface in the sun so that the south line points directly to the south.
5. Place the spool and pencil at the intersection of the lines on the paper, Figure 11-29B.
6. Measure the height of the pencil from the paper to the top of the pencil and record it on the Azimuth and Zenith angle handout.
7. Record the date the test was taken on the handout.

8. Take a reading about every hour. If you take the test in the summer, more frequent readings will need to be taken. Take 7 to 12 readings, depending upon the time of the year.

9. At each reading, mark the position of the sun shown by the pencil's shadow (tip) on the paper. Refer to Figure 11-29C.

10. Continue to take readings each hour during the day, plotting and labeling each point.

11. After all readings have been taken, connect a straight line from each point plotted, through the center point on the paper and into the southern quadrant, Figure 11-29C.

12. The position of each line in the southern quadrant is the position of the sun, called the *azimuth angle*. Measure the Azimuth angle and record each line and record in the table on the Azimuth and Zenith angle handout.

13. Measure the distance that each plotted point lies in the northern quadrant from the center point. Record this distance as "A" on the handout for each time.

14. Divide each distance labeled "A" into the height of the pencil from the paper. The result of the calculation is called the tangent. Record it on the handout.

15. Using trigonometric tables, determine the zenith angle by looking up the tangent and reading the corresponding angle in degrees. If you need help reading trigonometric tables, ask your instructor. As an example, a tangent of .6 is equal to 31 degrees for a zenith angle. Record each zenith angle on the Azimuth and Zenith angle handout.

REVIEW QUESTIONS

1. Which angle is required to determine the length of an overhang on a home?
2. Which angle changes throughout the day?
3. Which angle changes most throughout a year?

 # SOLAR ENERGY LOST THROUGH GLASS

INTRODUCTION

Most solar designs require the use of various glazings or glass to hold the solar heat inside. Various materials can be used, some of which are much better than others. This activity is designed to test how much solar energy passes through different materials.

TECHNOLOGICAL LITERACY SKILLS

Problem solving, data collection, data analysis, predicting, experimentation, mathematical analysis, instrumentation.

OBJECTIVES

At the completion of this activity, you will be able to:

1. Define transmittance and translucence.
2. Measure and compare the amount of solar energy passing through four different materials.
3. Determine the transmittance of double-pane and angled glazings.

ADDITIONAL INFORMATION

Transmittance is defined as a material's ability to pass radiant energy through its structure. *Translucence* is defined as a characteristic of a material to transmit radiant energy diffusely or imperfectly. It is difficult to distinguish objects clearly through a translucent material.

MATERIALS

1. One solar insolation meter capable of reading in Btu/sq.ft/hr.
2. Four pieces of glazing material no larger than 3″ × 3″. Examples may include:
   a. Low-iron glass
   b. High-iron glass
   c. Hard plastic, such as Plexiglas
   d. Reinforced polyester glazing
   e. Translucent materials, such as Mylar or Teflon
3. Hand calculator
4. One light source (either the sun or a spotlight) capable of producing at least 200 Btu/sq. ft/hr.
5. Solar Energy Lost Through Glass handout.

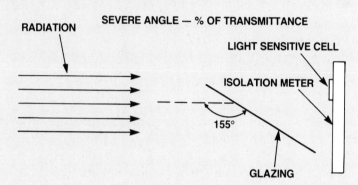

FIGURE 11-30 When the glazing is at an angle, less solar energy is transferred through the glass.

PROCEDURE

1. Set the insolation meter in the presence of the light source and adjust its position to read an even Btu/sq.ft/hr. Record this number on the Solar Energy Lost Through Glass handout.
2. Now place each of the four materials individually about 1 inch above the meter. Record the Btu/sq.ft/hr. on the table in the handout.
3. Using the best transmittance material, place it in front of the insolation meter and slowly rotate it away from direct radiation. Rotate it about 45 degrees from the perpendicular. The effect is to cause the sun's rays to hit the glass at an angle, as shown in Figure 11-30. Observe the insolation meter readings and record on the handout.
4. Place two pieces of glazing in front of the insolation meter to represent a double-pane window. Observe the readings on the insolation meter and record on the handout.
5. Subtract the Btu/sq.ft/hr. recorded in each test from the original readings taken in Step 1. The result is the amount of solar energy lost through the material(s).
6. Using the following formula, calculate the transmittance percentage of each test and record on the handout.

$$\text{Transmittance \%} = \frac{\text{Btu/sq.ft/hr. coming through}}{\text{Btu/sq.ft/hr. original}} \times 100$$

REVIEW QUESTIONS

1. Which material had the best transmittance?
2. What happens when the sun hits a glass or glazing at an angle?
3. What happens when two pieces of glass, such as a double-pane window, are used?

SOLAR PAYBACK-COMPUTER SPREADSHEET

INTRODUCTION

The concept of payback is often used to help consumers make decisions about buying energy equipment. This activity will help you to develop a spreadsheet for calculating payback for a solar domestic hot water system.

TECHNOLOGICAL LITERACY SKILLS

Problem solving, mathematical analysis, data analysis, predicting information.

OBJECTIVES

At the completion of this activity, you will be able to:
1. Analyze data to determine cost payback on a solar system.
2. Develop a spreadsheet to determine cost payback.
3. Determine how cost payback is affected by changing interest, increases in inflation, and initial capital cost.

MATERIALS

1. Computer — just about any computer and program that can produce a spreadsheet will work.

PROCEDURE

1. To complete this activity, it is necessary to be familiar with the spreadsheet program on the computer used.
2. To develop a spreadsheet, various necessary statistical data include:
   a. Average yearly fuel bill = $960.00
   b. Annual percentage of increase in fuel bill = 8%.
   c. Percentage of total energy bill that is consumed by hot water usage = 15%.
   d. Percentage of hot water that solar energy will assume = 60%.
3. Set up a spreadsheet on your computer similar to the example shown in Figure 11-31.

SOLAR DOMESTIC HOT WATER PAYBACK

Row	A Yearly Bill	B Percent Increase	C Hot water Dollars	D Percent Hot water .15	E Solar Amt. $	F Percent Solar .6	G Savings Dollars	H Payback Year
4	960	1.08	+A4*D3		+C4*F3		+E4+0	one
5	+A4*B4		+A5*D3		+C5*F3		+E4+E5	two
6	+A5*B4		+A6*D3		+C6*F3		+G5+E6	three
7	+A6*B4		+A7*D3		+C7*F3		+G6+E7	four
8	+A7*B4		+A8*D3		+C8*F3		+G7+E8	five
9	+A8*B4		+A9*D3		+C9*F3		+G8+E9	six
10	+A9*B4		+A10*D3		+C10*F3		+G9+E10	seven
11	+A10*B4		+A11*D3		+C11*F3		+G10+E11	eight
12	+A11*B4		+A12*D3		+C12*F3		+G11+E12	nine
13	+A12*B4		+A13*D3		+C13*F3		+G12+E13	ten
14	+A13*B4		+A14*D3		+C14*F3		+G13+E14	eleven
15	+A14*B4		+A15*D3		+C15*F3		+G14+E15	twelve
16	+A15*B4		+A16*D3		+C16*F3		+G15+E16	thirteen
17	+A16*B4		+A17*D3		+C17*F3		+G16+E17	fourteen
18	+A17*B4		+A18*D3		+C18*F3		+G17+E18	fifteen

FIGURE 11-31 This spreadsheet is a model to use for this activity. It is used to calculate the payback when considering using a solar hot water system.

4. Label the columns of the spreadsheet:
   a. Yearly Fuel Bill
   b. Percent Increase
   c. Hot Water Dollars
   d. Percent Hot Water
   e. Solar Amount
   f. Percent Solar
   g. Savings Dollars
   h. Payback Year

5. Place the following information as a guide in the cells identified. Cells are identified as the index between a column (A, B, C, D,...) and a row (1, 2, 3, 4,...).
   a. Cell A4 = The average yearly fuel bill, in dollars.
   b. Cell B4 = An average percent of increase on the yearly fuel bill. 1.08 is the multiplication factor for 8%.
   c. Cell D3 = The percent of hot water cost on the bill (.15).
   d. Cell F3 = The percent of the hot water bill that solar will assume (.6).

6. Now put in calculations for each cell. The following example illustrates the complete calculation (blocked in cells).
   a. In cell A5, $960 (A4) will be multiplied by 1.08 (B4) showing the next year's bill, if there is an 8% increase in fuel cost.
   b. In cell C4, $960 (A4) will be multiplied by 15% (D3) to get the cost of hot water each year.
   c. In cell E4, the hot water cost (C4) is shown if 60% (F3) comes from the solar system.
   d. In cells G4, G5, G6, etc. the savings (E4, E5, E6,...) is added to get total savings in dollars.

7. Each column is then continued through 15 years.

8. If the cost of a solar system was $1,500.00, how many years under existing data did it take before the savings reached $1,500 or more? This is your payback. Now change the variables, such as the monthly bills, percent of increase, percent of hot water, and other factors, and determine new paybacks.

REVIEW QUESTIONS

1. What happens to the payback time if the cost of heating goes up? Goes down?
2. What happens to the payback time if the percent that solar assumes increases?
3. What happens to the payback if more people use hot water in a home, increasing the percent of hot water used?

 ## SOLAR CELLS

INTRODUCTION
Solar cells are used to convert radiant sunlight into electrical energy. This activity experiments with solar cells and tests their efficiency under various conditions.

TECHNOLOGICAL LITERACY SKILLS
Problem solving, collection of data, data analysis, mathematical calculations, experimentation.

OBJECTIVES

At the completion of this activity, you will be able to:

1. Determine the efficiency of solar cells.
2. Identify the effect different zenith and azimuth angles have on solar cells.
3. State the effect the distance from the light source has on solar cells.
4. Compare the efficiency of solar cells under artifical light as compared to sunlight.

MATERIALS

1. A solar cell array able to produce at least three volts under direct sunlight (can be obtained from most electronic stores)
2. Voltmeter and ammeter capable of reading milliamperes
3. A load to place on the solar cell, (could be a small motor or resistor connected to the solar cells)
4. An insolation meter that can be read in Btu/sq.ft/hr.
5. A light source (spotlight)
6. Ruler
7. Protractors to determine zenith and azimuth angles
8. Solar Cell handout

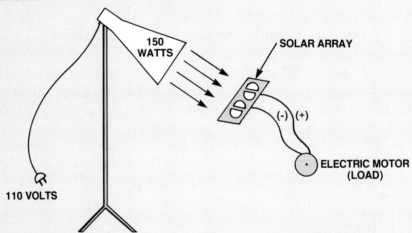

FIGURE 11-32 An example of testing the solar cell array hookup for your laboratory activity.

PROCEDURE

1. The solar cell array should be hooked up as is shown in Figure 11-32.
2. Make sure there is at least a 150-watt spotlight for the radiant energy source. Record the wattage on the Solar Cell handout.
3. Adjust the light source to get the maximum output voltage and current under load. Keep the light source six inches away from the solar cells. Do not keep the light source on the cells for more than one minute.
4. Read the voltage and the current being produced on the output of the solar cell.
5. Calculate the efficiency under these conditions by dividing the input power (150 watts) into the output power (solar cell voltage × current), and multiply by 100 to get percent efficiency. Record your findings on the Solar Cell handout as "short term efficiency."
6. Allow the light source to remain on the cells for at least 5 minutes. Now, calculate the efficiency when the cells are heated. Record on the Solar Cell handout.

7. Keeping the zenith and azimuth angles the same, move the light source back to 9, 12, and 15 inches; calculate and record efficiency for each distance.

8. Plot the information calculated on the chart shown on the Solar Cell handout.

9. Readjust both the azimuth and zenith angles off by 10 degrees; calculate and record the efficiency.

10. Place the solar array directly in clear sunlight. Calculate the efficiency, using the following steps:

    a. Measure the insolation (Btu/sq.ft./hr.)

    b. Determine the exact surface area of the solar cells.

    c. Since insolation is measured per square foot, and the solar cells are probably less than one square foot, the input insolation must be reduced. Reduce the input insolation by multiplying according to the following formula:

$$\text{Input} = \text{Insolation} \times \frac{\text{Solar area}}{144}$$

    d. To convert the input to the same unit as the output, multiply the input Btu × .2929 to get watts input.

    e. Calculate the efficiency under direct sunlight, using the aforementioned figures, and record on the handout.

REVIEW QUESTIONS

1. What happens to the efficiency as the solar cells heat up?

2. What happens to the efficiency as the zenith and azimuth angles change?

3. Why is there such a great difference in efficiency between the light source and natural sunlight?

CHAPTER 12

Renewable Energy Resources

OBJECTIVES

After reading this chapter, you will be able to:

■ Analyze hydroelectric dams as a renewable energy resource.

■ Identify the different forms of technology used to generate wind energy.

■ Define the four types of biomass and identify how biomass can be used as an energy resource.

■ Examine wood as a biomass energy resource.

■ Identify Ocean Thermal Energy Conversion systems as a renewable energy resource.

■ Compare the different methods used to extract geothermal energy resources from the ground.

KEY TERMS

Hydroelectric	Tip Speed Ratio	Cord
Turbine	Megawatt	Secondary Combustion
Head	Yaw	Creosote
Penstock	Pitch	Refrigerant
Darrieus Wind Turbine	Carbohydrates	Geothermal
Power Coefficient	Anaerobic Decay	

Introduction

Several additional renewable energy resources are being tested and used today. These are sometimes called alternative energy resources. They are mostly considered nondepletable or renewable energy resources because they will never be used up and are continually renewing themselves.

This chapter looks at several of these renewable energy resources, such as hydroelectric, wind, bio-mass, wood, ocean thermal energy conversion and geothermal resources. Not all of these resources are economically advantageous. However, as the price of existing fossil fuels and nonrenewable resources increases, the resources discussed in this chapter will become more feasible. Today, the total renewable energy resources makes up about six to eight percent of the total energy used in our society.

Different Forms of Energy

In the future, our society will have to rely on many renewable or nondepletable energy resources. These are resources that will never be used up, and are continually renewing themselves. Many forms of renewable energy forms are available to our society.

This photo shows four types of energy resources that are considered renewable: solar, wind, biomass, and geothermal energy resources. Solar energy systems capture the sun's energy directly. Wind energy captures the mechanical energy in the wind to turn a generator. Biomass is the process of using the energy in garbage, manure, and other waste materials. Geothermal energy uses the heat energy below the surface of the earth. Note, however, that before any of these renewable resources are commercially available, they must be economically attractive as well.
Courtesy of American Petroleum Institute

Hydroelectric Energy Resources

Hydroelectric energy is considered a renewable form of energy. This means that as long as there is rain with varying weather patterns, hydroelectric energy will continue to exist. Hydroelectric energy systems have been around for many years. In fact, hydroelectric dams have been providing electric power for more than 60 years. Figure 12-1 shows a typical hydroelectric dam in operation.

Hydroelectric energy is defined as using water flowing through a dam to produce electricity. Typically, water is used to turn a turbine. The turbine is used to turn a generator and thus produce electricity. About four to five percent of the total energy supplied to our society is provided by hydroelectric energy resources. This amount has shown little increase in the last few years. Most of the hydroelectric dam sites have been used and are already in operation. Only in the past few years have smaller dams been built or existing dams renewed for improved operation and efficiency.

FIGURE 12-1 Hydroelectric dams such as this one have been providing electricity for many years.
Courtesy of American Petroleum Institute

Hydroelectric Dams and the Systems Model

As with all the other technologies discussed, a hydroelectric dam can also be studied by relating it to the systems model of technology. The "input" or objective of a hydroelectric dam is to change falling water into electricity. The "processes" (the actual plant) uses various materials, tools, machines, people, capital, and so forth to process the energy. The "output" is the actual electricity produced from the generators. The "feedback" includes the controls for the water gates, the generator and turbine speed controls. "Impacts" include low-cost electricity, lost land usage from the reservoir, and increased recreational use on the water.

Dam Size

Hydroelectric dams work on several very simple principles. Naturally draining water is held in a reservoir. As the water falls through a dam on the reservoir, the force of gravity from the water causes various types of turbines to turn. It is important to have the water fall a predetermined distance. This distance, called *head,* determines the commercial usability of a dam. Figure 12-2 illustrates a comparison of high-head and low-head dams.

Energy is extracted from a hydroelectric dam because of gravitational forces. The amount of energy in falling water due to gravitational forces depends upon two factors. First, the more mass (more water), the greater the amount of energy. Second, the faster the water falls, (velocity) the greater the energy. Hydroelectric dams are designed and built to maximize these two principles.

The greater the head, the greater the amount of energy available. The lower the head the lesser amount of energy available. In the early 1970s, the price of fuel was so low that only dams with heads of more than 50 feet were built. Today, however, many hydroelectric dams are being built with smaller heads. The price of other fuels has increased to such a point that low-head dams are now usable and profitable to build and operate.

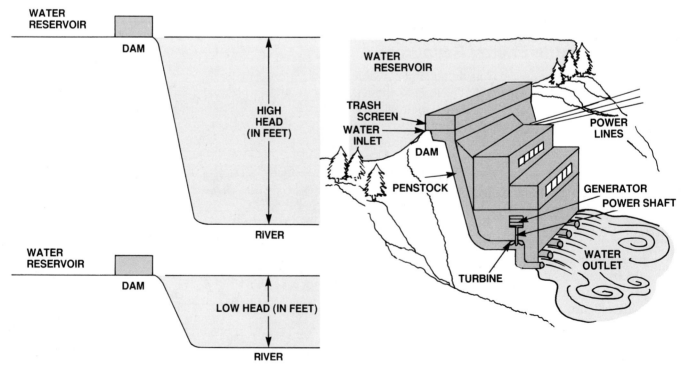

FIGURE 12-2 A comparison of high-head and low-head dams.

FIGURE 12-3 The major parts of a typical hydroelectric dam are shown.

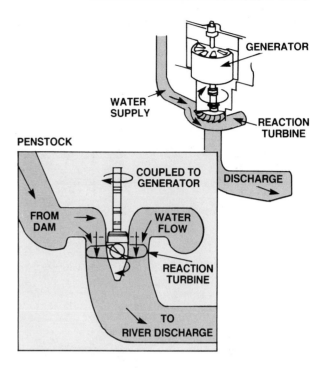

FIGURE 12-5 The reaction turbine is used in a hydroelectric power station to convert the force of falling water into torque to turn the generator.

FIGURE 12-4 This power shaft connects the turbine to the generator on a hydroelectric dam. *Courtesy of Department of Energy*

Parts of a Hydroelectric Dam

The major parts of a typical hydroelectric dam are shown in Figure 12-3. The water in a *reservoir* is held back by the dam. As water passes through the *trash screen*, debris is removed. The water then flows through *penstocks*. The penstocks (there are several, depending upon the size of the plant) direct water to the *turbine* area. Here, water turns the

turbine causing a *generator* to produce electricity. Figure 12-4 shows the interior of a hydroelectric dam where the power shaft connects the turbine to the generator. Electrical energy is then sent out to consumers by power line.

Hydroelectric Turbine

The turbine in a hydroelectric power plant is used to change the falling water into rotary forces *(torque)* used to turn a generator. Turbines are manufactured in many styles and types. Figure 12-5 shows an example of a reaction turbine. As the water from the penstock turns the turbine, the generator is also turned.

Wind Energy Resources

Wind results from the uneven heating of the earth and its atmosphere from the sun. Uneven heating causes pressure differences to occur which produces wind. In some cases, wind energy can be classified as solar energy. Wind energy is considered a

FIGURE 12-6 A wind turbine being tested by U.S. government agencies. *Courtesy of NASA*

nondepletable or renewable energy resource. About two percent of all the solar energy radiation hitting the earth is converted to wind energy. It is estimated that by the early twenty-first century, wind may be providing between five and ten percent of the total energy needs of our society. Figure 12-6 shows a wind turbine being tested by the Department of Energy and NASA.

TECH LINK

The amount of energy available from a wind turbine depends upon the amount of air passing through the turbine blades for a specific time period. This amount of air is determined by several factors. These include:

- The velocity of the wind.
- The mass of the wind.
- The area of the wind turbine blades.

Wind turbines are designed to maximize these factors to get the highest efficiency and maximum output from the wind-energy machine.

Many years ago, wind provided significant amounts of energy up until the mid-1930s. From that date on, energy was mainly supplied by other means such as fossil fuels. Today, however, wind energy is showing signs of increased popularity. This is because the cost of existing fossil fuels has increased steadily.

Vertical and Horizontal Turbine Systems

Two major types of wind turbine systems are: the horizontal shaft and the vertical shaft types. The horizontal system has a number of turbine blades attached to a horizontal shaft. As the wind hits the turbine blades, the shaft spins. This provides mechanical energy to turn a generator.

Figure 12-7 shows a popular vertical shaft turbine. This system is called a *Darrieus wind turbine*. The system is capable of producing about 50 kW in a wind of 30 mph. The blades are about 55 feet in diameter. As the wind flows through the blades, a driving torque is produced, regardless of the wind direction.

FIGURE 12-7 This Darrieus vertical shaft wind turbine is able to capture the wind from any direction. *Courtesy of Department of Energy*

Efficiency and Power Coefficient

All wind turbines are rated by a power coefficient. The *power coefficient* is a measure of the wind turbine system's efficiency. It is normally accepted that only about 59% of the input energy of the wind can be converted to mechanical energy. Laws of physics prevent greater efficiencies. Practically, a wind turbine's efficiency is more like 35 to 40%. Losses occur because of blade inefficiencies and mechanical friction.

The power coefficient is a measure in percentage of the amount of energy actually extracted from the 59%. For example, a power coefficient of 55% (.55) means that 55% of the energy is being produced from the 59% maximum efficiency. A power coefficient of 100% (1.00) means that all of the 59% energy in the wind is being captured by the wind turbine.

Wind Turbine Tip Speed Ratio

An important characteristic of wind turbines is called tip speed ratio. *Tip speed ratio* is defined as the tip of the blade at its outer diameter in relationship to the wind speed. For example, a tip speed ratio of 5 means the tip speed is moving 5 times as fast as the wind speed. Normal tip speed ratios are between 1 and 7. Figure 12-8 shows a comparison of the tip speed ratios of both the horizontal and vertical axis wind turbines. Notice that the optimum tip speed ratio produces the maximum power coefficient. This suggests that there is a most efficient speed at which all wind turbines can operate.

FIGURE 12-9 This wind turbine generator test site was designed to help private industry test, develop, and build prototype wind turbine systems. *Courtesy of Department of Energy*

Wind Energy Research

Wind energy has been undergoing testing for many years. Figure 12-9 shows a small wind development center. This site was established to help private industry develop, test and build experimental wind machines. Normally, these tests are on turbines that produce 100 kW or less.

Annual Average Wind Power

Generally, the higher the wind speed, the more energy available. Wind energy can be used in many spots throughout the United States. However, certain parts of the United States have higher average wind speeds than others. Thus, wind energy is only useful in certain geographical areas.

Wind Projects

Wind energy projects are many. However, they can be subdivided into three major categories:

1. Small Wind Systems
2. Intermediate Wind Systems
3. Large-scale Wind Systems

Small wind systems are typically used by farms, rural residences and remote communities. Small wind systems are able to produce up to about 100 kW of electrical power. It is hoped, through research and development, that in a few years electricity from these systems will be competitive with existing fuels.

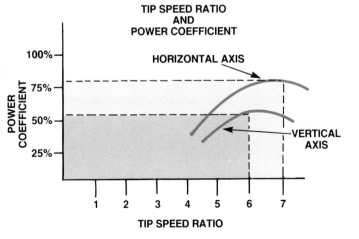

FIGURE 12-8 Tip speed ratios differ for both the horizontal and vertical axis wind turbines.

The intermediate class of wind turbines is being developed for irrigation and small utilities. These systems yield from 100 kW to 1 MW (megawatt). Systems such as these are providing valuable experience in the utilities' day-to-day operation of wind systems.

Large-scale wind systems have a capacity of at least 1 MW. These are still being designed and tested with rotor diameters up to 300 feet. These turbines are being designed for use in the utilities and industries of the future.

Storage System

The wind energy resource is not constant or continuous. Therefore, if a wind turbine is used on a residential dwelling, storage may be needed. Storage is accomplished by using DC batteries. This means that DC electricity must come from the wind generator. This can be done by changing AC voltage in the generator to DC or by using a DC generator. Either way, when the DC electricity is taken out of the batteries, it must be changed back to AC for use in the home. Cost is then one of the "impacts" of using wind energy in a home. Most often, wind generators have rather long payback periods, in the range of 10 to 20 years.

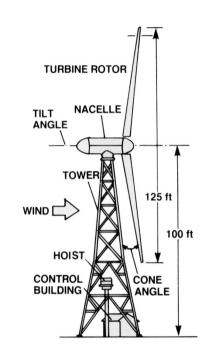

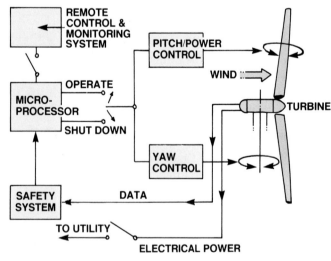

WIND TURBINE CONTROLS

FIGURE 12-10 This wiring schematic illustrates several important controls on a typical wind turbine. The yaw (turbine direction), and pitch (blade angle), are controlled by the microprocessor for best efficiency.

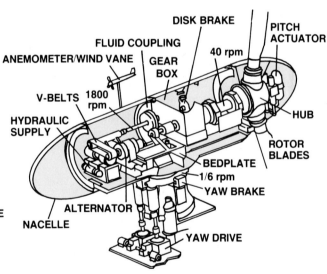

FIGURE 12-11 The major parts of a horizontal wind turbine.

Wind Turbine Controls

Several wind turbine controls are used on intermediate and large-scale generators, Figure 12-10. These controls help to improve the efficiency. *Yaw* control is needed to keep the entire assembly pointed into the wind. *Pitch* (blade angle) control is needed for several conditions, including startup, shutdown, and power control for optimum mechanical efficiency from the turbine blades. These variables are controlled by a microprocessor. The microprocessor receives signals (data) from the turbine assembly. The remote control and monitoring system is used to monitor and control the wind turbine operation from a remote location. This includes startup, shutdown, and data collection.

Wind Turbine System Parts

A large-scale wind turbine system has many parts. Figure 12-11 shows typical parts for a large, 200-kW large-scale horizontal wind turbine. Some of the more important parts include:

1. Nacelle — the housing of the turbine system assembly.
2. Pitch actuator — Used to change the pitch of the blades for improved efficiency.
3. Rotor blades — Used to capture the wind energy and convert it to mechanical rotation.
4. Gear box — Used to change the rotor speed to a constant 1,800 r/min needed for the generator in order to keep the electricity at 60 cycles.
5. Yaw drive — Used to turn the entire machine at the best angle into the wind.
6. Bedplate — Used to support the entire rotor-nacelle assembly.
7. Disk brake — Used to stop the rotor from turning and to keep the rotor from turning.

Biomass and Wood Energy Resources

Biomass Energy

Biomass or bioconversion is another major energy resource gaining in popularity. Biomass, also considered a form of solar energy, is produced by the process of photosynthesis. Green plants convert solar energy, carbon dioxide, and water into carbohydrates. The energy is stored in a variety of plant and animal organic matter. Forest materials, Figure 12-12, residues, grains, crops, animal manures and aquatic plants are the principal resources of biomass.

These raw materials can be transformed into liquid or gaseous fuels and petrochemical substitutes. From this point, thermal energy (heat), electricity, and steam can be produced. The primary

FIGURE 12-12 Forest waste, including trees, is considered a form of biomass energy resource. *Courtesy of Sun Co. Inc.*

purpose for using biomass is to supplement fossil fuel resources. This is done through the growth, harvest, and use of plant and animal residues. Today, biomass is already providing about two percent of our energy needs. Much of this two percent comes from the direct combustion of wood in residential homes.

Amount of Biomass

A great deal of biomass energy is available in the world. Approximately 100 billion tons of biomass is produced in the world each year. This energy, if converted to fuel, would be six times the energy required for all our energy needs.

Categories of Biomass

All biomass energy resources can be divided into four major categories, as shown in Figure 12-13. These categories are: urban and industrial waste, agricultural and forestry waste, land and fresh-water farming, and ocean farming.

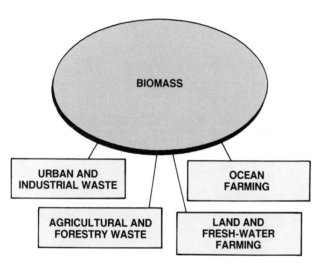

FIGURE 12-13 The four major resources used for biomass.

Urban and Industrial Waste. These waste materials include garbage, Figure 12-14, sewage, and various industrial waste products such as wood. These resources can be burned to produce heat or converted to natural gas for heating. For example, sewage can be fermented to produce methane gas for heating. One of the environmental "impacts" when using this resource is that fewer refuse disposal sites are needed.

Agricultural and Forestry Waste. Various animal waste, such as manure from cows and chickens, can be processed (digested) and converted into methane gas. Forestry waste are defined as dead or excess wood (wood taken out for thinning) for producing heat.

Land and Fresh-water Farming. These resources include field crops, such as grain, and animal waste. Grain, for example, is distilled to produce alcohol that is mixed with gasoline to make gasohol. For example, gasohol is a mixture of 90% gasoline and 10% alcohol. Also, certain types of algae and other lake plants can be grown, dried, and burned to produce thermal energy.

FIGURE 12-14 Garbage can be burned as a resource of energy. *Courtesy of American Gas Association*

Ocean Farming. An ongoing testing program is taking place to determine the potential of seaweed and other ocean plants as an energy resource. Some plants grow more than two feet per day. These can be harvested to produce the needed fuel.

Extracting Energy from Biomass

Energy can be extracted in two ways from biomass energy resources. One method is simply to burn the organic waste by the conventional combustion process. The waste is heated until it begins to release gases which burn.

A second method is by allowing the waste to decay. One method of decay is called *anaerobic decay* or decay without oxygen. When anaerobic decay occurs, methane gas is usually a by-product. Other by-products include glucose (sugar), oil, and heavy tars. Glucose is then converted to alcohol to be used as a fuel.

Methane Digester

Figure 12-15 shows a methane digester. First, the organic materials are shredded and made into a slurry (a watery mixture of insoluble matter). The slurry solution is then fed into the digester. Here, the organic materials decay and produce a methane gas. The methane gas, also called product gas, is sent to the combustion area. The remaining sludge and liquid are separated and recycled.

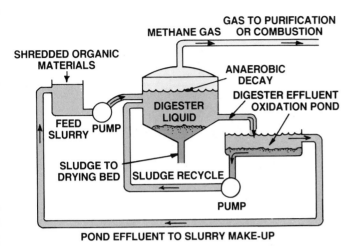

FIGURE 12-15 This system is called a methane digester. It uses shredded organic materials as the energy resource. During the decaying process, methane gas is produced in the digester.

Wood as an Energy Resource

Wood is also considered a biomass energy resource. A great deal of information is known about wood burning. Wood today is mostly used in the residential sector for space heating. However, several wood product companies burn waste sawdust as an energy resource. Thermal energy can be extracted from wood by increasing its temperature until gases are produced. As the gases burn they give off thermal energy.

Advantages and Disadvantages of Using Wood

Wood, as with other fuels, has both advantages and disadvantages to its uses.

Advantages

- Wood is a renewable resource.
- Many times the fuel is free, or less expensive than other fuels. However, this may change as the demand for wood increases.
- The heating value of wood is generally high.

Disadvantages

- Wood is bulky and difficult to handle.
- For best performance, wood must be dried. This takes time and proper storage.
- Wood fires may be unsafe in a home, and usually require stoking and periodic checking.
- Wood burning causes ash to be produced.

Measuring Wood

Wood is measured by the cord. There are two types of cords. One is called the field cord or standard cord. The other is called a face cord or short cord. One *field cord*, as shown in Figure 12-16, is a stack of wood 4 feet wide, by 4 feet high, by 8 feet long. Actually, there are three layers of 18-inch logs stacked 4 feet high and 8 feet in length. If two of these layers were removed, the resultant stack would be called a face cord. Thus, a *face cord* is a stack of wood 18 inches deep, 4 feet high, and 8 feet wide. A face cord is considered one-third of a full cord. A standard cord has about 128 cubic feet of wood. A face cord has about 42.6 cubic feet of wood.

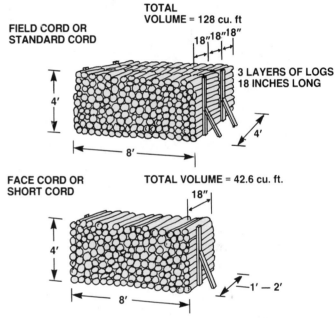

FIGURE 12-16 A field or standard cord of wood measures 4′ × 4′ × 8′ or 128 cubic feet. A face cord measures 18″ × 4′ × 8′.

Wood Characteristics

Among the many types of wood, some are excellent to burn, whereas others are considered poor for combustion. Wood has several characteristics. One characteristic is the weight per cubic foot. Generally, the heavier the wood the denser it is. The denser, the greater the Btu per pound. Typically, a good quality dry wood may be able to produce upwards of 200,000 to 250,000 Btu per cubic foot of wood. Using this as a gage, hickory and black birch are extremely good woods for burning. Other characteristics to consider when selecting wood are:

- Ease of splitting
- Amount of smoke produced
- Moisture content (dryness)
- Ease of ignition (birch, maple and oak are good)
- Sparking danger (cedar and pine should be watched)

WOOD ENERGY CONTENT

Species	Available Heat per cord in Millions of Btu		Percent more heat from air-dried wood
	Green Wood	Air-Dried Wood	
Hickory	21	25	19
Oak, White	19	23	18
Beech, Amer.	17	22	26
Maple, Sugar	18	21	16
Oak, Red	18	21	19
Birch, Yellow	17	21	23
Pine, Yellow	14	21	44
Ash, White	17	20	21
Maple, Red	15	19	22
Birch, Paper	15	18	NA
Fir, Douglas	13	18	38
Elm, American	14	17	20
Pine, E. White	12	13	10
Aspen	10	12	25

FIGURE 12-17 Green wood does not contain as much energy per cord as dry wood. Note the percentage of increase in heat when dry wood is used.

Figure 12-17 shows selected woods and the amount of available heat per cord in millions of Btu. Notice the difference in heat availability and percentage of increased heat between dry and green wood.

How Wood Burns

Wood burns in three stages, Figure 12-18. During the first stage, heat drives water from the wood. This heat does not warm the stove or room. In the second stage, charcoal and volatile gases are formed. The gases must be heated to about 1,100°F and mixed with sufficient oxygen to burn. During the third stage, the charcoal continues to burn and produce heat.

Burning Rate of Wood

A given amount of wood contains a certain amount of chemical energy. If the wood is burned com-

STAGES OF WOOD BURNING

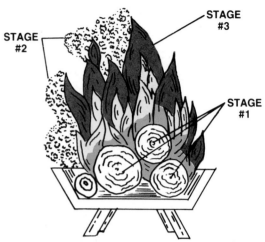

STAGE #1	The wood is heated to evaporate and drive off moisture. This heat does not warm the stove or room.
STAGE #2	The wood starts to break down chemically at 500°F and volatile matter is vaporized. These vapors contain between 50-60% of the heat value of the wood. At 1100°F these vapors burn. This high temperature must be maintained for maximum efficiency of combustion.
STAGE #3	Following the release of volatile gases, the remaining material is charcoal, which burns at temperatures exceeding 1100°F.

FIGURE 12-18 The three stages of wood burning. Note the temperatures needed for improved efficiency during Stage 2.

pletely, a given amount of heat will be released. When burned quickly, this given amount will be produced at a high rate for a brief time. When burned slowly, the same amount of heat will be produced, only at a slower rate for a longer time. The best situation is to burn the wood slowly so that the heat can be released over a longer period of time.

Efficiency

Many types and designs are used for wood-burning appliances. This causes a wider range of efficiencies on fireplaces and wood-burning stoves. Many older fireplaces are less than 10% efficient. This means that only 10% of the heat available from the wood is released into the room. The main reason for an inefficient fireplace is because the gases are not retained long enough to burn completely. By controlling the amount of input and output air to the stove, efficiencies can be increased. Some wood-burning stoves can obtain efficiencies in the 55 to 65% range. Figure 12-19 shows combustion efficiencies for various styles of heating units.

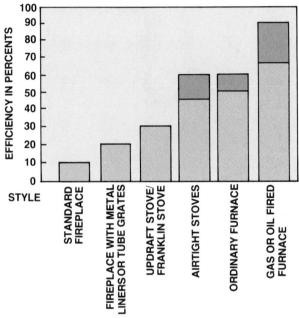

FIGURE 12-19 Different types of fireplaces and wood-burning stoves have varying efficiencies. Note that airtight stoves are very high in efficiency by comparison.

Wood Burning Stove Designs

Several designs should be considered when purchasing a fireplace or wood-burning stove. By considering the following designs, efficiencies can be improved significantly:

1. Make sure the fireplace or wood-burning stove has glass doors. Without glass doors, the efficiency of the appliance may be close to only ten percent or less. Figure 12-20 shows the heat loss that occurs when there are no glass doors or an open hearth is used.

2. Make sure there is a control for the input air. If the input air is controlled, the burn rate and, thus, efficiency can be controlled.

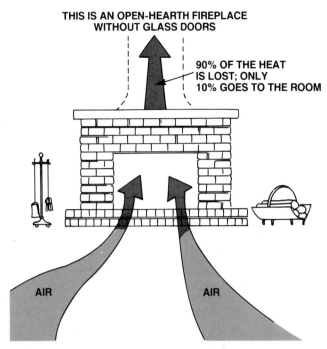

FIGURE 12-20 In an open-hearth fireplace without glass doors, most of the heat escapes up the chimney.

3. Make sure there is a control for the output air or exhaust. If the output air is controlled, burn rate and, thus, efficiency can be controlled. Output air can be controlled by using a variable damper, as shown in Figure 12-21.

4. Consider the use of outside air for combustion. When outside air is used for the combustion oxygen, it is cold air not warm air that has already been heated.

5. The use of a secondary combustion chamber has a positive effect on efficiency. *Secondary combustion chambers* retain the gases in the

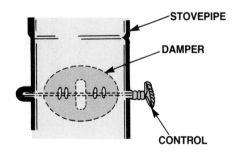

FIGURE 12-21 An air control damper in a stove is used to control the amount of outgoing exhaust air.

stove longer, causing them to burn more completely. Secondary combustion is usually achieved by using various baffles in the stove, so as to control the hot gases for secondary burning.

6. The use of a fan to remove the heat from the combustion chamber or from the stove surface area improves efficiency. Quite often an air-to-air heat exchanger is used, Figure 12-22.

7. Generally, the thicker the stove metal the better the stove retains the heat. The stove then has a tendency to give off heat for a longer period of time after the fire slows down.

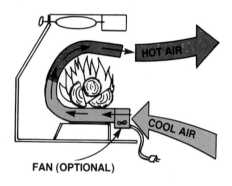

CONVECTION TUBES INCREASE THE
HEAT FLOW INTO THE ROOM

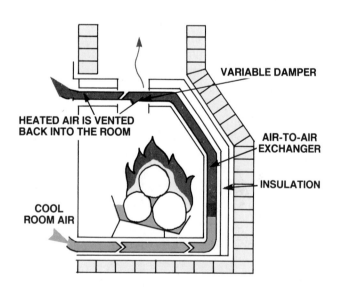

FIGURE 12-22 An air-to-air heat exchanger is one method used to increase the efficiency of a stove. This is done by convection or by using a fan.

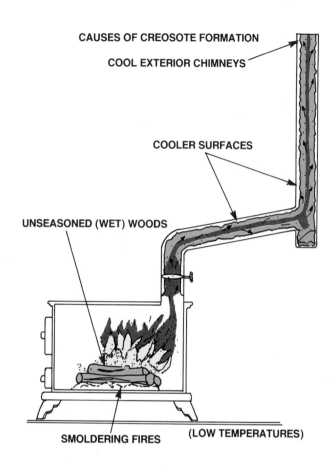

FIGURE 12-23 The causes of creosote buildup include green wood, smoldering fires, and cool surfaces.

Creosote Buildup

When wood burns, the combustion process is never complete. The smoke usually contains unburned gases and a sustance called *creosote*. Creosote is one of the negative environmental "impacts" of burning wood as an energy resource. The creosote gases condense and plug up the inside of the stove exhaust pipe. Creosote looks like a black, tar-type liquid inside of the chimney. It can also take on other forms, such as flakes or bubbles. Also, layers can develop inside of the chimney.

The amount of creosote condensing inside the chimney varies. It depends upon the temperature of the inside chimney surface, the dryness of the wood, and the density of the smoke. Thus, long and slow burning usually produces more creosote. Quick, hotter fires cut down on the creosote accumulation.

Creosote deposits in the chimney will burn with intense heat. This could be a dangerous situation and may cause a chimney fire. Reduce creosote buildup by:

1. Burning dry wood.
2. Stoking a hot fire every 15 to 30 minutes to keep the fire hotter.
3. Eliminate cool surfaces on the chimney.

Figure 12-23 shows the causes of creosote formation.

Catalytic Converter-type Combustor

The catalytic converter-type combustor is one of the more recent innovations in wood burning. Similar to the emission controls on a car, the catalytic converter reduces emissions and improves efficiency. The catalytic combustor chemically reduces the temperature at which smoke burns. This has the same effect as increasing the combustion temperature. The result is less pollution and more efficient heating. The catalytic combustor usually fits in the upper part of the stove just ahead of the exhaust chimney pipe. Figure 12-24 shows an example of a small catalytic combustor used in a stove pipe.

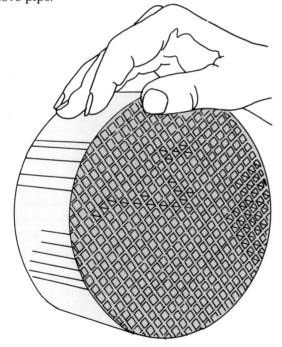

FIGURE 12-24 The catalytic converter combustor used in some stoves helps to improve efficiency and reduce pollution.

Pollution from Burning Wood

The exhaust from burning wood is typically unclean. The exhaust gases contain, among others, such chemicals as hydrogen, carbon monoxide, methane, acetic acid, formaldehyde, and pine tar. Figure 12-25 shows each of these chemical pollutants, along with the temperatures at which they ignite. To reduce such pollution, burn at higher temperatures or use catalytic converters.

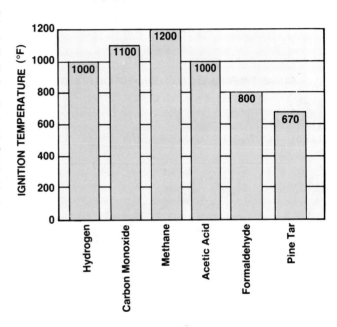

FIGURE 12-25 These pollutants are formed when wood is burned in a fireplace or wood-burning stove.

Ocean Thermal Energy Conversion (OTEC)

Ocean thermal energy conversion, also called OTEC, is another type of energy resource that may be used in the future. OTEC is defined as extracting energy from the ocean. Consider the ocean near the equator to be a massive water solar collector. The sun keeps the water near the equator at about 80 to 85°F. At the bottom of the ocean, the water is usually very cool, about 35 to 40°F. A simple thermodynamic concept is used. When there is enough of a temperature difference between the upper and lower layers of water, energy can be extracted. Normally, this difference in temperature is about 40°F. At present, this energy resource is being tested to see if the concept can become a reality.

OTEC Operation

Figure 12-26 shows a schematic diagram of how an OTEC plant operates. Warm water from the top of the ocean is pumped into the plant. As the warm water passes by the large heat exchanger on the left, thermal energy (75 to 80°F) is transferred into a liquid refrigerant. Most refrigerants (such as ammonia) have a very low boiling point, usually below 80°F. The refrigerant turns into a low-pressure gas. The gas is used to turn a low-speed turbine. Electricity is produced when a generator is attached to the low-speed turbine shaft.

FIGURE 12-27 Older vessels such as this are being rebuilt to test the OTEC concepts. *Courtesy of Department of Energy*

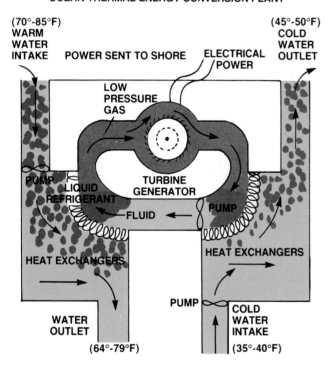

OCEAN THERMAL ENERGY CONVERSION PLANT

FIGURE 12-26 This schematic illustrates how an OTEC plant operates.

The warm water is then exhausted. Cool water (35 to 40°F) is pumped up from the bottom of the ocean. This cool water is used to condense the refrigerant gas back to a liquid state. This process continues as long as warm water heats and cool water condenses the refrigerant. Warm water is drawn into the top, cool water is drawn into the bottom for operation. Today, older ships are being redesigned as testing units. Figure 12-27 shows a typical vessel used to test the OTEC concept.

Advantages and Disadvantages of OTEC

The OTEC concept has several advantages and disadvantages.

Advantages

1. A great deal of energy is available around the equator.
2. Many existing technologies can be used in the power plant itself.
3. If many plants were to be built, mass production of the plants could lower the cost of the plant and thus reduce electricity costs.

Disadvantages

1. The structure of the power plant would have to be capable of handling ocean conditions such as salt.
2. Algae and marine life often clog the inlet screens.
3. The cold bottom water being mixed with the warm water on top kills off certain marine life.

Geothermal Energy Resources

Geothermal energy is defined as the thermal energy in the ground, caused by the decay of radioactive

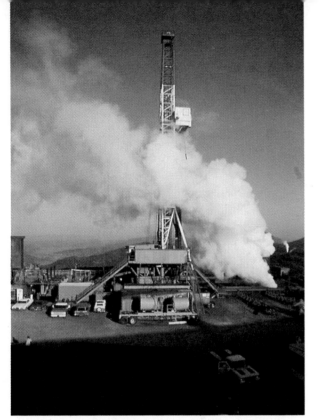

FIGURE 12-28 This drilling rig is used to drill down through nonpermeable rock to bring the geothermal energy to the surface. *Courtesy of American Petroleum Institute*

materials. Quite often, this thermal energy is close enough to the surface of the earth to be extracted. Figure 12-28 shows a typical steam well drilling rig used to release geothermal energy. When the energy is released, it is used as steam to turn a turbine/generator and produce electricity.

Types of Geothermal Energy Resources

Three types of geothermal energy resources are commonly found. *Hydrothermal* reservoirs are those that usually have naturally circulating hot water or steam. *Geopressured* reservoirs are high-temperature, high-pressure reservoirs of water. The resource is trapped beneath a nonpermeable rock area. *Hot-Dry rock* is buried deep in the earth close to the extremely hot molten materials. All three types are being investigated. However, only hydrothermal reservoirs are being used at the present time.

Geothermal Plant Operation

Geothermal plants are rather simple in design. A hole is drilled much the same as for natural gas. After the drill is capped off, the steam is connected

Drilling Rig for Geothermal Energy

The technology associated with oil well and natural gas well drilling can be transferred to other uses. Geothermal energy is one area that also uses drilling technology. *Geothermal energy* is produced by extracting heat from below the surface of the earth to heat water. Holes must be drilled to depths similar to oil drilling.

This drilling rig is capable of drilling to depths of 20,000 feet, and is being used to locate geothermal energy resources. Heated, pressurized water and natural gas are found below the 14,500-foot level of the well. The temperature at the bottom of the well is about 300°F. Tapping into this energy resource can provide additional renewable energy resources for our society. *Courtesy of U.S. Department of Energy*

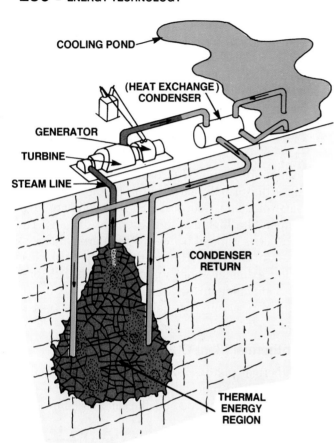

COOLING POND

(HEAT EXCHANGE)
CONDENSER

GENERATOR

TURBINE

STEAM LINE

CONDENSER
RETURN

THERMAL
ENERGY
REGION

FIGURE 12-29 Geothermal plant operation.

to a turbine and generator unit, Figure 12-29. Steam from the geothermal reservoir turns the turbine and generator unit. The remaining steam is sent to a condenser where it is cooled. Water from a cooling pond extracts the remaining heat. A standard heat exchanger is used. The remaining water is sent back into the reservoir to be reheated and possibly used again.

Summary

- Hydroelectric energy resources, considered renewable, make up about four to five percent of all energy.
- The penstock on a hydroelectric dam is used to channel the falling water to the turbines.
- More low-head dams are being built as prices of other fuels increase.
- The reaction turbine is used to convert the force of falling water to torque.
- Both vertical and horizontal wind turbines are being tested to extract the energy from the wind.
- Only 59% of the wind's energy can be extracted and used in a wind turbine.
- Power coefficient is the amount of energy (from the 59%) that can be extracted from the wind.
- The *tip speed ratio* is defined as the ratio of the tip of the wind turbine blade compared to the wind speed.
- Three types of wind energy projects are currently being tested. They are: small, intermediate, and large-scale wind projects.
- A wind energy system for a residential dwelling must use a storage battery because of the inconsistency of wind.
- Biomass energy is the process of extracting energy from organic materials, to produce heat or methane gas.
- The four types of biomass being used and tested today are urban and industrial waste, agricultural and forestry waste, land and fresh-water farming, and ocean farming.
- When organic material is shredded and put into a digester, methane gas is produced. This by-product results from the process of anaerobic decay.
- Wood, measured in cords, can also be considered a form of biomass energy.
- Hickory is one of the best woods to burn.
- It is best to burn only seasoned or dry woods.
- It is best to burn wood slowly.
- Efficiency of wood-burning units can be increased by using glass doors, controlling air input and output, using a heat exchanger, and having a secondary combustion chamber.
- Creosote buildup is caused by burning slow and cool fires, burning green wood, and by having cool stove pipes.
- The catalytic combustor is used to reduce pollu-

tion and improve combustion efficiency.

■ The ocean thermal energy conversion (OTEC) concept needs a temperature difference of approximately 40°F between the warm and cool sides of the power plant.

■ Today, older vessels are being reconstructed to test the OTEC principle.

■ Geothermal energy is produced by extracting hot water and steam from the earth's center.

■ Geothermal plants are designed by drilling deep holes into the earth. Steam is extracted and used in a turbine generator unit. The steam is cooled by a condenser or heat exchanger. The cooler water is then pumped back into the geothermal reservoir.

REVIEW

1. What actual amount of energy is extracted from the wind if there is a power coefficient of 68%?

2. A trailer full of wood measures 8 feet by 6 feet by 2 feet. If three trailer loads of wood were purchased, _____ chords of wood were obtained.

3. Using the information calculated in question number 2, how many Btu does this wood contain if the wood is air-dried white oak?

4. Using the information calculated in question number 3, how many Btu could be extracted if all of the wood were burned in a stove having a 49% efficiency rate?

5. Using the information calculated in question number 4, for how many hours would this amount of wood heat a home that requires 12,000 Btu per hour to heat?

6. Why are more hydroelectric dams being built with lower heads?

7. Identify the major parts and operation of a hydroelectric dam.

8. What is the difference between the vertical shaft and horizontal shaft wind turbines?

9. What is the definition of *power coefficient*?

10. Why is it important to consider tip speed ratio when designing wind turbine systems?

11. Define the energy resource called *biomass* and state the type of energy extracted.

12. Define the four categories of biomass and give examples of at least two.

13. How is wood quantity measured?

14. Identify five factors in the design or process of burning wood that will improve efficiency.

15. State how the OTEC system works.

CHAPTER ACTIVITIES

 ## COST OF WOOD BURNING

INTRODUCTION

Wood can help significantly as a fuel in residential dwellings. This activity is a mathematical problem to determine how much wood is needed to heat a home for the winter months.

TECHNOLOGICAL LITERACY SKILLS

Data Analysis, mathematical analysis, drawing conclusions.

OBJECTIVES

At the completion of this activity, you will be able to:

1. Calculate how many Btu are used in a home during the winter.
2. Analyze an energy bill.
3. Determine the amount of wood necessary to heat a home during the winter.

MATERIALS

1. Energy bills for a winter period
2. Hand calculator
3. Pencil and paper
4. Wood Burning handout

ADDITIONAL INFORMATION

This activity is a mathematical analysis problem to determine how much it would cost to heat a home with wood rather than natural gas. If you have an electrically heated home, then the electricity must be converted to Btu.

PROCEDURE

1. Obtain your home's energy bills for the last year for October, November, December, January, February, and March.
2. Locate the amount of energy needed each month. This is usually indicated by the unit ccf or therm. A ccf or therm is equal to 100,000 Btu. If you use other forms of heat, such as oil or electricity, you will need to convert these forms of fuel into Btu.
3. Record the information (ccf/therms), Btu, and price in the table of the Wood Burning handout.
4. Now calculate the total Btu needed for this six-month period. Record on the handout.
5. Determine the number of Btu that can be extracted from a cord of wood if the one cord of wood has 20,900,000 Btu and the wood-burning stove is only 30% efficient. (20,900,000 × .3). Record on the handout.
6. Calculate the number of cords of wood needed during this six-month period by dividing the Btu extracted from the cord of wood into the total number of Btu required from your energy bill.
7. Identify the price of a cord of wood in your area and record on the handout.
8. Multiply the price per cord of wood times the number of cords needed for the six-month period. This is your total cost to heat with wood for the six-month period.

REVIEW QUESTIONS

1. Is it more or less expensive to heat your home with wood or with natural gas?
2. If the efficiency of the wood-burning stove increased to 40%, how much would you save?
3. If the wood used had a higher Btu content, would the cost be higher or lower?
4. Plug in different numbers, such as a 50% efficient stove, more ccf, and so forth, and determine the cost.

SAVONIUS WIND GENERATOR

INTRODUCTION

This activity is designed to build and test a Savonius wind generator. This generator uses a set of baffles, as shown in Figure 12-30. Two curved baffles are used to catch the wind and rotate the center shaft. The two curved baffles are adjustable. Figure 12-31 shows how the airflow increases the torque as the baffles are moved. When the baffles are together, less power is produced. When the baffles are apart (shown at the bottom), air pressure pushes both baffles to produce increased power.

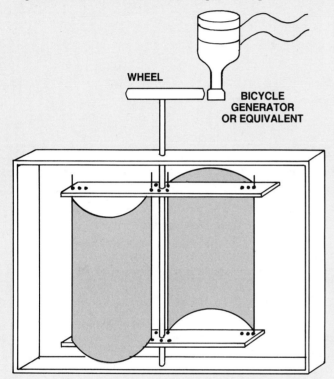

WHEEL

BICYCLE
GENERATOR
OR EQUIVALENT

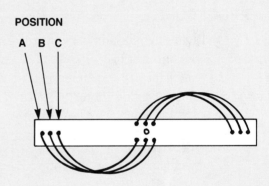

POSITION

A B C

FIGURE 12-30 An example of the Savonius wing generator.

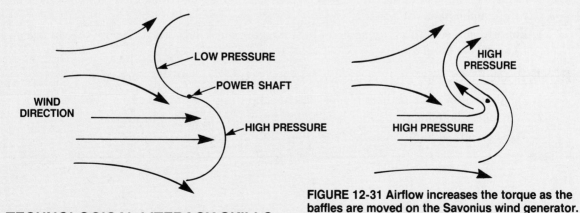

LOW PRESSURE

POWER SHAFT

WIND
DIRECTION

HIGH PRESSURE

HIGH
PRESSURE

HIGH PRESSURE

FIGURE 12-31 Airflow increases the torque as the baffles are moved on the Savonius wind generator.

TECHNOLOGICAL LITERACY SKILLS

Problem solving, creativity, data analysis, design, collection of data.

OBJECTIVES

At the completion of this activity, you will be able to construct and test a Savonius wind generator.

MATERIALS

1. Bicycle generator or equivalent
2. Voltmeter
3. Aluminum sheets
4. Wood for the wind generator frame
5. Dowel rods for the center shaft
6. Assorted fasteners, glue and metal for assembly
7. A woodworking and metal working laboratory
8. Small wheel for drive mechanism
9. Support brackets to hold the generator in place
10. Large house fan to produce air pressure
11. Savonius Wind Generator handout.

PROCEDURE

1. Divide the class into groups of two or three students. Each group will build and test a Savonius wind generator.
2. Sketch the size and dimensions necessary for your wind generator. Remember that the object is to turn the wind generator to produce electricity. A good size is about 18 to 24 inches high.
3. After the dimensions have been established, build the wind generator using the appropriate tools.

   ▶ **CAUTION:** Always wear safety glasses when working with tools in the laboratory. Also, make sure you know the correct operation of all tools used in the laboratory. If not, check with your instructor.

4. Make sure that the two baffles can be adjusted into three positions.
5. Using a house fan, operate the wind generator to produce voltage with the baffles in the outermost position. Note the voltage produced and record it on the Savonius Wind Generator handout. Also, count the r/min and record on the handout.
6. Reposition the baffles into the center position and retest the voltage. Record the voltage and r/min on the handout.
7. Reposition the baffles into the inner position and retest the voltage. Record the voltage and r/min on the handout.

REVIEW QUESTIONS

1. What position produced the highest voltage and r/min on the Savonius wind generator?
2. Why does changing the baffles have an effect on the voltage and r/min?
3. What could you do to increase the voltage output? The r/min output?

CHAPTER 13

Nuclear Energy

OBJECTIVES

After reading this chapter, you will be able to:

- Discuss the extent to which nuclear energy is used today, and how it may be used in the future.
- Describe how fuels produce nuclear energy.
- Define *half life*.
- Analyze the process of making nuclear fuel.
- Compare different types of nuclear reactors.
- Identify the problems of nuclear waste.
- Compare fission and fusion nuclear energy.
- Analyze the process and requirements for nuclear fusion.

KEY TERMS

Waste Management	Fusion	Breeding
Isotopes	Fission	Moderator
Electrons	Control Rods	Secondary Loop
Protons	Yellow Cake	Primary Loop
Neutrons	Enriched	Rem
Theory of Relativity	Plutonium	Laser
Uranium		

Introduction

Nuclear energy is one of the more controversial energy resources of today. Even though nuclear energy is often debated, it is predicted to increase considerably in the next 10 to 20 years. This chapter is about the principles and concepts of nuclear energy. In order to make technological decisions about the use of nuclear energy, several important concepts should be known. These concepts include the basic chemistry of nuclear energy, nuclear fuels, different types of reactors, and waste problems. These subjects are discussed in this chapter.

FIGURE 13-1 Nuclear power plants such as these will increase in usage over the next few years. *Courtesy of New York Power Authority*

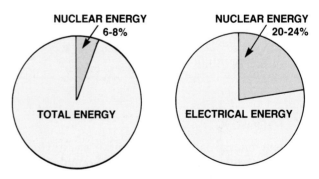

Nuclear Energy

Nuclear Energy Supply

The demand for electrical energy usage has increased over the past few years. The total energy demand from all sources increases about 3% each year. However, the demand for electrical energy increases between six and seven percent each year. Power plants using nuclear energy help to meet this additional demand, Figure 13-1. Although statistics vary, nuclear energy provides about six to eight percent of the total energy within the United States. More specifically, nuclear energy provides about 20

NUCLEAR ENERGY
6-8%

TOTAL ENERGY

NUCLEAR ENERGY
20-24%

ELECTRICAL ENERGY

FIGURE 13-2 Nuclear energy today provides about 6 to 8% of the total energy and about 20 to 24% of all electrical energy.

to 24% of all the electrical power in the United States. These data are shown in Figure 13-2. Although this may not seem like much, most projections show a large increase in nuclear power in the next two decades.

Figure 13-3 shows the number of plants and their locations throughout the United States in a particular year. The fact that many plants are either planned or on order suggests that the nuclear industry will grow rather significantly in the future.

Nuclear Energy Used in Other Countries

The Unitd States is not the only country that utilizes nuclear energy. Figure 13-4 shows a bar chart and the average nuclear energy share used by several selected countries. Note that the United States presently is not as reliant on nuclear energy as many other countries. The reason, of course, is that the power industries in the United States believe it

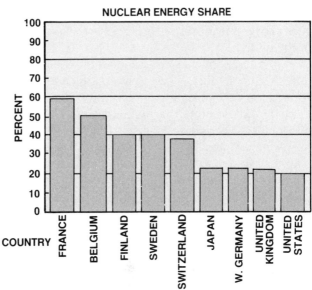

FIGURE 13-4 The United States produces only about 20% of its electricity by nuclear energy. Other countries are much higher and more reliant on nuclear energy.

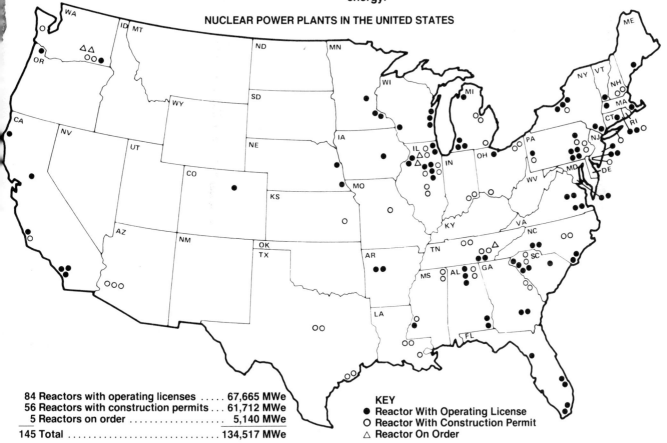

84 Reactors with operating licenses	67,665 MWe
56 Reactors with construction permits ...	61,712 MWe
5 Reactors on order	5,140 MWe
145 Total	134,517 MWe

KEY
● Reactor With Operating License
○ Reactor With Construction Permit
△ Reactor On Order

FIGURE 13-3 Nuclear power plants are located throughout much of the United States. *Courtesy of Atomic Industrial Forum*

is important to use other types of energy as well. Nuclear energy is considered one of several resources for the future.

Figure 13-5 shows a second chart. This bar chart indicates the number of countries and the number of power plants presently in operation. On this chart, the United States has the largest number of power plants. This is due to the demand of electrical energy in the United States. By combining these two charts, it can be seen that 85 U.S. nuclear power plants supply about 20% of the electrical energy. By comparison, France requires about 30 plants to produce about 59% of its electrical energy.

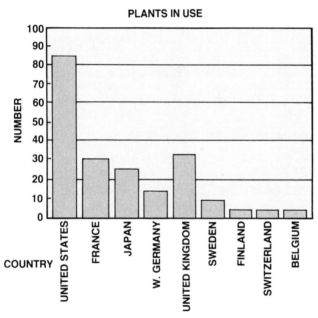

FIGURE 13-5 Although the U.S. is less reliant on nuclear energy than other countries, it has the greatest number of power plants.

Price of Nuclear Energy

Nuclear energy at the present is considerably less expensive than other forms of energy. Figure 13-6 shows a comparison of the price of electrical energy produced from four major resources. The data used to get these prices include such factors as:

■ Transportation costs
■ Fuel costs
■ Electrical generator efficiency
■ Capital cost of power plant
■ Cost of waste management
■ Operating and maintenance costs

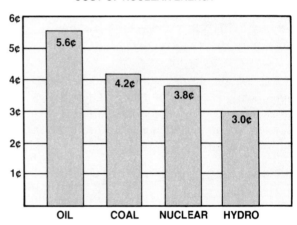

FIGURE 13-6 Nuclear energy is one of the least expensive methods used to produce electricity.

Nuclear Chemistry

Isotopes

To understand nuclear fuels, isotopes must first be studied. An *isotope* is a type of atom identified by the number of neutrons. Isotope atoms have additional neutrons in the core. All atoms have an equal number of protons, electrons, and neutrons. *Protons* are the positive charges, *electrons* are the negative charges, and *neutrons* have no charge. The weight of any atom is primarily made from the weight of the protons and the neutrons. Electrons are very light, and thus make up little weight on the atom. It is important for each atom to have a balance between the number of protons and electrons. However, an atom may have a different number of neutrons. This is the case with many types of atoms called isotopes.

Figure 13-7 shows a comparison of several atoms used as fuel in nuclear reactions. There are three types of hydrogen atoms: hydrogen, deuterium, and tritium. In comparison to hydrogen, deuterium has an extra neutron, and tritium has two extra neutrons. This makes both of them heavier than the light hydrogen atom. Deuterium and tritium are both considered isotopes of the basic hydrogen atom. They are also called *heavy hydrogen* atoms.

The same is true for different isotopes of uranium, also a nuclear fuel. Three of the many isotopes of uranium are also shown in Figure 13-7. Each has 92

ISOTOPES OF NUCLEAR FUEL

	(NUMBER LOCATIONS) ATOMIC WEIGHT X NEUTRONS PROTONS	(+) = PROTON (-) = ELECTRON • = NEUTRON SYMBOL	
HYDROGEN	$^{1}_{1}H_0$	(+)(-)	
DEUTERIUM	$^{2}_{1}H_1$	(•+)(-)	HEAVY HYDROGEN
TRITIUM	$^{3}_{1}H_2$	(•+•)(-)	HEAVY HYDROGEN
U-234	$^{234}_{92}U_{142}$	(-)92 (+92 •142)	
U-235	$^{235}_{92}U_{143}$	(-)92 (+92 •143)	
U-238	$^{238}_{92}U_{146}$	(-)92 (+92 •146)	

FIGURE 13-7 These isotopes are all used for the production of nuclear energy.

electrons and protons, but they differ in the number of neutrons. The isotope U-234 has 142 neutrons, U-235 has 143 neutrons and U-238 has 146 neutrons. Type U-235 is most used in a nuclear power plant.

Nuclear Energy Formula

A very simple formula will help to understand nuclear energy. This formula is shown as:

$$E = M C^2$$

where: E = Energy
M = Mass of the fuel
C = Speed of light

TECH L I N K

The formula $E = M C^2$ is known as the *theory of relativity*. It says that mass (M) and energy (E) are merely two different forms of the same thing. Each can be converted to the other. Theoretically, mass or matter can be transformed into energy and energy can be transformed into mass.

In a nuclear power plant, a certain amount of uranium (M) is converted to energy (E). The speed of light (C) is normally considered to be 186,000 miles per second. With this number so high, and by using the formula, a very small amount of uranium (M) can be converted to a very large amount of energy (E). Typically, one pellet of uranium (approximately ½ inch long by ⅜ inch in diameter) is equal to the same amount of energy in 1,780 pounds of coal, 149 gallons of oil, or 15,856 cubic feet of natural gas.

Fusion and Fission

At present, two types of nuclear reactions can create energy: fusion and fission. Both processes are designed to change mass to energy. Referring to Figure 13-8, *fusion* is the process of binding elements together to convert mass to energy. *Fission* is the process of splitting elements apart to convert mass to energy. Fission is being used in power plants today, whereas fusion is still considered experimental.

Fission

Today's nuclear power plants all use the fission process to extract energy from molecules. Fusion reactors are still being tested and are discussed later in this chapter. Fission is the process used to produce large amounts of energy from small amounts of uranium.

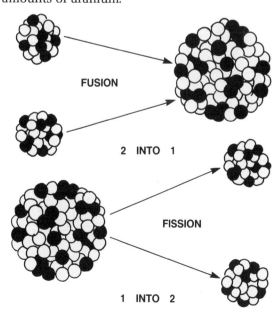

FUSION

2 INTO 1

FISSION

1 INTO 2

FIGURE 13-8 Fusion is the binding together to obtain energy. Fission is the splitting apart to obtain energy.

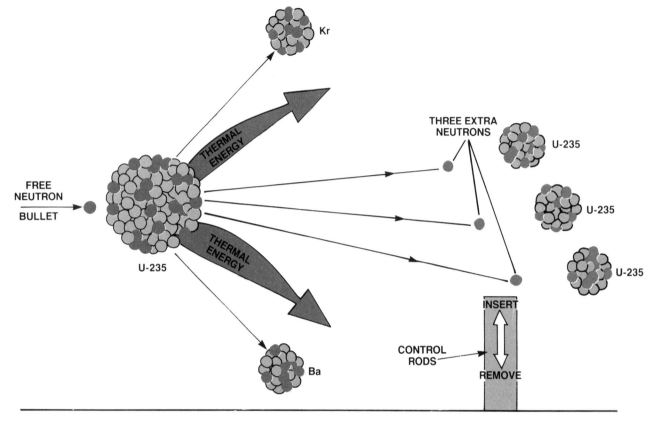

FREE
NEUTRON

BULLET

U-235

THERMAL ENERGY

THERMAL ENERGY

Kr

Ba

THREE EXTRA
NEUTRONS

U-235

U-235

U-235

INSERT

CONTROL
RODS

REMOVE

FIGURE 13-9 In a fission process, when a U-235 atom is hit by a free neutron, the atom splits. During the splitting of the atom, some of the mass is converted to thermal energy.

Referring to Figure 13-9, a uranium (U-235) element is shown. As a free neutron bullet strikes the U-235 atom on the left, the reaction is quite unusual; there is now an imbalance of neutrons. This causes the atom to split (fission) apart into two new elements, krypton and barium. In addition, three extra neutrons also fly out. When the weight of the krypton, the barium and the free neutrons are added together, their combined weight is less than the original weight of the U-235 atom. The loss in mass has been converted (by fission) into thermal energy. This is represented by the energy arrows. Thus, mass (M) has been converted to energy (E). It should be noted that a very small mass has changed to a very large amount of energy.

To continue the process, if the three extra neutrons were to hit three more U-235 elements as shown, even more energy would be developed. This is called a *chain reaction*. If this process continued uncontrolled, a nuclear explosion would be created, Figure 13-10.

FIGURE 13-10 An uncontrolled nuclear fission process results in a nuclear explosion. *Courtesy of American Petroleum Institute*

Controlling the Nuclear Energy Reaction

The best method for controlling the nuclear reaction is to absorb some of the free neutrons. If these neutrons are stopped before they hit another uranium element, the reaction process slows down. Nuclear power plants use *control rods* for this purpose. As the control rods (see Figure 13-9) are inserted in a nuclear core, they absorb the extra neutrons. The reaction now slows down. As the control rods are removed from the nuclear core, the reaction speeds up.

Nuclear Fuel Processing

Uranium is mined much like coal. It can be extracted by both surface and underground mining techniques. In nature, the majority of uranium is the U-238 isotope, not the U-235. However, U-238 is not usable in a power plant in its natural or present state, although U-235 is. Normally about .25% of natural uranium is U-235. The remaining amount is mostly U-238, plus certain impurities. The natural amount of U-235 is not sufficient to sustain the fission chain reaction previously mentioned.

To solve this problem, the mined uranium must be U-235 enriched to about 3%. If 3% of the uranium is U-235, a chain reaction can occur. The nuclear fuel cycle for producing the right type of uranium is shown in Figure 13-11. The process is as follows:

Stage 1. The uranium ore is mined. It includes the uranium isotope chemically identified as U_3O_8 (uranium oxide) and various impurities.

Stage 2. The uranium is shaped into blocks called *yellow cake* for ease of shipping. At this point, 70 to 90% of the ore is made of uranium isotopes.

Stage 3. The uranium is then changed to a gaseous state in preparation for the enrichment process. Uranium gas is referred to as UF_6.

Stage 4. The uranium gas is enriched from .25% U-235 to 3% U-235.

Stage 5. The enriched fuel is shaped, purified, and machined into pellets.

Stage 6. The uranium pellets, shown in Figure 13-12, are then used in a nuclear power plant.

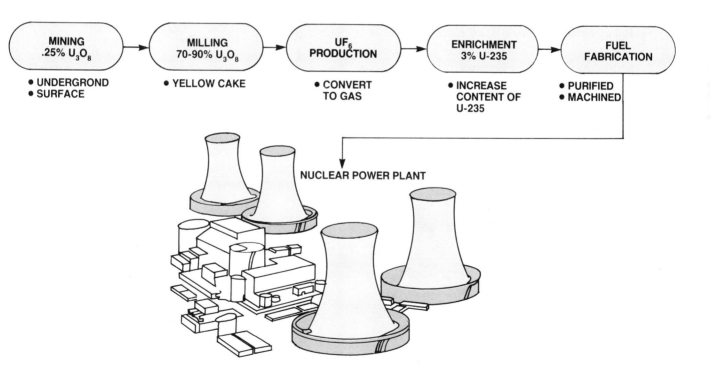

FIGURE 13-11 The process of producing uranium for a power plant is shown.

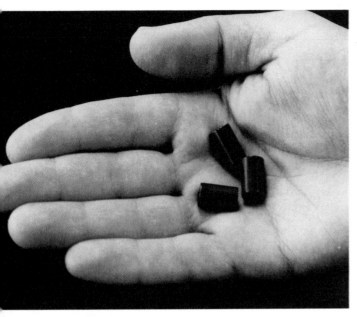

FIGURE 13-12 These are simulated uranium pellets of the type used in a nuclear power plant. *Courtesy of New York Power Authority*

Plutonium as a Nuclear Fuel

Plutonium can also be used as a nuclear fuel inside of a nuclear reactor. Plutonium is not found naturally, but is manufactured. The chemical symbol for plutonium is Pu-239. Plutonium is produced inside of a nuclear reactor in the following manner. Referring to Figure 13-13, when an excess U-238 atom is hit by a free neutron, it becomes very

unstable. The unstable element immediately changes into plutonium 239. This element, if now hit by another free neutron, will behave the same as does U-235 in a fission process.

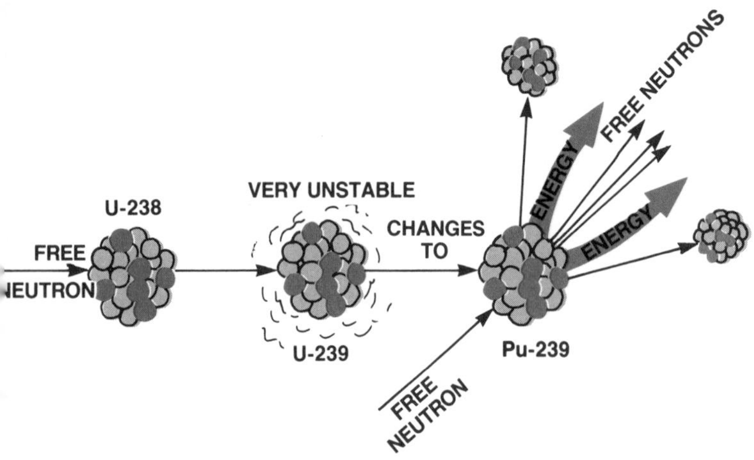

Breeding Fuel

Breeding fuel means that more fuel is actually produced than that which is used. Figure 13-14 shows how breeding fuel can occur. After a fission of U-235 occurs, the free neutrons may hit U-238, changing immediately to Pu-239. In actual practice, a specific ratio of new fuel (Pu) is being produced. For example, 10 atoms of U-235 surrounded by ample atoms of U-238 will make 12 atoms of Pu-239.

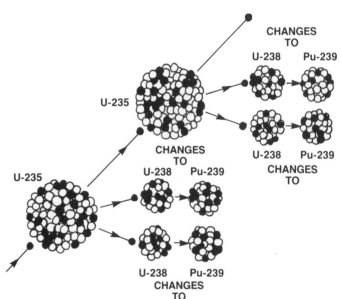

FIGURE 13-14 Breeding fuel occurs when U-238 is hit by neutrons, converting them into Pu-239.

Types of Nuclear Reactors

Several types of nuclear reactors are being used commercially, and several designs are being tested. A nuclear reactor can be studied by using the systems model.

1. The "input" or objective (command) is to convert the energy in a nuclear fuel into electrical energy.
2. The "process" (the actual power plant) is designed to accomplish the objective. It requires people, capital, energy, tools and materials, among others.

FIGURE 13-13 When a free neutron hits a U-238 atom, it becomes very unstable, turning immediately into Pu-239.

3. The "output" is the actual energy that has been created by the nuclear power plant.
4. The "feedback" includes the control rods, pressures, temperatures, and other factors fed into the computer control room to operate the power output of the plant.
5. The "impact" includes the radiation produced from the waste products in the nuclear reactor.

Reactor designs are based upon a number of considerations that include:

- Use and purpose — For example, nuclear reactors can be used for commercial electrical power or for power in nuclear ships.
- Type of neutron — There are two types of neutrons, fast and slow. The faster the neutron the less chance of it hitting a U-235 atom.
- Moderator and control rods — The moderator and control rods can be made from different materials and liquids. Water is a good moderator, and graphite or carbon makes a good control rod.
- Coolant — Water is typically the coolant. Various gases as well as liquid sodium are also used.
- Fuel — The most used fuel is U-235. However, some reactors may use different isotopes of uranium.
- Fuel arrangement — The fuel rods can be arranged physically in several ways.

Boiling Water Reactor

Figure 13-15 shows the simplest type of nuclear reactor: the boiling water reactor system. In operation, fuel is placed in the core, surrounded by water as a moderator and coolant. Once the control rods are removed, the nuclear reaction starts. The heat produced by fission causes the water to boil. The boiling water is sent to the turbine generator unit. Here, electricity is produced and sent into the commercial power grid. A cooling tower, as shown in Figure 13-16, or condenser is used to reduce the temperature of the steam. The steam now turns back into water. The water is pumped back into the

FIGURE 13-16 A cooling tower is used to cool down hot water before it reenters the nuclear core. *Courtesy of American Petroleum Institute*

BOILING WATER REACTOR SYSTEM

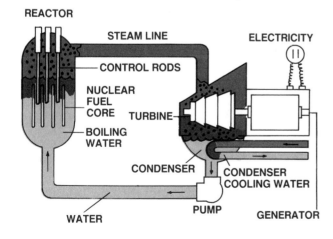

FIGURE 13-15 Schematic of a boiling water reactor. *Courtesy of Northern States Power Company*

FIGURE 13-17 The core of a nuclear reactor houses the fuel and control rods, as well as the water. *Courtesy of American Petroleum Institute*

core of the nuclear reactor. Figure 13-17 shows a view looking down into the core of a reactor during refueling.

Pressurized Water Reactor

The pressurized water reactor, compared to the boiling water reactor, has higher temperatures and pressures inside of the core. This reactor system is more efficient than the boiling water reactor. Figure 13-18 shows a schematic of a typical pressurized water reactor. Besides having higher temperatures

and pressures, a steam generator is also used. The steam generator operates as a heat exchanger. Any heat produced in the primary loop is exchanged to the secondary loop. This system is much safer than the boiling water reactor. With the heat exchanger, there is less chance of radioactive water getting into the turbine/generator system.

Nuclear reactors of these designs also must have a rather complex control room. Figure 13-19 shows a typical computerized control room. Throughout

FIGURE 13-19 The control room of a nuclear power plant monitors many temperatures, pressures, and flow rates for correct operation. *Courtesy of Vt. Yankee Nuclear Power Plant*

PRESSURIZED WATER REACTOR SYSTEM

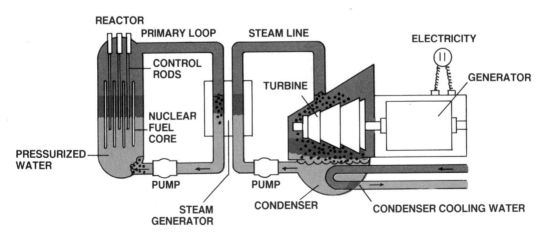

REACTOR
PRIMARY LOOP
STEAM LINE
ELECTRICITY
CONTROL RODS
TURBINE
GENERATOR
NUCLEAR FUEL CORE
PRESSURIZED WATER
PUMP
PUMP
CONDENSER
CONDENSER COOLING WATER
STEAM GENERATOR
CONDENSER

FIGURE 13-18 This pressurized water reactor has an additional steam generator (heat exchanger) to protect the turbines from radiation. *Courtesy of Northern States Power Company*

the plant, hundreds of readings are taken and sent to the control room. An example of some of the data includes:

Turbine speed	Turbine load
Primary loop temperatures	Secondary loop temperatures
Pump pressures	Core temperatures
Control rod position	Heat exchanger temperature

Experimental Reactors

Several experimental reactors are currently being tested. The *high-temperature gas reactor* uses helium as a thermal energy transfer fluid. Tests show that this type of reactor may be even more efficient than the pressurized water reactor. A second type of reactor being tested, called the *breeder reactor*, uses liquid sodium as a heat transfer medium. In addition, the fuel arrangement is designed to use the plutonium being developed inside of the reactor for more fuel.

Nuclear Waste Management

Radiation

Radiation is one of the by-products (negative "impacts") of a nuclear power plant. *Radiation* is a very broad term; it often includes electromagnetic waves such as X rays, light waves, radio waves, and so forth. In the nuclear industry, radiaiton means to ionize. *Ionize* means to add or subtract electrons in an atom. A material that is hit by radiation produces charged particles called *ions*. Because of these ions, certain types of radiation can be a health hazard.

Among the various types of ionizing radiation, the most common are alpha, beta and gamma radiation. Atoms that emit these types of radiation are said to be *radioactive*. Figure 13-20 shows the penetration of radiation.

Radiation Measurement

Several units are used to measure radiation doses. One common unit is called the *rem*, representing the radiation absorbed dose. The rem is often measured as the millirem. For example, rocks, soil, and building materials account for about 40 millirems per year exposure for the average person in the United States.

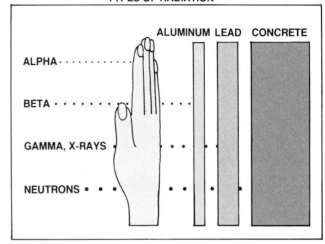

TYPES OF RADIATION

FIGURE 13-20 The penetration power of radiation. The weakest type of radiation is the alpha particles.
Courtesy of International Atomic Energy Agency

In our daily lives, we are all being bombarded by radiation in various millirem doses. For example, approximately 30% of all radiation comes from medical facilities; natural background accounts for about 68% of all radiation to a person. Other sources of radiation include fallout, occupational exposure, and miscellaneous sources which account for about 2% of all radiation exposure to humans.

Half Life

All radioactive materials have a half life. *Half life* is the time it takes for half of the radioactive material to decay. For example, refer to Figure 13-21. This

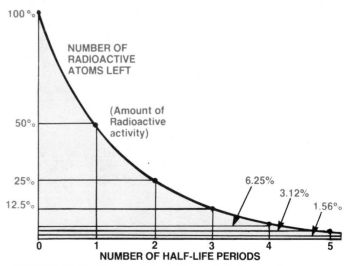

FIGURE 13-21 After each half-life period, the number of radioactive atoms is cut in half.

chart shows that after one half life, 50% of the radioactive atoms has decayed. After two half-life periods, only 25% of the original radiation is present, and so on. A half life is important because it indicates how long a certain element will be radioactive. For example, some elements have as short a half life as one minute or less. Other radioactive materials have a half life of more than 30,000 years.

TECH LINK

Half lives can be considered the opposite of exponential growth, discussed in an earlier chapter. The difference is that, rather than exponential growth, half lives can be called exponential decay. Rather than "doubling time," "halving time" is used. In any given period of time, the same percentage of decrease takes place as radioactive materials decay.

Refueling Operations

Part of the waste of a nuclear power plant is the spent or partially used fuel rods. Figure 13-22 shows an example of the spent or used-up fuel rods being replaced. This is called *refueling operations*. Refueling operations occur about every 18 months or so on a nuclear power plant. Every 18 months, the partially spent or used-up fuel rods are removed and replaced. Although there is not much mass involved with this type of nuclear waste, the rods are very radioactive.

Types of Nuclear Waste

Typically, two types of waste are by-products of using nuclear energy: low-level waste and high-level waste. Both types have radioactivity. *Low-level waste* do not contain significant amounts of long-lived isotopes. For example, half lives may be between one minute and 30 years. Example of low-level waste include tools, clothing, valves, and other maintenance items that have come in contact with the radioactive materials.

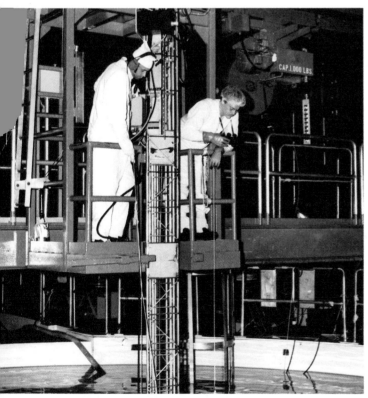

FIGURE 13-22 Spent fuel rods in a nuclear power plant must be removed and replaced every 18 months or so. *Courtesy of New York Power Authority*

FIGURE 13-23 Spent fuel rods are currently being stored in a waste pool such as this at the plant site. *Courtesy of New York Power Authority*

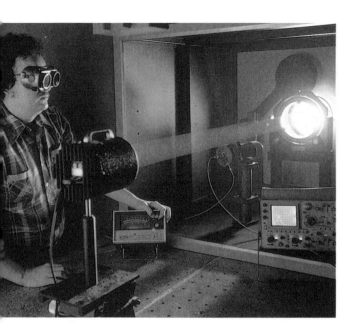

FIGURE 13-24 Lasers are currently being used to separate the isotopes of uranium for storage. *Courtesy of Department of Energy*

High-level waste has a high content of long-lived radioactive isotopes. They require long-term isolation from the environment. For example, high-level waste may have a half life of 5,000 up to 30,000 years, depending upon the isotope. Spent fuel rods are one example of high-level waste.

These wastes from power plants are currently contained within a spent fuel pool being stored temporarily at the plant sites. Figure 13-23 shows a spent fuel pool where the high-level waste is stored. These waste materials are awaiting the development of a spent fuel reprocessing plant. At present, such plants are not completed yet. However, the plan is to reprocess the spent fuel rods. The remaining fuel would be removed, while the waste would be stored in a permanent facility. It is also planned that reprocessing plants be used to upgrade the fuel for future use. These future plants are intended to serve as centralized spent fuel and nuclear waste consolidation and packaging facilities.

As part of reprocessing fuel, a significant amount of research is continuing to help separate isotopes of radioactive materials from uranium. This can be done by using a laser. Figure 13-24 shows a cylindrical, high-speed copper vapor laser. It is being used to stimulate isotopes of uranium for separation.

Nuclear Fusion

As mentioned previously, fusion is the opposite of fission. Fusion creates energy by combining molecules together to form one element. When two molecules are forced near each other under very high temperatures, they fuse together. The combined weight of the original two elements is greater than the weight of the resultant single element. Figure 13-25 shows an example of how two atoms of deuterium are fused together. As the atoms come closer together, they have a tendency to repel each other. When heat is applied (about 1,000,000°C) the two will fuse together. The technology used to achieve these temperatures is still being researched and tested.

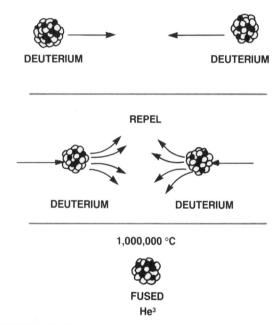

FIGURE 13-25 Fusion occurs when two deuterium atoms are forced together under very high temperatures.

Fuels for Nuclear Fusion

The fuels being considered for use in a fusion power plant are very light as compared to uranium. These fuels include deuterium and tritium. As stated previously in this chapter, both of these isotopes are heavy hydrogen atoms. Heavy hydrogen (deuterium) is found naturally in sea water. It is estimated that if nuclear fusion were ever feasible, there would be enough energy to supply our world with energy for 50 billion years.

Magnetic Fusion Reactor

Fusion energy has been researched extensively in the past few years. Although not yet technologically available, many fusion reactors have been tested. The fusion program goal is to produce useful electrical power at appropriate temperatures for a specific period of time. A fusion reactor requires a temperature of 100 million°C. A confinement time of one second has been produced.

This Tokamak Fusion Test Reactor (TFTR) will be the first magnetic fusion system in the United States. The TFTR experiment is considered to be a link between the current technology and the first experimental fusion power reactor in the future. *Courtesy of U.S. Department of Energy*

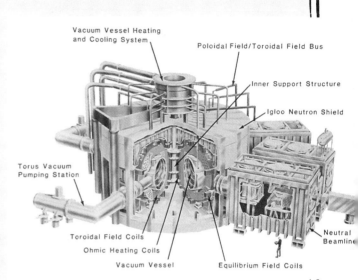

Plant Operation

Fusion nuclear plants are being tested to see if the concept actually works. Figure 13-26 shows an example of a fusion reactor. The reactor, called the Tokamak Fusion Test Reactor, was able to sustain a fusion reaction of one second. Figure 13-27 shows a particle beam fusion accelerator. It is designed to deliver at least 100 trillion watts of power for producing a fusion reaction. It has 36 pulse generators arranged in a spoke fashion around a central hub. The diameter is about 108 feet. The generators pulse electricity to a center point. For about 30 billionths of a second, the 100 trillion-watt pulse is stronger than the world's total generating power. The electrical discharges shown in the photo are a result of air breaking down at the surface of the water. It is hoped that this technology will speed the development of nuclear fusion in the future.

FIGURE 13-26 An example of a fusion reactor. *Courtesy of Department of Energy*

FIGURE 13-27 A particle beam fusion accelerator. Its pulse generators create very high temperatures (1,000,000°C) so fusion can occur. *Courtesy of Department of Energy*

Summary

- Nuclear energy will supply more electrical energy in the future.
- Although the U.S. has more plants, it is less reliant than other countries on nuclear energy.
- The price of nuclear energy is less than coal and oil, but more expensive than hydroelectric.
- Isotopes are atoms that have additional neutrons in the core.
- Nuclear energy is based upon the principle that mass can be converted into energy and energy can be converted into mass. This is called the *theory of relativity.*
- The type of nuclear energy used today is called *fission. Fusion* is now being tested to determine its feasibility.
- *Fission* is the process whereby a U-235 atom is hit by a free neutron. The atom splits and produces thermal energy.
- The nuclear fission process is controlled by inserting control rods to slow down the process.
- To prepare uranium for use in a power plant, it must first be enriched so that the chain reaction can continue.
- Any U-238 that is hit by a free neutron turns into Pu-239, which can also be used as a nuclear fuel.
- The most common types of reactors used today are the boiling water reactor and the pressurized water reactor.
- Two experimental reactors are being tested: the high-temperature gas reactor and the breeder reactor.
- Radiation from a nuclear power plant is measured in rems or millirems.
- Nuclear power plants are refueled every 18 months or so. The spent fuel rods are currently stored at the plant in a water pool.
- A nuclear power plant produces both low- and high-level waste that must be managed.
- Nuclear fusion is the process of combining two deuterium molecules which, when fused together, produce energy.
- The greatest challenge with nuclear fusion is to create the heat necessary to fuse deuterium molecules together. It takes about 1,000,000°C for this operation.

REVIEW

1. If a uranium U-234 isotope has 92 electrons, it has _____ neutrons.
2. The word fission means to _____ nuclear elements to produce energy.
3. Uranium must be _____ to about 3% to be used in a nuclear power plant.
4. Refueling a nuclear power plant takes place about every _____ .
5. A _____ is used in a nuclear power plant to transfer the heat in the primary loop to the secondary loop.
6. There are several types of common radiation, including alpha, beta and _____ radiation.
7. Explain why the United States has the most nuclear power plants, yet is less reliant on nuclear energy than other countries.
8. Describe an isotope in relation to hydrogen atoms.
9. Define the theory of relativity.
10. What is the difference between fusion and fission?
11. Describe the six stages used for processing nuclear fuel.
12. Describe how breeding fuel occurs.
13. Identify all parts of a boiling water reactor and describe how the system operates.
14. What three types of radioactive particles produce radiation?
15. Compare the differences between low- and high-level radioactive waste produced from a nuclear power plant.
16. Describe how fusion occurs. What temperature is needed for fusion?

CHAPTER ACTIVITIES

 NUCLEAR ENERGY DEBATE

INTRODUCTION

Nuclear energy is one of the more controversial energy resources being used. One way to analyze many of the issues is to debate the various concepts of nuclear energy. This activity is designed to have you debate the important concepts of nuclear energy and how they relate to our social/economic systems.

TECHNOLOGICAL LITERACY SKILLS

Creativity, technical research, group analysis, interpersonal skills.

OBJECTIVES

At the completion of this activity, you will be able to:

1. Research a particular topic dealing with nuclear energy.
2. Analyze these data and develop arguments for and against the issue.
3. Effectively debate the issue and justify your comments.

MATERIALS

1. A library from which students can obtain information about nuclear energy
2. Pencil and paper for notes
3. Nuclear Energy Debate Evaluation handout

ADDITIONAL INFORMATION

To establish a debate on nuclear energy, a difference of opinion must be evident. This can be accomplished, for example, by having one debating team approach a topic from a "consumeristic" point of view. The other debating team approaches the issue from a "capitalistic" point of view. The consumeristic viewpoint suggests "back to the basics, smaller industrial plants, decentralization, environmental emphasis, profits not important," and so forth. The capitalistic viewpoint suggests "profits, large industries, growth, and large corporations."

PROCEDURE

1. Divide the class into four equal groups. Identify them as group 1, 2, 3, and 4.
2. Group 1 will take the "consumeristic" point of view on the issue..
3. Group 2 will take the "capitalistic" point of view on the issue.
4. Group 3 will devise two-four questions about nuclear energy that can be answered by both sides. This group will also ask the questions during the debate. An example of a debate question is: "Should we as a society continue to use nuclear energy and build more plants, or should we divert money to the development of alternative forms of energy?"
5. Group 4 will evaluate the debate on the Nuclear Energy Debate Evaluation handout.
6. Time should be given in class to research and discuss the questions, and to prepare logical and justifiable answers from both points of view.

7. When both teams are ready and prepared, start the debate. The instructor should be a moderator and time checker.

8. Use the following time schedule:
   a. 3-4 minutes for Team 1 answer
   b. 3-4 minutes for Team 2 answer
   c. 1-3 minutes for Team 1 rebuttal
   d. 1-3 minutes for Team 2 rebuttal
   e. 4-5 minutes for both teams to debate and ask questions of the other team.

9. When debating, use the following guidelines:
   a. Each student should have a name tag.
   b. Role playing is encouraged during the debate. This means that the consumeristic and capitalistic groups should dress their part.
   c. Statistics should be used to justify viewpoints.

10. Group 3 should be observers during the debate.

11. Group 4 will be evaluating the debate.

12. When the debate is completed, Groups 3 and 4 exchange places with groups 1 and 2. Have a second debate so that all students have a chance to research and debate a topic on nuclear energy.

REVIEW QUESTIONS

1. What effect does nuclear energy have on our environment?

2. Is nuclear energy more or less expensive to produce electricity than other forms of fuel such as coal, oil, and natural gas?

3. If we decide to no longer build nuclear power plants, what type of energy will take its place and how much will this energy cost?

CHAPTER 14
Energy Conservation

OBJECTIVES

After reading this chapter, you will be able to:

■ State the major principles of how to save energy in any system, including heat loss, gain, and other thermal properties.

■ Examine methods used to save energy in the commercial sector of society.

■ Describe the most common methods used to save energy in the residential sector of society, and identify the use of several energy-saving appliances.

■ Cite several tips on how to save energy in the transportation sector of society.

KEY TERMS

Kilocalorie	Degree Days	Caulking
Heating Unit	Median	Sill
Heat Loss	Payback	Threshold
R Value	Infiltration	Setback Thermostat
U Value	Superinsulated Home	Flue
Coefficient	Attic Ventilators	Bimetal

Introduction

Energy problems in our society can be solved in many ways. One method is to educate people who use energy to practice energy conservation techniques. In the past few years, energy conservation practices have improved. In some cases, certain states even showed a reduction in energy usage by improved energy conservation practices. As indicated in a previous chapter, approximately 50% of all energy is being wasted. This suggests that there is a great need to conserve or save energy. There have been many technologies as well as behavior changes made to help save energy. This chapter looks at many of the accepted methods and techniques used to save energy in the transportation, residential, and commercial energy sectors.

Fuel Cells

Many technologies have been designed to save the existing fuels in use today. One such method is to create energy by using fuel cells. A fuel cell is an electrical-type power plant that uses hydrogen, carbon dioxide, and oxygen to produce electrical power. Hydrogen, carbon dioxide, and oxygen are extremely abundant elements in our environment for creating fuels. Fuel cells have been used as a power source in spacecraft for several years.

This 4.8 megawatt fuel cell power plant contains a fuel processor for enriching hydrocarbon fuels with hydrogen. This type of power plant is also suited to urban and other densely populated areas. It is modular in design, easy to transport by truck, and easily assembled in a small area. A great deal of research data from the space program has been transferred to such units to study them for commercial use. If found practical and economically advantageous, fuel cells could help reduce our reliance on fossil fuels in the future. *Courtesy of U.S. Department of Energy*

Principles of Energy Conservation

Need for Energy Conservation

The need for energy conservation increases every day. The balance between energy supply and demand is very critical. One method used to keep the two in balance is to educate society to reduce its demand for energy. This is not easy for people to accept. To use less energy requires a certain amount of behavior change for each individual. At present, our total society is wasting about 50% of all its available energy, Figure 14-1. Of course, a certain amount of this loss is due to entropy or energy becoming more random. However, much of this energy can actually be saved.

FIGURE 14-1 Our society wastes approximately one-half or 50% of all its available energy.

Human Values and Energy Conservation

The United States is considered to have about 16% of the world's population. However, U.S. citizens use about 33% of the world's energy supply. Part of this amount is used to produce goods and services for underdeveloped countries. Nevertheless, the U.S. still uses more energy per person than any other

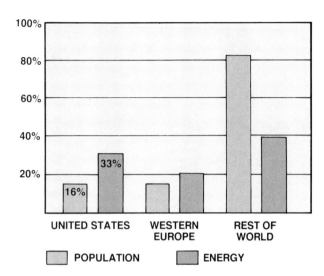

FIGURE 14-2 The United States uses about 33% of the world's energy, having only 16% of the world's population. Other countries use much less energy for greater populations.

TECH L I N K

Each individual in a home can reduce heat losses in a home by:

1. Opening the curtains on south-facing windows of a home to gain solar heat during sunny days.
2. Closing the curtains on all windows during the nighttime to eliminate heat losses.
3. Closing the curtains on north-facing windows during the day to reduce heat losses.
4. Keeping all doors closed whenever possible to eliminate large amounts of infiltration.
5. Looking for frost buildup inside the home during extremely cold days and nights. This indicates infiltration is occurring at that point.

country, as shown in Figure 14-2.

For example, let's assume that all of a person's activities with energy use oil. If this were the case, each person would consume about 7 gallons of oil every day to live. This includes energy used for transportation, food, recreation, heating, manufacturing, and others. By contrast, people in many parts of Africa use only about .7 gallons each day. As indicated by the amount of energy being used, people in the United States have become increasingly materialistic.

To change this imbalance, individual human values must be changed. To change values, a strong education is needed. In the future, all citizens must be educated to conserve energy on the systems that are so often being misused. When the basic values of a society change, then and only then will that society realize the tremendous need for saving more energy.

Thermal Energy Measurement

In the study of energy conservation, several units are used to describe the quantity of thermal energy. These units include Btu, calories, and heating units. The Btu stands for British thermal unit. One *Btu* is the amount of thermal energy used to raise one pound of water one degree Fahrenheit. A wooden match, if burned completely, will produce about one Btu, Figure 14-3. Normally a residential dwelling takes about 20,000 Btu per hour to heat on a cold winter day. A natural gas furnace that runs for one hour may produce about 100,000 Btu.

A calorie is the metric heating unit. One *calorie* is the amount of thermal energy needed to raise one gram of water one degree Celsius. Because a calorie is such a small unit, the *kilocalorie* (kcal) is quite often used as the base unit. One kilocalorie equals 1,000 calories. Normally, 1 Btu is equal to about 252 calories.

When measuring larger amounts of thermal energy, often the heating unit can be used. One *heating unit* is equal to 100,000 Btu. Figure 14-4 shows four types of energy and the amount of each necessary to produce one heating unit. For example, 15 pounds of coal or 1 gallon of oil will produce 100,000 Btu. Heating unit measurements are often used to show the amount of heat lost from a residential building.

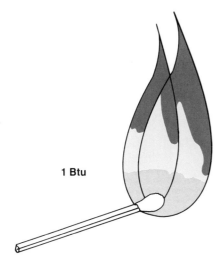

FIGURE 14-3 If one wood match were burned from end to end, approximately one Btu of thermal energy would be created.

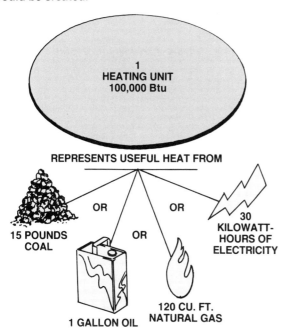

FIGURE 14-4 One heating unit can be produced from four different types of fuel.

including fossil fuels, cooking with electricity, wood stoves, solar gain, and others. Generally, the heat loss and the heat gain must be equal to keep the temperature inside the dwelling constant. It is evident that one goal of energy conservation would be to minimize heat loss as much as possible.

Several factors affect the amount of heat loss in a building. These include:

1. The amount of wind — the higher the wind outside, the greater the heat loss.
2. The temperature difference between the inside and outside of the building — the greater the difference, the greater the amount of heat loss.
3. The type of materials used in walls and ceilings of the building — the greater resistance to heat flow, the less heat loss.

Figure 14-5 shows an example of various heat losses that may occur in a typical home. For example, approximately 25-35% of the home's heat is lost through the roof. The windows and doors lose about 20-30%. About 20-30% is lost through the walls. About 15-20% is lost through the chimney and other vents. About 3-5% is lost through the floor to the cold outside ground.

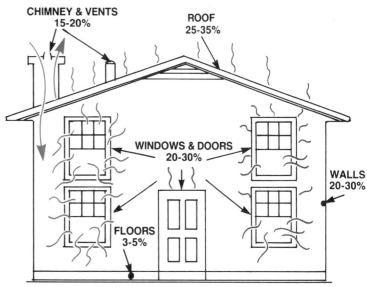

FIGURE 14-5 Average heat loss percentages from various parts of a home.

Heat Loss and Heat Gain

The expressions heat loss and heat gain are used in the study of energy conservation. *Heat loss* is defined as the amount of thermal energy in a building lost to the outside air. *Heat gain* is defined as the amount of thermal energy being put into the building. This input can be from any energy resource,

Direction of Heat Flow

When studying energy conservation, it should again be noted that thermal energy always flows from a warmer to a colder material. This can be shown by standing near a large window on a cold day. It appears that the air is cooler by the window. This suggests that the cool air has come in through the window. Actually, thermal energy has conducted from the inside to the outside of the window. There is now an absence of thermal energy near the window, as shown in Figure 14-6.

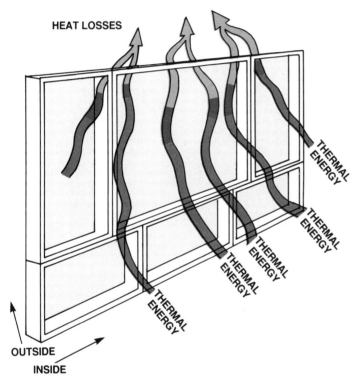

FIGURE 14-6 Heat losses occur near windows. Actually, the thermal energy is being conducted from the warmer air inside the building, through the windows, to the colder air outside.

R and U Values

The R value and the U value are two units commonly used to measure the actual amount of thermal energy during heat loss.

The R value of a material is a unit that measures the resistance to heat flow for a particular material. All manufacturers normally indicate the R value for any material used for insulation. Generally, the

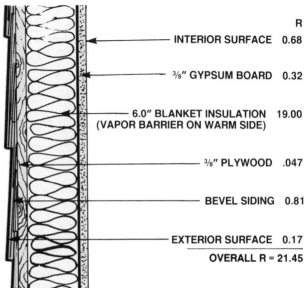

	R
INTERIOR SURFACE	0.68
⅜″ GYPSUM BOARD	0.32
6.0″ BLANKET INSULATION (VAPOR BARRIER ON WARM SIDE)	19.00
⅜″ PLYWOOD	.047
BEVEL SIDING	0.81
EXTERIOR SURFACE	0.17
OVERALL R =	21.45

FIGURE 14-7 This six-inch wall has a total R value of 21.45.

higher the R value, the greater the resistance to heat flow. Figure 14-7 shows an example of various materials used in a six-inch wall and the R value for each. Figure 14-8 shows R values for different types of building materials.

The U value is defined as the *coefficient* or opposite of R value. The lower the U value, the better the insulation quality. U values are needed to help determine the amount of heat loss in a building, an important consideration in energy conservation. The U value indicates the amount of heat flow through an entire assembly. For example, referring to Figure 14-9, the ceiling shown has a total R value of 39.03. The R value for each material has been added together to get the total R value for the ceiling. To calculate the U value of this wall use the formula:

$$U \text{ value} = \frac{1}{R} \text{ value}$$

$$U \text{ value} = \frac{1}{39.03}$$

$$U \text{ value} = .0256$$

Normally, one square foot of space is used for determining heat losses. This means that the ceiling

R-VALUES OF DIFFERENT KINDS OF INSULATION	R/Inch	Inches Needed For					
Loose Fill — Machine Blown		R11	R19	R22	R34	R38	R49
Fiberglass	R2.25	5	8.5	10	15.5	17	22
Mineral Wool	R3.125	3.5	6	7	11	12.5	16
Cellulose	R3.7	3	5.5	6	9.5	10.5	13.5
Loose Fill — Hand Poured							
Cellulose	R3.7	3	5.5	6	9.5	10.5	13.5
Mineral Wool	R3.125	3.5	6	7	11	12.5	16
Fiberglass	R2.25	5	8.5	10	15.5	17	22
Vermiculite	R2.1	5.5	9	10.5	16.5	18	23.5
Batts or Blankets							
Fiberglass	R3.14	3.5	6	7	11	12.5	16
Mineral Wool	R3.14	3.5	6	7	11	12.5	16
Rigid Board							
Polystyrene Beadboard	R.36	3	5.5	6.5	9.5	10.5	14
Extruded Polystyrene (Styrofoam)	R4-5.41	3-2	5-3.5	5.5-4	8.5-6.5	9.5-7	12.5-9
Urethane	R6.2	2	3	3.5	5.5	6.5	8
Fiberglass	R4.0	3	5	8.5	8.5	9.5	12.5
Liquid Foam Urea-Formaldehyde	R4.8 (35°F)	2.5	4	4.5	7	8	10.5

FIGURE 14-8 This chart shows different types of insulation materials, the R value per inch, and the amount of insulation needed for specific total R values. *Courtesy of Northern States Power Company*

shown in Figure 14-9 will transfer .0256 Btu for each square foot of ceiling. Heat loss is measured in Btu/sq.ft/hr/°F. In the ceiling example, the heat loss is then stated as .0256 Btu/sq.ft/hr/°F difference across the ceiling.

If the temperature difference across the ceiling at a particular time of day is 40°F (65°F inside and 25°F outside) then the exact amount of heat loss can be determined. This is done by multiplying the U value by the temperature difference. Thus:

Heat Loss = U value times the temperature difference.
Heat Loss = .0256 × 40°F
Heat Loss = 1.024 Btu/sq.ft/hr

Thus, a ceiling that has an R value of 39.03 and a U value of .0256, will transfer 1.024 Btu for each square foot of material, each hour, when there is a 40°F temperature differential. If the total ceiling area is equal to 1,120 square feet, the total heat loss per hour on the ceiling is 1,146.88 Btu (1,120 × 1.024).

TYPICAL
CEILING SECTION

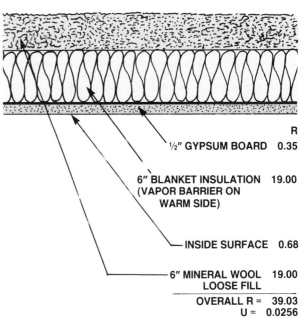

	R
½″ GYPSUM BOARD	0.35
6″ BLANKET INSULATION (VAPOR BARRIER ON WARM SIDE)	19.00
INSIDE SURFACE	0.68
6″ MINERAL WOOL LOOSE FILL	19.00
OVERALL R =	39.03
U =	0.0256

FIGURE 14-9 This ceiling has a total R value of 39.03. The U value is equal to .0256 (one divided by the total R value).

TECH L I N K

When measuring heat loss in buildings, at times the k value is needed. The *k value* is defined as the thermal conductivity of a material. It is measured in Btu per hour per square foot per Fahrenheit degree difference across the material per inch of thickness. Examples of various materials and their conductivity, determined in a laboratory situation, include:

Hardboard . . . . (.73)
Glass Fiber . . . . (.25)
Particle board . . . . (.94)
Polystyrene . . . . (.20)

In this example, particle board will conduct the greatest amount of thermal energy, whereas polystyrene will conduct the least amount of thermal energy.

Recommended R Values for Buildings

A recommended amount of insulation is required throughout the United States. Figure 14-10 shows a map indicating insulation R values for ceilings, walls, and floors. These figures are minimum R values. For instance, in northern regions, although R-38 is recommended in the ceiling, most homes have up to R-60.

The maximum amount of insulation is mostly determined by the price of existing fuels. As fossil fuel prices increase, more insulation can be used. For example, if fuel prices increase, payback for adding insulation decreases. Thus, more insulation could be added. When prices of fossil fuels were low many years ago, maximum insulation was about R-17. However, as fossil fuel prices increased over the years, the maximum amount of insulation increased to today's standards.

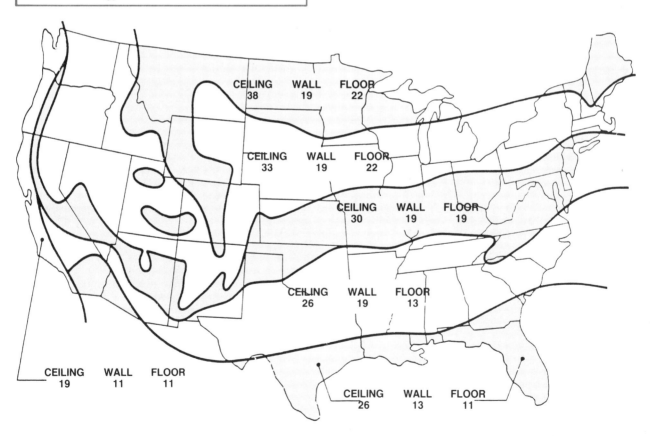

FIGURE 14-10 This map shows the recommended insulation R values for various parts of the United States.
Courtesy of Owens/Corning Fiberglas Corporation

Degree Day

When comparing heating bills from one year to another, quite often the severity of the weather may vary. One method used to help determine the severity of the winter is by using degree days. These can be both heating degree days and cooling degree days. Heating degree days are available from most national weather stations. The *degree day* is the difference between a fixed, set-temperature (65°F) and the daily median temperature, Normally, a home requires no heating or cooling if the temperature is 65°F. The heating degree days for each day are added together throughout the heating season. The formula used is:

$$\text{Degree Day} = 65°F - \frac{\text{High + Low Temperature}}{2}$$

For example, if the high temperature of the day was 55°F and the low temperature of the day was 15°F, 30 heating degrees would have been accumulated. Figure 14-11 shows a table with the average heating degree days for selected cities. Other cities throughout the United States also have data available for degree days.

HEATING DEGREE DAYS

CITY/STATE	TEMP
DENVER, COLO	6283
DAYTONA BEACH, FLORIDA	879
PORTLAND, MAINE	7511
BALTIMORE, MARYLAND	4654
MINNEAPOLIS, MINN	8382
LAS VEGAS, NEV	2709
NEW YORK, NEW YORK	4471
SEATTLE, WASHINGTON	4424

FIGURE 14-11 This table shows a number of selected cities and their seasonal heating degree days.

Payback Periods

In the study of energy conservation, many decisions are made based upon the payback of the item. *Payback* is defined as the amount of time in heating seasons (or years) it takes for the savings in energy to pay off the initial cost. Normally, as the price of fossil fuels increases, the payback period will decrease in years. Another way to define payback is by stating it as a formula, as shown in Figure 14-12.

For example, the payback period could be calculated if more insulation were put into the ceiling of a home. Let's say the cost of more insulation is $600.00. The total heating cost per year

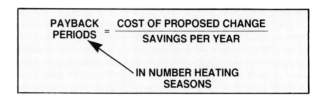

$$\text{PAYBACK PERIODS} = \frac{\text{COST OF PROPOSED CHANGE}}{\text{SAVINGS PER YEAR}}$$

IN NUMBER HEATING SEASONS

FIGURE 14-12 Payback on any energy conservation technology is found by dividing the original cost of the item by the savings per year.

saved by the increase in insulation is $150.00. When the cost of the insulation is divided by the savings each year, the payback is four heating seasons. This means that the initial cost would be paid back after four heating seasons. After four years, $150.00 will be saved each heating season.

Infiltration

Infiltration is one source of heat loss in many homes. *Infiltration* is defined as the process that occurs when cold air from outside enters a building through cracks, windows, doors, and foundations. This is caused by the *chimney effect*, Figure 14-13. As warm air rises and escapes due to convection, cold air is drawn in. The cold air must be heated to the room temperature to keep the comfort level constant in the home. Wind also has a tendency to increase infiltration.

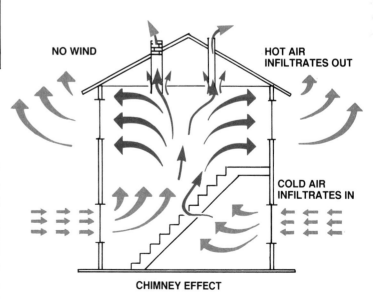

FIGURE 14-13 Infiltration in a home due to the chimney effect. Warm air rises and escapes past and through all vents in the roof causing cold air to be drawn in.

All buildings continually exchange inside air with the outside air during the winter months. Outside air leaks in, and inside air leaks out. Infiltration is usually measured as the number of air changes per hour. The minimum is one-half air change per hour. However, most buildings have much more than this. Typical "loose" homes may have from two to three complete air changes per hour due to infiltration. On the other hand, if a home is too tight, say one-quarter air change per hour, the home may be a health hazard. The home may lack oxygen, causing illness, nausea, and, in some cases, death. Several documented cases have shown highly insulated homes may actually not have enough air for normal living conditions.

Outside Air for Combustion

One of the greatest causes of infiltration is the use of oxygen inside the home for combustion. Several household appliances require oxygen. These include furnaces, water heaters, wood-burning stoves, fireplaces, and clothes dryers. Each time a cubic foot of air is burned and exhausted outside, a new, cold, cubic foot of air must enter the home by infiltration. To offset this heat loss, all appliances that use air for combustion should use outside air. Although not practical for all appliances, the more outside air that is used, the less heat loss that occurs. Figure 14-14 shows outside air used for combustion in a natural gas furnace.

Humidity in Homes and Buildings

Humidity is a very important factor in heating homes. When the level of humidity in a home is correct, the temperature can be lowered. The higher the humidity, the greater the comfort level. In fact, because it is more comfortable, the thermostat can be lowered to save energy. A properly humidified home usually is as comfortable at 68 degrees as a dry home is at 72 degrees.

Two factors cause the comfort level to increase with humidity. First, dry air without humidity absorbs moisture from the skin at a more rapid rate. This produces a chilling effect. On the other hand, high humidity helps a body to hold heat better. Second, thermal energy is transferred more easily through moist air. The dryer the air, the more difficult it is to transfer heat. To provide humidity in a home, a humidifier is a good investment. Typic-

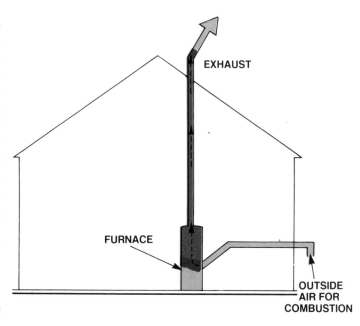

FIGURE 14-14. Whenever possible, outside air for combustion should be used for furnaces, fireplaces, wood-burning stoves, water heaters, and dryers.

ally, humidifiers have a payback in the range of three to four years.

Energy Conservation-Residential/ Commercial Sector

Attic Ventilation

Many techniques and appliances can help save energy within the residential and commercial sectors of society. One such device is called an attic ventilator. This device removes air in the attic area of a building. Normally, energy is saved by cooling the attic in the summer months. This will help to reduce the amount of air-conditioning cost. Figure 14-15 shows the effects of using an attic ventilator. When a ventilator is not used, the attic becomes very hot during the day. This heat conducts down into the rooms below, keeping them very warm at night. When an attic ventilator is used, the hot air is removed. This helps keep the rooms cooler in the evening hours.

Many types of attic ventilators are available. Certain types remove excess heat; others remove excess moisture. Control of both these conditions is very important for correct home operation. There should be at least one square foot of ventilation

WITHOUT
VENTILATOR

WITH
VENTILATOR

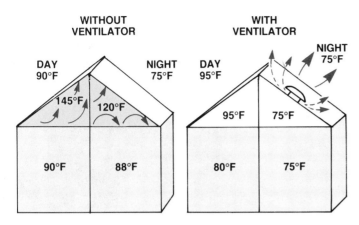

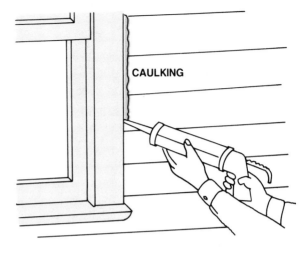

CAULKING

FIGURE 14-15 An attic ventilator cools the air in the attic during the summer. This helps to reduce air-conditioning costs.

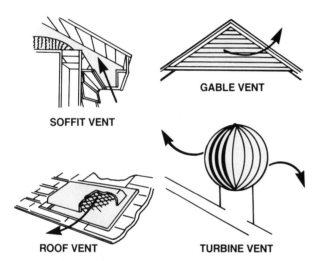

SOFFIT VENT

GABLE VENT

ROOF VENT

TURBINE VENT

FIGURE 14-16 Examples of attic ventilation systems used in various buildings.

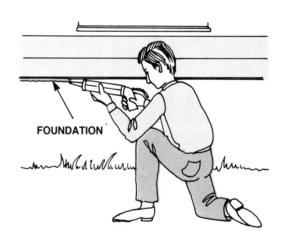

FOUNDATION

FIGURE 14-17 Caulking various cracks in a building can help reduce infiltration significantly.

area for each 150 square feet of roof space. Figure 14-16 shows examples of attic ventilation systems used in various buildings.

Caulking

Caulking the home or commercial building can reduce infiltration to a great degree. There are many types of commercial caulking materials. With an inexpensive caulking gun, a good caulking compound and a putty knife, one can seal a home in a few hours. Areas that may need caulking are:

■ Joints between windows and frames, Figure 14-17.
■ Between window and door drip caps and siding.
■ Joints between door frame and siding.

■ Sills where the wood structure meets the foundation, as shown in Figure 14-17.
■ Between windowsills and siding.
■ Around water faucets.
■ Where the chimney and main body of the house meet.
■ At corners formed by siding.

Many leaks in a home are also caused by openings made to install bathroom vents, lights, and other features. All pipes, tubes, electrical service areas and vents should be adequately caulked to help eliminate infiltration.

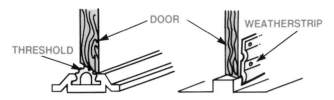

FIGURE 14-18 The threshold at each door should be checked for damage. Adequate weatherstripping should be put on all doors to eliminate infiltration.

Weatherstripping

Most doors have a rubber seal at their base, also called the *threshold,* Figure 14-18. However, many windows and doors can use additional weatherstripping. For example, make sure that all windows and doors are completely sealed with the correct type of weatherstripping.

The most common types of weatherstripping include: felt strips, foam rubber, flexible vinyl, and spring bronze.

FIGURE 14-19 Many types of insulation are used in a building. Some have a paper backing, others have foil, and some may be filled with rigid board or use blown-in wood. *Courtesy of Owens/Corning Fiberglas Corporation*

Insulation

Many types of insulation are used in homes today. *Insulation* is used to reduce the heat losses in various parts of the home or commercial building. Many areas should be checked for the correct amounts of insulation. Make sure to check:

■ The ceiling.

■ The walls.

■ Concrete basement walls.

■ Around wall outlets.

■ Any unfinished attic floors.

■ The perimeter basement ceiling between the joists.

■ Any crawl spaces.

Figure 14-19 shows various types of insulation commonly used in a building. These types of insulation are used to control both thermal and sound energy.

Setback Thermostats

A setback thermostat is another good energy conservation device. Setback thermostats can be considered part of the "feedback" or "control" loop on the systems model used to study technology. Thermostats adjust the times at which a furnace turns on and off.

This type of themostat is used to set back the temperature of the dwelling during periods when heat is not needed. The times heat is not usually needed include during periods of sleeping or extended absence, or when no one is home during the day.

Figure 14-20 shows selected cities and the amount of setback savings. The chart is read for both 5°F setback and 10°F setback. Setback times are usually stated for an 8-hour period. Normally, a 10°F setback for an 8-hour period will save about 10% of a monthly energy bill.

SET-BACK SAVINGS

CITY	5°F	10°F
BOSTON, MA	7	11
CINCINNATI, OH	8	12
DALLAS, TX	11	15
DENVER, CO	7	11
LOS ANGELES, CA	12	16
MINNEAPOLIS, MN	5	9
NEW YORK, NY	8	12
SALT LAKE CITY, UT	7	11
WASHINGTON, DC	9	13

FIGURE 14-20 The percentage of savings is shown when the thermostat is set back either 5°F or 10°F.

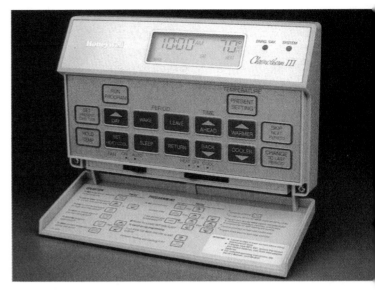

FIGURE 14-21 This setback thermostat sets the furnace temperature back at predetermined times throughout a 24-hour period. *Courtesy of Honeywell, Inc.*

Figure 14-21 shows an example of a typical setback thermostat. Two types are the mechanical and electronic setback thermostats. During installation, the regular thermostat is replaced with the setback thermostat.

Flue Dampers

In any furnace or water heater, a certain amount of heated air convects and escapes through the flue. Some companies estimate that approximately 10 to 20% of the heat in a building goes up a flue when the appliance is shut off, Figure 14-22. A *flue*

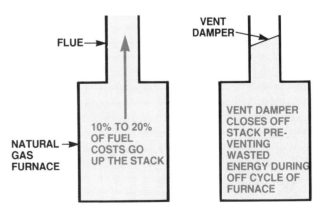

FIGURE 14-22 Flue dampers save energy by closing off the vent when the furnace is not operating. This saves 10 to 20% of the fuel costs.

damper is used to close the flue and stop the loss of heat. Flue dampers are often used on furnaces and water heaters.

Figure 14-23 shows the operation of a typical flue damper. When there is no heat from the appliance in the flue, the damper closes and reduces heat losses. When the appliance turns on, the exhaust heat from the appliance heats a bimetallic coil. As the bimetallic coil expands, it causes the vent to open, allowing exhaust gases to escape. When the appliance shuts off, the temperature is removed from the bimetallic coil. This causes the vent to close again, preventing or reducing heat losses.

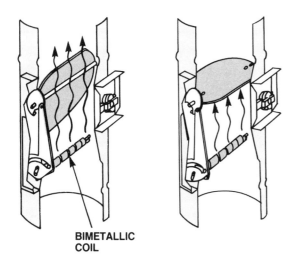

FIGURE 14-23 This flue damper automatically closes the flue vent during the off cycle, preventing wasted energy. *Courtesy of Hy-Temp Manufacturing, Inc.*

Air-to-air Heat Exchangers

As homes are designed to reduce infiltration, they become much tighter. This causes fewer air changes per hour to occur. Lack of fresh air can cause health problems. Whenever cold fresh air is allowed to come into a dwelling, the result is wasted energy and higher energy costs. To offset this problem, air-to-air heat exchangers are being used. Although mostly used in commercial buildings to reduce heat losses, more homes are using them each year.

Figure 14-24 shows how heat loss is reduced while fresh air is entering the building. Air at a temperature of 72°F enters the heat exchanger and is exhausted. Fresh air from outside at 20°F is

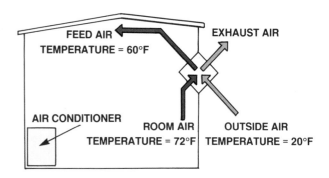

FIGURE 14-24 Air-to-air heat exchangers are used to bring in fresh air without losing thermal energy in the process.

heated by the heat exchanger before it comes into the home. The air now entering the home is 60°F rather than 20°F. Notice that there is very little heat loss, while still allowing fresh air to enter the building.

Dryer Vents

Most homes today have a clothes dryer. Normally, the dryer uses either electrical energy or natural gas. The exhaust of this appliance can become a very good heat source for most homes. Typically, when

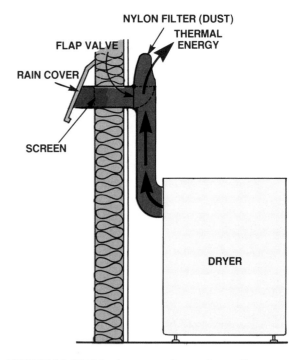

FIGURE 14-25 This dryer vent is used to redirect thermal energy from the dryer back into the room.

the dryer is in operation, the exhaust is sent outside and wasted. The exhaust usually has two major properties: moisture and thermal energy.

A dryer vent is used to redirect the dryer exhaust back into the building, Figure 14-25. Both the recaptured thermal energy and the moisture are excellent for improving energy efficiency in a home.

Insulating the Water Heater and Pipes

Normally, it pays to insulate the water heater and pipes in any home or building that uses hot water. Typical paybacks are from one to three years. Make sure to wrap all hot-water pipes with insulation. In addition, both electric and natural gas water heaters should be insulated if the heater feels warm to the touch. Figure 14-26 shows both types of water heaters and a hot-water pipe wrapped in an insulation blanket.

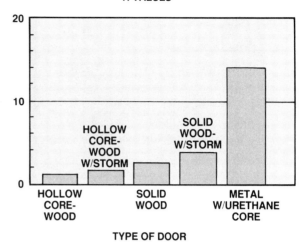

FIGURE 14-27 External doors on buildings can be a great source of heat loss. Always use a door with the maximum amount of R value.

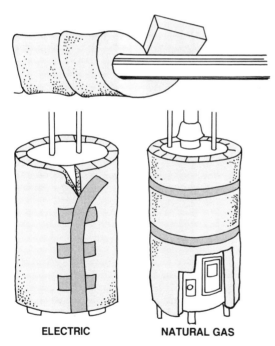

FIGURE 14-26 Hot-water pipes and the hot-water heater should be adequately wrapped in insulation.

Air-lock Entry

An air-lock entry is another technique for saving energy in both commercial buildings and residential homes. Its purpose is to keep out cold air in the winter when the doors are opened. The air lock uses two doors for people to pass through. By using two doors, infiltration is reduced; thus, heat loss can be reduced significantly. In addition, different types of outside doors have different R values, as shown in Figure 14-27. An external door should always have insulation inside.

Energy Conservation Tips

Individuals can conserve energy in many ways. The following are some of the more important techniques a person can use:

1. Dust all light bulbs regularly.
2. Switch lights off when not in use.
3. Use larger-wattage bulbs in lamps; they are more efficient.
4. Reduce the temperature in the home to 68°F.
5. Close off heating vents in rooms that are not used.
6. Close drapes at night to eliminate heat loss through windows.
7. Replace furnace filters regularly.
8. Wash and dry only full loads of laundry.
9. Install flow restrictors on faucets and showers.
10. Fill refrigerators and freezers to capacity; they operate at maximum efficiency when full.

Energy Conservation — Transportation Sector

Transportation Tips

Most of the energy conservation techniques in the transportation sector depend upon the individual. The following is a list of suggestions that help to save energy in the transportation sector.

1. Have automobiles professionally tuned. Special attention should be given to cleaning oil filters and air filters. A dirty air filter can reduce gasoline mileage by 10%.

2. Inflate automobile tires to the recommended pressure. A pressure of 1 to 2 pounds above the recommended level may also have advantages on long trips, provided the maximum rating is not exceeded.

3. Remove all excess baggage from the trunk. For each 400 pounds, the gasoline mileage goes down by one mile per gallon. If a new car is purchased, remember that the lighter the car the better the gasoline mileage.

4. Do not idle the engine for more than one minute. When the engine is at idle, the gasoline mileage is zero.

5. Accelerate and brake gradually. A good method of accelerating correctly is to imagine that an egg is between the foot and the accelerator. During slow acceleration, gasoline mileage can be improved by 50%.

6. Combine several small errands into one single trip. Take friends and neighbors along if you can. Short-distance driving can use 70% more gasoline than highway driving.

7. Consider a set of radial tires if tires need to be purchased. Radial tires increase gasoline mileage by 6%.

8. Drive at the correct speed posted on the highway. Figure 14-28 shows the effect on gasoline mileage when driving either too slow or too fast. The most efficient speed is from 45 to 50 mph.

9. Consider using mass transportation such as a bus or a train.

10. Use carpooling whenever possible for saving energy. Unfortunately, most people still prefer to drive to work alone. However, carpooling is generally increasing in use.

11. Stay in as high a gear as possible. Keep the r/min of the engine as low as possible.

12. Use cruise control if possible.

13. Keep the brakes of the vehicle correctly adjusted. Brakes that are set too tight increase fuel consumption, and wear will also occur.

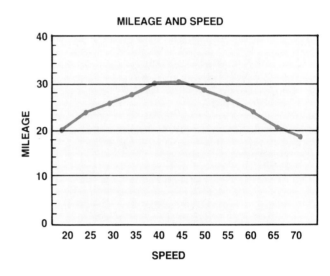

FIGURE 14-28 Gasoline mileage is directly affected by the speed of the vehicle.

Summary

- One of the best ways to keep the supply and demand of energy equal is to conserve energy, thus reducing the demand.

- In order for energy conservationn to work effectively, the behavior of each individual must change. Behavior is changed by education and, thereby, changing one's values.

- Thermal energy units include the Btu, calorie, and heating unit.

- One major principle of energy conservation is to reduce heat losses in buildings.

- The majority of heat loss in a home is through the roof.

- Heat always flows from a warmer to a colder material.

- Both R and U values are used to determine the amount of insulation and heat losses.

- When insulation is being added to a building, always put in at least the minimum amount recommended.

- Degree days help to determine the severity of weather.
- Payback periods are used to determine if an energy conservation improvement is worthwhile.
- Infiltration occurs when cold air is drawn into a building and then must be heated.
- One of the most energy effective ways to reduce infiltration is by using outside air for combustion.
- Humidity levels in a home should always be carefully maintained, which, in turn, will help to conserve energy.
- Attic ventilators are used to remove excess heat in the attic area and to give proper ventilation as well.
- Caulking a building with the correct type of caulking material can help to reduce infiltration.
- Always make sure doors and windows have adequate weatherstripping to eliminate infiltration.
- Insulation should be placed in all parts of the home, including the ceiling, walls, crawl space, and basement.

- Setback thermostats reduce energy consumption if set back for a period of 8 hours.
- Flue dampers are used to eliminate naturally rising warm air through vents and exhaust pipes.
- Air-to-air heat exchangers are used to bring in fresh air to a building without causing heat losses.
- Dryer vents are used to capture lost heat when drying clothes.
- Water heaters and hot-water pipes should be insulated for maximum efficiency.
- Many buildings are using air-lock entries to help reduce infiltration when doors are opened and closed.
- Some energy conservation tips for individuals include dusting light bulbs, using only full loads on appliances, and closing off heat to unoccupied rooms.
- Energy conservation tips in the transportation sector include keeping cars tuned properly, keeping the car as lightweight as possible, not idling the car for more than one minute, and combining several trips into one.

REVIEW

1. A natural gas furnace runs for 20 minutes of each hour. The Btu rating of the furnace is 120,000 Btu/hour. This home requires _____ Btu to operate during the day.

2. A wall in a building has an R value of 28.9. The U value is equal to _____ .

3. A temperature difference across a wall equals 42 degrees. The U value of the wall is .029. The heat loss is _____ Btu/sq.ft/hour.

4. The high temperature of a winter day was 48°F. The low temperature of that day was 15°F. The number of heating degree days for this day was _____ .

5. _____ are devices used to control the furnace to operate only at certain times of the day.

6. The lack of fresh air in highly insulated homes can be improved by the addition of an _____ .

7. For each _____ pounds transported in a vehicle, gasoline mileage drops by _____ mile per gallon.

8. What is the relationship between supply and demand and energy conservation?

9. Define three thermal energy units used to measure energy.

10. What is the relationship between heat loss and heat gain?

11. What four factors cause an increase in heat losses?

12. What is the difference between R values and U values?

13. Define the term *heating degree day.*

14. State at least four ways that will cause infiltration to increase.

15. What is the relationship between humidity and comfort level?

16. Identify four areas in a home that should be checked to see if they need caulking.

17. Describe how a setback thermostat works.

18. Describe the operation of a flue damper.

19. List three items that can be added to a home to save energy.

20. List at least four factors that can help save energy in the transportation sector of society.

CHAPTER ACTIVITIES

 HEAT EXCHANGERS

INTRODUCTION

Many types of heat exchangers are used in energy equipment. For example, air conditioners, heat pumps, solar collection systems, and so forth all use heat exchangers. Heat exchangers are used to transfer thermal energy from one substance to another. This activity is designed to test how a liquid-to-air heat exchanger operates.

TECHNOLOGICAL LITERACY SKILLS

Data collection, data analysis, instrumentation usage.

OBJECTIVES

At the completion of this activity, you will be able to:
1. Measure the temperature difference across a liquid-to-air heat exchanger.
2. Measure how flow rate affects the heat exchanger operation.

MATERIALS

1. A demonstration model heat exchanger
2. A hot water source, such as a faucet
3. An electronic temperature indicator
4. Heat Exchanger handout

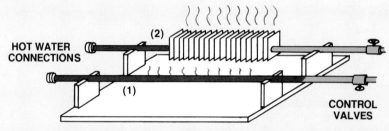

HOT WATER
CONNECTIONS

(2)

(1)

CONTROL
VALVES

FIGURE 14-29 An example of a liquid-to-air heat exchanger used in the laboratory activity.

PROCEDURE

1. Without the use of heat exchanger, turn on the hot water and measure its temperature. This is the input temperature and should remain constant. Record it on the Heat Exchanger handout.
2. See Figure 14-29 for an example of the demonstration model heat exchanger. Hook-up the model heat exchanger provided by the instructor to tube 1.
3. Turn the control valve to allow only a small amount of water to flow through the tube.
4. Measure the temperature output by placing the electronic thermometer probe on the output tube. Record it on the handout.
5. Determine the drop in water temperature across the tube from input to output. Record it on the handout.
6. Measure the radiant temperature approximately two inches above the tube and record it on the handout.
7. Now repeat steps 3 through 6 using tube 2 (with baffles) and record on the handout.
8. Now repeat steps 3 through 7 using a high flow rate of water. Record on the handout.

REVIEW QUESTIONS

1. Which tube, with or without baffles, gives up the greatest amount of heat?
2. What happens to the heat exchange process if the water flow is increased?
3. How could more heat be exchanged in the liquid-to-air heat exchanger?

 TESTING INSULATION

INTRODUCTION

Many types of insulation are used today to conserve energy. This activity is designed to have the student test and compare different types of insulation in the laboratory.

TECHNOLOGICAL LITERACY SKILLS

Problem solving, creativity, data analysis, data collection, predicting.

OBJECTIVES

At the completion of this activity you will be able to:
1. Measure the thermal energy transferred through different forms of commercial insulation.
2. Identify the best type of insulation to use.
3. Plot temperatures on both sides of a section of insulation.

MATERIALS

1. Two electronic temperature indicators
2. Heat loss testing unit
3. Electrical power to operate heaters in the demonstration model heat loss unit.
4. Testing Insulation handout (pages 1 and 2).
5. At least three different insulation types.
6. Plotting paper or computer "plotting" program.

ADDITIONAL INFORMATION

In this activity, you will be testing different types of insulation in a heat loss tester. The heat loss testing unit is shown in Figure 14-30. Heaters are used to produce thermal energy on one side of the insulation being tested. The entire testing section is surrounded by rigid foam insulation. When the heaters are turned on, the "hot side" will increase in temperature. The "cold side" will keep relatively cool.

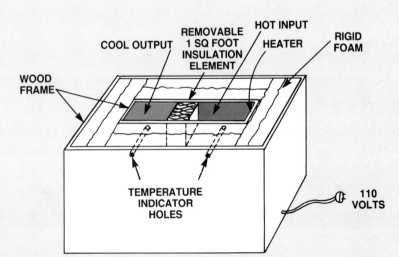

FIGURE 14-30 Heat loss testing unit. When an insulation element is placed in the center of this test box, the amount of heat transferred through it can be calculated.

PROCEDURE

1. During this activity, you will be taking readings over a period of time. Typically, readings should be taken every 15 minutes over a one- to two-hour period of time. Plan accordingly.
2. Remove the one square foot insulation element. Place your first type of insulation to be tested into the removed element and replace it in the heat loss tester.
3. Place the cover on the heat loss tester.
4. Turn on the electric heaters.
5. Every 15 minutes, take input and output temperature readings using the temperature indicators. Record on the Testing Insulation handout, page 1.
6. Continue taking readings until the input temperature is 180°F.
7. Shut off the electrical heaters and allow them to cool.
8. Continue to take readings for approximately one hour (during cooling) after being shut-off.
9. Now remove the insulation element and replace it with another type of insulation.
10. Repeat the test. Variations involved in the insulation element can include manufacturers, fiberglass or rigid board, four- or six-inch sections, and so on.
11. When all three tests have been taken, plot the data on the graph shown on the Testing Insulation handout, page 2. Note, that if you are able to use a computer plotting program, the data can be easily plotted.

REVIEW QUESTIONS

1. Are there any inaccuracies in the testing procedure? How could the test be improved?
2. What is the purpose of having so much insulation around the inside of the heat loss tester box?
3. Were there any differences in the cooling-down times for each type of insulation and if so, why?

 # MINI ENERGY AUDIT

INTRODUCTION

Many homes and buildings are being given an energy audit. An *energy audit* is the process of analyzing how energy is being used in a building. There are many types of energy audits. Some are very complex and require large amounts of time. Others simply look at various energy devices and analyze how they are used. This activity will help you to do a mini-energy audit for your family.

TECHNOLOGICAL LITERACY SKILLS

Data analysis, problem solving, predicting, and collecting data.

OBJECTIVES

At the completion of this activity, you will be able to:
1. Define how energy is being used in your home.
2. Analyze where energy is being lost in your home.
3. Determine some simple measures to reduce the energy used in your home.

MATERIALS

1. Paper and pencil

2. A standard residential home that uses energy for heating, cooling and appliances
3. Mini-audit handout

PROCEDURE

1. This activity must be done in a home, so first find a time in which you can be in your home with someone who can help you answer a series of questions.
2. Ask each of the questions listed on the Mini-audit handout.
3. Check off either a "yes" or a "no" for each question.
4. After all questions have been answered, show the home owner how energy efficiency can be improved.

REVIEW QUESTIONS

1. What items could be added to the list of questions on the Mini-audit handout?
2. How would you calculate the payback in years of a new thermostat or other device if the home owner needed to know.

SECTION FOUR

POWER TECHNOLOGY

Power technology is used to convert and transform energy into useful power. The power systems discussed in this section are mainly related to transportation technology. However, power technology is also used in communication and production systems as well.

Power technology, as with transportation and energy technology, can be studied using the systems model. For example, the systems model can be related to a small gasoline engine on a lawn mower.

1. The "input" is the command to convert chemical energy in the fuel to mechanical energy to turn a lawn mower blade and propel the mower forward.
2. The "process" to convert the energy to power is the workings of the engine.
3. The "output" is the actual power being produced by the lawn mower. "Impacts" include pollution from manufacturing, pollution from burning a fossil fuel and depletion of natural resources, among others.
4. The "feedback" system or control includes the throttle and carburetor, the on and off switches, the governor, and other parts.

Most systems in the area of power technology can be studied using this systems model.

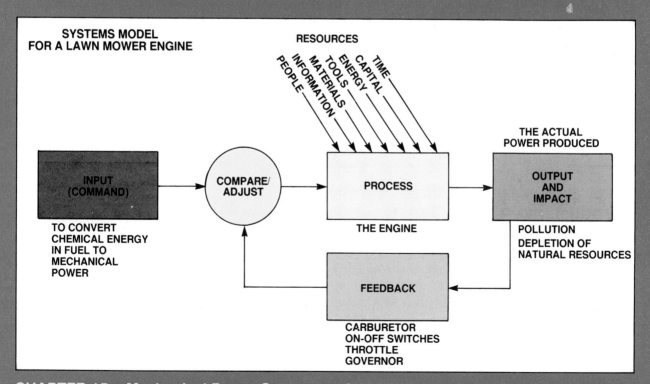

SYSTEMS MODEL
FOR A LAWN MOWER ENGINE

RESOURCES

TIME
CAPITAL
ENERGY
TOOLS
MATERIALS
INFORMATION
PEOPLE

THE ACTUAL
POWER PRODUCED

INPUT
(COMMAND)

COMPARE/
ADJUST

PROCESS

OUTPUT
AND
IMPACT

TO CONVERT
CHEMICAL ENERGY
IN FUEL TO
MECHANICAL
POWER

THE ENGINE

POLLUTION
DEPLETION OF
NATURAL RESOURCES

FEEDBACK

CARBURETOR
ON-OFF SWITCHES
THROTTLE
GOVERNOR

CHAPTER 15

Mechanical Power Systems

OBJECTIVES

After reading this chapter, you will be able to:

- Define several terms used to describe power, including *work, force, power, torque,* and the several terms for *horsepower.*

- Describe how horsepower is measured.

- Analyze the technologies used to change power to different torques and/or horsepower.

- Define how power is controlled in a mechanical energy system.

KEY TERMS

Power	Horsepower	Gear Ratio
Mechanical Converter	Frictional Horsepower	Hypoid
Torque	Dynamometer	Kinetic
Efficiency	Fulcrum	

Introduction

Energy comes to us in many forms. Usually, though, it does not come in the correct form to produce power for our transportation systems. For example, a transportation device usually needs different types of mechanical power. One type is needed to push it forward, whereas other forces are required to operate a generator or an air conditioner. This chapter is about how energy is converted to power for use in transportation technology. Most often, combustion-type engines are used to create the necessary power. To understand power, one must study such terms as work, force, pressure, torque, gearing, friction, and so on. The purpose of this chapter is to define the many terms used to describe mechanical energy systems. In addition, the chapter discusses measuring power, changing power and controlling power.

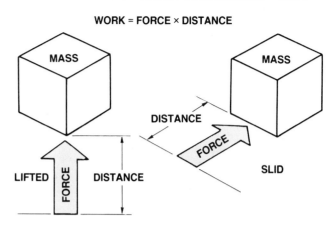

WORK = FORCE × DISTANCE

FIGURE 15-2 Work is defined as the result of moving a certain mass a certain distance. The movement can be a lifting or sliding motion.

FIGURE 15-1 An engine is being tested on a dynamometer, an apparatus used to measure mechanical power. *Courtesy of Chrysler Corporation*

Defining Mechanical Power

Energy Defined

Most energy converters, such as gasoline and diesel engines, are designed to accomplish one purpose: to convert energy into useful work. *Energy* is defined as the ability to do work. For example, energy is contained in the fuel used in engines. The function of the engine is to take the energy from the fuel and convert it into a form of power. The power is used to propel the vehicle forward. Figure 15-1 shows an engine being tested on a dynamometer which is used to measure the work produced from an engine.

Power Defined

Power is defined as a measure of the work being done. Power is the final output of an engine after it has converted the energy in the fuel into work. A common term used to describe output power is horsepower. *Horsepower* is a measure of the work being done by a mechanical converter, such as a diesel engine.

Many types of horsepower are used in relation to mechanical converters. When comparing engines, brake horsepower is used. When discussing efficiency, frictional and indicated horsepower are used. When analyzing gasoline mileage, road horse-

power is used. These and other horsepower definitions are further defined later in this chapter.

Work Defined

Work is defined as the result of applying a force to move a mass a certain distance. This force is created by the combustion of a source of fuel, such as gasoline. Work is produced when the force moves a certain mass a certain distance. The definition of work is shown in Figure 15-2. Referring to this figure, force is measured in pounds, distance is measured in feet. When the two units are put together they become *foot-pounds* (ft-lb), the energy needed to move a certain number of pounds a certain distance. Work then is measured in ft-lb. For example, if any transportation object is moved 50 feet by a force of 20 pounds, then 1,000 ft-lb of work have been produced. See Figure 15-3.

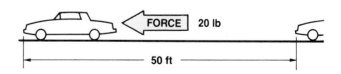

WORK = FORCE × DISTANCE
WORK = 20 × 50
WORK = 1,000 ft-lb

FIGURE 15-3 When a vehicle is pushed a distance of 50 feet by 20 pounds of force, 1,000 foot-pounds of work are created.

FIGURE 15-4 These torque wrenches produce a twisting force on bolts. The reading is measured in ft-lb. *Courtesy of Snap-On Tools Corporation*

Torque

Torque is one way to measure work. *Torque* is defined as the twisting force on a shaft. For example, a torque wrench produces a twisting force, measured in ft-lb, Figure 15-4. Torque is also produced on the output shaft of engines because of the combustion of fuel. The combustion of gases pushes internal pistons downward. This causes a crankshaft to rotate, producing torque. This force also causes other objects to rotate. Torque is the force that turns transmissions and wheels, boat propellers and lawn mower blades, for example.

Torque is actually available at the rear of the engine, Figure 15-5. Since torque is expressed in foot pounds, an engine is said to have 500 ft-lb of torque at a certain speed. Speed on a gasoline or diesel engine is measured in revolutions per minute (r/min). Torque can be measured directly from a rotating shaft. A dynamometer is used to obtain this measurement. Dynamometers are discussed later in this chapter.

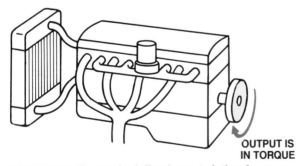

OUTPUT IS IN TORQUE

FIGURE 15-5 Torque is defined as a twisting force. The work an engine produces is measured as torque at the back of the engine. *Courtesy of DCA Educational Products*

Converter Efficiency

Several types of efficiency are used for mechanical converters. Efficiency generally refers to how well a particular job can be done. Generally, *efficiency* is expressed as a ratio of input to output, as shown in Figure 15-6. Other specific types of efficiency include *mechanical efficiency*, *volumetric efficiency*, and *thermal efficiency*.

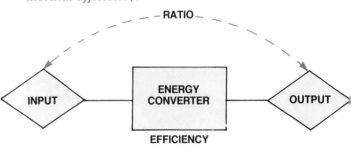

FIGURE 15-6 Efficiency is a ratio of the input energy to the output energy.

Efficiencies are expressed as percentages, which are always less than 100%. The difference between the percent efficiency and 100% is due to the percent loss incurred during the process of converting power. Efficiency is important because it shows how much energy is being wasted. This is especially important when there is a shortage of energy.

Mechanical Efficiency

One way of determining the efficiency of a machine is by analyzing its mechanical systems. For example, the machine can be a motorcycle, as shown in Figure 15-7. *Mechanical efficiency* is a relationship

FIGURE 15-7 A motorcycle has a certain mechanical efficiency. Mechanical efficiency is a measure of the actual work versus the theoretical work needed to run the motorcycle. *Courtesy of Harley-Davidson, Inc.*

between the theoretical (mathematically calculated) amount of work to move the motorcycle, and the actual amount of work to move it. For example, if the motorcycle requires 35 units of actual work and 55 units of theoretical work, the mechanical efficiency can be calculated. The formula to calculate mechanical efficiency is:

$$\text{Mechanical efficiency} = \frac{\text{Actual work}}{\text{Theoretical work}} \times 100$$

$$\text{Mechanical efficiency} = \frac{35}{55} \times 100$$

$$\text{Mechanical efficiency} = 63.6\%$$

The losses on any mechanical system are primarily due to friction. If friction can be reduced, then the mechanical efficiency will increase. If friction increases, the mechanical efficiency will decrease.

Volumetric Efficiency

Another way to measure efficiency is related to how easily air for combustion flows in and out of an engine. *Volumetric efficiency* measures the airflow conditions in an engine. The formula for measuring volumetric efficiency is:

$$\text{Volumetric efficiency} = \frac{\text{Actual air used}}{\text{Maximum air possible}} \times 100$$

For example, at a certain engine speed, 40 cubic inches (40 in³) of air enters the cylinders. However, under ideal conditions, 55 cubic inches (55 in³) should enter. Using these two numbers:

$$\text{Volumetric efficiency} = \frac{40}{55} \times 100$$

$$\text{Volumetric efficiency} = 72\%$$

Factors that will affect the volumetric efficiency of engines are:
1. Exhaust restrictions
2. Air-cleaner restrictions
3. Carbon deposits on cylinders and valves
4. Shape and design of valves
5. Amount of restriction by curves in the intake and exhaust ports

Thermal Efficiency

Thermal efficiency tells how effectively an engine converts the thermal energy in its fuel into actual power at the output shaft. Thermal efficiency is expressed as a ratio of the input energy to the output energy. It takes into account all of the losses on the engine, including thermal, mechanical, and volumetric losses. For this reason, thermal efficiency is sometimes called *overall efficiency*. It is the most common form of efficiency used to compare engines and other energy converters.

TECH LINK

Thermal efficiency is found by using the following formula:

$$\text{Thermal efficiency} = \frac{\text{Actual output}}{\text{Heat input}}$$

When using this formula, always make sure that the input and output are expressed in the same units of measurement. The input and output are expressed in Btu. (Recall that one British thermal unit is the amount of energy needed to raise one pound of water one degree Fahrenheit.)

Relating this efficiency to a gasoline engine, approximately 25% of the input energy is available at the output. Referring to Figure 15-8, the remainder

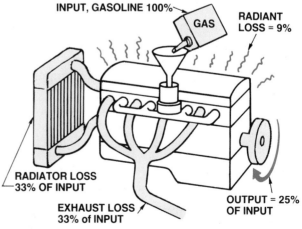

FIGURE 15-8 A gasoline engine loses much of its energy to other systems. The radiator, exhaust, and radiant heat make up most of the losses. The remaining power is the output. *Courtesy of DCA Educational Products*

EFFICIENCIES OF DIFFERENT ENGINES	
Gasoline Engine	25-28%
Diesel Engine	35-38%
Aircraft Gas Turbine	33-35%
Liquid Fuel Rocket	46-47%
Rotary Engine	20-22%
Steam Locomotive	10-12%

FIGURE 15-9 All machines have an overall efficiency. This shows average efficiencies of various mechanical converters.

of the input energy is lost through various ways. The cooling system absorbs a certain percentage of the input energy. The exhaust system carries away a certain amount of energy. Nine percent of the input energy is lost through radiation. When all of these losses are considered, the output energy drops to about 25%. Figure 15-9 shows a comparison of efficiencies for several mechanical converters.

Measuring Mechanical Power

Once the base definitions of mechanical power are expressed, it can now be measured. This section looks at how mechanical power is measured. More specifically, this section defines different types of horsepower, and how horsepower is measured on a dynamometer.

Horsepower Defined

Horsepower (hp) is described as the rate at which the output work is being done in a mechanical system. It is also a unit or measure of the work done within a certain time period. When something is measured by rate, time must be considered. Therefore, it may be said that horsepower is also a measure of how long it takes to do any work. For example, the dragster shown in Figure 15-10 is required to race a certain distance in the least amount of time. This requires a certain amount of horsepower.

One horsepower is the measurement of the amount of work needed to lift 550 pounds one foot in one second. An example is shown in Figure 15-11. If this work is measured per minute (rather than per second), one horsepower is then measured as the amount of work needed to lift 33,000 (60 × 550) pounds, one foot, in one minute. These two measurements are considered the standard ways of defining horsepower. It is important to note that the direction of motion is in a straight line when horsepower is applied. However, remember that torque is always related to rotation, Figure 15-12.

FIGURE 15-10 This dragster requires high horsepower to race through the track. *Courtesy of Dodge Division, Chrysler Motors*

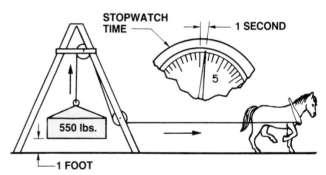

1 hp = 550 lbs./sec./ft.

FIGURE 15-11 One horsepower is defined as the amount of work required to raise 550 lbs one foot in one second.

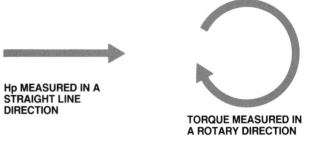

Hp MEASURED IN A STRAIGHT LINE DIRECTION

TORQUE MEASURED IN A ROTARY DIRECTION

FIGURE 15-12 Horsepower is measured in a straight line. Torque is measured as a twisting force.

Brake Horsepower

Brake horsepower (bhp) is defined as the actual horsepower measured at the rear of an engine under normal conditions. For example, a lawn mower or outboard motor has a certain bhp available at the output of the engine. It is called brake horsepower because a brake is used to slow down the shaft inside of a loading device. Brake horsepower is often used to compare engines and their characteristics. Engine manufacturers use brake horsepower to show differences in engine outputs. For example, an engine sized at 235 cubic inches produces less bhp than one sized at 350 cubic inches. Other factors that may change bhp include the type of carburetion, the quality of combustion, the compression in the engine, the type of fuel used, and the air to fuel mixture quality.

Indicated Horsepower

Indicated horsepower (ihp) is defined as theoretical horsepower. Indicated horsepower has been calculated by the engine manufacturers. Ihp represents the maximum horsepower available from the engine under ideal or perfect conditions. Ihp is calculated based on the engine size, displacement, operational speed, and the pressure developed theoretically in the cylinders. Indicated horsepower values will always be higher than bhp values.

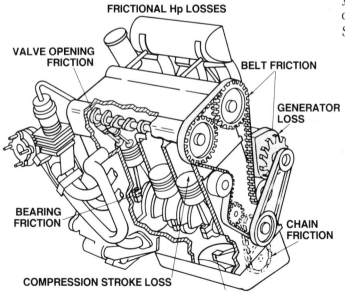

FRICTIONAL Hp LOSSES

VALVE OPENING FRICTION

BELT FRICTION

GENERATOR LOSS

BEARING FRICTION

CHAIN FRICTION

COMPRESSION STROKE LOSS

FIGURE 15-13 Frictional horsepower is created in an engine. Some sources include bearings, compression stroke, belts, generators, valves, and so on. *Courtesy of Peugeot Motors of America, Inc.*

Frictional Horsepower

Frictional horsepower (fhp) is defined as the horsepower exerted to overcome internal friction. Friction is produced whenever two objects touch each other while moving. The friction that is present in any engine must be overcome with more energy. Sources of frictional horsepower include bearings, pistons sliding inside cylinders, the compression stroke, the generator, fan, water pump, belts, air conditioner, and others. Figure 15-13 shows an engine cut-away view and various sources of friction.

Other sources of frictional hourspower on a vehicle include the wind (drag), tire rolling resistance and road conditions, among others. All of these have a tendency to slow down the engine. They make up the total frictional horsepower.

Frictional horsepower should be reduced as much as possible. The more frictional horsepower that must be overcome by the engine, the more power needed to operate the vehicle. More frictional horsepower results in poorer fuel mileage on any transportation vehicle.

Reducing Frictional Horsepower

Frictional horsepower on transportation vehicles has been analyzed very carefully. Research efforts have found that poor fuel mileage occurred because of great amounts of frictional horsepower. In past years, a considerable number of changes in vehicle design have been made to reduce frictional losses. Some of these include:

1. Reducing the rolling resistance on tires. Computers are used to design tires to reduce the rolling resistance. Radial tires also reduce rolling resistance.
2. Reducing the air drag on a vehicle. The vehicle then has less wind resistance. Figure 15-14 shows an example of a vehicle designed for minimum wind resistance and improved aerodynamics.
3. Making the vehicle lighter. On the average, one mile per gallon of fuel is lost for every 400 pounds on the vehicle. This is called the power-to-weight ratio.
4. Changing the undercarriage of the vehicle to reduce the air drag underneath.

These and other designs have aided the engine manufacturers to improve the fuel mileage on some vehicles from 12 to 15 miles per gallon to more than 50 miles per gallon.

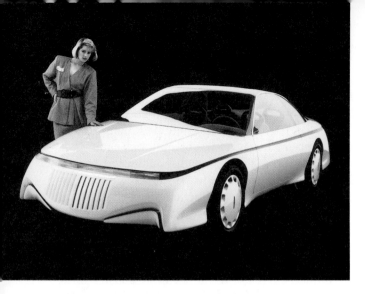

FIGURE 15-14 This car is designed to minimize frictional losses from wind resistance. *Courtesy of Ford Motor Corp.*

Road Horsepower

Road horsepower is defined as the horsepower available at the drive wheels of any vehicle. Road horsepower is always less than bhp. The difference between road horsepower and brake horsepower is due to frictional horsepower. Frictional horsepower losses are produced in transmissions, drive shafts, and differential assemblies, Figure 15-15. Road

horsepower can then be shown as:

Road hp = bhp - fhp through the drive train

Definition of Dynamometers

Work must occur in order to measure horsepower. This means a load must be put on the engine while it is operating. Typical examples of loading an engine include:

- Pulling a trailer up a steep hill
- Mowing through thick grass with a lawn mower
- Plowing through water in a boat

A *dynamometer* is a device which attaches to the back of an engine to absorb the power being created by the engine. When an engine is at idle, it is impossible to determine how much horsepower or torque can be produced. When an engine is run on a dynamometer, it can be loaded to simulate actual working conditions. The dynamometer measures the brake horsepower and torque at the output of the engine.

Another type of dynamometer is one which is used to measure road horsepower. It is called a chassis dynamometer. A *chassis dynamometer* measures the road horsepower and torque available

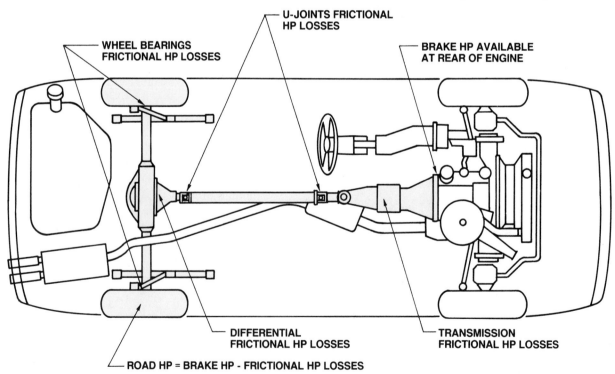

U-JOINTS FRICTIONAL HP LOSSES

WHEEL BEARINGS FRICTIONAL HP LOSSES

BRAKE HP AVAILABLE AT REAR OF ENGINE

DIFFERENTIAL FRICTIONAL HP LOSSES

TRANSMISSION FRICTIONAL HP LOSSES

ROAD HP = BRAKE HP - FRICTIONAL HP LOSSES

FIGURE 15-15 Road horsepower is the difference between the brake horsepower minus all of the frictional losses. *Courtesy of Mazda Corporation*

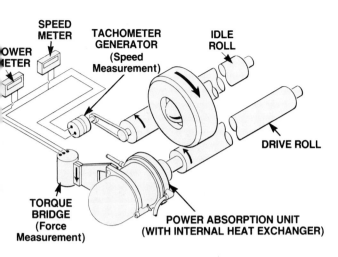

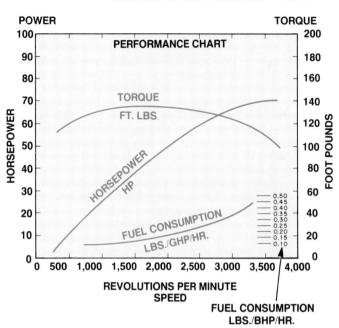

FIGURE 15-16 A chassis dynamometer is used to measure the road horsepower. The tires roll directly on the idle roll and the drive roll. The power absorption unit loads the system. *Courtesy of Clayton Industries*

FIGURE 15-18 A performance chart shows the amount of horsepower and torque an engine can produce for a range of r/min. Fuel consumption is also shown. *Courtesy of DCA Educational Products*

at the drive wheels of any vehicle. Figure 15-16 shows the mechanical layout of a chassis dynamometer. In this example, the tires roll on two rollers: the idle roll and the drive roll. The power absorption unit is used to absorb the energy, and acts as the load on the vehicle. Both speed (r/min) and torque are measured on the scales shown. Figure 15-17 shows a vehicle being tested on a chassis dynamometer.

Performance Charts

Gasoline, diesel, and other engines each have certain operating characteristics. This means that they have different torque, horsepower and fuel consumption at different r/min. By using a dynamometer, a *performance chart* (also called characteristic curve) can be developed. Figure 15-18 shows a standard performance chart. The lower scale shows the r/min of the engine. The right scale shows the torque on the engine. The left scale shows the horsepower being produced on the engine. A fuel consumption scale is included at the lower right.

When the engine is loaded with a dynamometer, a certain maximum torque and horsepower can be produced at a specific r/min. For example, referring again to Figure 15-18, this particular engine is capable of producing about 135 ft-lb of torque at 1,500 r/min. Also, this engine can produce about 70 horsepower at 3,500 r/min. This chart shows the characteristics of the engine throughout its r/min range. A fuel consumption curve is also shown. This curve indicates the amount of fuel used in pounds per brake horsepower per hour. This unit is sometimes referred to as BSFC or brake specific fuel consumption.

FIGURE 15-17 This vehicle is being tested on a chassis dynamometer. *Courtesy of Clayton Industries*

Phanthom View of Vehicle

This is a phanthom view of a current automobile. Phanthom views and illustrations are made to show the internal workings and location of complex systems of technology. There is considerable demand by industries to hire graphic artists to produce phanthom views of various products. By using this type of photo, many technological systems can be viewed as to their location and shape in the vehicle.

In this photo, the propulsion, suspension, and control systems can be observed. As discussed in this chapter, the propulsion system is used to produce the necessary horsepower and torque for correct and efficient engine operation. *Courtesy of Ford Motor Company*

TECH LINK

A dynamometer can only measure the torque being produced at the rear of an engine or at the drive wheels of a vehicle. The dynamometer does not measure horsepower. In order to obtain horsepower readings the following formula is used:

$$\text{Horsepower} = \frac{\text{Torque} \times \text{r/min}}{5252}$$

The number 5252 is a constant, and is related to how torque is measured on the diameter of a rotating shaft ($5252 = 33,000/2\pi$)

Altering Mechanical Power

In most mechanical systems the type of power used may need to be altered. For example, when starting a vehicle, high torque is needed. After the vehicle is moving, less torque is needed and more horsepower is needed. This section addresses ways in which power can be altered or changed to meet a desired need.

Levers and Forces

A *lever* is a device that changes the forces and distances of mechanical motion. For example, in Figure 15-19A, a lever has an input, a fulcrum and

INPUT = OUTPUT

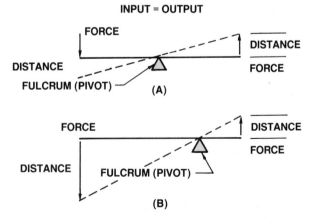

FIGURE 15-19 A lever mechanism is used to change forces and distances. If the pivot point is moved to the right, the force increases on the output. The distance, however, decreases.

an output. The *fulcrum* is the support about which a lever turns. When a force is applied to one side (input) over a certain distance, a resultant force (output) is produced within a certain distance on the other side. Force times distance on the input always equals force times distance on the output. Therefore, work input always equals work output.

If the fulcrum is positioned farther to the right, as shown in Figure 15-19B, several actions occur. First, the work input again equals the work output. However, the output force is much greater, whereas the input distance is much greater. By changing the position of the fulcrum, different forces can be obtained on the output.

Mechanical Advantage (MA)

Mechanical advantage (MA) is defined as the gain in forces or distances in a mechanical system. If a set of levers increases the force by 5, then the mechanical advantage is 1 to 5. All mechanical lever systems are designed to accomplish a certain mechanical advantage. However, remember that for any gain in force, a loss in distance must occur.

Classes of Levers

Three types of levers are used in mechanical systems: the 1st, 2nd, and 3rd class lever. Depending upon the type of lever, either force or distance can be gained. Figure 15-20 shows the three types of levers. The difference among them is in the location

FIGURE 15-21 A robot uses many types of levers for its operation. *Courtesy of Arvin Industries, Inc.*

of the fulcrum, input, and output forces. All machines used today are based upon the application of these three levers. Examples include:

- Wheelbarrow — 2nd class lever
- Wrench — combination of 1st and 2nd class levers
- Scissors — 1st class lever
- Windshield wiper — mostly designed as a 3rd class lever
- Dentist chair and equipment — all three levers

Levers are also used extensively in the design of robots, as shown in Figure 15-21. Several classes of levers are combined to move the various arms and to gain either force or distance motion.

Torque Multiplication

The principle of levers can also be applied to gears. A *gear* can be considered a set of spinning levers. A set of gears can increase or decrease torque in the same way that levers increase or decrease force. In Figure 15-22A, one lever pushes a second lever. Its

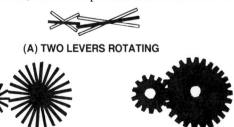

(A) TWO LEVERS ROTATING

(B) MANY LEVERS ROTATING   **(C) GEARS ROTATING**

FIGURE 15-22 Gears are also used to increase torque just as levers are used to increase force. *Courtesy of General Motors Corporation*

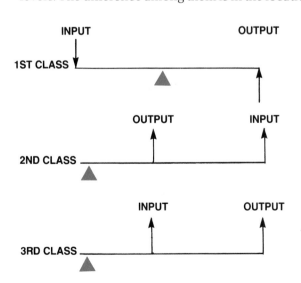

FIGURE 15-20 All machines are made of one or more of these types of levers. The three types are 1st, 2nd, and 3rd class levers.

action is like the motion of a 1st class lever. The length of each lever determines how much force will be created on it. For example, if the short lever pushes against the long lever, the longer lever will move a lesser distance but will have more force. If a series of levers were constructed, as shown in Figure 15-22B, then a continuous torque can be developed. When applied to gears, as shown in 15-22C, a small gear can increase torque in a larger gear. However, as with levers, the larger gear moves a lesser distance than the input gear.

Gear Ratios

The required change in torque depends upon the relative size of the gears. The size of the input gear in relation to the output gear is called the *gear ratio*. The best way to identify a gear ratio is by counting the number of teeth on each gear. Figure 15-23 shows a set of gears. The input gear has 12 teeth and the output gear has 24 teeth. It will take two revolutions on the input gear to turn the output gear one revolution. The speed of the output gear will be one-half the speed of the input gear. However, the torque will be doubled on the output gear. The gear ratio would be stated as 24:12 or 2:1. This means that the input gear will turn twice as the output gear turns once.

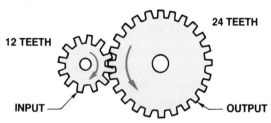

GEAR RATIO = 2:1
(2 REVOLUTIONS INPUT TO
1 REVOLUTION OUTPUT)

12 TEETH   24 TEETH

INPUT   OUTPUT

FIGURE 15-23 Gear ratios are determined by the number of teeth on the output compared to the input. This gear ratio is 24:12 or 2:1.

Types of Gears

Several types of gears are used in mechanical systems, Figure 15-24. Spur gears were used in past applications. These gears are very noisy. In order to reduce noise, helical gears are now being used. Helical gears have the teeth set at an angle, which allows a smoother meshing of teeth between the two gears. It also creates more surface contact

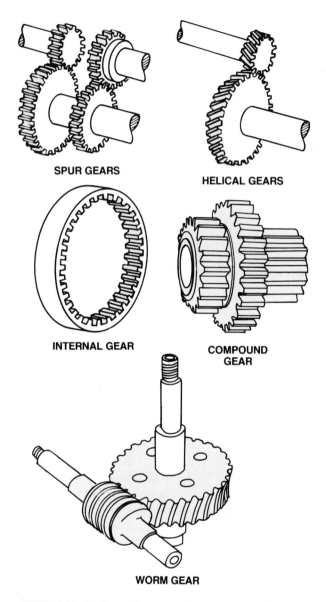

SPUR GEARS   HELICAL GEARS

INTERNAL GEAR   COMPOUND GEAR

WORM GEAR

FIGURE 15-24 Several types of gears are used on mechanical systems. Shown here are spur, helical, internal, worm and compound gears.

between the teeth, making them stronger. Most manual transmissions used in automobiles use helical gears. In the internal gear, the teeth are machined inside of a ring. A compound gear is composed of several gears of different sizes placed on the same shaft. Each gear spins at the same speed. The worm gear is used to gain high torque and low speed.

Figure 15-25 shows an example of a hypoid gear used often in differentials for cars, trucks, boat drives, tractors, and other applications.

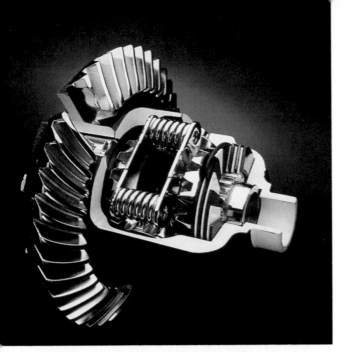

FIGURE 15-25 This differential uses a hypoid gear (curved piece). *Courtesy of Eaton Corp.*

Controlling Mechanical Power

Control is a necessary part of any mechanical system. Control systems for mechanical power are also part of the systems model. Control systems are considered part of the "feedback" technology. *Control* is used to stop and start (regulate) the flow of mechanical power. This section discusses various examples of controlling technology (feedback loops) in mechanical power systems.

Friction

Friction is defined as a resistance to motion between two objects. Friction results when two surfaces rub against each other, Figure 15-26. The amount of friction depends upon two factors: the roughness of the surfaces and the amount of pressure between the two surfaces.

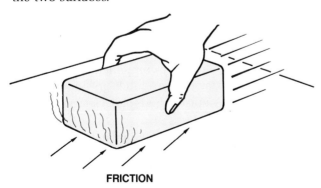

FRICTION

FIGURE 15-26 Friction is produced when two surfaces rub together.

From an energy viewpoint, when there is friction, kinetic energy (power or work) is converted into thermal (heat) energy. The larger the amount of power or work that must be brought to rest (controlled), the greater the amount of heat produced. Examples of control technology that use friction include brakes, bands, discs, and clutches.

Braking Systems

In any braking system, the amount of friction is being controlled by the pressure on the frictional parts. By varying friction, for example, rotating shafts can be stopped as well as modified in speed. The control for friction is obtained by forcing a stationary brake shoe or pad against a rotating drum or disc.

In a vehicle, for example, as the operator presses harder on the brake pedal, friction increases. When the wheel is being slowed down by the brake friction, the tire is also slowed down. However, friction is also being produced between the tire and the road. The friction on the brakes must be matched by the friction between the tires and the road. If the tires cannot produce the friction, the wheels will lock and the vehicle will skid. Locked wheels can produce dangerous results, especially since there is no driver control over the friction between the tires and the road. Computer-controlled brakes are now being used to control the friction at each wheel. This will control skidding during braking.

Drum Brakes

A drum brake assembly consists of a cast drum

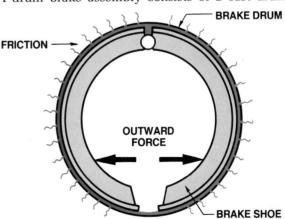

BRAKE DRUM

FRICTION

OUTWARD FORCE

BRAKE SHOE

FIGURE 15-27 On a drum brake system, the brake shoes are forced outward against a brake drum to produce friction.

which is bolted to the wheel and rotates with it. Inside, there is a stationary backing plate with a set of brake shoes attached to it. Other components attached to the backing plate include a hydraulic cylinder and several springs and linkages. The brake shoes are lined with frictional material that contacts the inside of the drum when the brakes are applied, Figure 15-27. When the brakes are applied, the brake shoes are forced outward, producing friction against the inside of the drum.

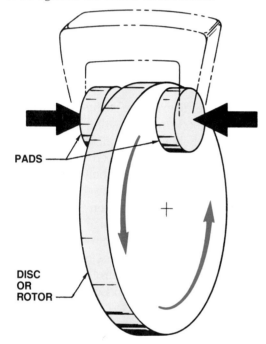

PADS

DISC
OR
ROTOR

FIGURE 15-28 A disc-type brake system uses two pads working against a rotor to produce friction. *Courtesy of EIS Brake Parts, Division Standard Motor Products, Inc.*

Disc Brakes

Today, disc brakes are used on many transportation vehicles. Disc brakes are used on the front of the vehicle, whereas drum brakes are used on the rear. Disc brakes resemble the brakes used on a ten-speed bicycle. The friction is produced by using pads, as shown in Figure 15-28. The stationary pads are squeezed or clamped against a rotating wheel. The disc, also called the rotor, is attached to the rim and tire. The rotor is made of cast iron that is machined on both sides. The pads are attached to metal plates which are actuated by pistons from the hydraulic system. Figure 15-29 shows a motorcycle with disc brakes on the front.

FIGURE 15-29 This motorcycle uses disc brakes on the front for stopping the vehicle. *Courtesy of Harley-Davidson, Inc.*

Transmission Band

A clutch is another type of mechanical power control. A *clutch* is a device used to control the speed of a rotating shaft. Clutches are often used in transmissions in cars, trucks, motorcycles, and other vehicles. One type is called the *transmission band*. It is made of a flexible piece of steel wrapped around a clutch housing or drum. The inside of the band has a frictional surface to help grip the clutch housing (drum) or other rotating part. The band is tightened or loosened to hold or free the housing or drum.

Multiple-disc Clutch

A *multiple-disc clutch* is another common motion control used in many applications, such as transmissions. It is made of a series of friction discs placed between steel discs. The exact number depends upon the application. The friction discs or composition-faced plates have rough gripping surfaces on a metal base. The steel discs have smooth metal surfaces. These two components make up the input and output of the clutch. In addition, the clutch pack has a piston and return spring to aid in operation.

When fluid pressure is applied to the clutch, the piston moves and compresses all of the clutch discs together. The action locks the input and output of the clutch. When the pressure is released, the spring helps to remove the pressure on the discs. This action unlocks the clutch.

Overrunning Clutch

The *overrunning clutch* is used to prevent backward rotation of certain parts on a gear system. The overrunning clutch shown in Figure 15-30 is made of the inner hub, outer cam, and a series of balls and springs. It operates in such a way as to allow rotation in only one direction. For example, as the inside hub attempts to rotate counterclockwise, the balls become wedged and locked, stopping the rotation. When the rotation is in the opposite direction, the balls are free and rotation continues.

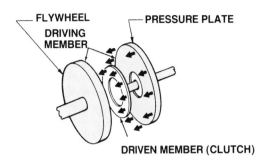

FIGURE 15-31 When the clutch is engaged, the driven member is squeezed between the two driving members. *Courtesy of General Motors Corporation*

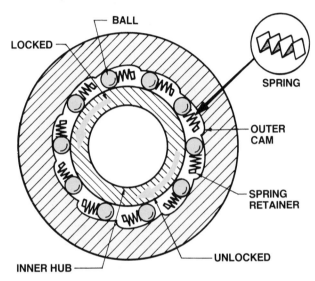

FIGURE 15-30 The overrunning clutch assembly is used to provide rotational control. When the inner hub tries to rotate counterclockwise, the balls become wedged and locked.

Purpose of Friction Disc Clutches

Disc clutches are used most often to connect the output of an engine to a transmission or other application. While the engine is running, there are times in which the output must not turn. The clutch is used as a mechanism to engage or disengage the transmission and drive wheels. If clutches were not used, every time the vehicle stopped, the engine would stop. Since this is not practical, the operator can engage or disengage the clutch when needed.

The clutch is designed to engage the transmission or other application gradually. This eliminates jumping abruptly from no connection at all to a direct, solid connection to the engine. This is done by allowing a certain amount of slippage between the input and the output shaft on the clutch. Several components are needed in order to do this. These

include the pressure plate, driven plate also called the clutch or friction disc, and engine flywheel. These parts are shown in Figure 15-31.

The left side is considered the driving member or input to the clutch. It is composed of the flywheel and pressure plate. The output is the center driven member or clutch. The output of this shaft drives the transmission. When the pressure plate is withdrawn, the engine can revolve freely and is disconnected from the driving member and the transmission. However, when the pressure plate moves in the direction of the arrows, the clutch is forced to turn at the same speed as the input or driving member. Figure 15-32 shows an actual clutch system used in heavy-duty trucking applications. This system uses two friction plates and two pressure plates.

FIGURE 15-32 This truck clutch system uses two discs and two pressure plates. *Courtesy of Dana Corporation*

Summary

- *Energy* is defined as the ability to do work.
- *Power* is defined as a measure of the work being done.
- *Work* is defined as a force that moves a mass a certain distance.
- *Torque* is defined as a twisting force.
- Efficiency of any converter is usually expressed as a ratio of input to output.
- The three types of efficiency are mechanical, volumetric, and thermal efficiency.
- *Horsepower* is defined as the amount of work done per time unit.
- Several types of horsepower include brake, indicated, frictional, and road horsepower.
- A dynamometer is used to load an engine under simulated load conditions to determine the torque and horsepower characteristics.
- All machines need levers to operate. Levers have both an input and output. Work input always equals work output.
- The three types of levers are the 1st, 2nd, and 3rd class levers.
- Gears are used to obtain torque multiplication.
- The most common gears include the spur, helical, compound, worm, and internal gears.
- Controlling mechanical power is accomplished by applying friction.
- Drum and disc brakes are both used to stop rotation of spinning shafts.
- Transmission bands use a steel band around a housing or drum as a brake.
- The overrunning clutch is used to allow rotation in one direction, while locking or stopping the rotation in the opposite direction.

REVIEW

1. If it takes 55 units of actual work and 75 units of theoretical work to produce power, the mechanical efficiency is _____ percent.
2. Thermal efficiency is measured by dividing the actual power output by the thermal _____ .
3. When 80 foot-pounds of torque are produced at 3,200 r/min, _____ horsepower are being produced.
4. A gear system that has 14 teeth on the input gear and 26 teeth on the output gear is said to have a _____ gear ratio.
5. Braking systems and clutches are considered systems that _____ mechanical systems.
6. A _____ gear is used in a car differential.
7. Describe the difference between energy and power.
8. What is the difference between work and horsepower?
9. List and describe the three most common types of efficiency used on power converters.
10. State and describe at least three types of horsepower.
11. Identify three ways in which frictional horsepower can be reduced.
12. Describe the operation of a dynamometer.
13. Describe how levers work on the input and output in relation to force and distance.
14. Define gear ratio.
15. Describe the operation of at least three frictional controlling devices used on power converters.
16. Define the operation of an overrunning clutch.

CHAPTER ACTIVITIES

 PEDAL POWER

INTRODUCTION

This activity is an experiment to determine the mechanical advantage (MA) of a bicycle, and to compare the MA between different gears (sprockets).

TECHNOLOGICAL LITERARY SKILLS

Problem solving, data analysis, data collection, experimentation.

OBJECTIVES

At the completion of this activity, you will be able to:
1. Describe the advantages and disadvantages of bicycles as a means of transportation.
2. Explain the term *mechanical advantage.*
3. Calculate the mechanical advantage of several gears on the bicycle.

MATERIALS

1. One 10-speed or equivalent bicycle
2. Tape measure
3. Paper and pencil
4. Chalk
5. Pedal Power handout

PROCEDURE

1. Divide the class into groups of two or three students each.
2. When placed in your group, discuss the advantages and disadvantages of using a bicycle rather than a car for your transportation needs. Include the following:
   a. Cost of original purchase
   b. Cost of operation and maintenance
   c. Age and skill requirements
   d. Traffic laws
   e. Support technology
   f. Convenience
   g. Environmental impacts.
3. Now obtain one bicycle per group.

> ▶ **CAUTION:** Always wear safety glasses when working with the bicycle and keep fingers away from the moving sprockets.

4. Set-up the bicycle in such a way that you can measure the distance the pedal travels in one complete revolution. This is called the *circumference.*

5. Measure the distance from the center of the sprocket to the center of the pedal axis. This is the *radius* of the pedal, Figure 15-33. Place this data on the Pedal Power handout.

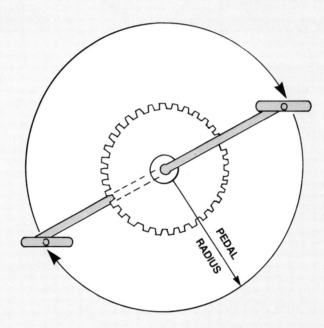

FIGURE 15-33 When working on the pedal power activity, you will need to determine the radius of the pedal on your bicycle.

6. The circumference is calculated by the formula ($2\pi r$, or $2 \times 3.14 \times$ radius). Place the circumference on the handout.
7. Place the gear shift lever so that the bicycle is in first or lowest gear.
8. Now determine the distance the bicycle travels in one revolution of the pedal.
   a. Put the bicycle on the floor and mark the starting position with chalk.
   b. Rotate the pedal exactly one revolution.
   c. When the bicycle stops, mark the end of the distance.
   d. Measure the distance from the start to the end of the distance the bicycle moved. Enter the distance in the table provided on the Pedal Power handout.
9. Calculate the mechanical advantage (MA) by dividing the pedal travel distance by the bicycle distance. Enter the MA in the table on the Pedal Power handout.
10. Now calculate the MA for each of the remaining gears on the bicycle, and enter in the table on the handout.

REVIEW QUESTIONS

1. When a gain of torque or starting power is developed using the gears on a bicycle, what is given up or lost?
2. Which gear produces the greatest amount of torque?
3. Which gear produces the greatest amount of distance?

MEASURING ENGINE PERFORMANCE

INTRODUCTION

Gasoline and diesel engines produce both horsepower and torque. Each engine has somewhat different characteristics, also called performance. This activity is designed to produce a performance chart of a small gasoline engine.

TECHNOLOGICAL LITERACY SKILLS

Problem solving, data collection, data analysis, instrumentation, plotting data on charts.

OBJECTIVES

At the completion of this activity, you will be able to:
1. Operate a dynamometer.
2. Graph a performance chart.
3. Determine engine characteristics by changing various settings and comparing performance charts.

MATERIALS

1. A small 1 to 5 horsepower gasoline engine or diesel engine (operational).
2. A small engine dynamometer with either water, hydraulic fluid, or electrical load application.
3. Torque meter and tachometer.
4. Appropriate dynamometer manuals, if available.
5. Gasoline or diesel fuel.
6. Adequate engine exhaust system.
7. Engine Performance handout.
8. Weather instruments used to measure air temperature, barometric pressure, and relative humidity.
9. Masking tape.

PROCEDURE

 NOTE: All performance tests should be taken under the same atmospheric conditions to obtain comparative results.
1. Locate the dynamometer manuals and review the principles of operation of the specific dynamometer in your laboratory.
2. Make sure the engine is properly bolted to the dynamometer and to the frame.

 ▶ **CAUTION:** Always wear safety glasses when working in the laboratory. Also, remember that engines have hot exhaust parts that can burn the hands. In addition, be careful not to touch the spinning parts (crankshaft) with your hands as injury may result.

---

3. Start the engine on the dynamometer and check all systems for correct operation. These include ignition, fuel, air, lubrication, exhaust, and the load sensor on the dynamometer. Enter the air temperature, barometric pressure, and relative humidity on the Engine Performance handout.
4. Set the carburetor adjustments to obtain the highest r/min setting set by the governor.

5. Hold the engine throttle full open with no load applied to the engine.

6. Enter this r/min on the chart located on the Engine Performance handout. This is the maximum r/min. Label the r/min scale in equal increments down to zero r/min.

7. Increase the load in small and equal increments.

8. Each time the r/min drops 500 r/min, take a torque and r/min (tachometer) reading, and record on a scrap piece of paper.

9. Continue reducing the r/min by increasing the load until the engine stalls under heavy load.

10. Based upon the torque readings, label the torque scale on the handout from the maximum to the minimum torque.

11. Plot the torque readings on the chart to produce a standard torque curve. Label as "Standard Torque."

12. For each torque reading, a horsepower reading should now be calculated. Horsepower is calculated by using the following formula:

$$\text{Horsepower} = \frac{\text{Torque} \times \text{RPM}}{5252}$$

NOTE: Some commercial dynamometers use different figures than in the formula given. Some use the figure 10,000 rather than 5252 and measure one-half foot-pound rather than one foot-pound.

13. Set the scale and plot the horsepower on the chart as well. Label as "Standard Horsepower."

14. Now produce a partial air restriction inside of the air cleaner. This can be done by using masking tape to close off approximately two-thirds of the air inlet.

15. Run a second performance chart (both horsepower and torque) and plot on the same chart on the handout. Record the graphs as "Partial Air Restriction."

16. Remove all tape, and put the engine back into its original condition and settings.

REVIEW QUESTIONS

1. Was there any difference between the "standard" and "partial" test?

2. Why is it necessary to take the test using the same air temperature, barometric pressure and relative humidity?

3. What other variations in the test (changes you could make on the engine) could be used to compare engine performance?

CHAPTER 16

Heat Engine Design

OBJECTIVES

After reading this chapter, you will be able to:

■ Compare different types of engines, including internal, external, intermittent, continuous, reciprocating, rotary, and other classifications.

■ Define the basic parts of any engine.

■ State the requirements for combustion on heat engines.

■ Analyze the differences between two- and four-cycle engine designs on both gasoline and diesel engines.

■ State the operation of the rotary engine design.

■ Identify the operation of several continuous combustion engines, including the Stirling, gas turbine, and steam turbine.

KEY TERMS

Internal Combustion	Rich Mixture	Air Box
Reciprocating	Lean Mixture	Swash Plate
Piston	Engine Displacement	Turbine
Crankshaft	BMEP	Compressor
Timing	Reed Valve	Regenerator
Air-fuel Ratio	Scavenging	Axial

Introduction

Many types of heat energy converters are used to power our transportation technologies. This chapter looks at several types of engine converters that are commonly used. They are called *heat engines* because they convert the thermal energy in fuel into mechanical energy for motion. This chapter discusses basic heat engine principles and terminology, combustion requirements, two- and four-cycle engines, diesel, rotary, and continuous combustion engines.

Types of Engines

Heat engines can be classified in several ways. These classifications are based on the location of the combustion, the type of combustion, and the type of internal motion.

Internal Combustion Engine

An *internal combustion engine* (ICE) is so named because the combustion occurs internally in the engine. For example, a gasoline engine used in a chain saw is considered an internal combustion engine. The combustion process occurs directly on the parts that must be moved inside the engine. Small lawn mower engines, snowmobile engines, and motorcycle engines are all also considered internal combustion engines. Internal combustion directly touches the parts that must be moved in order to produce mechanical energy. The burning of fuel takes place internally in the engine, Figure 16-1.

External Combustion Engine

In an *external combustion engine*, the combustion occurs indirectly on the parts that must be moved. For example, a boiler is an external combustion engine; the combustion is not touching the piston, Figure 16-2. Actually, the thermal energy in an external combustion engine heats another fluid. In this case, it is water which is converted to steam. Steam pushes against the piston to create the power.

Intermittent Combustion Engine

In an *intermittent combustion engine*, the combustion within the engine starts and stops many times

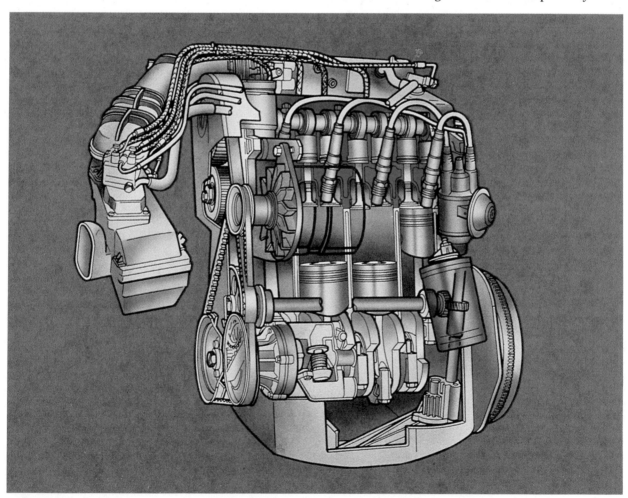

FIGURE 16-1 This engine is considered an internal combustion engine because the combustion occurs internally in the engine. *Courtesy of Volkswagen of America*

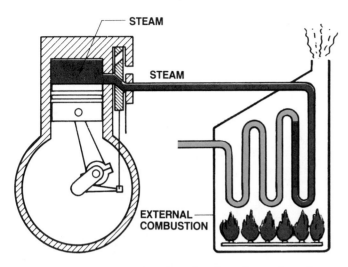

FIGURE 16-2 The combustion chamber of an external combustion engine is located separately from the internal parts of the engine.

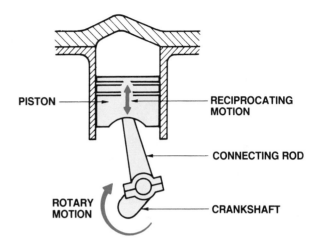

FIGURE 16-3 In a reciprocating engine, a piston moves up and down, causing rotary motion at the crankshaft.

during operation. A standard gasoline engine has an intermittent combustion design. Diesel engines are also intermittent combustion engines. Diesel engines are used primarily by large trucks and heavy equipment. They have also been used in automobiles by several automobile manufacturers.

Continuous Combustion Engine

A *continuous combustion engine* has a combustion process that continues constantly without stopping; it keeps burning continuously. A propane torch is one example of continuous combustion. Engines that use continuous combustion include turbine engines, rocket engines, stirling engines, and jet engines. Turbines, for example, are used in many industrial applications for pumping processes, and for aircraft applications.

Reciprocating Engine

A *reciprocating engine* is one in which the motion produced from the energy within the fuel moves parts up and down. The motion reciprocates or moves back and forth. Gasoline and diesel engines are considered reciprocating engines. In these operations, the power from the air and fuel starts the internal parts (piston) moving. The piston starts, then stops, then starts, then stops, over and over again. In this type of engine, the reciprocating motion must then be changed into rotary motion. A

crankshaft is designed to change this motion. Figure 16-3 shows the basic parts of a reciprocating heat engine.

Reciprocating engines can also be related to the systems model of technology. For example:

1. The "input" in this system is the command to change chemical energy to mechanical energy.
2. The "process" is the engine and its parts. The engine processes chemical energy into mechanical energy. It requires parts, materials, tools, knowledge, energy, and other factors.
3. The "output" is the mechanical energy produced at the crankshaft.
4. The "feedback" is the carburetor, throttle, on/off switch, governor, and other controls required to control the engine.
5. The "impact" is the pollution produced from burning fossil fuels, the depletion of natural resources, and the social impacts of using cars that have engines, among others.

Rotary Engine

A *rotary engine* has continuous rotation of the parts that are moving. For example, a turbine engine and a Wankel engine are considered rotary engines. The mechanical motion of the parts is in the shape of a circle. The crankshaft operation in Figure 16-3 is also an example of rotary motion.

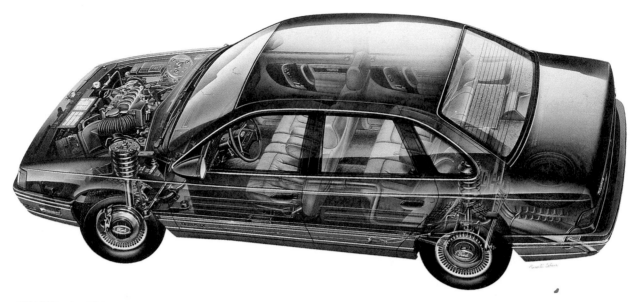

FIGURE 16-4 This car uses an internal combustion, intermittent combustion, reciprocating-type engine.
Courtesy of Ford Motor Company

Other Heat Engine Classifications

Heat engines can also be classified additionally by:

1. Cycles — There are two- and four-cycle engines.
2. Cooling systems — There are liquid-cooled and air-cooled engines.
3. Fuel system — There are gasoline-fueled and diesel-fueled engines.
4. Ignition systems — There are spark-ignition and compression-ignition engines.

All of these methods of classifying engines can be combined with those previously mentioned.

Most Common Engine Classifications

The most common engines used today are the gasoline or diesel engines. The gasoline and diesel engines used in cars, trucks, buses, lawn mowers, and so forth, are considered internal combustion, intermittent combustion, reciprocating-type engine designs. Figure 16-4 shows a phantom view of a car with such an engine. If the rotary (Wankel) engine is used, it is considered an internal combustion, inter- mittent combustion, rotary design. These engines are also considered four cycle, either liquid or air cooled.

Heat Engine Parts and Systems

In order to understand the principles of heat engines, certain parts must be defined. These parts are considered the major components of any re- ciprocating heat engine. They include the cylinder block, cylinders, pistons, connecting rod and crank- shaft, cylinder head, combustion chamber, valves, flywheel, and carburetor/fuel injection.

Cylinder Block

The *cylinder block* is defined as the foundation of any heat engine, Figure 16-5. The cylinder block is made of cast iron or aluminum. All other com- ponents of the engine are attached to the cylinder block. The cylinder block has several internal passageways to allow cooling fluid to circulate around the cylinders. It also has several large holes machined into the block where the combustion occurs.

Cylinders

The *cylinders* are defined as internal holes in the cylinder block, Figure 16-5. These holes (cylinders) are used as combustion chambers. The number of holes indicate the number of cylinders used on an engine. For example, on small gasoline engines, such as lawn mowers, there is one cylinder. Auto- mobiles usually use four, six or eight cylinders. Some engines used on heavy equipment have as many as 24 cylinders.

Pistons

Pistons are defined as the round piece that slides up and down in a cylinder, Figure 16-5. There is one piston for each cylinder. Pistons are made of lightweight material, such as high-quality aluminum, that can withstand high temperatures. When combustion of fuel occurs above the piston, the expansion of heated gases forces the piston downward. This downward motion of the piston converts the energy in the fuel into mechanical energy. Pistons are equipped with seals or rings, which are used to stop any combustion from passing by the side of the piston.

Connecting Rod and Crankshaft

The connecting rod is attached to the bottom of the piston, as is shown in Figure 16-5. The main purpose of the *connecting rod* is to attach the piston to the crankshaft. The crankshaft changes the reciprocating motion of the piston and connecting rod to rotary motion. Rotary motion is used as the output power of a heat engine.

Cylinder Head

The *cylinder head* is the part that fits over the top of the cylinder block, Figure 16-5. All reciprocating engines have some form of cylinder head. It usually houses the valves and ports that allow fuel and air to enter into the cylinder. The spark plug is also attached to the cylinder head. The cylinder head is made of cast iron or aluminum. When it is bolted to the cylinder block, it seals the cylinders so that the air and fuel flow can be controlled in and out of the cylinder.

Combustion Chamber

The combustion chamber is where the combustion takes place inside the cylinder. When the cylinder head has been attached to the cylinder block, the area inside of the cylinder head and block is called the *combustion chamber*. On some engines, the combustion chamber is located inside the head. Other engines have the combustion chamber located inside the top of the piston; this is especially true on diesel engines. On certain types of turbine engines, the combustion chamber is a separate unit.

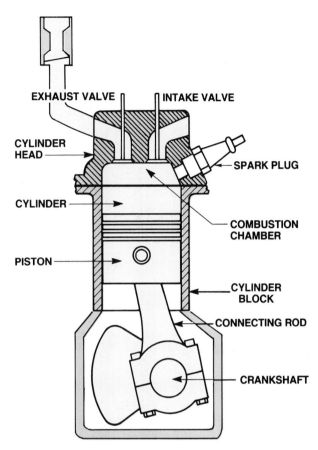

FIGURE 16-5 The cylinder block is the foundation for all of the basic parts of a reciprocating engine.

Valves and Ports

Valves and *ports* are located inside of the cylinder head and block. Their purpose is to allow air and fuel to enter and leave the combustion area. The valves are shown in Figure 16-5. Valves are designed so that when they are closed the port is sealed perfectly. They must also be designed so that they can be opened exactly at the right time. The valves are opened by using a camshaft, and closed by using springs. An intake valve allows fuel and air to enter the cylinder, and an exhaust valve allows the burned gases to exit the cylinder.

Camshaft

The *camshaft* is used to open the valves at the correct time. Cam lobes, or slightly raised areas, are machined on the camshaft to open the valves so that air and fuel can enter the cylinder. The valves are then closed by springs on each valve. The

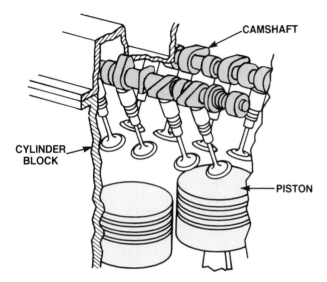

FIGURE 16-6 A dual overhead camshaft is used on some engines to operate the intake and exhaust valves.

camshaft is driven by the crankshaft. This means that the camshaft must be timed to the crankshaft, so that the valves will open and close in correct time with the position of the piston. One lobe is placed on the camshaft for each valve that must be opened and closed.

The camshaft may be mounted in the block or mounted directly on top of the cylinder head. When mounted on top of the cylinder head, it is called an overhead camshaft (OHC). A dual overhead camshaft is shown in Figure 16-6.

Flywheel

The *flywheel*, which is located on the end of the crankshaft, is designed to act as a weight to keep the crankshaft rotating once power has started. The flywheel is usually heavy. It smooths out any intermittent motion from the power pulses. The flywheel is a good example of Newton's law of motion. This law says that an object in motion tends to remain in motion, whereas an object at rest tends to remain at rest. Once the flywheel is in motion, it tends to remain in motion.

Carburetor/Fuel Injection

The carburetor is placed on the engine to mix the air and fuel in the correct proportion. This is called

the *fuel induction* system. On heat engines today, fuel induction can also be done by *fuel injection*. Air and fuel must be mixed correctly for the engine to operate efficiently. The carburetor's or fuel injector's job is to mix the air and fuel during cold weather, warm weather, high altitudes, high humidity, low- and high-speed conditions, and acceleration.

Engine Systems

All engines require several mechanical, fluid, and electrical systems to operate. These systems are usually considered part of the engine. Without the following systems, the engine would not run correctly or efficiently.

Cooling System. The cooling system is designed to keep the engine temperature at a constant and most efficient temperature. Both liquid-cooled and air-cooled designs are used. Figure 16-7 shows a typical cooling system in a multiple-cylinder reciprocating engine.

Fuel System. The fuel system is used to monitor and precisely control the amount of fuel being fed into the engine. Carburetors and fuel injectors are now generally controlled by computers.

Lubrication System. The lubrication system is used to keep all internal moving parts well lubricated.

Ignition System. The ignition system is used to provide the necessary spark for combustion of the air and fuel mixture. The ignition system must also provide the spark at the correct time during engine operation.

Starting System. The starting system is used to crank the engine during starting conditions only. Usually, a battery and a direct-current starter motor are used in conjunction with switches and a solenoid.

Charging System. The charging system is used to provide electricity to charge the battery and operate the required accessory systems.

Air/Exhaust System. The air and exhaust systems are used to feed air into and out of an engine. Common components include air filters, turbochargers, mufflers, and catalytic converters. Figure 16-8 shows the exhaust system of a typical vehicle.

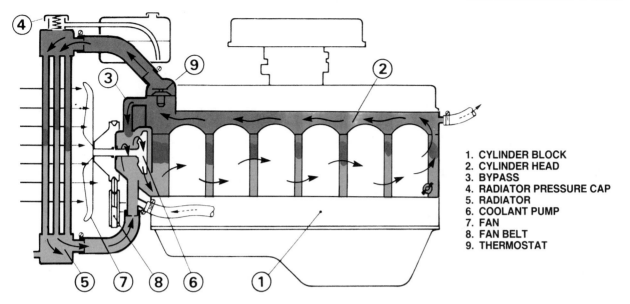

1. CYLINDER BLOCK
2. CYLINDER HEAD
3. BYPASS
4. RADIATOR PRESSURE CAP
5. RADIATOR
6. COOLANT PUMP
7. FAN
8. FAN BELT
9. THERMOSTAT

FIGURE 16-7 This cooling system is an example of one of the major systems used in a heat engine. *Courtesy of First Brands Corporation*

FIGURE 16-8 The exhaust system on a heat engine such as in this vehicle, is used to reduce noise and eliminate pollution. *Courtesy of Volkswagen of America*

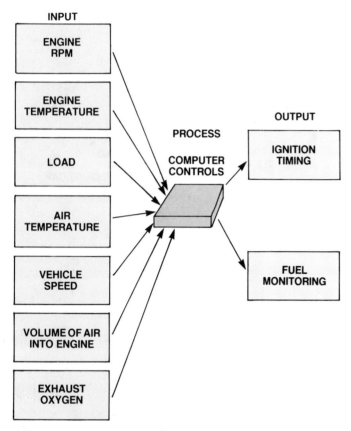

FIGURE 16-9 Computer controls (processor) are used on a heat engine to monitor ignition timing and the fuel.

Computer-controlled Systems. Many heat engines have computer controls (processor) to aid in precise operation. For example, ignition timing and fuel monitoring (outputs) are controlled by inputs from several sources as shown in Figure 16-9.

Pollution Control Systems. Many pollution control systems are used on heat engines today. Most engines produce carbon monoxide, nitrogen oxides, and hydrocarbon emissions. Pollution control systems include positive crankcase ventilation (PCV), controlled combustion systems (CCS), air injection reactors (AIR), exhaust gas recirculators (EGR), and others.

Combustion Requirements

To produce heat, some form of combustion is required. The quality of combustion has a direct effect on the efficiency of the heat engine. Several terms that relate directly to reciprocating-type engines help to describe combustion requirements.

In addition, several of these concepts are directly related to other types of heat engines as well.

Air, Fuel, and Ignition

All internal combustion-type engines have certain requirements for efficient operation. Every engine has three requirements for effective operation: 1) there must be sufficient air for combustion, 2) the correct amounts of fuel must be mixed with the air, and 3) some type of ignition is needed to start combustion. When these three requirements are met, combustion will take place, Figure 16-10. This combustion changes the chemical energy in the fuel to thermal energy. The thermal energy will then cause a rapid expansion of burning gases. This expansion pushes on the pistons or turbine blades. For example, these forces cause crankshafts to rotate or generators to turn. The rotary motion can then be used for moving transportation technology. If any one of these three requirements is missing, the engine will not run.

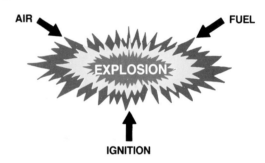

FIGURE 16-10 Air, fuel, and ignition are the three requirements for efficient combustion in a heat engine.

Timing

Timing is defined as the process of identifying the exact time when the air, fuel and ignition for combustion occurs. Most internal combustion engines require exact timing of certain events. This is done in relationship to the position of the piston and crankshaft. In order for the engine to operate efficiently, the air and fuel mixture must enter the cylinder at the correct time. This means that the intake valve must be opened and closed at the correct time. The exhaust valve must also be opened and closed at the correct time.

The ignition must also be timed. Ignition of the air and fuel must occur at a precise time. The timing of the ignition also changes with the speed and load of the engine. When the intake and exhaust valves are correctly timed, and the ignition occurs at the correct time, maximum power will be obtained in converting chemical energy into mechanical energy.

Air to Fuel Ratio

Air to fuel ratio is defined as the ratio of air to fuel mixed in any heat engine.. The air and fuel must be thoroughly mixed. Each molecule of fuel must have enough air surrounding it to be completely burned. If the two are not mixed in the correct ratio, engine efficiency will drop. Exhaust emission levels will also increase.

The standard air to fuel ratio should be about 15 parts of air to 1 part of fuel. This measurement is calculated by weight. Actually, the most efficient ratio is stated as 14.7:1. For every pound of fuel used, 15 pounds of air are needed, Figure 16-11A. In terms of size, this is equal to burning 1 gallon of fuel to 9,000 gallons of air.

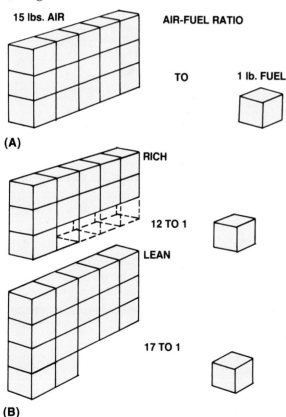

(A)

(B)

FIGURE 16-11 (A) Any combustion process works most efficiently when there is an exact air to fuel mixture. This mixture is usually 15 to 1 (exactly 14.7:1). (B) A rich air to fuel ratio has less air. A lean air to fuel ratio has more air.

Rich and Lean Mixtures. A low ratio of around 12:1 suggests a *rich mixture* of fuel. A mixture of 18:1 suggests a *lean mixture*. The rich and lean mixtures are shown in Figure 16-11B. Generally, rich mixtures are less efficient during combustion. The rich mixture is used during cold weather starting conditions. The lean mixture burns hotter than a rich mixture. Normally, the fuel acts as a coolant in the combustion process. With less fuel to cool, the combustion process gets hotter. A lean mixture can cause severe damage to the pistons and valves and other internal parts if not corrected.

Much has been done in the past few years to control the air to fuel ratio to exact requirements. Fuel systems are better able to keep the mixture under control with the use of computers and special types of fuel injection. By controlling air-fuel mixtures accurately, efficiency of the engine increases. For example, fuel mileage on cars can be increased well into the 40 to 50 miles per gallon range for smaller engine sizes.

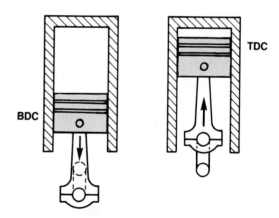

FIGURE 16-12 The position of the piston is shown at bottom dead center (BDC) and top dead center (TDC).

TDC and BDC

TDC stands for top dead center. BDC stands for bottom dead center. These terms are related to reciprocating piston engines. TDC indicates the position of the piston when it reaches the top of its upward motion. When the piston is at the bottom of its travel, it is at bottom dead center (BDC), Figure 16-12. These two terms are used to help identify the position of the piston during some of the timing processes.

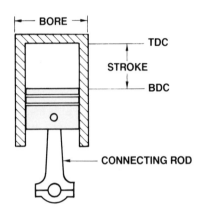

FIGURE 16-13 The bore and stroke of an engine.

Bore and Stroke

The bore and stroke of an engine help to identify its size, Figure 16-13. The *bore* of the engine is defined as the diameter of the cylinder. The *stroke* of the engine is a measurement of the distance the piston travels from the top to the bottom of its movement or the length from TDC to BDC.

The stroke is determined by the design of the crankshaft. The distance from the center of the crankshaft to the center of the crankpin is called the *throw*, Figure 16-14. This dimension, when multiplied by 2, is the same distance traveled by the stroke. If the stroke is changed on any heat engine, the crankshaft will have a different length throw.

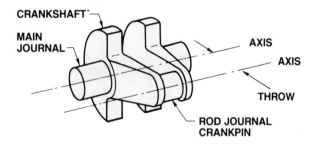

FIGURE 16-14 The throw is the distance from the center of the crankshaft to the center of the crankpin.

Engine Displacement

Engine displacement is defined as the volume of air in all of the cylinders of an engine. Each cylinder has a certain displacement.

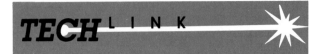

Displacement of a cylinder can be determined by using the following formula:

Displacement = 0.785 × bore² × Stroke in cubic inches

This formula gives the exact displacement in cubic inches of one piston from top dead center to bottom dead center. In order to calculate the displacement in metric units the formula is the same, only the bore and stroke are measured in centimeters.

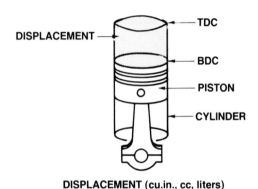

DISPLACEMENT (cu.in., cc, liters)

FIGURE 16-15 Displacement is the volume above the piston at bottom dead center.

Figure 16-15 shows a graphical example of the displacement of a cylinder. When there is more than one cylinder, the total displacement is multiplied by the number of cylinders.

Displacement is often calculated in cubic inches. However, today, many engines are sized by cubic centimeters (cc or cm³) and by liters. For example, today's engines are identified as 2.5 liters, 850 cc, and so on. The conversion from cubic inches to cc is:

$$1 \text{ in}^3 = 16.387 \text{ cc}$$

and

$$1{,}000 \text{ cc} = 1 \text{ liter}$$

Compression Ratio

During any heat engine operation, the air and fuel mixture must be compressed. This compression helps squeeze and mix the air and fuel molecules for better combustion. All heat engines require some form of compression for improved efficiency. Actually, the more compression of the air and fuel, the better the efficiency of the engine.

Compression ratio is a measure of how much the air and fuel has been compressed. *Compression ratio* is defined as the ratio of the volume in the cylinder above the piston when the piston is at BDC, to the volume in the cylinder above the piston when the piston is at TDC. Compression ratio is shown in Figure 16-16. Common compression ratios range anywhere from 6:1 on small gas engines and 8:1 on low-compression car engines, to 25:1 on diesel engines.

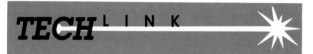

The formula for calculating compression ratio in any piston-type engine is:

Compression Ratio =

$$\frac{\text{Volume above the piston at BDC}}{\text{Volume above the piston at TDC}}$$

In many engines at TDC, the top of the piston is even or level with the top of the cylinder block. The combustion chamber volume is in the cavity in the cylinder head above the piston. This is modified slightly by the shape of the top of the piston. The combustion chamber volume must be added to each volume stated in the formula to give accurate results.

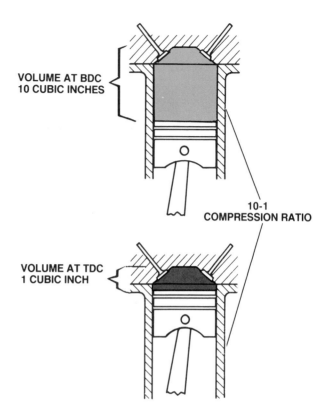

FIGURE 16-16 The compression ratio is the ratio of the volume at BDC compared to the volume at TDC.

BMEP

BMEP stands for the phrase b̲rake m̲ean e̲ffective pressure. This is an engineering term used to indicate how much pressure is applied to the top of any piston from TDC to BDC. It is measured in pounds per square inch. This term becomes very useful when analyzing the results of different fuels used in heat engines. For example, if diesel fuel is used in an engine, more BMEP is produced. This then produces more output power than if gasoline as a fuel were used. Also, as different injection systems, combustion designs, and new ignition systems are developed, they all affect the BMEP of the engine.

Four-Stroke Engine Design

The four-stroke engine is one of the most popular types of reciprocating-type heat engines. A four-stroke engine can also be called a four-cycle engine. The terms stroke or cycle can be used interchangeably. A four-stroke engine has a very distinct operation. The four strokes are titled intake, compression, power, and exhaust.

When the piston moves downward with the intake valve open, intake occurs. When the piston moves upward with both valves closed, compression occurs. When the spark ignites the mixture after combustion, the power stroke occurs. After the power stroke, the exhaust valve opens. As the piston moves upward, the spent gases are exhausted.

The next sections describe the four-stroke gasoline engine in detail. However, remember that there are also four-cycle diesel engines as well.

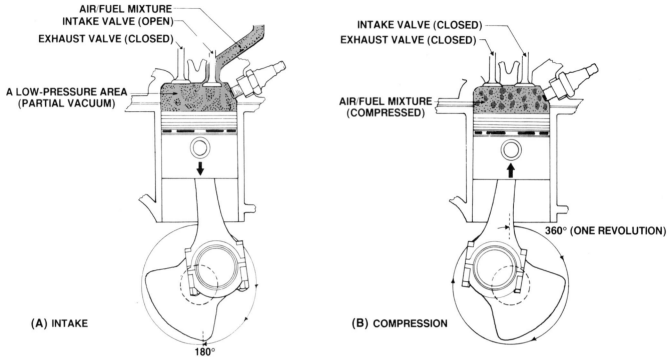

FIGURE 16-17 The four events of a four-stroke gasoline engine are: intake, compression, power, and exhaust. *Reprinted by permission of PWS-KENT Publishing Company, by Glen F. Ireland, Automotive Fuel, Ignition, and Emission Control Systems © 1981*

Intake Stroke

Refer to Figure 16-17A. To start, the location of the piston is near TDC. Note that the intake valve is opened. As the piston is cranked downward, called the *intake stroke*, air and fuel are brought into the cylinder. This occurs because, as the piston moves down, a vacuum is created. When any object is removed from an area, a vacuum is created. This vacuum (lower than atmospheric pressure) brings fresh air and fuel into the cylinder. It can also be said that higher air pressure outside of the engine pushes the air and fuel into the engine.

The air is first drawn through the carburetor. Here, the air is mixed with the fuel at the correct air to fuel ratio (14.7:1). When the piston gets to BDC, the intake valve starts to close. With the valve closed, the air and fuel mixture is trapped inside the cylinder area.

Compression Stroke

The piston now travels from BDC to TDC with the air and fuel mixture in the cylinder. This action is called the *compression stroke*. See Figure 16-17B. The compression stroke takes the air-fuel mixture and compresses it, according to the compression ratio of the engine. This compression causes the air

and fuel to be mixed very effectively. Actually, the higher the compression ratio, the greater the mixing of air and fuel. This leads to improved engine efficiency.

It is very important that there are no leaks through which the compression gases can escape. Possible leaks may occur by the valves, the gasket between the head and cylinder block, and past the rings on the piston. Note that at the end of the compression stroke, the crankshaft has revolved 360 degrees or one revolution.

During the compression stroke, the air and fuel are actually heated from the action of compression. It is like using an air pump to pump up a tire. As the air at the bottom of the pump is compressed, the air gets hotter. If the compression ratio is too high, temperatures within the combustion chamber may ignite the fuel. This process, referred to as *pre-ignition*, can cause pinging. This means that the combustion in the chamber started before the piston reached TDC.

It would be very helpful if compression ratios were increased. However, as long as air and fuel are being compressed, the compression ratios must be low so the air and fuel do not preignite. Higher compression ratio engines are discussed in the diesel section of this chapter.

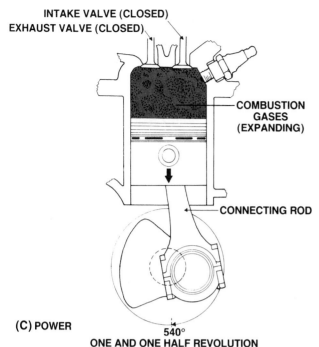

INTAKE VALVE (CLOSED)
EXHAUST VALVE (CLOSED)

— COMBUSTION GASES (EXPANDING)

— CONNECTING ROD

(C) POWER
540°
ONE AND ONE HALF REVOLUTION
FIGURE 16-17 Continued.

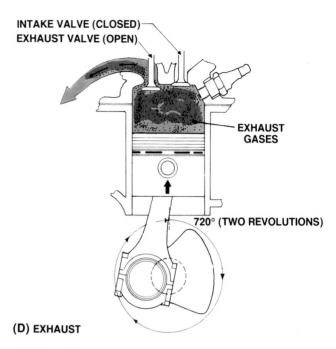

INTAKE VALVE (CLOSED)
EXHAUST VALVE (OPEN)

— EXHAUST GASES

720° (TWO REVOLUTIONS)

(D) EXHAUST

Power Stroke

During the *power stroke*, shown in Figure 16-17C, both the intake and exhaust valves remain closed. As the piston rises on the compression stroke, a spark will occur slightly ahead of TDC. At this point, air, fuel and ignition are present. This causes the air and fuel to ignite. When this happens, the expansion of gases during combustion pushes down on the top of the piston. This pressure pushes the piston downward through the power stroke. This is also when BMEP is created.

Exhaust Stroke

The final stroke in the four-cycle design is called the exhaust stroke, shown in Figure 16-17D. The *exhaust stroke* starts when the piston starts moving upward again. The crankshaft continues to rotate because of the flywheel weight. At the beginning of the exhaust stroke, the exhaust valve opens. As the piston travels upward, it pushes the burned or spent gases out of the cylinder as exhaust.

Near the top of the exhaust stroke, the exhaust valve starts to close. At this point, the intake valve is already starting to open for the next intake stroke. It is important to note that the crankshaft has revolved two revolutions at this point. Only one power stroke has occurred. If the engine is running at 4,000 r/min, then there are 2,000 power pulses for each cylinder per minute.

Timing Diagrams

A *timing diagram* is a method used to identify the times at which all of the four-stroke events occur. A timing diagram is shown in Figure 16-18. The

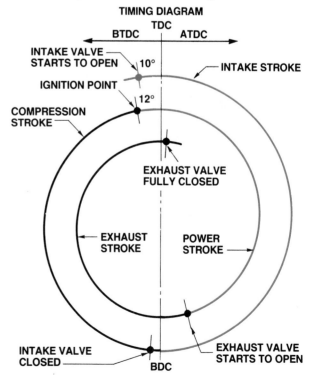

FIGURE 16-18 This timing diagram shows the point in degrees rotation that each event occurs on a four-cycle engine.

diagram is set on a vertical and horizontal axis. There are 360 degrees around the axis. Events of the four-cycle engine can be graphed on the circle. One way to look at the diagram is to think of these events in terms of the position of the crankshaft through 360 degrees rotation. For example, at the top of the diagram, the piston would be located exactly at TDC. Any event that happens before TDC is referred to as BTDC (before top dead center). Any event that happens after top dead center is called ATDC (after top dead center). The mark at the bottom of the graph would illustrate the position of the piston at BDC. Two circles are shown. This is because two circles represent two complete revolutions of the crankshaft. During the four strokes of operation, the crankshaft revolves two complete revolutions, or 720 degrees of rotation.

Four-stroke Timing Diagram Procedure

Referring again to Figure 16-18, follow through the four-stroke design on the timing diagram. Note that the events and degrees may vary with each engine and manufacturer. The cycle starts with the intake valves opening slightly before TDC. It should be fully open at TDC. It takes this many degrees of crankshaft rotation to open the intake valve completely.

As the piston travels downward on the intake stroke, the intake valve starts to close shortly before BDC. It is fully closed after BDC. At this point the intake stroke is completed.

The compression stroke starts when the intake valve is fully closed. The piston travels upward, compressing the air and fuel mixture. As the piston is traveling upward, the air-fuel mixture is being mixed by the compression of gases. Also, the temperature is rising inside of the combustion chamber. About 12 degrees before TDC, ignition from a spark plug occurs. The point of ignition is several degrees before TDC. It takes about 12 degrees for the combustion to actually build up to a maximum. At TDC, the combustion is at a maximum point. Now, the piston is ready to be pushed downward.

If the timing of the ignition were sooner, or more than 12 degrees before TDC, then the combustion would occur too soon. This would then reduce the BMEP during the power stroke. If the timing of the ignition were too late, or after TDC, then the BMEP would also be less. It is important that maximum power from the combustion of gases occurs just

when the piston is at TDC.

The power stroke starts when the piston starts downward. In this case, the power stroke is shown on the inside circle of the timing diagram. As the combustion occurs, the gases expand very rapidly. This expansion causes the piston to be forced down. This action produces the power for the engine.

Near BDC, at the end of the power stroke, the exhaust valve starts to open. By the time the piston gets to BDC, the exhaust valve is fully open. As the crankshaft continues to turn, the piston travels upward. This action forces the burned gases out of the exhaust valve, into the atmosphere. The exhaust valve is fully closed a few degrees after TDC. The time in which both the intake valve and the exhaust valve are open, (near TDC) is called *valve overlap*.

Advance and Retarded Timing

The timing of the ignition is the only part of the timing on most engines that can be adjusted. If the ignition time is moved or adjusted more BTDC, the condition is called *advance timing*. If the ignition time is moved or adjusted toward or after TDC (ATDC) the condition is called *retarded timing*.

Two-Cycle Engine Design

The two-cycle engine design is used on many small engines, such as outboard motors, lawn mowers, chain saws, snowmobiles, cycles, and other recreational vehicles.

Two-cycle Engine Operation

Figure 16-19 shows an example of two-cycle engine operation. Note that many of the engine parts are the same as for the four-cycle engine. One difference is that the cylinder does not use the standard type valves to allow air and fuel to enter the engine. In order to follow the operation, consider the events both on the top and on the bottom of the piston. In operation, as the piston in Figure 16-19A moves upward, compression is produced above the piston. A vacuum is also created within the crankcase area below the piston. The vacuum is used to bring in a fresh charge of air and fuel past a reed valve. Note that oil must be added to the air-fuel mixture at this point. This is because there is no oil in the crankcase as with four-cycle engines. The oil in the fuel acts as the lubricant. Normally, an oil to gas ratio of between 20:1 up to 50:1 or higher is used, depending upon the year and manufacturer of the engine.

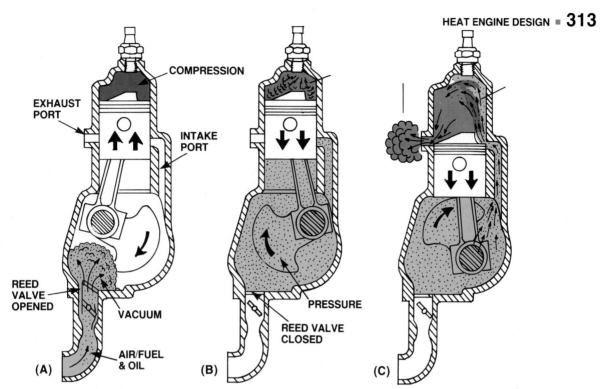

FIGURE 16-19 The two-cycle engine uses the pressure and vacuum created below the piston to draw in a fresh charge of air/fuel/oil to be used in the combustion chamber. *Courtesy DCA Educational Products*

As the piston continues upward on the compression stroke, eventually, a spark and thus combustion occurs, Figure 16-19B. This pushes the piston downward. As the piston moves farther down, a high pressure is created in the crankcase area. The reed valve is forced closed by the pressure, sealing the crankcase area. When the piston gets low enough in its stroke, it eventually opens both the intake and exhaust ports, Figure 16-19C. *Ports* are simply holes cut into the cylinder to allow air and fuel to enter and exhaust escape.

When the ports are open, the crankcase pressure forces a mass of air/fuel/oil mixture into the combustion chamber. This mass also helps to remove any exhaust gases by way of the exhaust port. As the piston starts upward, the ports are closed. Compression and power continue on top of the piston, while suction and a small pressure continue on the bottom of the piston.

Two-cycle Timing Diagram

To better understand the two-cycle engine, a timing diagram is again used. Remember that the vertical axis represents the TDC and BDC point on the piston and crankshaft. The events of the two-cycle process can now be graphed on the timing diagram, as shown in Figure 16-20. Although each engine

diagram may differ slightly, the diagram shows several common points.

1. Timing for combustion occurs slightly before TDC.
2. During the power stroke, the exhaust valve opens slightly before the intake.
3. During the compression stroke the exhaust valve closes slightly after the intake port.
4. When the piston is at the bottom of its travel, both intake and exhaust are occurring.

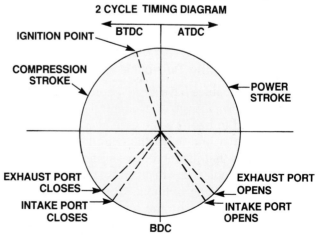

FIGURE 16-20 This timing diagram shows the events that occur during two-cycle engine operation.

Advantages and Disadvantages of Two-cycle Engines

There are several distinct advantages and disadvantages of the two-cycle engine.

Advantages

1. Two-cycle engines are very responsive because there is a power pulse every revolution. (Note that the two-cycle engine has a power pulse every revolution.) This means it takes less time to get from 500 r/min at idle, to say 4,000 r/min maximum speed.
2. Two-cycle engines are usually lighter in weight than four-cycle engines. This is because they usually have fewer parts.
3. Two-cycle engines can be operated at varying angles of operation. This is because there is no crankcase that holds oil. This is one among several reasons that two-cycle engines are usually found on recreational vehicles.

Disadvantages

1. Two-cycle engines lose some of their efficiency for several reasons. These include:
   a. Poor volumetric efficiency. Air and fuel can only enter the cylinder for a very short period of time. This reduces the total amount of air and fuel that can enter the engine, thus reducing efficiency.
   b. Poor combustion efficiency. The oil in the air/fuel mixture reduces combustion efficiency.
   c. Less BMEP. Total force during the power stroke will be reduced because the power stroke is shortened. The power stroke ends when the exhaust port is opened.

Loop Scavenging Two-cycle Engine

Two-cycle engines have been improved from the standard design. *Loop scavenging* is a two-cycle design used to improve the ease at which air and fuel can enter and leave the cylinder. The main difference is that the reed valve system previously discussed is replaced with an intake port located on the bottom of the cylinder. The intake port is opened and closed by the position of the piston skirt. Events occur both on top and bottom of the piston.

The events occur in three phases. In phase 1, the

FIGURE 16-21 One of the more popular applications for the two-cycle, loop scavenging-type engine is in a snowmobile. This is a three-cylinder, two-cycle engine. *Courtesy of Polaris Industries L.P.*

piston moves upward and the piston skirt opens the intake port in the cylinder. The vacuum below the piston draws in fresh fuel, air, and oil for lubrication. During phase 1, compression above the piston is also occurring. During phase 2, power is produced on top of the piston. Below the piston, compression occurs on the air/fuel and oil mixture. During phase 3, the exhaust port and the intake port to the cylinder are opened. This causes the air/fuel/oil mixture below the piston to enter the cylinder. The spent exhaust gases in the cylinder are also exhausted to the atmosphere. Figure 16-21 shows a typical example of a two-cycle, loop scavenging-type engine used in a snowmobile.

Diesel Engine Design

The diesel engine is much the same as the gasoline engine in many of its principles. It is considered a four-cycle engine. The diesel engine is considered an internal combustion engine. It is also considered a compression ignition engine rather than a spark ignition engine. One of the most common applications for diesel engines is in trucks, as shown in Figure 16-22.

Diesel Compression Ratio

One major difference between a diesel engine and gasoline engine is that the diesel engine has a very high compression ratio. Compression ratios of 20:1

(A)   **(B)**

FIGURE 16-22 Diesel engines are mostly used in trucks as well as in many other heavy-duty applications.
Courtesy of (A) Detroit Diesel Corporation and (B) Cummins Engine Co. Inc.

up to 25:1 are very common. This high compression ratio means that any fuel that is in the cylinder during compression will become ignited. Therefore, only air is brought into the cylinder during the intake stroke. A carburetor is not needed to mix the air and fuel; fuel is injected in a diesel engine. With high compression ratios, temperatures inside the combustion chamber may be as high as 1,000°F. This would be enough to ignite most fuels. This is why the diesel engine is called a compression ignition engine.

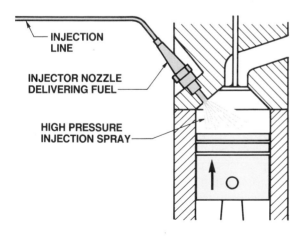

FIGURE 16-23 In a diesel engine, fuel in injected directly into the combustion chamber, under very high pressure, near the top of the compression stroke.

Fuel Injection

A fuel injector injects fuel into the combustion chamber on diesel engines, at or slightly before TDC. This process is called *fuel injection*. A *fuel injector* is a device that pressurizes fuel to nearly 20,000 pounds per square inch (psi). This fuel is injected into the combustion chamber, as shown in Figure 16-23. At this point, all three ingredients (air, fuel, and ignition) are present to produce combustion. The power and exhaust strokes are the same as for the gasoline engine.

Gasoline and Diesel Engines Compared

Figure 16-24 shows some common comparisons between the gasoline and diesel four-stroke or four-cycle engines.

1. The intake on the gasoline engine is an air-fuel mixture. The diesel engine has air only during the intake stroke.
2. The compression pressures on the gasoline engine are lower. This is because the compression ratios are also lower.
3. The air and fuel mixing point on the gasoline engine is at the carburetor or at the fuel injectors. The mixing point on the diesel engine is near top dead center or slightly BTDC by the fuel injector.
4. Combustion is caused by a spark plug on the

gasoline engine. The diesel engine uses the heat of compression for ignition.

5. The power stroke on the gasoline engine produces around 460 psi; the diesel engine produces nearly 1,200 psi. This is because there is more energy in diesel fuel as compared to gasoline.

6. The exhaust temperature of the gasoline engine is much higher. This is because some of the fuel is still burning when being exhausted. The diesel engine has a much cooler exhaust.

7. The efficiency of the diesel engine is about 10% higher than the gasoline engine. This is mostly because there are higher compression ratios and more energy in a gallon of diesel fuel.

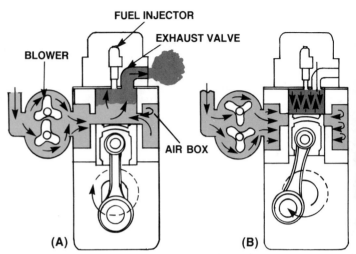

FIGURE 16-25 A two-cycle diesel engine is used in many heavy-duty applications.

COMPARISON BETWEEN GASOLINE AND DIESEL ENGINES		
	GASOLINE	**DIESEL**
Intake	Air-Fuel	Air
Compression	8-10 to 1 130 psi 545°F	16-20 to 1 400-600 psi 1,000°F
Air-Fuel Mixing Point	Carburetor or Fuel Injection	Near Top Dead Center By Injection
Combustion	Spark Ignition	Compression Ignition
Power	460 psi	1,200 psi
Exhaust	1,300°-1,800°F CO = 3%	700°-900°F CO = 0.5%
Efficiency	22-28%	32-38%

FIGURE 16-24 A comparison between gasoline and diesel engines.

GM Two-cycle Diesel Engine

Another type of two-cycle engine is manufactured by General Motors (GM). This two-cycle engine is shown in Figure 16-25. The major difference is that a blower forces air through an air box, ports, and into the cylinder when the piston is at BDC, as shown in Figure 16-25A. The piston then comes up on the compression stroke, Figure 16-25B.

Fuel is injected near TDC. The fuel is then ignited by the heat of compression. The power stroke forces the piston downward. At the end of the power stroke, the exhaust valves open. When the intake ports in the cylinder are uncovered, the fresh air pressure from the blower helps to push the exhaust gases out through the exhaust valves. The

advantage to the engine design is that no oil is mixed with the fuel, as with other smaller two-cycle engines. However, a significant amount of frictional horsepower is lost to operate and turn the blower to pump the air.

Rotary Engine Design (Wankel)

In the late 1960s a relatively new engine design was introduced into the power technology markets. Called the *rotary engine*, it is also referred to as the *Wankel engine*. The rotary design has been in existence for some time, and was most popular during the 1970s. Lately, because of improved materials, there has been a renewed interest in developing the rotary engine. In this heat engine, rotors instead of pistons are used to convert chemical energy into mechanical energy. The engine is an intermittent combustion, spark ignition, rotary design (not reciprocating).

Rotary Cycle Operation

Referring to Figure 16-26A, this is called the intake position. The upper port is called the intake port. The lower port is called the exhaust port. There are no valves. The position of the center rotor opens and closes the ports much as the piston does on a two-cycle engine. The rotor moves inside of an elongated circle. Because of the shape of the housing, certain areas are enlarged or compressed during rotation. As the rotor is turned, an internal gear causes the center shaft to rotate. This is the location of the output power.

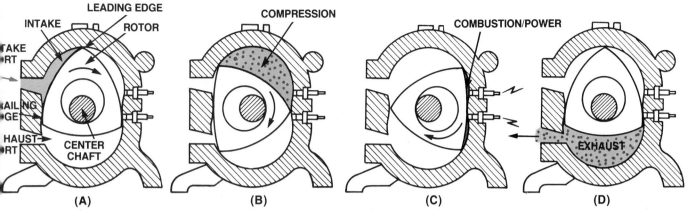

FIGURE 16-26 A rotary engine uses a rotor placed in a special-shaped housing. As the rotor turns, intake, compression, power, and exhaust occur.

When the leading edge of the rotor face sweeps past the inlet port, the intake cycle begins. Fuel and air (14.7:1 air to fuel ratio) is drawn into the enlarged area. This continues until the trailing edge passes the intake port.

As the rotor continues to rotate, the enlarged area is now being compressed. This is called the *compression position*, Figure 16-26B. The compression ratio is very close to that of a standard gasoline engine (8.5:1). This is because both air and fuel are being mixed.

When the rotor travels to the combustion/power position, Figure 16-26C, the air and fuel are completely compressed. At this point, ignition occurs from two spark plugs. Most often, two spark plugs are used for better ignition. All three ingredients for correct combustion are now available. The air and fuel ignite and the combustion causes expansion of gases. This expansion pushes the rotor face downward, causing the rotor to receive a power pulse.

Referring to Figure 16-26D, this is called the exhaust position. As the rotor continues to travel or rotate, the leading edge uncovers the exhaust port. The rotor's movement within the housing causes the exhaust gases to be forced out of the engine.

So far, only one side of the rotor has been analyzed. Note that when intake occurs, compression is occurring on another face of the rotor. Exhaust is also occurring on the third face of the rotor. This means that there are three power pulses for each rotation of the rotor.

The rest of the rotary engine uses many of the same components and systems as the standard gasoline or diesel engine. The carburetor design is the same. The starter, alternator, and external components are the same.

Continuous Combustion Engine Designs

Although gasoline and diesel engines are quite common, other types of engines are also used as power sources in industry and technology. One engine studied for several years is the Stirling engine, a continuous combustion design.

Stirling Engine

The Stirling engine operates very smoothly with complete combustion and low emission characteristics. Both General Motors and Ford Motor Company have studied Stirling engines. Several designs have been tested. The most popular uses a swash plate design.

The engine has four pistons, as shown in Figure 16-27. An external combustion chamber is used.

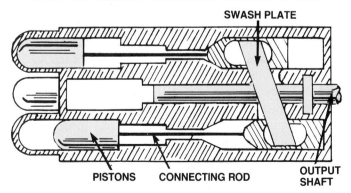

FIGURE 16-27 A Stirling engine has four pistons, a swash plate, and an external combustion chamber.
Courtesy from Energy Technology: Sources of Power, Davis Publications, Inc. 1980

The combustion is considered continuous. The heat from combustion causes the four pistons to be forced downward. Each piston is attached to a swash plate. Mechanically, the *swash plate* is a disc attached in an angular position to the output shaft of the engine. As the pistons are forced downward, the connecting rods sequentially push the swash plate in a rotary motion. The power pulses must occur in the correct order. Referring to Figure 16-28, as number 1 piston fires, it pushes the swash plate clockwise. Then number 4 piston must fire. Then number 3, then number 2, and so on. The engine runs smoothly because of the swash plate. The purpose of the swash plate is the same as the crankshaft action on a conventional internal combustion engine. It changes reciprocating motion to rotary motion.

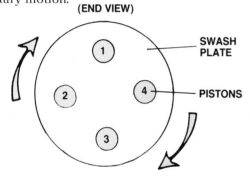

FIGURE 16-28 The swash plate is used to convert the motion of the pistons into rotary motion, needed for pushing a vehicle forward. *Courtesy from Energy Technology: Sources of Power, Davis Publications, Inc. 1980*

Stirling Gas Cycle

The Stirling gas cycle is shown in Figure 16-29. Thermal energy from any resource, such as coal, oil, or diesel fuel is applied to the heater. All heaters are connected together, although, in the diagram, they appear to be separated. The heat causes the gases to expand above the number 1 piston. Also, the area below the number 1 piston is connected to the cooler near the number 4 piston. This causes the gases below the number 1 cylinder to contract. The difference in pressure across the number 1 cylinder forces the piston downward.

As the number 1 piston moves down, the gases below the piston are forced through the cooler, generator and heater to the number 4 piston. As the gases pass through the cooler, they contract. The gases are then heated by the generator and heater.

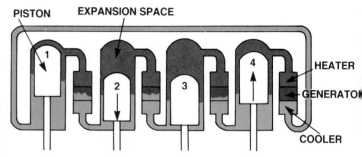

FIGURE 16-29 The Stirling engine has four pistons with a firing order of 1, 4, 3, 2. *Courtesy from Energy Technology: Sources of Power, Davis Publications, Inc. 1980*

The gases expand and build up pressure above the number 4 piston. At the same time, the gases below the number 4 piston are near the number 3 cooler. This contracts the gases. Now there is a pressure differential across the number 3 piston. This process continues to number 2, then to number 1 piston again. The firing order is then, piston #4, 3, 2, 1.

The Stirling engine gets four power pulses per revolution against the swash plate. There is also a suction on the bottom of the piston. This design has a great potential for even higher efficiency. The Stirling engine is considered a very quiet and smooth-running engine.

FIGURE 16-30 The gas turbine all-ceramic engine can operate at the high temperatures and speeds necessary for good fuel economy. *Courtesy of Garrett Corporation*

Gas Turbine Engine

Another type of heat engine used in both transportation and industrial applications is the gas turbine engine shown in Figure 16-30. This all-ceramic engine is classified as continuous and internal combustion. The motion produced by the turbine is considered rotary motion.

The gas turbine engine has been tested by several manufacturers in the past 15 years. However, because of its high cost, it still has not been used extensively in automotive markets. However, gas turbines are used in other transportation applications, including helicopters.

Gas Turbine Cycle

The layout of turbine parts is shown in Figure 16-31. The gas turbine burns diesel fuel. A centrifugal *air compressor*, rotating at 35,000 r/min, forces *pure* air (not air and fuel) into the engine. The heat of compression increases the temperature to about 500°F.

Air passes through the compressor and through a regenerator. The *regenerator* is designed to pick up excess heat from the exhaust. As the exhaust gases flow through the regenerator, the heat is conducted into the metal of the regenerator. The regenerator turns only 18 r/min so heat is easily absorbed. As the intake air passes through the regenerator, it picks up this excess heat. The process brings the air temperature up to about 1,200°F.

The air is then sent into the burner or combustion chamber. Air and fuel are added to an already burning flame. Coming out of the burner, the hot gases flow through a vortex chamber and into the gasifier or compressor turbine. The temperature at this point is nearly 2,100°F. The compressor turbine turns nearly 35,000 r/min. Its major purpose is to turn the air compressor at that speed.

The remaining energy in the gases from the first (gasifier) turbine enters the second turbine, called the *power turbine*. It is connected to the part of the application that requires torque. The temperature of the gases going into the power turbine is nearly 1,400°F. This energy turns the power turbine to produce torque. The gases then pass through the regenerator and out into the atmosphere.

The turbine engine also has potential for heavy-duty applications in the transportation sector. It averages about 45% efficiency. However, the cost of this engine is still well above that of a comparable gasoline or diesel engine. The advantages include smooth running, use of multiple fuels, higher efficiency, and no liquid cooling system. The disadvantages include high cost, no dealerships for repair, no parts distribution systems available, and too much power for the average vehicle.

Steam Turbine Engine

Another form of turbine is called the *steam turbine heat engine*. This engine is usually used in industrial generator applications. The big difference between

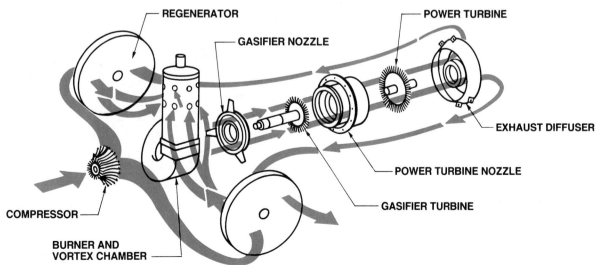

GAS TURBINE FLOW CHART

REGENERATOR — POWER TURBINE — GASIFIER NOZZLE — EXHAUST DIFFUSER — POWER TURBINE NOZZLE — GASIFIER TURBINE — COMPRESSOR — BURNER AND VORTEX CHAMBER

FIGURE 16-31 The gas flow is shown through the turbine parts. *Courtesy of General Motors Corporation*

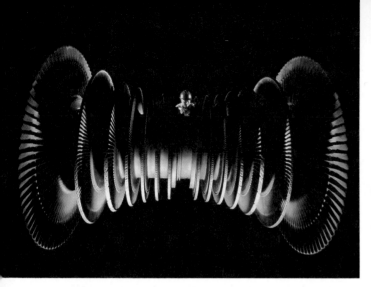

FIGURE 16-32 Turbine blades used in a steam turbine engine. *Courtesy of Union Electric Co.*

FIGURE 16-33 An example of a large steam turbine unit used in a nuclear power plant. *Courtesy of New York Power Authority*

a steam turbine and a gas turbine is the type of power used to turn the turbine. A steam turbine uses steam heated by coal or oil in a power plant system. The steam turbine is much larger than a gas turbine and produces a higher torque for turning the generator. Figure 16-32 shows an example of a set of turbine blades used in a commercial steam generator. Figure 16-33 shows a partial view of a large commercial steam turbine. Only half of the turbine is shown; the other half is below the surface of the floor. This steam turbine is used to turn a generator to produce electricity.

Air Force Jet

Reaction-type engines are used as propulsion to produce thrust. Many military aircraft also use jet engines for propulsion. A U.S. Air Force F-16C streams contrails off its forebody, as it climbs with maximum thrust (engine power) during a predelivery check over Fort Worth, Texas.

All aircraft are given a predelivery check to determine their operational characteristics, propulsion system operation, handling, safety, and maneuverability. These data are important to monitor the quality of each engine and propulsion system manufactured. *Courtesy of General Dynamics Corporation*

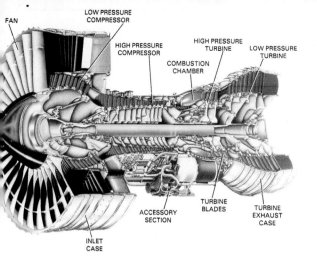

FAN
LOW PRESSURE COMPRESSOR
HIGH PRESSURE COMPRESSOR
COMBUSTION CHAMBER
HIGH PRESSURE TURBINE
LOW PRESSURE TURBINE
TURBINE BLADES
TURBINE EXHAUST CASE
ACCESSORY SECTION
INLET CASE

FIGURE 16-34 Cut-away view of a jet reaction-type engine. *Courtesy of Pratt & Whitney Aircraft Division*

Jet (Reaction) Engine

As stated earlier in the text, thrust is needed to propel a spacecraft forward. Thrust, also called *reaction*, can be produced by jet engines as well as rocket engines. Thrust can be explained by referring to Newton's second and third laws. Newton's second law states that "an unbalance of force on a body tends to produce an acceleration in the direction of the force." Newton's third law states that "for every force there is an opposite and equal force." These two laws working together cause a jet engine to produce thrust. An unbalanced condition is produced inside of the engine's combustion chambers. This causes acceleration of gases to escape. The force of the gases has an opposite and equal force toward the front of the engine. This causes the object to move forward.

Jet engines are designed much the same as smaller gas or steam turbines. The difference is in the type of compressor and the number of turbines. Figure 16-34 shows a typical cut-away view of a reaction-type engine. The compressor is made of several *axial* stages. Rather than one burner, several are used to ignite the fuel. As the hot gases leave the burners, they cause several turbine stages to turn. These turbine stages are usually used to turn the compressor. The remaining energy in the exhaust gases comes out of the rear of the engine. Because of the difference in pressure inside of the burners, thrust or reaction is produced. This thrust causes the vehicle to move forward.

Summary

- The types of heat engines include internal, external, intermittent, and continuous combustion, reciprocating and rotary engines.
- The basic parts of a heat engine are the cylinder block, cylinders, pistons, connecting rods and crankshaft, cylinder head, combustion chamber, valves/ports, camshaft, flywheel, and carburetor and fuel injectors.
- All engines have several systems that enable the engine to operate efficiently. These include the cooling, fuel, lubrication, ignition, starting, charging, air/exhaust, computer, and pollution control systems.
- Any combustion requires air, fuel and ignition mixed together at the right time for correct operation.
- The best air to fuel ratio is 14.7:1 by weight.
- A rich mixture of air and fuel is 13:1; a lean mixture is 17:1.
- The bore and stroke are used to calculate the displacement of a heat engine.
- Compression ratio is the ratio of the volume above the piston at TDC compared to the volume at BDC.
- The four-cycle engine has intake, compression, power, and exhaust cycles, all of which must occur at the correct time.
- Timing diagrams are used to graphically represent the events of two- and four-cycle engines.
- Two-cycle engines have a power pulse every crankshaft revolution, whereas four-cycle engines have a power pulse every other crankshaft revolution.
- Loop scavenging is another design used in a two-cycle engine to cause the air/fuel/oil mixture to enter the engine.
- Diesel engine compression ratios are much higher than they are for gasoline engines.
- Diesel engines use high-pressure injection to get the fuel into the cylinder.
- A two-cycle diesel is also manufactured by GM which uses a blower to get the air into the cylinders.
- The rotary engine uses a triangular rotor placed in a special housing to create intake, compression, power, and exhaust.
- Continuous combustion engines commonly used include the gas turbine, steam turbine, and jet (reaction) heat engine.

REVIEW

1. The order of events on a four-cycle engine are _____, compression, _____, and _____.

2. The carburetor is considered a/an _____ as part of the systems model.

3. The three ingredients necessary for an internal combustion engine to operate include, _____, fuel, and _____.

4. An engine has a bore of 3.5 and a stroke of 3.2. The piston displacement of this engine is _____.

5. The volume above a piston at BDC is equal to 10.5 cubic inches. The volume above the piston at TDC is equal to 1.3 cubic inches. The compression ratio of this engine is equal to _____.

6. The spark on a four-cycle engine usually occurs at about _____ degrees _____ top dead center.

7. The Stirling engine changes the piston motion to rotary motion by using a _____.

8. The _____ is used in a gas turbine to change the thermal energy in the combustion into rotary motion.

9. Identify six classifications of engines, and state the definition of each.

10. What are the purposes of the cooling, ignition, and computer systems used on a gasoline engine?

11. Define a rich and a lean air to fuel mixture.

12. Identify the difference between TDC and BDC.

13. Describe the four events on a four-cycle engine.

14. Describe how loop scavenging is different from using a reed valve two-cycle engine.

15. Draw a two-cycle timing diagram, and indicate when the intake, compression, power and exhaust occur. Also show when the intake and exhaust ports open and close.

16. State three differences between a diesel and a gasoline engine.

17. Describe the four events on a Wankel or rotary engine.

18. Define complete operation and parts of a gas turbine engine using regenerators.

CHAPTER ACTIVITIES

 ENGINE TIMING

INTRODUCTION

When studying internal combustion engines, the timing of the four-cycle events is very important toward understanding engine operation. During this activity, you will be able to identify and plot all timing events of a small, four-cycle gas engine.

TECHNOLOGICAL LITERACY SKILLS

Problem solving, data collection, data analysis, plotting data, instrumentation.

OBJECTIVES

At the completion of this activity, you will be able to:

1. Determine the points in the timing cycle for intake, compression, power and exhaust.
2. Determine the point of ignition in the timing cycle.
3. Identify the number of degrees for valve overlap.
4. Lay out a complete timing cycle with all points recorded.

MATERIALS

1. An operational four-cycle gasoline or diesel engine, between 1 and 15 horsepower, with the valves located in the block
2. A protractor for measuring degrees of crankshaft rotation
3. Various small engine tools for removal and reassembly of parts
4. A dial indicator
5. Engine Timing handout

PROCEDURE

1. Select a four-cycle engine that is able to rotate and produce spark.

▶**CAUTION:** Always wear safety glasses when working with tools in the laboratory. Also, make sure you know the correct operation of all tools and machines in the laboratory. If not, check with your instructor.

---

2. Using the proper tools, remove the cylinder head, exposing the valves and piston head.
3. Position the crankshaft at the top of its travel (TDC).
4. Mark the end of the crankshaft, so that readings on a protractor can be taken to determine the degrees of crankshaft rotation. This can be done by taping a small wire to the end of the crankshaft long enough to reach the protractor numbers easily. The wire will then point to the protractor numbers to show degrees rotation of the crankshaft. Make sure the wire is pointing directly vertical or upward.
5. Now rotate the crankshaft in the direction of engine operation and observe the operational characteristics of the piston and valves.
6. Position the piston at the bottom of its stroke (BDC) with the wire pointing down.
7. Put a dial indicator on the intake valve and adjust the dial to zero. The dial indicator is used to show when the valves start and stop moving.
8. Rotate the engine crankshaft to bring the piston up on the exhaust stroke. Watch at what point the intake valve starts to open.
9. Stop moving the crankshaft when the intake valve starts to open.
10. Using the protractor, measure the degrees BTDC (before top dead center) at which the intake valve starts to open. Measure the degrees of the position of the wire on the crankshaft.
11. Using the same type of procedure, measure the following:
    a. When the intake valve is fully closed.
    b. When the exhaust valve starts to open.
    c. When the exhaust valve is fully closed.
    d. The degrees of crankshaft rotation at which the intake and exhaust valves overlap.

12. Plot these points on the Engine Timing handout. Two circles are used because there are two complete revolutions of the crankshaft. Make sure the points are on the correct circle.
13. Determine the point of ignition in relation to the crankshaft position by the following procedure:
   a. Remove the spark plug and ground it out (touch to frame).
   b. Rotate the engine until the spark plug fires and note the degrees of rotation.
   c. If this method does not work, use a dwell meter or ohmmeter to determine exactly when the ignition points open. This is the time the plug fires.
   d. Note this position of degrees rotation on the handout provided.
14. On the Engine Timing handout, identify the starting and stopping points (degrees) for:
   a. Intake
   b. Compression
   c. Power
   d. Exhaust

REVIEW QUESTIONS

1. Why is the ignition timing usually before top dead center?
2. Looking at the timing diagram, how could the efficiency of the engine be improved?
3. What event on the timing cycle is adjustable?

 # COMPRESSION RATIO

INTRODUCTION

One important concept when studying gas and diesel engines is called compression ratios. This activity is designed to measure and test the compression ratio of a small gasoline engine.

TECHNOLOGICAL LITERARY SKILLS

Problem solving, data collection, data analysis, and experimentation.

OBJECTIVES

At the completion of this activity, you will be able to:
1. Determine the compression ratio of a small gas engine.
2. Compare this ratio to that which is stated in the maintenance manual.

MATERIALS

1. Small four-cycle gas or diesel engine between 1 and 10 horsepower and maintenance manual
2. Inside micrometer
3. Vernier caliper or scale used to measure the stroke on the engine
4. A small graduated cylinder measuring in milliliters or cubic inches
5. Assorted small engine tools
6. Compression Ratio handout

PROCEDURE

1. Select a small gasoline or diesel engine with which to do the compression ratio test.

   ▶ **CAUTION:** Always wear safety glasses when working with tools in the laboratory. Also, make sure you know the correct operation of all tools and machines in the laboratory. If not, check with your instructor.

2. Remove the cylinder head so that the piston and valves are exposed.
3. Using a vernier caliper, measure the stroke of the engine from TDC to BDC. Record the stroke on the Compression Ratio handout.
4. Using an inside micrometer, measure the bore of the cylinder. Record on the handout.
5. Using the following formula determine the piston displacement:

$$\text{Displacement} = \text{Bore}^2 \times \text{Stroke} \times .7854$$

   Record the piston displacement on the handout.
6. Check to see if the piston comes exactly to the top of the block (some do not). If it does not, calculate the additional volume of the cylinder using the formula given in step 5.
7. To determine the volume of the combustion area within the cylinder head:
   a. Fill the combustion chamber in the head with water or oil poured in from a graduated cylinder.
   b. Measure and record this information on the handout. If the graduated cylinder is in milliliters, convert to cubic inches (1 milliliter = .06103 cu in).
8. Add all volume calibrated in steps 5, 6, and 7. Record the total displacement on the handout. This is called "total displacement at BDC."
9. Now determine the displacement of the engine when the piston is at TDC. Use the same method stated previously. Record on the handout.
10. Using the following formula, determine the engine compression ratio and record it on the handout.

$$\text{Compression ratio} = \frac{\text{Displacement at BDC}}{\text{Displacement at TDC}}$$

11. Remember, compression ratios are stated as 6:1, 7:1, 8:1, and so forth.
12. Locate the manufacturer's stated compression ratio as listed in the maintenance manual, and record it on the handout.

REVIEW QUESTIONS

1. What error could occur when determining the compression ratio?
2. What physical changes could be made to the engine to increase the compression ratio?
3. What could cause the calibrated compression ratio to differ from the manufacturer's stated compression ratio?

CHAPTER 17

Electrical Power

KEY TERMS

Atoms	Electron Theory	Domains
Valence Ring	Conventional Theory	Diodes
Conductor	Ohm's Law	Transistor
Insulator	Watt's Law	Integrated Circuits
Semiconductor	Voltage Drop	Microprocessor

Introduction

When studying any transportation, energy, or power technology, many systems require an understanding of electricity. For example, storage batteries, ignition systems, charging systems, starting systems, vehicle controls, solar systems, speed controls and others all require a basic understanding of electricity. In fact, most transportation, energy, and power technology is becoming more and more controlled by electricity and electronics. In addition, our society uses an ever-increasing amount of electricity for buildings and other structures, homes, offices, and industries, Figure 17-1. This chapter is designed to help the student understand how electricity is applied to the study of transportation, energy, and power systems.

FIGURE 17-1 Electrical energy is used for lighting and operating buildings, offices, and other structures throughout our society. *Courtesy of NY Convention and Visitors Bureau*

Basic Electricity

Atomic Structure

The heart of all information concerning electricity is in the study of atoms and atomic structure. Everything is made up of atoms — water, trees, buildings, and so on. Atoms are very tiny particles about a millionth of an inch in size. Millions of them are in a single breath of air.

The structure of an atom is illustrated in Figure 17-2. Each atom has at its center a nucleus containing both protons and neutrons. This makes up the majority of the weight of the atom. Protons are said

to carry a positive charge (+). Neutrons carry no charge and are not considered in the study of electricity. In addition, electrons orbit around the nucleus and have centrifugal forces. Electrons are very lightweight in comparison to the nucleus, and carry a negative charge (-).

An attraction exists between the negative electrons and the positive protons. The attractive force and the centrifugal force causes the electron to orbit the nucleus or protons in the center, Figure 17-3.

The number of electrons in all orbits and the number of protons in the nucleus attempt to remain equal. If they are equal, the atom is said to be

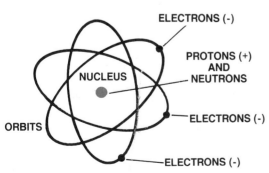

FIGURE 17-2 The structure of an atom.

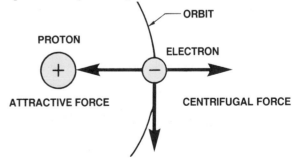

FIGURE 17-3 When an attractive force equals the centrifugal force, the electron will orbit around the proton.

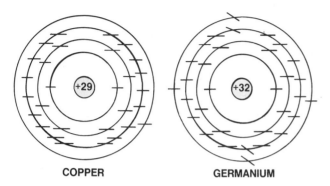

FIGURE 17-4 Atoms usually have an equal number of protons and electrons. Two balanced atoms are shown for comparison.

balanced or neutral. Figure 17-4 shows a copper atom and a germanium atom for comparison. Both are balanced and have an equal number of protons and electrons.

Valence Ring

In the study of electricity, the main concern is with the number of electrons in the outer orbit. The outer orbit of the atom is called the *valence ring*. It holds the outermost electrons. Electrons in the valence ring can be easily added or removed. Generally, an atom with several electrons missing will try to gain or capture other electrons. This will balance the atom. Also, if an atom has an excess number of electrons in the valence ring, it may try to get rid of them. This also helps to balance the atom.

Certain materials can lose or gain electrons rather easily. This depends upon the number of electrons in the valence ring when it is balanced. If an atom loses electrons easily, the material is called a good *conductor*. Copper wire is an example of a good conductor. Wires are used to carry electricity to homes, buildings, and offices throughout society. High line wires are shown in Figure 17-5. If the atom cannot lose electrons easily, the material is called a good *insulator*. An example of an insulator is shown in Figure 17-6. These insulators are used to hold the wires in place. Insulators and conductors can be defined as:

Three or less electrons . . . . . . *Conductor*
Five or more electrons . . . . *Insulator*
Four electrons . . . . *Semiconductor*

Note that the material that has exactly four electrons (semiconductor) in the outer orbit can be considered either a conductor or an insulator. Semiconductors are used in solid state components that are discussed later in this chapter.

FIGURE 17-5 High line wires are considered good conductors of electricity. *Courtesy of New York Power Authority*

FIGURE 17-6 Insulators are used on these wires to hold them in place. Insulators do not conduct electricity. *Courtesy of New York Power Authority*

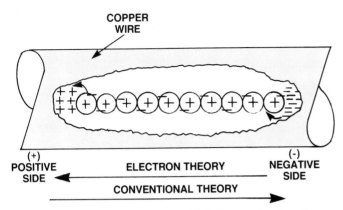

FIGURE 17-7 When a series of (+) charges is placed on one end of a copper wire, and (-) charges are placed on the other, electrons will move through the wire. This is called *electron flow* or *electricity*.

Electricity Defined

Knowing the previous information, *electricity* can be defined as the movement of electrons from atom to atom. This can happen only in a conductor material. An example is shown in Figure 17-7. Copper atoms are shown with only the valence ring. Copper is a good conductor. If an excess of positive charges or protons were placed on the left, one positive atom may try to pull the outer electron away from a copper atom on the left.

This action would make the far left copper atom slightly positively charged. There is one more proton than electron in the total atom. This positively charged atom then will pull an electron from the one on its right side. This atom also becomes positively charged. In total, when this action continues to occur, electrons are flowing from the right to the left. Remember, there must be an abundant number of protons on the left and electrons on the right for electron flow.

Electron Theory

In Figure 17-7, the electrons are flowing from a negative point to a positive point. *Electricity*, when defined this way, is called the *electron theory*. This means that electricity will flow from a negative point to a more positive point. This is one method of defining the direction of electrical flow.

Conventional Theory

Electricity can be defined another way. Electricity can be defined as flow from a positive point to a more negative point. This is called the *conventional*

theory. For example, referring again to Figure 17-7, while negative charges are flowing from right to left, positive charges are flowing from left to right. This means that electrical charges could also flow from positive to negative. In the automotive field, this method has been used to define the direction of electrical flow.

It is only important to be consistent with the method you choose. If electron theory is used, stay with electron theory; if conventional theory is used, stay with conventional theory.

Amperage Defined

Amperage is defined as the amount of electrons flowing from a negative point to a positive point in a given time period. This term is also called *current*. This term is similar to the example of water flowing through a pipe (electrons flowing through a wire). Amperage is further defined as the number of electrons passing any given point in the circuit in one second. The letter used to identify amperage or current is (I). This stands for intensity of current flow. The unit for expressing amperage is the ampere.

Voltage Defined

Voltage is defined as the push or force used to move the electrons. Referring again to Figure 17-7, the difference in charges between the positive and negative charges is called voltage. This difference in charges has the ability to move electrons through the wire. Figure 17-8 illustrates the definition of voltage. The unit for expressing voltage is the volt.

Voltage has other terms that help to describe it. Terms such as *potential difference*, *electromotive force* (emf), and *pressure* are all voltage terms. When the term voltage is compared to a water system, water pressure is used to push water through a pipe (voltage is used to push electrons through a

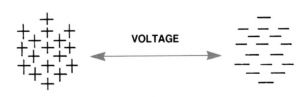

FIGURE 17-8 Voltage occurs when there is a difference in charges from one side of a conductor to another.

FIGURE 17-9 Generators in large power plants are used to produce the necessary voltage to push amperage through conductors. *Courtesy of New York Power Authority*

wire). Voltage is represented by the letter (E) which stands for electromotive force. Large generators in power plants, as shown in Figure 17-9, are used to produce voltage that will push amperage through conductors.

Resistance Defined

The third component in electricity is called resistance. *Resistance* is defined as opposition to current flow. Resistance is identified by the letter (R) which stands for resistance to electron flow. Certain materials, because of their atomic structure, offer poor conductivity. This, in turn, slows down the electrons. Actually, as the electrons move through a wire, they bump into other atoms in the conductor. As this occurs, the material heats up and causes even more resistance.

Various resistors, of different types and values, are designed today to control the flow of electrons. This depends upon how much current is needed to flow through a circuit. When comparing resistance to a water circuit, flow valves and faucets control or restrict water flow. Resistance in an electrical circuit controls or restricts electron flow.

Ohm's Law

The three components just described interact with one another. For example, if the resistance goes down and the voltage remains the same, the amperage will increase. Also, if the resistance stays the same and the voltage goes up, the amperage will also increase. These relationships can be identified by a formula called *Ohm's law*. It is a mathematical formula to show how voltage, amperage and resistance work together.

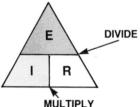

FIGURE 17-10 Ohm's law states that voltage (E) = amperage (I) × resistance (R).

The triangle shown in Figure 17-10 is a graphical way of showing this formula. It shows that if two electrical components are known, then the third can be easily found. For example, if resistance (R) and voltage (E) are known, cover the unknown (I) to see the formula. The amperage can be found by dividing the resistance into the voltage.

The following shows an example of how to calculate amperage using Ohm's law. If there are 120 volts and a resistance of 58 ohms, the amperage is calculated by:

$$\text{Amperage} = \frac{E}{R}$$

$$\text{Amperage} = \frac{120}{58}$$

$$\text{Amperage} = 2.068$$

If the amperage and resistance are known, voltage can be found by multiplying the amperage by resistance. In actual practice, many electrical circuits are designed so that, by changing the voltage or resistance, control of the current or amperage is maintained.

Watt's Law

The term wattage is also used to help analyze and measure electrical circuits. *Wattage*, expressed in watts, is a measure of the power (P) used in the circuit. Wattage is a measure of the total electrical work being done per unit of time. It is measured using *Watt's law*. When voltage (E) is multiplied by amperage (I), the result is wattage (P). Wattage, a measure of electrical power, may also be referred to in *kilowatts* (kW). 1,000 watts equal 1 kilowatt.

Figure 17-11 illustrates the relationship among

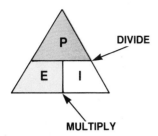

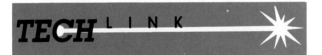

FIGURE 17-11 Watt's law states that wattage (P) = voltage (E) × amperage (I).

voltage, amperage, and wattage in a graphical form. If the amperage and wattage are known, cover the voltage to see the formula. If the voltage and wattage are known, amperage can be calculated. Figure 17-12 shows a wattmeter as it is used to measure the electrical use in an apartment complex.

TECH LINK

Wattage from a power plant is measured in watts. Because such a large number of watts are being produced, power plants are rated in megawatts. One megawatt is equal to 1,000,000 watts. Small hydroelectric power plants may be rated, for example, at about 30 to 50 megawatts. Large coal power plants and nuclear power plants are able to produce between 500 and 800 megawatts per power plant. In some cases, three such power plants may occupy one site or location, producing upwards of 2,400 megawatts at the total plant.

The following shows an example of how to calculate wattage when there are 120 volts and 22 amperes.

Wattage = voltage × amperage

Wattage = 120 volts × 22 amperes

Wattage = 2,640 watts

Basic Circuits

When studying electrical systems in transportation, energy, and power technology, circuits are used to show the operation of electrical components. A circuit normally consists of several components.

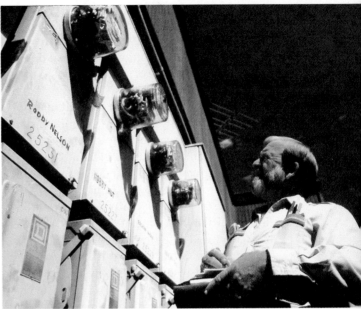

FIGURE 17-12 A wattmeter is used to measure the power used in an apartment complex. *Courtesy of Southern California Edison*

One, a power source is needed to provide the necessary voltage. Two, wire is needed to provide a path through which the electrons can flow. Three, a load is needed, which could be any kind of resistance. Lights, radios, solar controls, motors, and so forth are all examples of electrical loads. The load provides the resistance in the circuit. A motor is an example of a typical load. Figure 17-13 shows a typical load (motor) used in an electrical saw.

FIGURE 17-13 A motor in an electrical saw is the load in the electrical circuit. *Courtesy of Black and Decker (Blakeslee-Lane Studios)*

Deicer Element for Planes

In some instances recently, ice buildup on the wings of commercial aircraft has been determined to be the cause of several accidents. Ice buildup on wings changes the shape of the wing to such a point that improper lift may not be obtained during takeoff. Ice builds-up on aircraft wings because of cold temperatures combined with moisture in the atmosphere.

In this photo, a technician inspects the ribbon element for an electrothermal ice protection system at a company's deicer production facility. When placed on an aircraft, the heat generated helps to prevent ice buildup on the wings. In operation, the ribbon material has electrical resistance. As amperage flows through the ribbon, the resistance in the material causes heat to be generated. The heat is then used to melt ice. *Courtesy of the BF Goodrich Company*

Simple Circuit

A simple circuit consists of a power source, a single unit or load to be operated (a light bulb), and the connecting wires. Figure 17-14 shows a simple circuit. The power source is a battery. However, the power source could also be a generator to produce the voltage. Note that the wires must be connected to complete the circuit. In this example, electricity flows from the positive terminal on the battery, through the wire, to the light bulb, and back to the negative terminal of the battery (conventional flow).

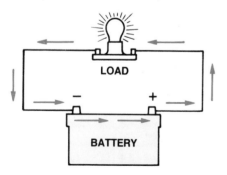

FIGURE 17-14 A simple circuit shows amperage flowing through the light bulb, causing it to operate.

Voltage Drop

When testing and troubleshooting any electrical circuit, *voltage drop* is usually measured. In order for the amperage to flow through a resistor, voltage must be present. Voltage is dropped across each resistor or load through which it pushes amperage. In order to determine the voltage drop across any one resistor or load, simply use Ohm's law again. Only in this case, use the voltage, amperage and resistance at that particular resistor. Voltage drop at any one resistor is then shown as:

Voltage drop = resistance × amperage (I × R)

The following is an example of calculating voltage drop when the resistance (R) is 35 ohms and the amperage (I) is 1.4 amperes.

Voltage drop = voltage × amperage

Voltage drop = 35 ohms × 1.4 amperes

Voltage drop = 49 volts

Voltage drop can also be measured by using a voltmeter. Usually the voltmeter leads are placed across the component to be checked.

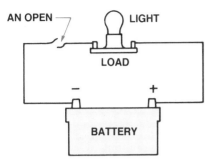

FIGURE 17-15 An open circuit stops all current from flowing through the circuit.

Opens, Shorts, and Grounds

Electrical systems may develop an open, shorted, or grounded circuit. Each of these conditions will render an electrical circuit ineffective.

An *open circuit* is one that has a break in the wire, called a break in continuity, Figure 17-15. If the circuit is open, there is an incomplete path for the current to flow through. An open circuit acts the same as if the circuit had a switch in the open position. The voltage drop across an open circuit is always the same as the source or maximum voltage.

A *shorted circuit* is one that allows electricity to flow past part of the normal load. An example of this is a shorted coil in a motor or generator, Figure 17-16. The internal windings are usually insulated from one another. Figure 17-17 shows the internal windings of a generator and the insulation around each wire. If the insulation breaks and allows the windings to touch one another, part of the coil would be bypassed. Any load can be partially or fully bypassed by having a shorted circuit. If a load is fully bypassed, then the voltage dropped across the load would be zero.

A *grounded circuit* is a condition that allows current to return to the voltage source (battery) before it has reached its intended destination. An example might be a grounded tail light on a truck. If

FIGURE 17-17 The internal windings of a generator showing how each is insulated. If the insulation breaks down, the wires would touch one another, causing a shorted circuit. *Courtesy of Madison Gas and Electric Company, Reed Design/Mike Rebholz Photo*

a wire leading to the light were broken and touching the frame of the vehicle, the electricity would be shorted back to the voltage source (battery), Figure 17-18. Grounded circuits can cause excessive current to be drained from the battery or voltage source.

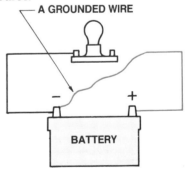

FIGURE 17-18 A grounded wire can cause excessive drain on a battery.

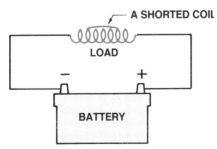

FIGURE 17-16 A shorted circuit bypassses part of the load. In this example, the load is a coil in a motor or generator.

Series Circuit

A *series circuit* consists of two or more resistors connected to a voltage source with only one path for the electrons to follow. An example is shown in

Figure 17-19. The series circuit has two resistors (loads) placed in the path of the electrons. The resistors are shown as R_1 and R_2. (The jagged line is a symbol used to represent a resistor). All of the amperage that comes out of the positive side of the battery must go through each resistor, then back to the negative side of the battery. In a series circuit, the resistors are added together to obtain the total resistance (R total).

Series circuits are characterized by the following facts:

1. The resistance is always additive. R total is equal to $R_1 + R_2 + R_3$, and so forth.
2. The amperage through each resistor is the same. The amperage will then be the same throughout the circuit.
3. The voltage drop across each resistor will be different if the resistance values are different.
4. The sum of the voltage drops of each resistor equals the source voltage.

SERIES CIRCUIT

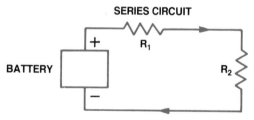

FIGURE 17-19 A series circuit has one path for current to flow.

Parallel Circuit

Parallel circuits provide two or more paths in which the current can flow. Each path has a separate load or resistor, and operates independently from the other parallel paths. In a parallel circuit the amperage can flow through more than one load at a time. An example of a parallel circuit is shown in Figure 17-20. Note that if one branch of the circuit

PARALLEL CIRCUIT

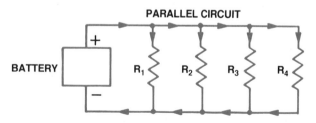

FIGURE 17-20 A parallel circuit has more than one path for current flow.

breaks or has an open circuit, the remaining resistors can still operate. The resistance in a parallel circuit is calculated by the formula:

$$R \text{ total} = \frac{1}{1/R_1 + 1/R_2 + 1/R_3 + 1/R_4 \text{ and so on}}$$

For example, the total resistance when the following resistors are placed in parallel would be shown as follows:

$$R_1 = 15, \quad R_2 = 5, \quad \text{and } R_3 = 3$$

$$R \text{ total} = \frac{1}{1/15 + 1/5 + 1/3}$$

$$R \text{ total} = \frac{1}{1/15 + 3/15 + 5/15}$$

$$R \text{ total} = \frac{1}{9/15}$$

$$R \text{ total} = \frac{15}{9}$$

$$R \text{ total} = 1.66 \text{ ohms}$$

When calculating the total resistance in a parallel circuit, the result will always be less than the smallest resistor. Most electrical circuits are parallel circuits. If more resistors are added to the circuit, the total resistance will decrease. A parallel circuit can be characterized by the following:

1. The total resistance is less than the lowest resistor.
2. The amperage through each resistor will be different if the resistance values are different.
3. The voltage drop across each resistor is the same. This is also the source voltage.
4. The sum of the separate amperages in each branch equals the total amperage in the circuit.

Series-parallel Circuit

A series-parallel circuit is designed so that both series and parallel combinations exist within the same circuit. Figure 17-21 shows four resistors connected into a series-parallel circuit. To calculate total resistance in this circuit, first calculate the parallel portions, then add the result to the series portion of the circuit. Total current flow is determined by the total resistance and the total source voltage.

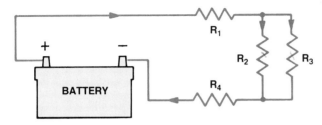

FIGURE 17-21 A series-parallel circuit. Resistors R_2 and R_3 are in parallel. The total resistance of R_2 and R_3 in parallel is added to R_1 and R_4, which are in series with R_2 and R_3.

Ground Symbol

When analyzing electrical circuits in transportation technology, sometimes a *ground symbol* is used. This means that the circuit is connected to the steel structure of the vehicle. The ground symbol is shown in Figure 17-22. The symbol indicates that the electricity is returning to the voltage source (battery) by using the frame of a vehicle. Any steel structure of the vehicle can actually act as the "wire" that returns electricity to the battery. Such structures include the body sheet metal, the frame, the engine block, the transmission case, or other metal parts.

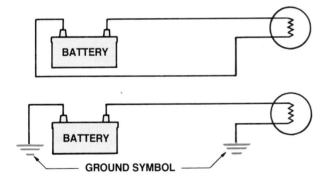

FIGURE 17-22 A ground symbol is used in electrical circuits on transporation technology to indicate that the circuit is connected to the metal structure of the vehicle.

Electrical Symbols

In more complex circuits, many types of electrical symbols are used. Symbols are used in wiring diagrams to represent meters, batteries, switches, fuses, circuit breakers, motors, generators, light bulbs, and other parts. As more involved circuits are analyzed, it will be necessary to become acquainted with electrical symbols.

Magnetism

Magnetism is one important area of study in all electrical systems. This is because the principles of magnetism are integrated into motors, generators, solenoids, and other electrical components in transportation, energy, and power systems. Figure 17-23 shows an example of an air conditioning compressor with a motor inside. This motor operates on the principles of magnetism. Magnetism can be best understood by observing some of its effects.

The effects of magnetism were first observed when fragments of iron ore, referred to as *lodestones*, were attracted to pieces of iron. It was further discovered that a long piece of iron would align itself so that one end always pointed toward the earth's North Pole. One end of the bar was called the north (N) pole, and the other end was called the south (S) pole. This was then called a *bar magnet*.

FIGURE 17-23 Motors are used in an air-conditioning compressor. They operate on the principles of magnetism. *Courtesy of Copeland Corporation*

Domains

Internally, the bar magnet consists of many small domains. *Domains* are minute sections in the bar where the atoms line up to produce a magnetic field. In a bar magnet, most of the domains must be lined up in the same direction to form a magnetic

WEDway People Mover

Mass transportation systems are being built to meet very specific needs of the consumer. Quite often, mass transportation systems are built at airports to move masses of people.

This transportation system is called the WEDway People Mover. Located both at Houston's Intercontinental Airport and Walt Disney World, this system uses linear induction propulsion and control systems. These motors and controls are designed on basic electro-magnetic principles. Characteristics include a speed of 15 miles per hour and an acceleration of 22 feet per second, using 240-volt, 60-Hz motors. Braking is developed through the use of linear motor reverse polarity. *Courtesy ©1987 The Walt Disney Company*

field. Figure 17-24 shows a bar of metal with the domains random and one with the domains lined up.

Lines of Force

Magnets can be further defined by the lines of force being produced. Referring to Figure 17-25, the *magnetic field* is defined by the invisible forces that come out of the north pole and enter the south pole. These forces are known as the *lines of force*. The shape of the magnetic lines of force can be illustrated by sprinkling iron filings on a piece of paper placed on top of the bar magnet. When the paper is tapped, the iron filings align to form a clear pattern around the bar magnet. Note that the lines of force never touch one another. Note also, that the lines of force are more highly concentrated at the ends of the magnet.

Repulsion and Attraction

If two bar magnets are placed together with unlike poles, they will attract each other and snap together. If the ends have like poles, the two poles will repel each other. See Figure 17-26.

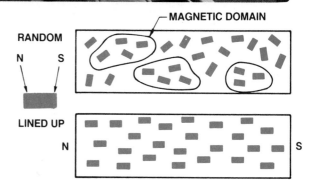

FIGURE 17-24 Domains in a bar. When they are not lined up (random) no magnetism is produced. When they are lined up, magnetism is produced in the bar.

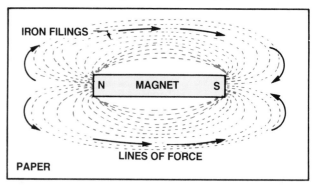

FIGURE 17-25 A bar magnet with iron filings shows the invisible lines of force around a magnet. Magnetic lines of force always flow from the north pole to the south pole.

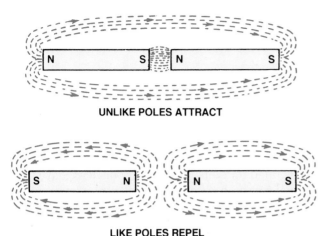

FIGURE 17-26 Unlike poles attract each other. Like poles repel each other.

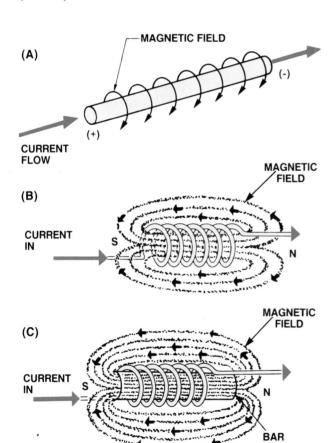

FIGURE 17-27 (A) A small magnetic field is produced around a wire that has electricity flowing in it. (B) If the conductor is placed in the shape of a coil the magnetic field is additive at the center. (C) Inserting an iron bar will increase the strength of the magnetic field.

Electromagnetism

The bar magnet previously discussed is called a *permanent magnet*. However, temporary magnets can also be made from electricity. This is done by wrapping an electrical wire around an unmagnetized bar. This bar then is called an *electromagnet*. Producing magnetism this way is called *electromagnetism*.

When any wire has electricity flowing through it, a magnetic field is developed around the wire. This is shown in Figure 17-27A. If the wire were then placed in the shape of a coil, as shown in Figure 17-27B, the magnetic field in the center of the coil would be additive. If a nonmagnetized metal bar is placed in the center, the bar will also become magnetized, Figure 17-27C.

Electromagnetic Induction

Through experimentation, it was discovered that a conductor (copper wire) moving across or cutting a magnetic field would produce a voltage. This event is called *electromagnetic induction*. Actually, an electromotive force (emf) is induced or generated within the wire. Internally, a generator is converting mechanical energy to electrical energy. Figure 17-28 shows a large generator in a power plant producing electricity.

FIGURE 17-28 The generator in a power plant produces electricity, based upon the principles of electromagnetic induction. *Courtesy of New York Power Authority*

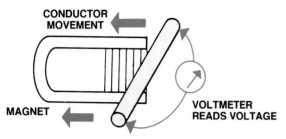

FIGURE 17-29 As a conductor moves or cuts through a magnetic field, a voltage is produced. If applied to a circuit with a load or resistance, a complete circuit can be produced. *Courtesy of Delco Remy Division of General Motors Corporation*

In the simplest form, Figure 17-29 shows how voltage is produced with a magnet. The direction of current flow produced from the voltage can be reversed if the movement is also reversed. In fact, if the motion of the wire were rapidly moved back and forth, the result would be an alternating current.

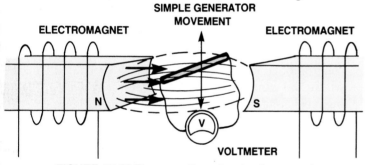

FIGURE 17-30 The operation of a simple generator.

Figure 17-30 shows a simple generator used to produce voltage in a wire. Note that rather than using permanent magnets, electromagnets are used. This voltage used to produce the magnetism is called the *field voltage*. If the conductor in the center moves up perpendicular to the lines of force from an electromagnet, a voltage will be produced on the voltmeter. If the conductor moves down, a reverse voltage will be produced.

Note that three requirements are needed to induce a voltage in a generator:

1. A magnetic field producing lines of force
2. A conductor
3. Movement between the conductors and the magnetic field so that the lines of force are cut

If any one of these requirements increases or decreases, the induced voltage will also increase or decrease. Also, note that the conductor could be stationary while the lines of force are moved. This

would still induce a voltage because the lines of force would be cut. Most large generators in power plants have the magnetic fields rotating in this manner.

Solid-State Components

Electronics is an area of electrical study that has grown in the past few years. Electronics is the study of *solid-state* devices such as diodes, transistors and integrated circuits. Solid-state devices have no moving parts, but operate on internal movement of electrons. Many of the solid-state parts are considered part of control or "feedback" circuits. In the systems model for studying technology, feedback control circuits are used to monitor and control the output.

It was mentioned previously that any material that has four electrons in the outer orbit is called a semiconductor. This means that the material could be either a good conductor or good insulator. Because of these characteristics, semiconductors are often used as switches. Circuits can be turned on and off by semiconductors with no moving parts.

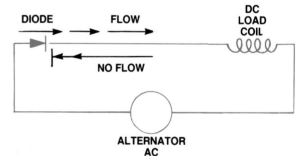

FIGURE 17-31 A diode in a circuit allows electricity to flow in only one direction.

Diode

The diode is one of the most common semiconductors. The *diode* permits current to flow through a circuit in one direction but not in the other. Diodes are used in many computer, generator/alternators and microprocessor circuits. Figure 17-31 shows a circuit with a diode inserted. Most generators, for example, produce voltage that flows back and forth 60 times per second. This is called AC voltage. However, direct current (DC) is needed at the load, (coil). The diode can be used to convert the AC to DC. Referring again to Figure 17-31, electricity is able to flow in the direction of the arrows shown at the top of the wire. However, if electricity tries to flow in the opposite direction, it will be stopped. This is shown by the arrows underneath the wire. There will be no current flow in the reverse direction.

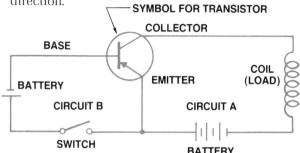

FIGURE 17-32 A transistor controls the on and off sequence of a coil or other load. Circuit B controls circuit A.

Transistor

The *transistor* is also a type of semiconductor. Only in this case, the transistor has some added semiconductor material. A circuit using a transistor is shown in Figure 17-32. In operation, the circuit to be turned on and off is identified as circuit A. Circuit B is the controlling circuit. The transistor has three wires: the *base*, the *emitter*, and the *collector*.

In operation, when the switch is closed, a small amount of current flows in the emitter circuit to the base circuit. Then the resistance between the

emitter circuit and the collector circuit now is zero. Circuit A is then turned on to operate the coil or other load. When the current stops flowing in circuit B (switch open), then the resistance between the emitter and collector is very high. This resistance shuts off circuit A.

Transistors can also be used to amplify an on and off sequence of signals. A small amount of current flowing on and off in circuit B can control a large amount of current flowing in circuit A. The on and off sequence would be amplifed from circuit B to circuit A.

Integrated Circuits

Over the past several years, engineers have found ways to make diodes and transistors extremely small. Because they are now so small, many diodes, transistors, resistors, and so forth can be placed on a board called an *integrated circuit*. Figure 17-33 shows a typical integrated circuit board. These circuits may contain many semiconductors. More recently the chip has been designed to incorporate even smaller components on the integrated board.

Some applications that use integrated circuits and chips in the transportation area include:

- Solid-state ignition
- Electronic fuel injection
- Electronic engine systems
- Computer-controlled combustion
- Speed and cruise controls
- Braking systems

FIGURE 17-33 Integrated circuits and chips are used in many applications in the transportation, energy, and power field today. *Courtesy of Matsushita Electric Industrial Co., Ltd.*

Microprocessors

Along with the addition of integrated circuits and chips, transportation, energy, and power systems are now using microprocessors. *Microprocessors are miniature circuits that can be used for a variety of tasks*. Microprocessors are often used in computers. Various sensors are provided that relay input information to the microprocessor. Figure 17-34 shows how a microprocessor can be used in an automobile. Everything from engine speed, temperature, outside weather conditions (barometric pressure), load and weight distribution of the vehicle, vehicle speed, throttle position, pollution amounts, and so on can be fed into the microprocessor. From these data, various decisions are made by the microprocessor to control the vehicle to its optimum performance. This microprocessor is considered part of the feedback in the systems model used to study technology.

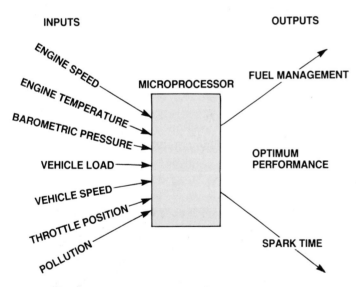

FIGURE 17-34 A microprocessor can be used to control transportation engine efficiency for optimum performance.

Summary

▪ This chapter investigates the basic principles of electricity and how they are related to transportation, energy, and power technology.

▪ *Electricity* is defined as the movement of electrons.

▪ Voltage, amperage and resistance are components used to control electricity. Both Ohm's law and Watt's law are defined and used to help determine the relationship among voltage, amperage, resistance and power.

▪ Several circuits are studied, including the series circuit, the parallel circuit, and the series-parallel circuit. Each type has specific characteristics.

▪ Types of circuits, voltage drop, opens, shorts, and grounds are also defined.

▪ As part of the study of electricity, magnetism is also defined. Domains, lines of force, electromagnetism and simple generators are discussed.

▪ The principles concerning magnetism are directly related to transportation, energy and power systems, such as starting and charging, ignition, and electronic controls.

▪ Semiconductors are also becoming a significant part of today's technology. Diodes, transistors, integrated circuits, and microprocessors are being used in all systems studied in transportation, energy, and power technology.

REVIEW

1. If 110 volts are used to push 15 amperes through a circuit, the resistance of the load is _____.

2. If 110 volts are used to push 15 amperes through a circuit, the power consumed by the load is _____.

3. The total resistance of a series circuit with resistors of 3, 18, and 1,000 is equal to _____.

4. A circuit has 15 amperes flowing through a load. The resistor or load is 15 ohms. The voltage dropped across the load or resistor is _____.

5. The total resistance of a parallel circuit with resistors of 20, 10 and 5 is equal to _____.

6. The _____ theory suggests that electricity flows from a _____ point to a negative point.

7. A circuit that has a break in the wire is called a (an) _____.

8. When the amperage is the same in all resistors or loads, it is called a _____ circuit.

9. Define Ohm's law.

10. Define and state the differences among an open circuit, a short circuit, and a grounded circuit.

11. Define voltage drop.

12. What are three characteristics of a series circuit?

13. What are three characteristics of a parallel circuit?

14. Define the purpose and operation of a diode.

15. What is the difference between a diode and a transistor?

CHAPTER ACTIVITIES

 KILOWATT-METER

INTRODUCTION

Electric kilowatt-meters are used to measure the amount of energy used in a residential or commercial building. This activity is designed to have you become familiar with a kilowatt-meter in a standard residential dwelling.

TECHNOLOGICAL LITERACY SKILLS

Collection of data, data analysis, plotting information.

OBJECTIVES

At the completion of this activity, you will be able to:

1. Read a kilowatt-meter.

2. Calculate electrical energy usage in dollars per month.

3. Plot a kilowatt-meter usage chart for a 10-day period.

4. Plot a kilowatt-meter chart for a 12-month period.

MATERIALS

1. A residential home with an electrical kilowatt-meter
2. Hand calculator
3. Electric utility bills for a period of 12 months
4. Ruler to plot data accurately
5. Kilowatt-meter handout

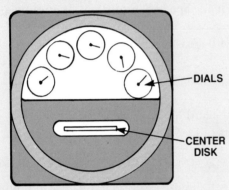

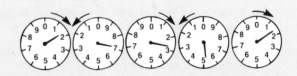

FIGURE 17-35 An example of a kilowatt-meter. It is always read from the number the pointer has just passed, and from the left dial to the right dial.

ADDITIONAL INFORMATION

Note that this activity is designed for you to take readings on a kilowatt-meter over a 10-day period. Plan your time accordingly.

The kilowatt-meter measures the amount of electrical power used in the home. An example of a kilowatt-meter is shown in Figure 17-35. It consists of a series of five dials and a center disk that rotates as kilowatts are being used. This unit is enclosed in a glass case. The meter is read from left to right. Read the last number the pointer passed in alternating clockwise and counterclockwise directions as shown by the arrows. The meter in Figure 17-35 reads 17251. If in one month the meter read 17738, 487 kilowatt-hours (kWh) were consumed (17738 - 17251). This is the amount that will be shown on the monthly statement.

PROCEDURE

1. Obtain electric bills for a residential building for a period of 12 monthly billings.
2. Determine the following from the energy bills and record on the kilowatt-meter handout.
   a. Average service period in days.
   b. Kilowatt price at the beginning of the year.
   c. Kilowatt price at the end of the year.
3. Using the monthly kWh shown on each statement, plot the kWh usage over the complete year on Chart A on the handout.
4. Plot the kWh used during a 10-day period on Chart B on the handout. Make sure to read and measure the kilowatts used at the same time each day.
   a. Take the initial start reading.
   b. Take a reading after one day.
   c. Subtract b from a and plot on the chart.
   d. Repeat this procedure each day for a 10-day period.

REVIEW QUESTIONS

1. What would cause any significant increases or decreases on a day-to-day basis?
2. What are some items in your home that consume the largest amount of kilowatts?
3. What could cause significant changes in kilowatt usage from month to month?

CHAPTER 18

Small Gas Engines

OBJECTIVES

After reading this chapter, you will be able to:

■ Identify applications where small gas engines are used today.

■ State the design variables used in small gas engines.

■ Identify the purpose and operation of small gas engine parts, such as the block, piston, cylinder heads, valves, and bearings.

■ Describe the purpose and operation of various engine systems, including ignition, cooling, fuel, lubrication, starting, governor, and air and exhaust systems.

■ Identify various service procedures and troubleshooting tips used on small gasoline engines.

KEY TERMS

Oil Injection	Micrometer	Diaphragm Fuel Pump
Reed Valve	Magneto Ignition	Butterfly Valve
Port Induction	Condenser	Governor
Cylinder Bore	Breaker Points	Solenoid
Compression Gasket		

Introduction

The small gas engine is used today in many applications of power and transportation technology. Small gas engines are those having from one to six cylinders. They are found in small to intermediate power applications often used in the transportation sector for moving vehicles. In addition, small gasoline engines are used in many industrial applications as a source of power. This chapter is about small gas engine technology, and how small gas engines operate.

FIGURE 18-1 Small gasoline engines are used to provide power for propulsion in many transportation devices such as these recreational vehicles. *Courtesy of (A) Polaris and (B,C) Kawasaki Motors Corp., U.S.A.*

Small Gas Engine Applications

Small gasoline engines are used for a variety of jobs both in transportation and industrial applications. In the area of transportation, small gasoline engines are most often found in recreational vehicles. Figure 18-1 shows examples of several recreational vehicles that use small gasoline engines for their power source. Probably the most popular include boats, motorcycles, wet bikes, and snowmobiles. All of these engines are usually designed to be used as a power source. They use either a two- or a four-cycle design.

Small gasoline engines are also used quite often to power various industrial applications. These applications include lawn mowers, chain saws, log splitters, pumps, snowblowers, garden tillers, generators, and others. Figure 18-2 shows examples of small gas engine industrial applications. All of these engines require small to intermediate power ranges for operation. Again, both two- or four-cycle engines are used for these applications.

Basic Engine Design Variations

Small gasoline engines must be made to fit many applications and power requirements. In addition, certain engine applications require quick response, whereas others may require more torque. These requirements have led manufacturers to build small gas engines in many shapes, sizes and designs.

All small gasoline engines are considered intermittent combustion, reciprocating-style power plants. However, many variables can be used to change the engine. These variables include:

1. The use of four-cycle designs. Many small gas engines today use the four-cycle design. It is mostly used in larger and heavier duty applications.

2. The use of two-cycle designs. Two-cycle designs are used in outboard motors, motorcycles, water bikes, and snowmobiles. One major reason for using the two-cycle is to get quick response.

3. Oil mix or oil injection. Today's two-cycle engines still need to have oil mixed with the gasoline. However, the oil can either be mixed at the gas tank, or it can be "oil injected." Depending upon the year and manufacturer, oil/gasoline mixtures are around 50 to 1 to as high as 100 to 1.

4. Single or multiple cylinder. When more horsepower or torque is required by the application, more than one piston can be used. Typical applications use between 1 and 4 pistons. However, 6 cylinders are used on some larger two-cycle outboard engines.

5. In-line and V-configurations. The pistons can be arranged in a single cylinder, in-line, or V-configuration. Smaller engines that require several pistons, such as outboard motors, often have a V-configuration. Figure 18-3 shows a single cylinder engine.

FIGURE 18-2 Small gasoline engines are used for a variety of industrial uses. The engine is used as a power source. *Courtesy of Polaris*

FIGURE 18-3 There are many configurations for small gas engines. *Courtesy of Tecumseh Products Company*

6. Liquid or air cooling. In the past, most small gasoline engines have been air cooled. However, today's applications require precise engine temperature control. This has prompted several manufacturers to incorporate liquid cooling systems.

7. Piston displacement. Piston displacements vary according to the applications. However,

it is not uncommon to have 200 or more cc (cubic centimeters) per cylinder.

8. Valve arrangement and number. Most four-cycle small gasoline engines have one intake and one exhaust valve. However, some manufacturers are designing engines with three and four valves per cylinder. A three-valve cylinder head is shown in Figure 18-4.

9. Reed or port induction system. On two-cycle engines, air can enter the crankcase area by one of two methods: *reed valves* or *port induction* can be used. Reed valves, as shown in Figure 18-5, are used on many small gas engines. Port induction controls the input charge by the position of the piston.

FIGURE 18-4 Some manufacturers of small gas engines are using three valves rather than two, per cylinder. *Courtesy of American Honda Motor Co., Inc.*

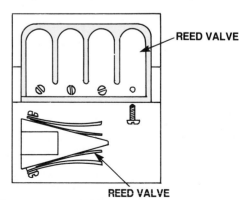

FIGURE 18-5 Reed valves are used on many two-cycle engines to control the intake of air/fuel into the crankcase.

The small gas engines used today may incorporate any combination of the aforementioned variables. For example, the engine shown in Figure 18-6 is an example of an in-line, two-cycle engine with liquid cooling. The oil is mixed not injected, and reed valves are used. The total engine displacement is 1,626 cc.

Mechanical Parts

Cylinder Block and Service

The *cylinder block* is the basic foundation of the small gas engine. The block is used to hold and house many of the engine parts, such as the pistons, valves, carburetor, and so forth. Figure 18-7 shows an example of a typical engine block. Note also that certain two-cycle gas engines are designed so the block can be split in half at the centerline of the crankshaft.

Several important checks can be made on cylinder blocks. Figure 18-8 shows how to check the cylinder bore using an inside micrometer. Certain engine manufacturers (not all) recommend that the block be honed. Honing helps new piston rings

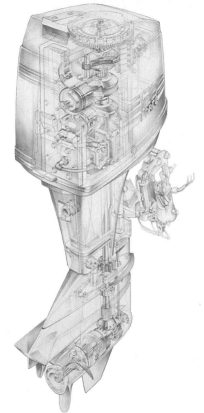

FIGURE 18-6 This engine incorporates several variables in design. It is a two-cycle, in-line engine. It is liquid cooled and uses a reed valve. *Courtesy of U.S. Marine Power Corporation*

Small Engine Testing/Sound Testing

Testing products is an important part of most manufacturing processes. It is important to test products to determine their characteristics. Small gas engines are also tested. Many tests are run on engines before they are sold to the consumer.

In photo (A) the engine is being tested for rattles. Photo (B) shows engines being run behind an insulated enclosure. This helps to reduce mechanical noise so that complete evaluation of mufflers can be obtained. In photo (C) exhaust noise is separated from mechanical noise by an *infinite* muffler. This permits quantitative evaluation of mechanical noise. *Courtesy of Briggs and Stratton Corporation*

(A)

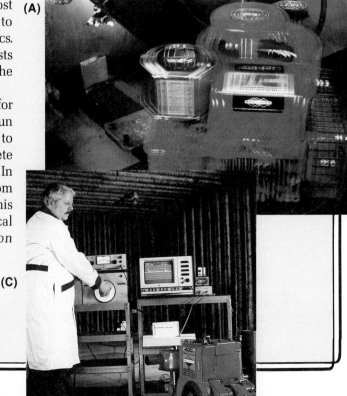

(B)

(C)

FIGURE 18-7 The block is the foundation of the small gas engine. All parts are attached to the block. *Courtesy of Outboard Marine Corporation*

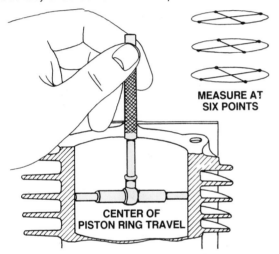

FIGURE 18-8 The cylinder bore can be checked with an inside micrometer. *Courtesy of Briggs & Stratton Corporation*

wear into the block (seating) quicker. A cylinder hone is shown in Figure 18-9.

Cylinder Head

The *cylinder head* is used to seal off the top of the cylinder so compression can be produced. The cylinder head is bolted to the cylinder block. A compression gasket is placed between the two during assembly.

Crankshaft and Service

The *crankshaft* is used to convert the reciprocating motion of the piston to rotating motion or torque. Figure 18-10 shows a typical crankshaft used in an outboard, two-cycle boat engine. Three types of bearings are used on crankshafts such as this. The

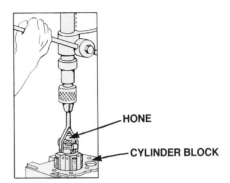

FIGURE 18-9 Certain manufacturers recommend honing the cylinder bore to help seat the rings. *Courtesy of Briggs & Stratton Corporation*

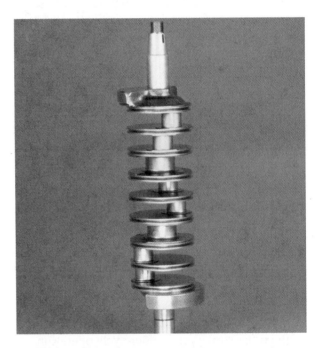

FIGURE 18-10 A crankshaft is used to convert the engine power into twisting motion. *Courtesy of Outboard Marine Corporation*

ends and center of the crankshaft are supported by both a roller bearing and a ball bearing. The connecting rod attaches to the crankshaft using smaller roller bearings called needle bearings. Most two-cycle engines today use similar bearings to aid in lubrication and the reduction of friction.

Smaller four-cycle engines use a simpler design for bearing surfaces. Bushings are used rather than roller bearings and ball bearings. Bushings are flat, soft metal surfaces that the crankshaft rides on. Several areas to check for wear on the crankshaft include straightness, diameters, and surface finishes.

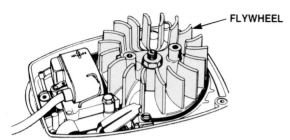

FLYWHEEL

FIGURE 18-11 The flywheel is used to smooth out the engine power pulses. *Courtesy of Tecumseh Products Company*

Flywheel

The *flywheel* is used for several purposes on small gas engines. The flywheel shown in Figure 18-11 has weights placed in the casting. The flywheel and weights act as a balance force to keep the engine running smoothly with less vibration.

TECH LINK

A flywheel on an engine has a tendency to keep the engine running smoothly as well as keeping the crankshaft turning during the intake, compression and exhaust strokes. This occurs because of Newton's first law of motion. This law says that a force in motion tends to remain in motion. Once the flywheel is in motion from the power stroke, it has a tendency to remain in motion. Because of its weight, this motion keeps the crankshaft rotating during the other strokes of the four-cycle operation.

The flywheel is also used to hold the magnets used for the ignition system and, in some cases, the charging system. In addition, the fins placed on the flywheel are used to move air around and through a shroud. This air is used for cooling and for governor operation.

Piston Assembly and Service

Figure 18-12 shows a typical piston assembly attached to the crankshaft by a connecting rod. The piston assembly normally includes the piston, connecting rod, piston pin and bearings, if used. Figure 18-13 shows a typical connecting rod used on a two-cycle outboard boat engine.

FIGURE 18-12 The piston assembly and connecting rod attaches to the crankshaft. *Courtesy of American Honda Motor Co., Inc.*

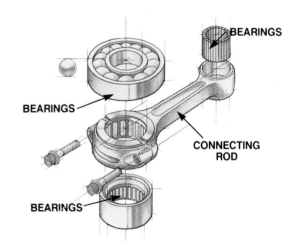

BEARINGS

BEARINGS

CONNECTING ROD

BEARINGS

FIGURE 18-13 The connecting rod connects the piston to the crankshaft. *Courtesy of U.S. Marine Power Corporation*

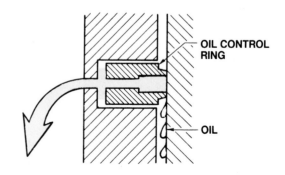

OIL CONTROL RING

OIL

FIGURE 18-14 The oil ring is used to scrape oil off the cylinder wall during the downward stroke of the piston.

Depending upon the type of engine, from two to four piston rings are used. The top rings (two to three) are used to seal in the compression and power pulses. The bottom ring is used to scrape the oil off the cylinder as the piston goes down. Figure 18-14 shows how oil is scraped off the cylinder wall and back into the crankcase area. Note, also, that on many two-cycle engines certain compression rings are kept in place by using a small dowel rod. This is shown in Figure 18-15.

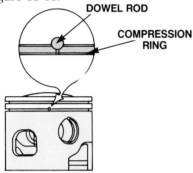

FIGURE 18-15 A small dowel rod is used to hold the rings in place on some two-cycle engines.

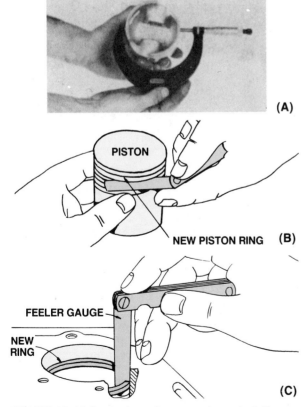

FIGURE 18-16 Several service procedures to follow on the piston assembly. *Courtesy of (A) Outboard Marine Corporation and (B,C) Briggs & Stratton Corporation*

There are several service procedures to follow on the piston assembly. First, the piston can be checked for wear, as shown in Figure 18-16A. A micrometer can be used to check the diameter. Two measurements are usually taken. Second, a check can be made on the piston ring grooves. Figure 18-16B shows how the ring grooves can be checked using a micrometer. Third, a check can be made on the piston ring end gap, Figure 18-16C. Normally, the compression ring is placed inside the bore and the end gap is checked with a feeler gage.

Camshaft and Service

The purpose of the camshaft is to open and close the valves. Camshafts are used only on four-cycle engines. Figure 18-17 shows an example of a typical small gas engine camshaft and cam gear. The camshaft is driven by the gear attached to the crankshaft. These gears are called timing gears. During assembly, the two gears must be aligned correctly. This alignment, shown in Figure 18-18, causes the valves to open and close at the correct time in relationship to the position of the piston.

Very little service is necessary on the camshaft. However, the height of the lobe on the camshaft should always be checked for wear. If the lobe is worn down, the valve will not open as far as it should. This could cause a loss in engine efficiency. In addition, the gear should be checked for any worn condition.

Valve Train

The valve operating mechanism, *valve train*, is used to cause the valves to open and close at the

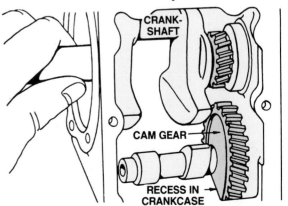

FIGURE 18-17 A typical small gas engine camshaft is used to operate the valve mechanism. It is located in the block on many four-cycle engines. *Courtesy of Briggs & Stratton Corporation*

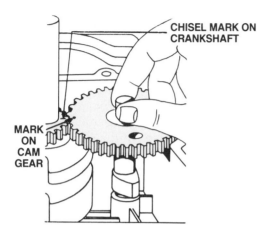

FIGURE 18-18 The crankshaft and camshaft must be carefully aligned for proper timing. Small marks on the gears are used for correct alignment. *Courtesy of Briggs & Stratton Corporation*

right time. The valve train is made up of several components. One common arrangement is called the I-head design. It includes a lifter, pushrod, rocker arm and shaft, valve spring, and valve. The valve is located in the top of the cylinder head. The parts are shown in Figure 18-19. As the camshaft lobe turns, the lifter is moved upward. The rocker arm shaft pivots at the center. This causes the valve to open downward.

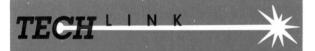

The motion of the rocker arm is considered a first-class lever. The input is on one side (cam side) and the output is on the other (valve) side. By designing the pivot point closer to the input, a greater distance will be moved on the output (at the valve). In practice, the valve can be opened farther than the lift of the cam by the design of the first-class lever.

A second common arrangement has the valves located directly in the block. This is referred to an an L-head design. Many small lawn mower engines use a similar design.

Valves and Service

Valves are very well-designed components in a small gas engine. The valves must be able to seal well enough to stand up to 500 pounds of pressure

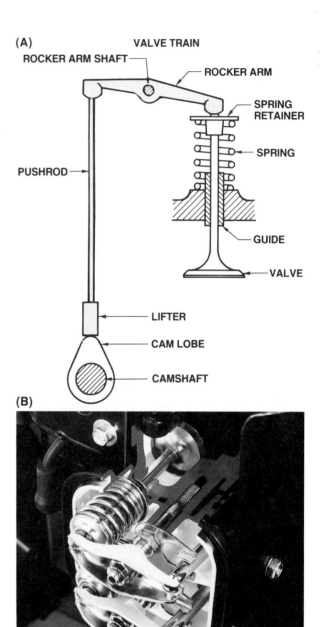

FIGURE 18-19 The parts of an I-head design. *Courtesy of (B) Tecumseh Products Company*

per square inch. The exhaust valve is also exposed to very high temperatures in excess of 2,500°F. Figure 18-20 shows the major parts of a valve. The compression seal occurs between the face and the seat of the assembly.

Valves are held to the spring using several designs. Figure 18-21 shows three common types used: pin type, collar type, and washer or retainer type.

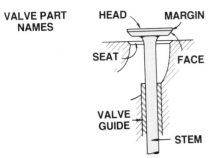

VALVE PART NAMES

HEAD   MARGIN

SEAT   FACE

VALVE GUIDE

STEM

FIGURE 18-20 The major parts of a valve. *Courtesy of Briggs & Stratton Corporation*

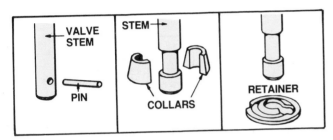

VALVE STEM

PIN

STEM

COLLARS

RETAINER

FIGURE 18-21 Design used to hold the valve in place on the spring. *Courtesy of Briggs & Stratton Corporation*

Valves should always be checked for failures. Figure 18-22A shows three common types of valve failure: burned, dished, or necked. Always check each valve for similar signs. The valve and seat should also be checked for correct dimensions. Figure 18-22B shows common dimensions for the margin and the valve seats. Always refer to the manufacturer's specifications when checking valve dimensions.

Engine Systems

Ignition System Principles

The major purpose of the ignition system is to produce a spark at the spark plug. The spark is used to ignite the air/fuel mixture. This is done using such components as the coil, switches, spark plugs, and wires.

Magneto Ignition System

The ignition systems on small gas engines have been redesigned considerably in the past few years. Most systems now are electronic and require very little service. However, the *magneto ignition* system is still used and, therefore, needs to be serviced on many engines.

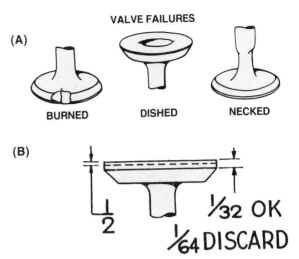

VALVE FAILURES

(A)

BURNED   DISHED   NECKED

(B)

$\frac{1}{32}$ OK
$\frac{1}{64}$ DISCARD

$\frac{1}{2}$

FIGURE 18-22 (A) Common valve failures and (B) correct dimensions for the margin and valve seats. *Courtesy of Briggs & Stratton Corporation*

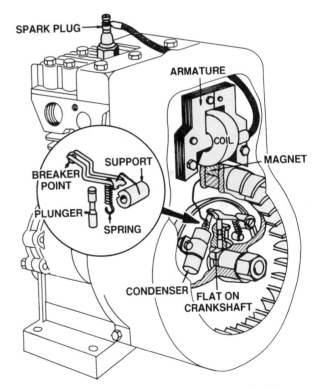

SPARK PLUG

ARMATURE

COIL

MAGNET

SUPPORT

BREAKER POINT

PLUNGER

SPRING

CONDENSER   FLAT ON CRANKSHAFT

FIGURE 18-23 The major parts of a magneto ignition system. *Courtesy of Briggs & Stratton Corporation*

Figure 18-23 shows the components of a typical magneto ignition system. This system operates by using a set of breaker points, a coil, a condenser and permanent magnets. The system consists of a primary circuit and a secondary circuit. Using

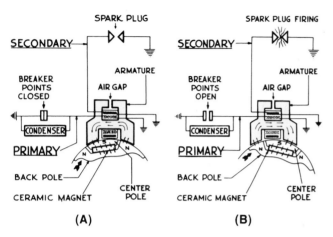

FIGURE 18-24 The events of operation for a magneto ignition system. *Courtesy of Briggs & Stratton Corporation*

Figure 18-24, the events of operation are described as follows.

1. As the center pole magnet spins in the flywheel, and when the breaker points are closed, a voltage is produced in the coil primary windings, Figure 18-24A.
2. When the breaker points are opened, the built-up magnetic field in the coil collapses and produces a voltage in the coil secondary windings, Figure 18-24B.
3. The ratio of windings in the primary and secondary increases the voltage from about 10 volts to about 20,000 volts.

Several important conditions will lower the amount of voltage produced at the spark plug. Causes that reduce or change the voltage include:

1. If the magnetic poles rotate too slowly, less voltage is produced.
2. If the breaker points are pitted, the collapse of the magnetic field will be slower, producing less voltage.
3. If the points are not adjusted to the correct gap, voltage will be reduced.
4. If the gap between the rotating poles and the stationary coil is increased, the voltage will be reduced.
5. If the key that holds the flywheel onto the crankshaft is slightly sheared, the flywheel will be positioned on the crankshaft incorrectly. This results in the voltage occurring at the wrong time.

Electronic Ignition Systems

Many small gas engine ignition systems now use solid-state systems, sometimes called capacitive discharge (CD) systems. These electronic ignition systems use transistors to turn the primary circuit on and off. A transistor can do this switching much faster than a set of breaker points. The result is that a higher voltage is produced for a longer period of time. Figure 18-25 graphically shows the difference between a standard magneto ignition system and an electronic ignition system.

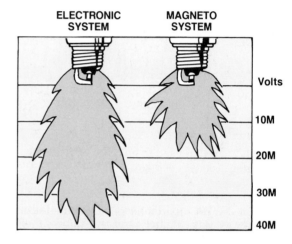

FIGURE 18-25 When an electronic ignition system is used, as compared to a standard magneto ignition system, the spark has a higher voltage over a longer period of time.

Spark Plugs and Service

The spark plug is one of the most important parts of any ignition system. Spark plugs are designed with different heat ranges. Generally, the longer the heat of the spark remains at the plug tip, the higher the heat range. It is important to always use the correct heat range spark plug. The numbers on the plug represent the heat range. Generally, the higher the number the hotter the plug. If the plug is too cold the engine will misfire. If the spark plug is too hot, pinging and preignition will occur. Refer to the manufacturer's recommended spark plug chart for the correct heat range and number.

The quality of the spark from a spark plug can be tested as shown in Figure 18-26A. This tool has different gaps that the spark will jump across. The spark should jump across the gap, as shown.

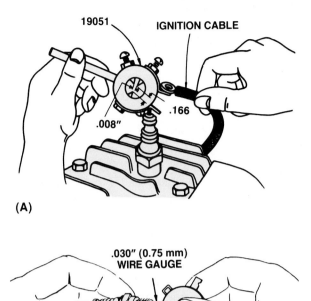

(A)

(B)

FIGURE 18-26 Two important service procedures on spark plugs include (A) checking the quality of the spark, and (B) checking the gap. *Courtesy of Briggs & Stratton Corporation*

The spark plug also should be checked for the correct gap. This is shown in Figure 18-26B. If the gap is too large or too small, the spark plug will misfire at different loads and speeds.

Fuel System Operation

The fuel system on most small gas engines uses a carburetor to mix the air and fuel at the correct ratio. This ratio is usually about 14.7 parts of air to 1 part of fuel (14.7:1). The fuel system is considered part of the "feedback" when studying the systems model. The carburetor and fuel system help to produce the correct amount of power required.

Many designs are used in the manufacture of carburetors. Some carburetors get fuel from a pump, whereas others get fuel from the force of gravity. On gravity-fed systems, the fuel tank is usually placed above the carburetor. On other systems, some form of pump must be used to transfer the fuel from the tank to the carburetor.

The parts of a typical carburetor are shown in Figure 18-27. Fuel, either gravity fed or from a pump, is sent into the lower part of the carburetor by the float. As the fuel fills this area, the inlet needle rises and shuts off the fuel coming into the carburetor.

Fuel transfers from the float bowl area to the air flow through the main nozzle and into a venturi. The venturi is the area on any carburetor that has a narrowing down on the main air channel. As air flows through a venturi, a vacuum is created. This vacuum is used to transfer fuel from the main nozzle into the air stream at the correct ratio.

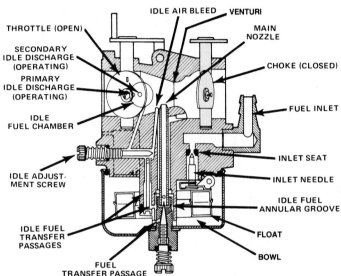

FIGURE 18-27 The principal parts of a small gas engine carburetor. *Courtesy of Tecumseh Products Company*

TECH LINK

A venturi causes a restriction in the flow of any fluid or gas, in this case air, going into a carburetor. This causes a vacuum to develop on the back of the venturi. The vacuum is produced according to Bernoulli's Theorem. This theorem states that when a gas or fluid flows through a restriction, its speed will increase. When speed increases, pressure decreases. The decrease in pressure (a vacuum) is used to bring fuel from the bowl area to the air flowing into the engine.

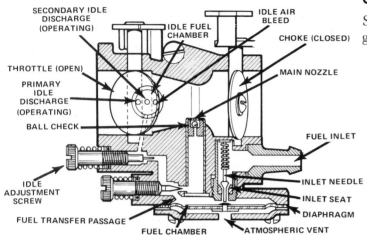

FIGURE 18-28 A diaphragm-type carburetor. The diaphragm on the bottom is used to pump fuel from the tank to the carburetor. *Courtesy of Tecumseh Products Company*

Diaphragm Fuel Pump

The *diaphragm fuel pump* is used on many two-cycle engines. The diaphragm system is shown in Figure 18-28. The diaphragm on the bottom of the carburetor is exposed to the engine crankcase vacuum and pressure on one side, and atmospheric pressure on the other. Because intake manifold pressure is constantly changing as the piston moves, the diaphragm also moves. This causes a pumping action to occur.

Carburetor Circuits

To help understand a carburetor, note that various circuits are used to increase control of the air and fuel mixture.

1. The choke circuit is used to bring in an additional amount of fuel used only for starting. Most carburetors have a *butterfly valve* on the intake. As the valve is closed, a greater suction is produced, and thus more fuel enters the carburetor.
2. During idle, the fuel comes from the fuel chamber on the bottom of the carburetor through an idle adjustment screw, and into the main stream of air near the throttle area.
3. The high-speed circuit allows more fuel to enter the air stream, especially at higher speeds. Fuel comes from the fuel chamber, through the main nozzle, into the air stream.

Carburetor Adjustments

Some of the adjustments that can be made on small gas engine carburetors include:

1. The idle adjustment screw — adjusted to get the best air to fuel ratio at idle conditions.
2. The main jet — adjusted to get the best air to fuel ratio during intermediate- and high-speed operation.
3. The level of the float — adjusted to get the correct level and amount of fuel inside of the float area. Too high a float setting will produce a rich mixture (too much fuel). Too low a float setting will produce a lean mixture (too little fuel). Both conditions will reduce the efficiency of engine operation. In addition, both conditions produce negative environmental impacts. An improper air to fuel ratio produces more carbon monoxide, nitrogen oxides, and hydrocarbons. These elements contribute to the reduction of air quality and increase pollution.

Cooling Systems

Many small gasoline engines are air cooled. When this is the case, the engine has many fins placed on the cylinder head and block. These fins increase the surface area and cool the engine. Air also flows over the fins to remove the excess heat.

More recently, however, liquid cooling is becoming more popular. Liquid-cooled engines are now used on motorcycles, snowmobiles, four wheelers, and others. The use of a small radiator to remove the heat from the cooling system is used on many liquid-cooled engines.

Outboard engines are also water cooled. Figure 18-29 shows the typical water route for cooling the engine. A small pump is used to bring in water and send it through the engine passageways.

Air System and Service

The air and exhaust system is used to get the air into the engine and the exhaust out of the engine. Air must be clean, so air cleaners are used on most land-operated engines. However, on outboard motors and winter use vehicles, such as snowmobiles, air cleaners are not needed as much.

Figure 18-30 shows a typical small engine air cleaner. This is called the poly-type air cleaner. The poly-type air cleaner element should be cleaned in a liquid detergent and water, or kerosene. Then the

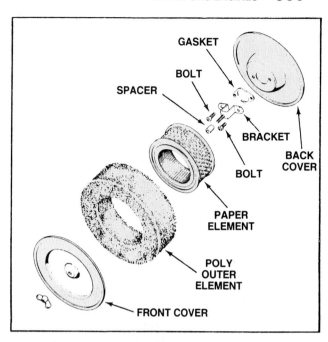

FIGURE 18-30 Type of air cleaner used on small gas engines. *Courtesy of Briggs & Stratton Corporation*

Governor Systems

The governor is a device used on many small gas engines to control the speed of the engine under different loads. The governor is also part of the "feedback" technology used to control the engine. The governor is designed to sense output speed. Based upon this speed, the governor readjusts the amount of fuel required for the application.

For example, a load is placed on the engine when a lawn mower goes through tall grass. As the engine speed decreases because of this load, the fuel setting must be increased to keep the speed at the correct r/min. When the load is removed, the engine has a tendency to increase in speed. The governor helps to decrease the throttle under these conditions to keep the engine at a constant r/min.

Mechanical Governor

Figure 18-31 shows how centrifugal counterweights are used to increase or decrease the throttle setting. In order to operate, the governor must sense the speed of the engine. The counterweights operate on an internal gear driven from the camshaft. As the speed increases, the weights move outward. The movement of the weights is connected to the fuel setting by linkages. The outward movement causes the fuel setting to decrease. As the speed decreases,

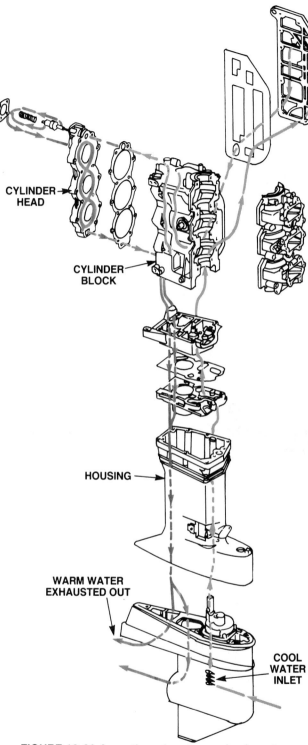

FIGURE 18-29 An outboard motor engine is water cooled. This diagram shows the water route to cool the engine. *Courtesy of Outboard Marine Corporation*

paper element should be soaked in engine oil and replaced on the engine. Other types include paper-type and foam-type elements. The paper-type air cleaner must be discarded and replaced with a new element when dirty.

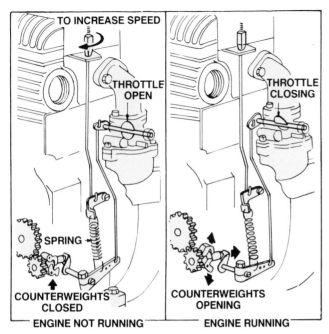

FIGURE 18-31 A governor helps to control the engine speed. The centrifugal weights sense engine speed and readjust the throttle (through linkage) when necessary. *Courtesy of Briggs & Stratton Corporation*

the weights move inward, causing the fuel setting to increase.

Air Vane Governor

Another method used to control the throttle setting is by sensing air pressure produced by the flywheel. The greater the air pressure, the faster the engine runs. The lesser the air pressure, the slower the engine runs. Figure 18-32 shows how the pressure moves an air vane. As the air vane is moved, the throttle setting is readjusted through linkage.

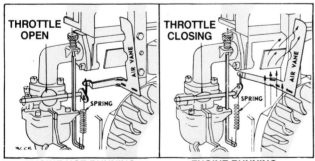

FIGURE 18-32 An air vane governor uses air pressure created by the flywheel to adjust the throttle setting. *Courtesy of Briggs & Stratton Corporation*

Lubrication System

The lubrication system on small gas engines is used to direct lubrication to certain engine parts during operation. Normally, however, lubrication systems are used only on four-cycle engines. Most two-cycle engines do not require a lubrication system. In a two-cycle engine, the oil is either mixed with the fuel or injected into the carburetor at about a 50 to 1 fuel to oil ratio.

Oil has four purposes. It cools, cleans, seals, and lubricates engine parts. In order for the oil to reach the parts that need lubrication, oil dippers are used on some engines. These are small pieces of metal bolted onto the connecting rod. The oil dipper splashes oil within the crankcase area as it dips through the oil.

A second method to distribute oil is by using an oil slinger. The oil slinger, similar to a gear, rolls through the oil and splashes oil throughout the crankcase area.

Some small four-cycle engines also use an oil pump built into the crankcase area. As the connecting rod rotates, it causes a small piston to produce a suction and pressure action. The oil is then directed to a specific spot for proper lubrication.

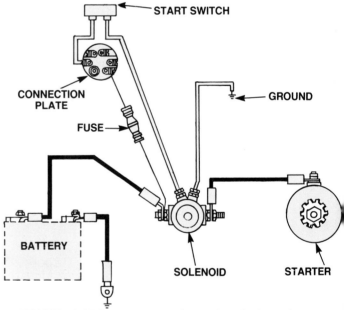

FIGURE 18-33 Common parts in an electrical starting system. *Courtesy of Outboard Marine Corporation*

Starting System

Many small gas engines use pull or mechanical rewind starters. However, on many other applications, an electrical starting system is used. Common parts in an electrical starting system are shown in Figure 18-33. They include the battery, solenoid, starter, fuse, and switch. In operation, the solenoid is used to make an electrical connection between the battery and the starter. The solenoid is energized by the start button or start switch. When the switch closes, the solenoid closes and electrical current from the battery causes the starter motor to turn. The starter motor then turns over the engine.

Charging System

The purpose of the charging system in a small gas engine can be used to provide electrical energy to:

1. Charge a battery for electrical starting systems.
2. Operate dash, head and running lights on boats, cycles, snowmobiles, garden tractors, etc.
3. Operate radios.
4. Operate handlebar warmers and facemask defoggers on snowmobiles.

Electrical energy is generated by placing several coils under the flywheel. Using these coils and permanent magnets, electromagnetic induction is produced in the wire. As the flywheel spins, electrical energy is generated in the coils. Figure 18-34 shows an example of the coils used in a charging system. The electrical energy is often controlled by using a regulator which uses transistors and diodes for voltage and current control.

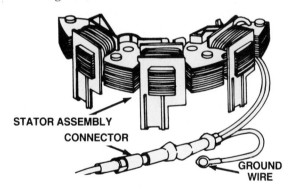

FIGURE 18-34 These coils, when placed under the flywheel, produce electricity for the charging system. *Courtesy of Briggs & Stratton Corporation*

Troubleshooting Small Gas Engines

Troubleshooting is the process of finding common or, at times, complicated problems in an engine. All manufacturers supply troubleshooting charts to aid the technician in locating problem areas. The following gives examples of common troubleshooting problems found in small gas engines.

Engine Fails to Start

1. Check for fuel in the tank.
2. Check for an obstruction in the fuel line.
3. Check for the fuel tank vent being closed off.
4. Check to see if the carburetor is overchoked.
5. Check the spark plug for fouling.
6. Check for poor compression.

Engine Misses under Load

1. Check for a fouled spark plug.
2. Check for improper spark plug gap.
3. Check for pitted breaker points.
4. Check for weak valve spring.
5. Check for improper valve clearance.

Engine Lacks Power

1. Check the choke position. It should be open when hot.
2. Check for improper carburetor jet adjustments.
3. Check for loss of compression.
4. Check for an air cleaner restriction.
5. Check for inaccurate valve timing.
6. Check for a dirty or damaged carburetor.

Engine Overheats

1. Check the timing on the engine.
2. Check the carburetor for improper adjustment (possibly too lean).
3. Check for an airflow restriction.
4. Check for carbon in the combustion chamber.
5. Check for a lack of lubrication.

Engine Surges or Runs Unevenly

1. Check the fuel cap vent hole for blockage.
2. Check the operation of the governor.
3. Check the carburetor linkage adjustment.
4. Check the carburetor for needle valve adjustments.
5. Check for intermittent spark at spark plugs.

Engine Vibrates Excessively

1. Check for broken engine mounts.
2. Check for a bent crankshaft.
3. Check for counterweights in the engine that are not properly aligned.

Engine Uses Excessive Amount of Oil

1. Check oil level, possibly too high.
2. Check the valve guides for signs of wear.
3. Check the compression and oil control rings.
4. Check for carbon in the ring groove area.
5. Check for glazing in the cylinder walls.

Oil Leaks from Engine

1. Check for hardening or worn seals.
2. Check for bent crankshaft.
3. Check for incorrectly installed seal.

Summary

- Small gas engines are used in a variety of applications from garden tractors, tillers and water bikes, to snowmobiles, cycles, and four wheelers.
- Small gas engines can have several designs. These include, two- or four-cycle, oil mix or oil injection, single or multiple cylinder, in-line or V-configuration, liquid- or air-cooled, various valve arrangements, reed or port induction, and different piston displacements.
- The cylinder block is used as the base of the engine.
- The cylinder head is placed on top of the cylinder block to seal the combustion chamber.
- The crankshaft is used to convert the piston motion to torque.
- The flywheel is used to reduce vibration, and provide air for air vane governors.
- The piston assembly has a connecting rod and bearings that attach to the crankshaft.
- The camshaft is used to operate the valve for correct operation.
- The valve train consists of lifters, pushrods, valves, and springs.
- The magneto ignition system uses permanent magnets to produce the necessary voltage in the primary.
- Many ignition systems today are electronic and do not use breaker points.
- Spark plugs have different heat ranges. Hotter plugs can cause pinging; cooler plugs can cause the plugs to foul out.
- The diaphragm fuel pump on certain carburetors is used to transfer fuel from the tank to the carburetor using vacuum and pressure pulses from the crankcase area.
- The important carburetor circuits include the choke, idle, and high-speed circuit.
- Important carburetor adjustments include the idle adjustment, float level, and main or high-speed adjustment.
- Small gas engines are either liquid or air cooled.
- A governor is used to sense engine speed and based upon this speed, readjusts the throttle setting accordingly.
- Governors sense speed by using counterweights, or air pressure from the flywheel fins.
- Most two-cycle engines today use a 50 to 1 or higher fuel/oil mixture for correct operation.
- The main starting system parts include the battery, solenoid, starter, switch, and fuse.
- The charging system uses a set of electromagnetic coils placed under the flywheel to produce a charging voltage.
- Troubleshooting small gas engines is a process of finding the correct solution when an engine problem occurs. Common engine problems include:

Won't start

Misses

Lacks power

Overheats

Surges or runs unevenly

Vibrates excessively

Uses excessive amounts of oil

Leaks oil

REVIEW

1. Air and fuel enter a two-cycle engine by either _____ valves or by _____ injection.
2. If a small gas engine is pinging and preignition occurs, the problem can be solved by _____ of the spark plug.
3. The _____ circuit on a carburetor is used to bring in additional fuel during cold starting.
4. Too high a float level in the carburetor will cause a _____ air/fuel mixture.
5. The governor is a device on small gas engines to control the _____ of the engine.
6. The lubrication system is designed to do four things. These include _____, _____, lubricate, and _____.
7. When an excessive amount of oil is being used, it is important to check the _____ on a small gas engine.
8. When a small gas engine misses under load, always check for a _____ spark plug.
9. List five applications in which small gas engines can be used for transportation or industrial purposes.
10. State at least five variables that can be found on small gas engine design.
11. List the major mechanical parts of a small gas engine.
12. What is the purpose of the flywheel on a small gas engine?
13. What is the difference between a standard magneto ignition system and an electronic ignition system?
14. Explain spark plug heat ranges and state what results if the wrong plug heat range is used.
15. Describe how a diaphragm fuel pump operates.
16. Identify two types of carburetor circuits and state how they work.
17. List at least three carburetor adjustments made on small gas engines.
18. What two types of cooling systems are used on small gas engines?
19. Describe how an air vane governor operates, what it senses, and what it controls.

CHAPTER ACTIVITIES

 ## MAGNETO IGNITION SYSTEM

INTRODUCTION

The magneto system on small gas engines is used to provide the spark for the ignition system. This activity will help you to become familiar with the parts of the magneto ignition system.

TECHNOLOGICAL LITERACY SKILLS

Problem solving, instrumentation, data analysis, data collection.

OBJECTIVES

At the completion of this activity, you will be able to:

1. Identify the components in a magneto ignition system.
2. Observe the output of a magneto ignition system.
3. Adjust components in the magneto ignition system.

MATERIALS

1. A magneto ignition system used on a small lawn mower or equivalent engine
2. Feeler gage
3. Ohmmeter
4. Maintenance manual for the engine
5. Assorted small engine tools
6. Magneto handout

PROCEDURE

▶ **CAUTION:** Always wear safety glasses when working with tools in the laboratory. Also, make sure you know the correct operation of all tools and machines in the laboratory. If not, check with your instructor.

1. Remove the flywheel of the engine and expose the magneto ignition system parts.
2. Using the information in this chapter, identify the purpose of the following parts on the Magneto handout:
   a. Permanent magnet
   b. Laminated core
   c. Primary windings
   d. Secondary windings
   e. Points or transistorized components
   f. Condenser, if used
   g. High-tension wire
   h. Spark plug
3. Disconnect all wires from the ignition system parts.
4. Using an ohmmeter, measure the resistance of the primary and secondary windings. Record on the handout.
5. Measure the spark plug gap and record on the handout.
6. From the engine manual, note the coil-to-flywheel air gap and record on the handout.
7. Set the coil air gap on the engine to the specification stated in the manual.
8. Position the crankshaft so the ignition points are fully open.
9. Check the actual gap and record on the handout.
10. Now check the manufacturer's gap and record on the handout.
11. Adjust the point gap to the manufacturer's specifications.
12. Reconnect all ignition system parts for correct operation.
13. Check for spark by grounding the spark plug on the engine frame and crank the engine by hand. You should be able to see a small spark occur across the spark plug gap. Identify the type of spark observed, and record on the handout.

REVIEW QUESTIONS

1. What form of energy does the flywheel rotation represent?
2. What type of energy is the flywheel motion converted to?

3. How does the number of windings in the coil affect the voltage produced?
4. Does the speed at which the magnets and flywheel turn affect the spark output voltage? How?
5. What effect would an increase in the coil-to-flywheel gap have on the spark plug voltage being produced?

 ## SMALL ENGINE PARTS IDENTIFICATION

INTRODUCTION

One method used to become familiar with the parts of a small gasoline or diesel engine is to measure the parts for wear. This activity will help the student to identify parts that are worn on a small gasoline or diesel engine.

TECHNOLOGICAL LITERACY SKILLS

Instrumentation, data collection, data analysis.

OBJECTIVES

At the completion of this activity, you will be able to:
1. Disassemble a small gasoline or diesel engine.
2. Identify the parts of the engine and evaluate their wear characteristics.
3. Determine the camshaft-to-crankshaft timing.
4. Assemble the engine to running condition.

MATERIALS

1. One small gasoline or diesel engine, preferably a four cycle, 1 to 10 horsepower.
2. Reference and maintenance manuals for the engine.
3. Standard small engine tools for disassembly and reassembly.
4. Small engine work stands, if available.
5. Various small engine special tools including:
   a. Flywheel puller
   b. Valve maintenance tools
   c. Torque wrenches
6. Small Engine handout
7. Cleaning solvent tank

PROCEDURE

1. Identify the engine's specifications, including the horsepower, manufacturer, model number and serial number, and record on the Small Engine handout.

   ▶ **CAUTION:** Always wear safety glasses when working with tools in the laboratory. Also, make sure you know the correct operation of all tools and machines in the laboratory. If not, check with your instructor.

2. Drain the oil in an appropriate oil drain container, and remove the fuel from the fuel tank.
3. Using the laboratory tools, disassemble the engine external parts. The exact procedure may vary depending upon the engine. Leave such subcomponents as the carburetor, starter, and so forth assembled as a unit.

4. To make sure all components have been removed, use the checkoff procedure on the Small Engine handout.

5. After the crankcase area has been exposed, notice the crankshaft-to-camshaft gear markings. These two gears must be timed correctly. Look for the marks on the teeth of the gears. Check the maintenance manual to determine exactly what to observe. On the handout, draw an example of how the gears should be timed.

6. Remove the piston and connecting rod, noting its position relative to the block of the engine. Also note the rod end cap markings, if visible.

7. Remove the crankshaft from the engine.

8. Clean all parts in the solvent tank.

9. Locate the specification for each part listed on the Small Engine handout, and then measure the parts using the correct measuring tools.

10. Begin assembling the engine. Make sure all bolts and nuts are torqued to the manufacturer's specification.

11. Install the crankshaft back into the engine.

12. Install the piston, connecting rod, and cam gear. Make sure this cam gear is correctly timed to the crankshaft.

13. Continue assemblying all parts of the engine.

14. Check the end play of the crankshaft and adjust according to the manufacturer's specification.

15. Continue assembling until the engine is complete and capable of running.

REVIEW QUESTIONS

1. What is the purpose for checking the ring end gap on the compression rings?

2. Why is it important to torque each bolt and nut during assembly?

3. How is the crankshaft end play adjusted?

CHAPTER 19

Fluid Power

OBJECTIVES

After reading this chapter, you will be able to:

■ Compare hydraulic and pneumatic fluid power systems.

■ Identify basic theories used to describe fluid power, including Pascal's law and Bernoulli's theorem.

■ Describe various fluid power principles, including force, pressure, and mechanical advantage.

■ Define various fluid characteristics, including viscosity, pour point and types of additives.

■ Compare the advantages and disadvantages of using synthetic fluids in fluid power systems.

■ Identify the operation of various fluid power components, such as check valves, hydraulic couplings, hydraulic clutches, pumps, regulator valves, bourdon tubes, filters, cylinders, and symbols.

KEY TERMS

Pneumatic	Viscosity Index	Axial
Atmospheres	Corrosion	Turbine
Bourdon Pressure Gauge	Inhibit	Stator
Fluidity	SAE	Differential Pressure

Introduction

Fluid power is an integral part of the study of power technology. *Fluid power* is used to transmit power from one point to another. Fluid power serves the same purpose as gears: both are used to transmit a certain type of power. Fluid power is used to transmit pressures, whereas gears are used to transmit torque. This chapter is about the principles, fluid characteristics, and components used in fluid power systems.

FIGURE 19-1 This log splitter uses a fluid power system to change rotary motion from the engine into force for splitting logs. *Courtesy of Huss Sales, Inc.*

Fluid Power Principles

Fluid Power Applications

All fluid power systems are used to transmit forces and motion from one point to another. For example, a log splitter, as shown in Figure 19-1, uses a fluid power system. The system takes the rotary motion of a gasoline engine and converts this power to forces needed to split a log. A system such as this also is used to multiply forces.

Hydraulic systems are also used in many transportation devices. A common example is that of a brake system on a car. The pressure produced by the driver's foot is transmitted to each brake on the wheels. Here the pressure is used to apply the brakes to stop the vehicle. Figure 19-2 shows a typical fluid power brake system on an automobile.

Large construction, agricultural and transportation equipment, such as cranes, front-end loaders, lift trucks, crawler tractors, field plows, and so forth also use fluid power systems. For instance, the power produced from a diesel or gasoline engine (torque) is used to raise and lower the blade, plow, or forks on a lift truck, Figure 19-3.

Robot technology is another application that

FIGURE 19-3 This lift truck uses fluid power to raise and lower the forks on the front of the truck. *Courtesy of Burlington Air Express*

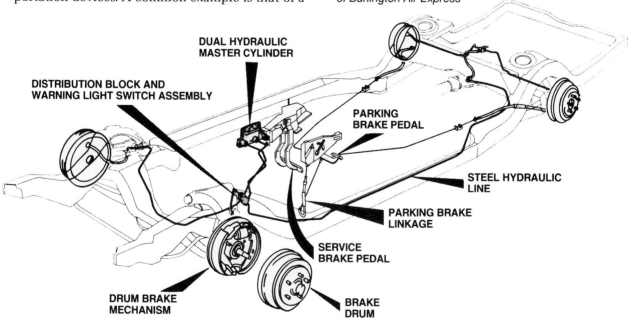

FIGURE 19-2 The automobile braking system uses fluid power to apply pressure to the brake drums.
Courtesy of Delco Moraine Division, General Motors Corporation

FIGURE 19-4 Industrial robots operate on fluid power systems. *Courtesy of ABB Robotics, Inc. (ASEA Brown Boveri)*

uses fluid power, Figure 19-4. The fluid power is used to move the grippers, body, and arms on the robot.

Hydraulic and Pneumatic Fluid Systems

Fluid power systems can be subdivided into two major types: hydraulic and pneumatic systems. *Hydraulic* systems are defined as those that use a liquid, such as a hydraulic fluid, as the transmitting medium. *Pneumatic* systems are those that use air or gas as the transmitting medium. Both systems are called "fluid" power, although each system uses a different fluid to transmit the forces. Some of the major differences are:

- Hydraulic fluids cannot be compressed.
- Pneumatic fluids are considered gases and are compressible.
- Hydraulic fluids must have complete hydraulic circuits. Return lines must be used, and a reservoir is needed to hold extra hydraulic fluid.
- Pneumatic fluids do not need complete circuits. The air is used for moving an object and it can be dumped into the atmosphere. No extra reservoir is needed as the atmosphere acts as the return.

Force and Pressure

To understand fluid power systems, both force and pressure must be defined. *Force* is defined as the pushing or pulling action of one object upon another. Force usually causes an object to move. Force is measured in pounds (lb).

Pressure is defined as a force acting upon an area. For example, the air pressure put into a bicycle

Repair of Automotive Robot

Fluid power is often used on different types of robots. Robots are playing an ever-increasing role in the manufacturing processes of many products. However, robots also are susceptible to failure and incorrect operation. A new career area has been developed in the service and repair of robot technology.

At the Ford Canada Essex Engine Plant, two employees repair a robot on the factory floor. They are helped by a portable computer by printing out a step-by-step program to pinpoint and repair the trouble in the robot. This is a good example of the interaction among robots, technology, and humans. *Courtesy of Ford Motor Company*

tire is said to be 60 pounds per square inch. This means that on each square inch of tire (area), 60 pounds of force are being applied. Pressure is then measured in pounds per square inch or (psi).

Types of Pressure

In the field of fluid power, two types of pressure are commonly used. These include:

1. Pressure per square inch-absolute (psia).
2. Pressure per square inch-gage (psig).

Absolute pressure (psia) is a measure of the pressure of a fluid starting at zero atmospheres and working upward to a maximum pressure. An atmosphere is a unit of pressure in which 14.7 pounds of pressure, absolute, is considered atmospheric pressure (barometric pressure) at sea level. The scale is shown in Figure 19-5. For example, each inch of a person's body is under 14.7 pounds of pressure (absolute) at sea level.

Gage pressure (psig) measures the pressure of a fluid above or below the pressure of the surrounding atmosphere. For example, a typical gage used to measure pressure reads zero when no pressure is exerted on the gage. (Of course, an absolute pressure is being applied to the gage but the gage does not read this pressure.) Both a pressure and a vacuum can be created on this scale. For example, any psia below 14.7 is considered a vacuum on the psig scale. Note that, in most cases, the (g) is dropped from the expression psig. Usually, only psi is used.

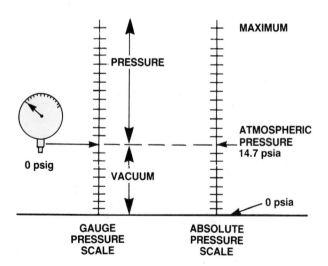

FIGURE 19-5 The psig and psia scales are two different types of pressure scales used in fluid power systems.

Pascal's Law

All fluid power systems follow certain predictable patterns. One law that helps to understand fluid power systems is called Pascal's Law. This law states that:

> A pressure applied to a confined fluid is transmitted undiminished to every portion of the surface of the containing vessel.

This law is illustrated in Figure 19-6. When a force is applied to the handle, the piston is forced downward. The pressure created in the fluid is equal and undiminished in all directions.

Pascal's law also states that pressure on a fluid is equal to the force applied divided by the area. This can be shown as:

$$P = \frac{F}{A}$$

Where P = pressure in psi

F = force applied in pounds

A = area to which force is applied

In Figure 19-6, if the force applied on the piston is 100 pounds, and the piston area is 1 square inch, then the pressure exerted inside of the cylinder is 100 psi.

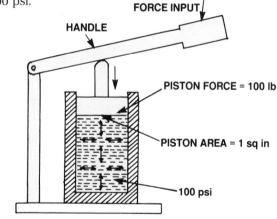

FIGURE 19-6 Pascal's law states that when a pressure is applied to a fluid, the pressure is the same at all points.

Fluid power systems use the fluid to transmit a force. Referring to Figure 19-7, when a force presses down on the brake pedal, a pressure is built-up in the master cylinder. This pressure is then transferred throughout the hydraulic lines to each wheel cylinder. Note that the pressure at each point in the system is the same.

In this fluid system, very little movement of fluid occurs. It is the pressure and the forces that do the work needed in the fluid system. In the Figure 19-7 example, the fluid is used to transfer the pressure of the operator's foot to the piston and friction pads.

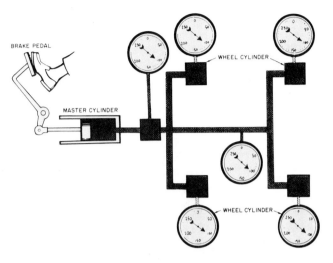

FIGURE 19-7 When a pressure is produced on the hydraulic brake system, the pressure is felt equally throughout the brake system. *Courtesy of Delco Moraine Division, General Motors Corporation*

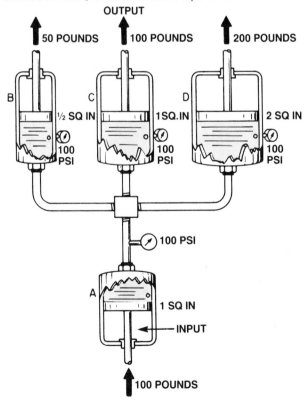

FIGURE 19-8 Pressure inside of a cylinder can be increased or multiplied by changing the size of the piston diameter. *Courtesy of EIS Brake Parts, Division Standard Motor Products, Inc.*

Boyle's Law

Another law that is often used to describe the properties of gases in a container is called Boyle's law. It has been found that a volume of gas is inversely proportional to its pressure. This means that as the pressure increases on a gas, the volume decreases. Boyle's law states that the volume of a gas varies inversely with the pressure applied to it, provided the temperature of the gas remains constant. Most often in a pneumatic fluid system, the pressure is created by pistons. Boyle's law is applied to other areas as well. Boyle's law helps to explain the characteristics of gases on top of a piston inside of a gasoline or diesel engine. The pressure of compression is increased as the piston reduces the volume of the gas.

TECH LINK

A scientific law that helps to explain the characteristics of gases in a fluid system is called the Charles law. This law states that as the temperature of a gas increases, the volume of the gas increases proportionally, keeping the pressure constant. For example, if the temperature of a gas doubled, the volume would also double. It also follows then, that as the pressure increases in a gas, the temperature also increases.

Force Multiplication (Mechanical Advantage)

Force can also be multiplied by using fluid systems. On many pieces of construction equipment, the force must be increased to do the required job. Figure 19-8 shows how this can be done. The principle is applied to different size pistons and cylinders in a hydraulic circuit. On the lower end, a piston size of 1 square inch is used as the input. When 100 pounds are applied, the ½ square inch, the 1 square inch, and the 2 square inch cylinders all have different output psi produced. The outputs are 50, 100, and 200 psi. Note that although the pressure per square inch is the same, the number of square inches in each output cylinder is different. This causes the output forces to be different.

Bernoulli's Theorem

Bernoulli's theorem is another law that affects fluid power systems. This law states that when a fluid flows through a pipe, pressure will remain constant unless the diameter of the pipe changes. Figure 19-9 illustrates this principle. Note how the diameter of the pipe changes in the center. In order to keep the flow rate constant, the fluid must flow faster through the restriction. When velocity of the fluid increases at the restriction, the static pressure is reduced at that point. A carburetor venturi, as discussed in a previous chapter, works on this principle.

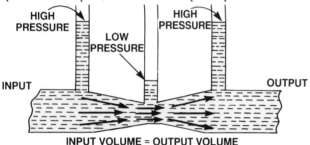

FIGURE 19-9 Bernoulli's theorum states that as the velocity of a fluid increases, the static pressure at that point reduces.

Measuring Pressure with a Bourdon Gage

All fluid systems must have certain controls. These controls are part of the "feedback" technology used in the systems model. Feedback and control systems need methods that can be used to read various pressures in fluid systems.

One method used to measure and read pressure in a fluid power system is by using a *Bourdon pressure gage*. Figure 19-10 shows a typical Bourdon gage. The tube is made of thin brass. The free end is connected to an indicating needle on the gage dial. As fluid pressure increases in the system, the tube has a tendency to become straightened. This causes the needle to read differently on the dial. This type of gage reading requires the fluid to be sent directly to the gage. Usually, a small copper or plastic tube is connected from the pressure point to the gage. A Bourdon gage can read either a pneumatic or hydraulic fluid pressure. However, the scales for each are calibrated differently.

Measuring Pressure with a Manometer

A second method used to measure pressure is by using a *manometer*. Manometers are also part of the "feedback" technology on the system model. A manometer is most often used to measure pneumatic pressure and vacuum readings. Figure 19-11 shows a typical manometer. It consists of a U-

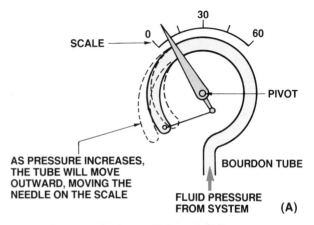

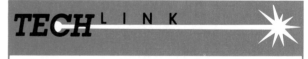

FIGURE 19-10 A Bourdon tube is used to measure and read the pressure inside a hydraulic system.

shaped tube with a fluid inside. A scale is used between the tubes. When a pressure or vacuum is connected to one end of the tube, the fluid has a tendency to move. The movement on the scale is an indication of the amount of vacuum or pressure. When small pressures or vacuums need to be measured, a water (H_2O) manometer is used. For higher pressures, a heavier liquid, such as mercury (Hg), is used. Normally, one pound of pressure will move water 27.7 inches. One pound of pressure will move mercury 2.036 inches.

TECH LINK

There are several conversion factors between water and mercury manometer readings and psig. The following numbers can be used for conversion from one to the other:

1" of water	=	.0735" of mercury
1" of water	=	.0361 psig
1" of mercury	=	.491 psig
1" of mercury	=	13.6" of water
1 psig	=	27.7" of water
1 psig	=	2.036" of mercury

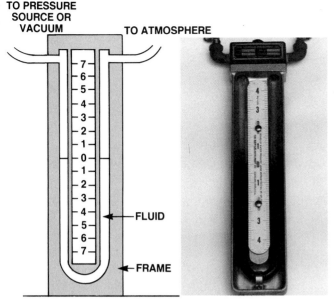

FIGURE 19-11 A manometer measures pressures and vacuum readings in a fluid power system.

Fluid Characteristics

To help understand fluid pressure, certain fluid characteristics are important to study. This section discusses various fluid properties and characteristics.

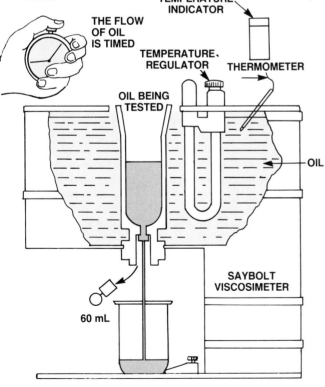

FIGURE 19-12 A Saybolt viscosimeter is used to measure the viscosity of a fluid. Time is measured for how long it takes a certain quantity of fluid, at a specific temperature, to flow through an orifice.

Viscosity

The *viscosity* of a fluid is defined as the fluidity or thickness of the liquid at a specific temperature. Viscosity, also defined as resistance to flow, is measured by a device known as the Saybolt universal viscosimeter. The operation of this device is shown in Figure 19-12. Viscosity is determined at a specific temperature of the fluid. The most common temperatures are 0°F, 150°F, 210°F. A sample of fluid is drained from the viscosimeter into a receiving flask. The time required for the sample to completely drain is recorded in seconds. The viscosity is given in Saybolt universal seconds (SUS) at a particular temperature.

Viscosity Index. As a fluid becomes colder, it becomes thicker. As a fluid becomes hotter, it becomes thinner. The *viscosity index* measures fluid thickness with different temperatures. Viscosity index (VI) is a measure of how much the viscosity of a fluid changes with a given temperature. Chemicals are added so that as the temperature of the fluid changes, the viscosity will not change as much. Usually, the higher the viscosity index, the smaller the relative change in viscosity with temperature. Viscosity index *improvers* are chemicals added to fluids to aid in making them more stable with temperature changes.

Pour Point

All fluid products must flow as a liquid in order to be used. Extreme cold conditions may increase viscosity until the fluid cannot flow. The temperature at which the fluid ceases to flow is defined as the *pour point*. As the temperature of the fluid approaches its pour point, it becomes thicker and more difficult to pump. This decreases the fluidity of the liquid. Additives are added to the fluid to control the pour point.

Fluid Additives

Antifoaming additives are added to fluids to reduce foaming. During normal operation in many fluid power systems, the fluid is pressurized and pumped through the circuit. This constant pumping may cause the fluid to foam. Any foam produced in the fluid power system reduces the efficiency of the system. In order to reduce foaming, specific chemicals are added to the oil.

Corrosion and *rust inhibitors* are added to

certain fluids to reduce or inhibit corrosion of the internal parts. Chemicals are added to help neutralize any acids produced. Rust inhibitors are also used to help remove water vapors.

Antiscuff additives are put in the fluid to help polish moving parts. This is especially important in new systems.

Extreme-pressure resistance additives are added to the fluids to keep the molecules from splitting apart under heavy pressures. During operation, fluids are constantly being pressurized, squeezed, and otherwise stressed. This may cause the fluid molecules to separate, thus reducing the fluid's lubricating and power transmission properties. The added chemicals react with metal surfaces to form very strong, slippery films which may be only a molecule or so thick. With these additives, protection is increased during moments of extreme pressure.

SAE Ratings

Most fluids and lubricating oil are rated by the Society of Automotive Engineers (SAE). *SAE ratings* are those that rate fluids in terms of the viscosity or thickness. SAE has applied the Saybolt Universal Seconds (SUS) test to their ratings. SAE ratings are determined by different temperatures. Fluids are tested for viscosity at 0°F, 150°F, and 210°F. The most common are 0°F and 210°F. A rating that has a letter W after it means that the viscosity is tested at 0°F. If there is no W after the ratings, the fluid has been tested at 210°F. For example, when two fluids are compared, the thicker fluid will have the higher SAE rating.

Other ratings are also used. The API (American Petroleum Institute) rates oils by the type of service such as SE, SF, etc. Military ratings are also shown on many oil containers.

Synthetic Fluids

In recent years, an increased use of synthetic fluids and lubricants has taken place. Synthetic fluids and lubricants are chemically made from mixing together alcohol, various acids, other chemicals and hydrocarbons. The hydrocarbons can be taken from coal, oil, natural gas, wood, or any agricultural resource. The result is a synthesized product capable of meeting and exceeding the fluid and lubrication needs of most applications.

Synthesize means to combine parts into a whole or to make complex compounds from a series of individual molecules. This is done within the chemistry of the fluid.

Synthetic fluid is manufactured by combining specific molecules into an end product tailored to do a specific job. These fluids are designed to meet or exceed the SAE or other recommendations.

Advantages and Disadvantages of Synthetic Fluids

Synthetic oils were initially designed for jet engine use because of their higher temperature and pressure characteristics. They are now used in many automobile and fluid power applications. This is because of their ability to withstand high temperatures with little change in the viscosity of the fluid. There are several advantages and disadvantages of using synthetic fluids.

Advantages

1. Increased thermal stability. For example, synthetic fluids can operate effectively within a range of from -60°F to +400°F.
2. Less evaporation. Only about 1% of the fluid is evaporated over a standard period of time, as compared to about 25% for other fluids.
3. Less viscosity change with temperature. This improves cold weather operation of fluid power systems.
4. Improved system efficiency. This is because synthetic fluids have less frictional resistance.
5. Less fluid loss and leakage. Synthetic fluids increase sealing characteristics.
6. Cleaner system parts. Parts remain cleaner. This results in less maintenance.

Disadvantages

1. Higher cost. The cost per quart for synthetic fluid is still higher as compared to conventional fluids. However, over the life of the system, the total cost will be about the same. The savings come from cleaner parts and more system efficiency.
2. Inability to be intermixed. It is not advisable to mix different brands of synthetic fluids. This may cause some inconvenience when trying to buy a particular brand.

Fluid Power Components

Many fluid power components are considered part of the "process" in the systems model. These components use various resources to accomplish a specific "output". These resources include materials, capital, tools, knowledge, human time, and other variables.

Fluid Pump

Fluid pumps are used to produce the pressure necessary in most fluid systems. In most cases, internal combustion engines are used to turn the pumps, although electric motors can also be used. For example, on a log splitter, the engine turns a pump in order to produce fluid pressure.

There are several types of fluid pumps. Some fluid pumps are defined as *positive displacement*. This means that for each revolution, an exact amount or volume of fluid will be pumped. As r/min increases, then fluid pressure will also increase.

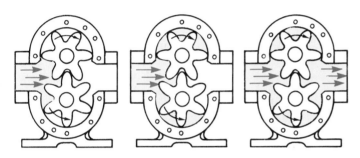

FIGURE 19-13 A gear-type positive displacement pump used on many fluid power systems.

Gear-type Pump

Figure 19-13 shows how a standard gear-type pump operates. In this example, the fluid is brought in on one side by a vacuum. The vacuum is created by the gear teeth disengaging. It could also be said that, because of the lower pressure (psia) or vacuum (psig), atmospheric pressure is forcing the fluid into the pump. It is then pressurized on the other side. The pressure is caused by the gear teeth meshing.

The eccentric gear-type pump operates on the same principle as the standard type. *Eccentric* means not having the same center. Figure 19-14 shows two gears. The centers of both gears are not at the same position. As the inside gear is turned, a suction is produced on one side, and a pressure is produced on the other side.

Vane Pump

Vane pumps are used on both hydraulic and pneumatic systems. Figure 19-15 shows a vane-type pump. Again, an eccentric design is used; however,

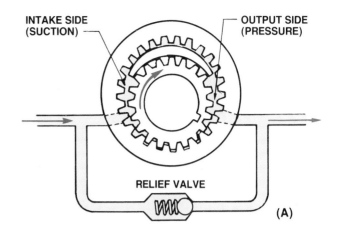

FIGURE 19-14 An eccentric gear-type pump is used to produce pressure in a fluid system.

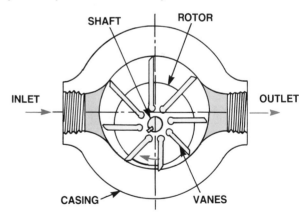

FIGURE 19-15 A vane-type pump uses an eccentric design to cause the suction and pressure for producing fluid pressure.

the vanes are acting as the gears. As the center rotor is turned, the vanes cause a suction and pressure to occur. The vanes can be held outward either by springs or by centrifugal force.

Axial Piston Pump

Another category of fluid pumps uses pistons to create a suction and pressure. Several types are

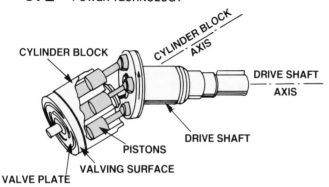

FIGURE 19-16 An axial system pump uses a set of pistons rotating on two shafts that are placed at different angles.

used. One common arrangement, called an axial piston pump, uses several pistons on two shafts that are placed at different angles, Figure 19-16. Similar arrangements are used on air-conditioning systems. As the drive shaft turns, the pistons also rotate. As they rotate, because of the angle, the pistons move up and down in a cylinder. This action creates a suction and pressure.

Hydraulic Coupling

A hydraulic coupling is another component used in many hydraulic systems. Hydraulic couplings are used most often in torque converters used in transportation vehicles.

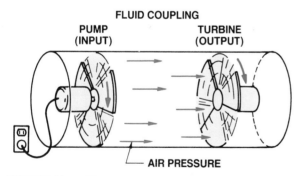

FIGURE 19-17 These two fans demonstrate the operation of a hydraulic coupling. They act as a torque converter. The pressures created from one side are used to turn the other side.

A common way of describing a fluid coupling is by using the action of two electric fans as an example. Referring to Figure 19-17, one fan is producing a pressure and blowing the air against the other fan. The air pressure produces enough energy to rotate the second fan. This action couples together the input and output. The first fan is called the *pump* or *impeller*. The second fan is called the

turbine. The faster the impeller turns, the better the fluid lock-up between the input and output. In the actual torque converter, a pump and turbine are used. And, in actual operation, hydraulic fluid is used rather than air as is used in the example.

Parts of the Torque Converter

Several parts make up a torque converter to produce an hydraulic coupling. Figure 19-18 shows the major parts: the pump (also called the *impeller*), the *turbine*, and the guide wheel or *stator*. Note that each part consists of a series of vanes used to direct fluid through the torque converter. These parts are contained in a sealed housing which is completely filled with oil. Motion and power are transferred by the pressure of the mass of the flowing oil. There is no direct mechanical contact between the input and the output drive, only a fluid connection. Because of this type of connection, torque converters operate wear-free.

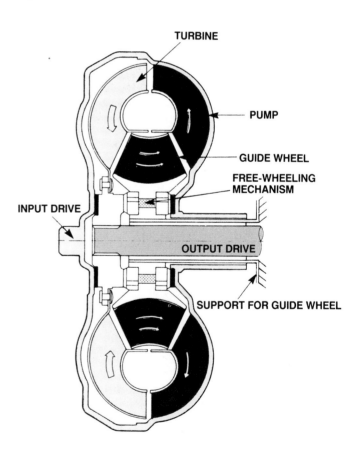

FIGURE 19-18 A torque converter uses a fluid to lock-up two spinning shafts. *Courtesy of Sachs Industries, Inc.*

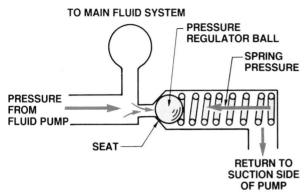

FIGURE 19-19 A pressure regulator valve sends fluid back to the suction side of the pump to reduce the pressure when it gets too high.

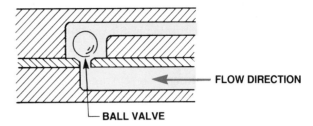

FIGURE 19-20 Ball check valves are used to stop the fluid flow in one direction, while allowing the fluid to flow in the opposite direction.

Pressure Regulating Valve

Because most fluid power pumps are positive displacement types, a pressure regulator valve must be used. A *pressure regulator valve* is used to keep the pressure within the system at a constant maximum value. As the r/min of the pump changes, the amount of pressure produced will also change. In addition, as the fluid thickens because of cold weather, pressure may also increase. The pressure regulator valve helps to maintain a constant maximum pressure. Any time pressure is increased above this maximum, the regulator valve opens to reduce the pressure.

Figure 19-19 shows how a pressure regulator valve works. As the fluid pressure increases in the pump, the pressure pushes against a ball or valve held in place by a spring. When pressure is greater than the spring tension, the ball lifts off its seat. At this point, some of the fluid is returned back to the suction side of the pump. This reduces the pressure, which seats the ball again. The spring tension is designed to set the fluid pressure at the manufacturer's specifications. If a stronger spring is used, the pressure will increase. If the spring pressure is decreased, or the spring is broken, the pressure will decrease.

Ball Check Valves

Ball check valves are used to control the flow of fluid through a circuit in a fluid power system. Check valves prevent flow in one direction while allowing fluid to flow in the opposite direction. They also close passages to prevent back-flow of hydraulic fluid. Figure 19-20 shows the action of a ball check valve.

Filters

In any fluid system, the hydraulic oil must be cleaned constantly. *Fluid filters* are used to clean the dirt particles out of the fluid.

There are two types of filtering systems. One is called the *full-flow system*, and the other is called the *bypass system*. Full-flow systems filter all of the fluid before it enters the system. Bypass systems filter only a part of the fluid during operation.

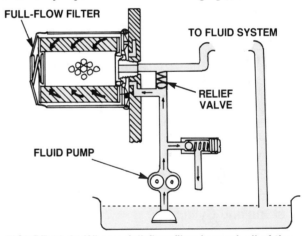

FIGURE 19-21 When a full-flow filter is used, all of the fluid is sent through the filter before it enters the main fluid system.

Full-flow Filter System. Figure 19-21 shows the full-flow filter system. In this system, all of the fluid must pass through the filter before entering the system. If the filter gets plugged with dirt, fluid pressure will increase before reaching the filter. The higher pressure will lift the ball and spring it off its seat. The result is that all of the fluid flows back to the fluid reservoir through the regulator or ball check valve.

To eliminate this, a relief valve is used. The relief valve is designed to open at a specific pressure across the filter. This is called differential pressure. *Differential pressure* is the difference in pressure between the inlet and outlet of the filter. The inlet pressure is always controlled by the regulator valve. As the filter plugs up, the pressure on the other side of the filter will drop. When the difference is equal to the relief valve setting, a certain amount of fluid will then pass the filter and enter the fluid system. This means that even if the filter becomes plugged, the system will still receive fluid.

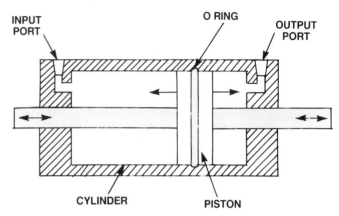

FIGURE 19-23 Pistons and cylinders are used to convert the pressure in a fluid to linear motion on a piston.

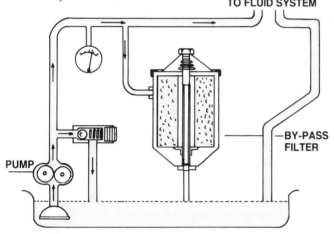

FIGURE 19-22 A bypass filter filters only part of the fluid in the circuit.

Bypass Filter System. Figure 19-22 shows the bypass filter system. Approximately 90% of the fluid is pumped directly into the system. Only about 10% is sent into the filter to be cleaned. If this filter becomes plugged, none of the fluid will be filtered. However, fluid will still be pressurized and sent into the system.

Pistons and Cylinders

Pistons and *cylinders* are used in a variety of applications in fluid systems. Generally, they are used to convert the pressure of a fluid into linear or rotary motion. For example, *hydraulic cylinders* are used on many construction vehicles to raise and lower buckets. Figure 19-23 shows a typical cylinder and piston arrangement. When a pressure fluid is applied to the right side of the piston, the piston moves to the left. When the pressure is reversed, the piston will move to the opposite direction.

Spool Valve

Spool valves are used in most fluid circuits to control the directions of fluid flow. For example, when using hydraulic cylinders, fluid must flow to one side of a piston, then reverse and flow to the

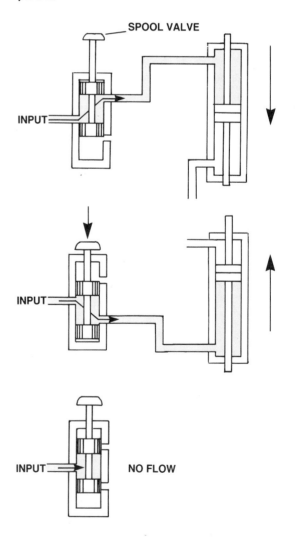

FIGURE 19-24 Spool valves are used to control the direction of fluid flow in many fluid power systems.

other side. Figure 19-24 shows an example of a spool valve operation. When the spool valve is lifted, fluid flows into the cylinder in one direction. When the spool valve is pushed down, the fluid flows to the opposite side of the hydraulic cylinder. When the spool valve is positioned in the center, there is no flow to the hydraulic cylinder.

Complete Fluid Circuit

Up to this point, only the individual parts of a fluid system have been defined. Figure 19-25 shows an example of a complete fluid system. This system uses hydraulic oil to raise and lower a landing gear on a small airplane. Although, in reality, the system is more complicated, the operation can be simply explained. Hydraulic fluid is drawn from the reservoir and pressurized by the gear-type pump. The pressure is controlled by the pressure relief valve. The pressure is then sent to the spool valve. Depending upon its position, the spool valve directs fluid to the double-acting hydraulic cylinder. The movement of the cylinder piston lifts or lowers the landing gear.

restrictions, pressure gages, and other parts. These and many other symbols are used to help technicians and engineers work on and design fluid circuits. Figure 19-26 gives an example of a simple pneumatic power circuit with several symbols shown for reference. This simple circuit is used to move a robot arm. Many other components are used in power circuits. The degree of complexity and control needed determines the exact components and the design of the circuit.

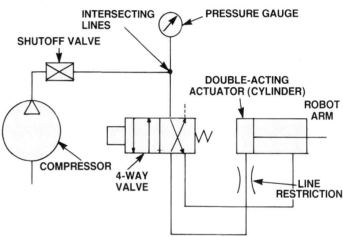

FIGURE 19-26 This common fluid power circuit is used to extend and retract a robot arm.

Summary

- The major purpose of a fluid power circuit is to transmit power from one point to another.
- The two major types of fluid power circuits include the pneumatic (air) and hydraulic (liquid) types.
- *Force* is defined as the pushing or pulling action of an object.
- *Pressure* is defined as a force acting upon an area.
- Two types of pressure are psia and psig.
- Pascal's law states that a pressure in a confined fluid is transmitted equally to all parts of the fluid.
- Fluid power circuits are also designed to achieve mechanical advantages.
- Bernoulli's theorem states that pressure in a fluid flowing through a pipe changes as the diameter changes.
- Pressure in a fluid system can be measured by a Bourdon gage and a manometer.

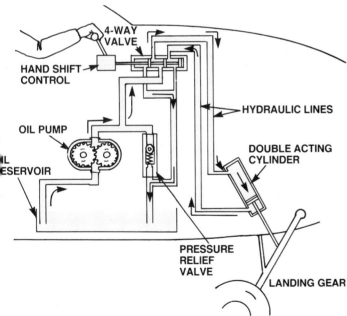

FIGURE 19-25 In this complete fluid circuit, a double-acting cylinder and piston are used to raise and lower the landing gear on a small airplane.

Fluid Symbols

Symbols are used to represent the actual parts when studying fluid power circuits. Symbols are used to show fluid power pumps, shutoff valves, line

- *Viscosity* is defined as the fluidity or thickness of a fluid.
- Viscosity index is a measure of how easily a fluid changes its viscosity with temperature.
- Pour point is the temperature at which a fluid will not pour because of cold temperatures.
- Many additives are chemically mixed with fluids.
- SAE viscosity ratings measure the thickness of the fluid at different temperatures.
- Synthetic fluids have many advantages and disadvantages for their use in fluid power systems.
- Common fluid pressure pumps include the gear-type, vane-type, and axial piston-type.
- A hydraulic coupling is also considered a fluid component used in fluid power systems.
- A pressure regulator valve is used to control the pressure output of a fluid pump.
- Ball check valves are used to control the flow of fluid in one direction through a fluid power circuit.
- Both bypass and full-flow filters are used in fluid power circuits.
- Pistons and cylinders are used in fluid power circuits to change the fluid pressure into reciprocating motion.
- Spool valves are used to control the direction of fluid into different circuits.
- All fluid power components can be identified by using symbols. These, and other symbols are then connected together to make fluid power circuit diagrams.

REVIEW

1. When a hydraulic force applied to a piston is 200 pounds, and the piston area is 4 square inches, the total pressure the piston can lift is equal to _____.
2. A psia reading of 27.2 at sea level is the same as a psig reading of _____.
3. A manometer reads 6.8 inches of mercury. This pressure in psig is equal to _____ .
4. The _____ is a measure of how much the viscosity of a fluid will change at a given temperature difference.
5. An oil has a viscosity rating of 5W30. This means that the oil has a viscosity rating of _____ at 0°F and a viscosity rating of _____ at 210°F.
6. The pour point of a fluid is the temperature at which the fluid _____ .
7. When a gas in a pneumatic system is compressed and reduced in volume, the _____ increases.
8. When a gas in a pneumatic system is increased in temperature, the pressure of the gas will _____.
9. A hydraulic system has two pistons. The input has 50 lb applied to a 1 square-inch piston. The output piston is 7 square inches. The total output pressure that can be lifted is _____
10. Explain the purpose for using fluid power systems.
11. What are some of the differences between a pneumatic system and a hydraulic power system?
12. State the difference between psia and psig pressures.
13. Describe how forces can be multiplied in a fluid power system.
14. State at least three fluid characteristics, and give a definition of each.
15. State how fluids are rated using SAE standards.
16. Identify at least two advantages of using synthetic fluids.
17. Describe how an axial piston pump operates.
18. State the operation of at least two types of valves used in a fluid power system.
19. What is the difference between a bypass filter and full-flow filter?

CHAPTER ACTIVITIES

⚛ OIL VISCOSITY

INTRODUCTION

Oil and hydraulic fluids have different thicknesses depending upon their temperature. The thickness of a fluid is called its viscosity. Oil viscosity or its thickness changes with different temperatures. This activity is designed to show how to test oil viscosity, and to show how the viscosity changes with different temperatures.

TECHNOLOGICAL LITERACY SKILLS

Data analysis, research, predicting, collection of data.

OBJECTIVES

At the compeltion of this activity, you will be able to:

1. Define SAE viscosity ratings.
2. Calculate the viscosity of oil.
3. Compare viscosity ratings to SAE ratings.

MATERIALS

1. Three samples of oil, SAE 30, 5W30 and 20W40
2. Viscosity tester, provided by the instructor
3. Heating device used to increase the oil temperature to 210°F
4. Thermometer
5. A cooling chamber, such as a freezer to cool oil samples to near 0°F
6. Stopwatch
7. Viscosity handout

ADDITIONAL INFORMATION

Viscosity is a measure of the resistance to the flow of oil. It is measured in a device known as a Saybolt universal viscosimeter. A sample of oil is placed in the meter. The time is measured to drain out 60 milliliters of oil. The time will change if the oil is cold or hot. The oil is tested at 0°F and 210°F. An oil tested at 0°F has a W placed after its viscosity. Oils tested at 210°F have no letter after the number. Figure 19-27 shows a chart used to compare the amount of seconds to drain different oils.

VISCOSITY RANGE, SAYBOLT UNIVERSAL SECONDS				
SAE Number	(0°F) Min.	Max.	(210°F) Min.	Max.
5W		4,000	39	
10W	6,000	12,000	39	
20W	12,000	48,000	39	
20			45	58
30			58	70
40			70	85
50			85	110

FIGURE 19-27 These numbers represent a comparison of the seconds for the oil to pass through the meter at different temperatures.

PROCEDURE

1. Select three different oil viscosities to test and record on the Viscosity handout.

    ▶ **CAUTION:** Always wear safety glasses when working with oils and fluids. Also be careful not to spill oil on the floor, as slipping may cause injury.

2. Using the viscosity meter provided by the instructor, check the viscosity of all three oils. See Figure 19-28.

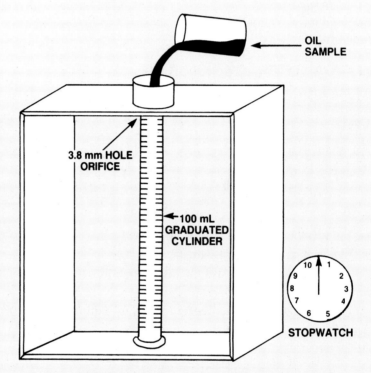

FIGURE 19-28 Oil viscosity can be checked by placing the fluid sample in the can and allowing it to drain into the graduated cylinder. Measure the seconds to drain 60 milliliters of oil.

  a. Measure out at least 80 ml of the test oil.
  b. Heat to 210°F.
  c. Pour the hot oil into the container.
  d. Using a stopwatch, measure the time in seconds for 60 milliliters to drain into the graduated cylinder.
  e. Record the data in the table on the handout.
  f. Now test the oil at 0°F and record.
  g. Test the two other oil samples using the same procedures (a-f), and record on the handout.

REVIEW QUESTIONS

1. What happens to the oil as it becomes hotter and colder?
2. If a cold oil were used in an engine, what would happen to frictional resistance inside the engine?

SECTION FIVE

THE FUTURE

Studying the future is one way to have control over our advancing technology. Many technologies are being researched and tested today to determine their feasibility in the future. However, the growth and direction of future transportation, energy, and power technology will determine the future impacts that this technology has on our society. The figure illustrates how the future fits into the systems model. For example, any new technology will be evaluated by the impacts it has on our society. Common concerns include economic gain, environmental damage, customer convenience, and depletion of natural resources.

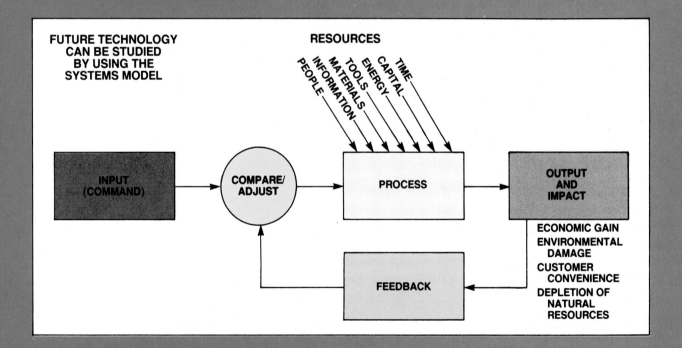

FUTURE TECHNOLOGY CAN BE STUDIED BY USING THE SYSTEMS MODEL

RESOURCES

TIME
CAPITAL
ENERGY
TOOLS
MATERIALS
INFORMATION
PEOPLE

INPUT (COMMAND)

COMPARE/ ADJUST

PROCESS

OUTPUT AND IMPACT

ECONOMIC GAIN
ENVIRONMENTAL DAMAGE
CUSTOMER CONVENIENCE
DEPLETION OF NATURAL RESOURCES

FEEDBACK

CHAPTER 20 ■ Future Transportation, Energy, and Power Technology

CHAPTER 20

Future Transportation, Energy, and Power Technology

OBJECTIVES

After reading this chapter, you will be able to:

■ Identify the major components that will affect the future of transportation, energy, and power systems.

■ List the major directions of change in transportation, energy, and power.

■ Describe possible technologies that will evolve in the future in the area of transportation technology.

■ Describe possible technologies that will evolve in the future in the area of energy technology.

■ Describe possible technologies that will evolve in the future in the area of power technology.

■ Identify how the future will change in regard to the systems model of technology.

KEY TERMS

Forecasting	Levitate	Heat Pump
Scenarios	Aerospace	Superconductivity
Vortex	Active Suspension	Synthetic
Waste Heat Recovery	Cogeneration	
Navigational	Absolute Zero	

Introduction

Technology is growing at a very rapid pace. Many scientists, engineers, and technologists suggest that technology is doubling every four to five years. This is also true in the area of transportation, energy, and power technology. Each day, new and innovative designs are being built and tested for feasibility.

This chapter is about some of the possible future technologies in the area of transportation, energy, and power technology. This chapter also introduces the major goals of change, and some possible alternatives in transportation, energy, and power technology.

Forecasting Future Technology

Looking at the Future

Determining the future is something that humans have been trying to do since the beginning of time. Looking into the future can be a very important tool. The more that is studied about the future, the better chance there is to control the future. Forecasting is one method used to look into the future. *Forecasting* is usually done by looking at the past and then projecting into the future. Quite often, the future is a continuation of the past.

Developing scenarios are also a method used to determine the future. *Scenarios* are often developed by asking the question, "What would happen if . . . ?" Quite often when studying future energy problems, both positive and negative scenarios are developed to observe possible conditions in the future. Both forecasting and developing scenarios help us look into future possibilities.

How Transportation, Energy, and Power Changes

When studying transportation, energy, and power, certain changes have occurred in the past. These changes in all probability will continue to occur in the future. Some of the major changes expected to occur in the future include:

- Reduction in Friction — All transportation, energy, and power technology will continue to change by reducing friction. Developments will include low-friction bearings, working to lower the coefficient of drag on vehicles and less internal friction in engines, among others. For example, Figure 20-1 shows a simple vortex design being tested for cars and airplanes. The *vortex* has a tendency to keep the airflow over the car close to its surface. The small fins placed on the roof help to direct the airflow more efficiently. This will in turn reduce the air drag on the vehicle, improving fuel mileage. Figure 20-2 shows an example of the shape of future vehicles that will have low wind resistance.

- Improved Engine Efficiency — Engines will continue to become more efficient. Engines of the future will continue to be controlled by computers, only with more control and power. Engines will also use lighter materials so that better fuel mileage can be achieved. Eventually, it is predicted that engines will have efficiencies in the range of 50 to 70%.

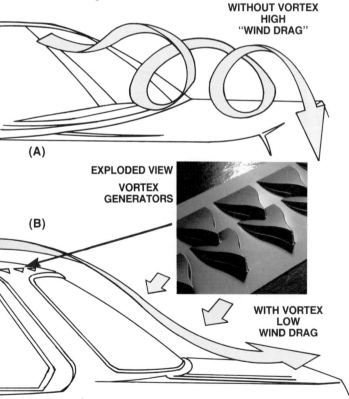

WITHOUT VORTEX HIGH "WIND DRAG"

(A)

EXPLODED VIEW VORTEX GENERATORS

(B)

WITH VORTEX LOW WIND DRAG

FIGURE 20-1 The reduction of friction will be one area of change in the future. These vortex generators force the air against the curved surfaces of a vehicle. The result is less wind drag. They may be used on airplanes as well. *Reprinted from Popular Science with permission © 1988 Times Mirror Magazines, Inc.*

FIGURE 20-2 Eventually, vehicles will be designed to slip through the air with little wind resistance. The vehicle shown is designed to have a minimum coefficient of drag. *Reprinted from Popular Science with permission © 1988 Times Mirror Magazines, Inc.*

■ Lightweight Materials — There are continuous developments in new synthetic and composite materials. *Synthetic* and *composite* means artificial and other materials are mixed together to produce a certain structural characteristic. These materials will be lighter in weight and stronger, and have better thermal shielding and greater usability than those presently available. These materials will be applied to engines, bearings, structures, and other transportation vehicle parts. For example, Figure 20-3 shows a specially designed tire used to reduce rolling resistance, thereby producing better fuel mileage.

■ Waste Heat Recovery — In the area of energy, much of the new development in the future will be centered around saving heat. Industries will continue to improve conversion efficiency while finding more uses for the wasted heat.

■ Improved Computer Control — In all areas, the use of computer controls will continue to increase. Eventually, many of the human controls now used will be transferred to the computer.

FIGURE 20-3 This specially designed tire will have less rolling resistance, thereby improving fuel economy. *Reprinted from Popular Science with permission © 1984 Times Mirror Magazines, Inc.*

Wind Tunnel

Wind tunnels are used to produce rapidly moving air to simulate a vehicle's operation through the wind at high speed. The wind tunnel shown here is an advanced design wind tunnel used to monitor and test wind resistance of passenger vehicles. Wind speeds of up to 112 mph and temperatures from -22°F to 113°F can be created. In addition, humidity up to 95% can be created in this tunnel.

Based upon data collected from this wind tunnel, car shapes and designs can be improved to produce the minimum wind resistance, and thus improve fuel economy. Data from wind tunnels such as this provide information to determine the coefficient of drag ratings, a very important characteristic on vehicles today. *Courtesy of Volkswagen of America*

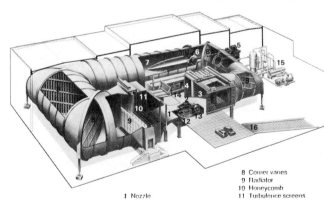

1 Nozzle
2 Test section
3 Collector
4 Movable test section cover
5 Electrical drive with transmission
6 Fan
7 Diffuser

8 Corner vanes
9 Radiator
10 Honeycomb
11 Turbulence screens
12 Balance
13 Roller dynamometer
14 Control room, process control computer
15 Refrigeration plant
16 Access to test section

FIGURE 20-4 In the future, AGVs (automated guided vehicles) will help to reduce materials handling costs in manufacturing plants of the future. *Courtesy of Caterpillar, Inc.*

Future Technology in Transportation

Robot Transportation

Transportation technology will continue to improve in the future. As an example, automated guided vehicles (AGVs) as a form of transportation will continue to be used more in the future. These vehicles are designed to follow a certain set path over and over again. Computers are used for control and memory. The AGV shown in Figure 20-4 will help to reduce material handling costs in many manufacturing plants in the future. As robots are refined, they will be used for more applications as well.

Navigational Systems in Automobiles

All navigational technology in transportation vehicles is considered part of the "feedback" in the systems model. Navigational systems are those that provide guidance and control over the vehicle's direction, speed, torque, horsepower, and so forth.

The future holds a great deal of change in this area. Eventually, automobile navigational systems will be able to monitor the vehicle's position as an aid to route guidance. A map (local/regional) will be displayed on the computer video screen in the dashboard, Figure 20-5. Signals from the car computer will be sent to satellites and beamed back to the vehicle. The position of the vehicle will then be shown on the map.

FIGURE 20-5 Navigational systems in cars will continue to improve. Eventually, cars will have video screens that show maps as well as the vehicle's position on the map. *Reprinted from Popular Science with permission © 1988 Times Mirror Magazines, Inc.*

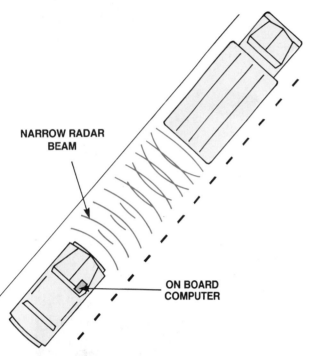

NARROW RADAR
BEAM

ON BOARD
COMPUTER

FIGURE 20-6 Vehicles of the future will use a narrow radar band to detect vehicle speeds to the front. The information is sent to an on-board computer. If the two vehicles are at different speeds, an alert light is flashed and a buzzer sounds.

Automatic Braking System

Future automobiles and other passenger vehicles will use a form of radar to monitor the distance between themselves and vehicles in the front. The system monitors and detects differences in the speed of two vehicles. The radar signals are transmitted to an on-board computer. Based upon the rate of difference between two vehicles, warning lights are flashed to tell the driver about a vehicle in front. Figure 20-6 shows an example of such a system. Eventually, there will be no need to warn the driver, as the car will automatically slow down.

Magnetic Levitation

In the past few years, a great deal of research has been developed to produce superconducting materials. *Superconducting materials* are those that produce little or no resistance to the flow of electricity. These advancements are leading the way to improved and highly efficient magnets. These magnets can then be used to *levitate* or raise vehicles on a magnetic field. Instead of pounding along on tires or rails, the vehicle floats four inches

Mark IV Monorail at Disney World

The future holds many advances in transportation systems. One such system that may eventually find its way into commercial use is the monorail system. This monorail system at Walt Disney World near Orlando, Florida is an advanced transportation system to move masses of people.

The system uses 600-volt, DC motors rated at 100 hp (8 per train). The vehicles are guided by a saddle-type monorail system. The concrete rails serve both as a guideway and the running surface for the vehicles. The monorails are controlled by one person and all cars include both heating and air conditioning. *Courtesy © 1987 The Walt Disney Company*

above its guideway on a cushion of magnetism. This will make the vehicle much more efficient.

One such system is shown in Figure 20-7. This system is designed for a train. A set of lifting magnets is used to raise the vehicle up on the magnetic cushion. The propulsion magnets are used to propel the vehicle forward. As the development of superconducting materials improves, magnetic levitation will certainly become more feasible.

MAGNETIC LEVITATION

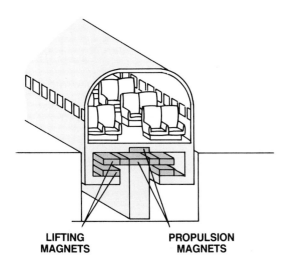

LIFTING   PROPULSION
MAGNETS   MAGNETS

FIGURE 20-7 Magnetic levitation will lift this train by a strong set of magnets. The vehicle will then float on magnetism, making it much more efficient.

Solar-powered Vehicles

One area that is receiving much attention is to propel a vehicle (automobiles or planes), by solar power. Solar cells are being developed with greater efficiency. In addition, battery technology is constantly improving. With these two technologies, solar-powered vehicles may soon become a reality. A solar vehicle is shown in Figure 20-8. A great deal of research must still be done on solar cells. In addition, friction of the vehicle must be held to a minimum. Some companies believe that, in the future, many vehicles will be able to run efficiently and reliably on solar cells.

One of the big advantages of using a solar-powered vehicle is the reduction of pollution.

FIGURE 20-8 The future may also have cars that operate by electricity developed from solar cells. This solar cell vehicle was tested in a recent design competition. *Courtesy of General Motors Corporation*

Remember that pollution is part of the "impacts" on the systems model for studying technology. If vehicles could be powered by solar cells, the amount of carbon monoxide, nitrogen oxides, and hydrocarbons would be greatly reduced. This could have a significant and positive impact on the environment of our society.

Aerospace Plane

Some experts are predicting that aerospace planes will be used by the early 2000s. *Aerospace planes* are those that can operate in space, but take off from conventional airports. The plane will be able to either work in space or to transport passengers and goods from city to city via space. These planes are planned to travel at six times the speed of sound and at altitudes of 20 miles or higher. The suggested

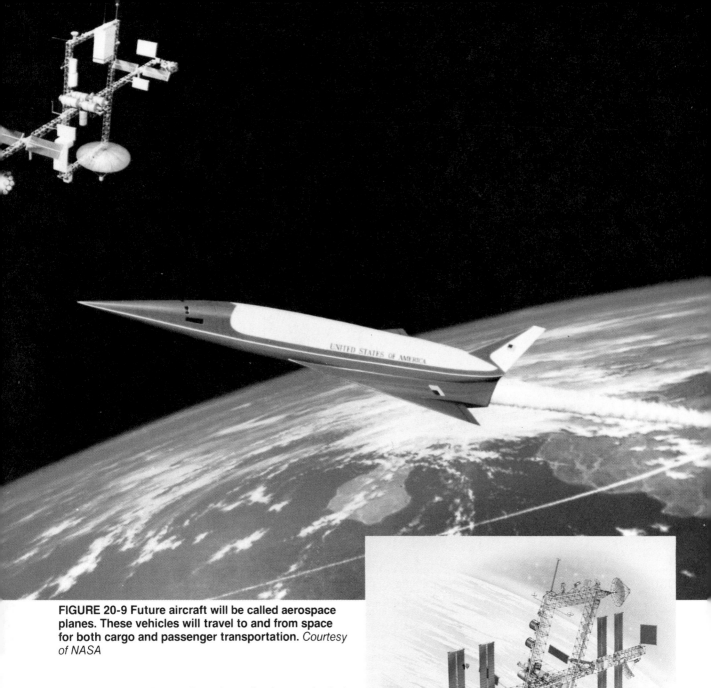

FIGURE 20-9 Future aircraft will be called aerospace planes. These vehicles will travel to and from space for both cargo and passenger transportation. *Courtesy of NASA*

propulsion will be air-breathing, hydrogen-fueled ramjet engines. Figure 20-9 shows an aerospace plane being planned by NASA.

Space Stations

One area that is projected to develop is the use of space stations. Figure 20-10 shows an example of a space station planned for the future. The space station will be an orbiting, multipurpose system for manned and unmanned research experiments. As our transportation continues to develop in both atmospheric and space, these stations will play an ever-important role.

FIGURE 20-10 Space stations such as this will also be a part of future space transportation systems.
Courtesy of Martin Marietta Manned Space Systems

Other Advancements in Transportation Technology

Many other advancements will occur in the transportation sector of society. Several innovations are now being tested for use in society. Future developments include the following:

1. Suspension of vehicles will become more controlled by on-board computers. These are called active suspension systems. The result will be to offer more comfortable and safer rides for passengers.
2. Four-wheel steering will become more developed for automobiles. This will improve control and movability of vehicles.
3. Boats will continue to use improved propeller design. The propeller design will improve efficiency and performance.
4. Wing shapes on airplanes will be developed to improve fuel efficiency and performance.
5. Hull design on power boats, sailboats, and other marine transportation will be more efficient with less frictional losses. Figure 20-11 shows a computer-generated hull design for a sailboat used in the America's Cup. This computer program is able to apply stresses to check for stability in water.

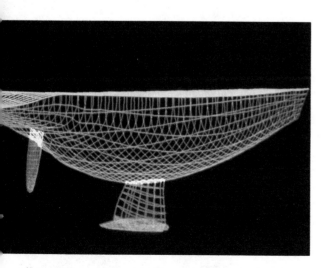

FIGURE 20-11 This computer-generated hull design is used to check a sailboat's stability under various stresses. *Reprinted from Popular Science with permission © 1987 Times Mirror Magazines, Inc.*

Future Technology in Energy

Cogeneration

Cogeneration will be developed more in the future. In all power plants, both electrical and thermal energy are produced from fossil fuels. In fact, a typical power plant is only about 32 to 38% efficient. The remaining power is lost as heat, called wasted thermal energy. The wasted heat contributes significantly to the thermal pollution of our planet. *Cogeneration* is the process of using the lost or wasted heat from a utility to operate other processes in the plant. A noncogenerating power plant simply vents waste heat to the atmosphere.

A cogenerating power plant uses the waste heat to help produce a variety of thermal energy end products. These may include process steam, hot water, cold water or air conditioning, among others. Overall power plant efficiency can, in some cases, be doubled. Figure 20-12 shows an example of a cogeneration unit.

FIGURE 20-12 This cogeneration plant uses the waste heat to produce various thermal energy products for use in the power plant. *Courtesy of Enron Corp. (Steve Brady Photographer)*

Ground Source Heat Pump

Ground source heat pumps will play an important role in the future. It is generally accepted that there is thermal energy in any substance down to *absolute zero* (-273°C). Any temperature above absolute zero actually has thermal energy in it. The object is to design a way to extract this heat.

A heat pump is a device that is much like a refrigerator or air conditioner. The *heat pump* is able to extract heat from substances such as water or air. Heat can be extracted from air efficiently to about 5°F. Heat can be extracted from water down to about 35°F. Many air heat pumps are used to heat homes. These heat pump units can be used for heating in the winter and air conditioning in the summer. Figure 20-13 shows the basic flow of heat in a home for summer and winter.

In operation, the ground-water heat pump extracts thermal energy from cool water circulated underground. Water is circulated through many feet of pipe that are buried about five feet underground. The pipes snake back and forth on the residential lot. The water heats up to approximately 50°F. A heat pump is then used to extract thermal energy from the 50-degree water. The thermal energy taken from the water is used to heat a residential home. The cooler water (after heat has been extracted) is then sent through the underground pipes to again be heated by the thermal energy in the ground.

Waste Heat Management

Many industries are now looking at waste heat management. Any wasted heat contributes to thermal pollution of our society. Waste heat is considered a negative impact in the use of technology.

Waste heat management is a system used to capture any lost heat from buildings and process plants. The heat can then be used for various end products, including heating the building.

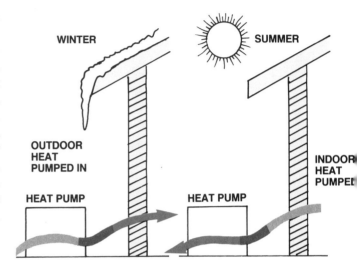

FIGURE 20-13 A heat pump extracts thermal energy from the outdoors in the winter and pumps it inside. In the summer, thermal energy is extracted from inside and pumped outside.

Superconductivity on Airplane Wing

Superconductivity is the process of cooling a material to a temperature in which no electrical resistance is evident. A great deal of research has been done to raise the superconducting temperature. As such temperatures rise, more and more products and manufacturing processes will use superconductivity. Superconducting technology is presently being considered for use in the aircraft industry.

Here superconducting technology will help in the study and design of an airplane wing extension and winglet. Information gained from such tests will help engineers to improve the design of wings for faster, safer, and more efficient wing designs. *Courtesy of The Boeing Company*

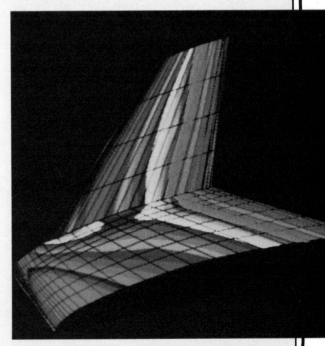

Home Energy Innovations

The residential dwelling will undergo many changes in the future. The primary direction of change will be to eliminate energy losses. For example, changes will occur in such areas as window design, passive solar gain, solar orientation, and insulation types. One area that shows promise is that of air-to-air heat exchangers. As homes are built with more insulation, infiltration is reduced. In fact, homes can become too tight and unable to "breathe" properly. This can cause many health problems. Air-to-air heat exchangers are being used to exchange air regularly, without losing the heat in the air. The thermal energy in the exhaust air is transferred to the incoming air. Figure 20-14 shows an example of an air-to-air heat exchanger.

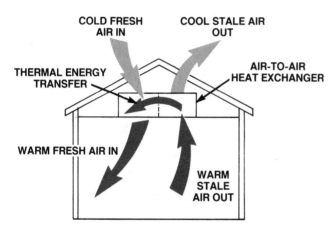

FIGURE 20-14 Air-to-air heat exchangers are used to exchange air regularly in a home without losing thermal energy.

Other Advancements in Energy Technology

Many other advances in the area of energy will take place. The following list is only an example of some of the changes that will occur.

- Batteries will be designed to store more energy per pound.
- Wind turbines will be designed to be more efficient, at lower cost.
- Special foam blocks will be used in home foundations. These blocks will be designed to reduce most heat losses that normally occur in the building foundation.

- Many new furnace and fireplace designs will be tested and manufactured. These will include:
  a. Alternative fuel stoves.
  b. Rock furnaces for thermal storage.
  c. Computer pulse controls for improved efficiency.

Future Technology in Power

Superconductivity

One of the most promising breakthroughs in electrical power is called superconductivity. *Superconductivity* is defined as the lack of all resistance to the flow of electricity in a material. Typically, all materials that carry electricity have a certain amount of resistance. This resistance has limited the conductivity of electrical circuits considerably. Superconductive materials have a great potential for transportation, (magnetic levitation) computer speed, microcircuits, fusion, electrical storage and transmission, and instrumentation.

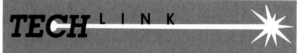

The resistance of most materials increases with an increase in temperature. The reverse is also true. As a temperature of a material is reduced, its resistance also is reduced. At or near absolute zero, many materials have no resistance to electricity. A ring of lead (as the conductor) was tested for more than a year, and kept at 7.2 degrees Kelvin. 0° Kelvin is considered absolute zero. Once the current started in the ring, it continued without diminishing. When the temperature increased, the current stopped immediately. Thus, the advantage of having superconductivity: less energy is needed for electrical systems.

It has been known that resistance in a conducting material can be reduced by dropping its temperature. For example, there is no resistance in a material when it is at absolute zero (-273°C or -460°F). In the past few years, much has been done to increase the temperature at which superconductivity occurs. This temperature is called the *transition temperature*. The goal is to develop a material

SUPERCONDUCTORS

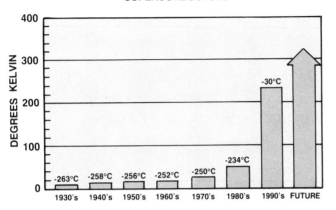

SUPERCONDUCTOR ADVANCEMENTS IN TEMPERATURE

NOTE: 0° KELVIN = 273°C OR -460°F

FIGURE 20-15 Progress toward developing super-conductive materials at atmospheric temperatures continues to develop. In the future, superconductivity will be achieved at a very low cost at or near atmospheric temperatures.

that has no resistance at near atmospheric temperatures. When this happens, the effects will be dramatic. Electrical circuits will be extremely efficient without the losses that now occur. Figure 20-15 shows how progress has been made over the years. Recently, materials have been produced that have minimum resistance at -33°C. One such material is a complex oxide, called the lanthanum-strontium copper oxide. Other materials are being tested to see if superconductivity can be achieved at even higher temperatures in the future, with a practical cost factor for industries.

Synthetic Engines

In the future, engine parts and, eventually, the entire engine will be made of synthetic materials. The object of using synthetic materials is to be able to increase the internal temperatures of the engine. The higher the internal temperatures, the less need for a cooling system. This means that less heat will be lost, and higher engine efficiency will result. Problems still arise concerning a material's ability to resist warping and still maintain the needed strength.

At present, several manufacturers are designing synthetic engine parts. Eventually, the entire engine will be made of synthetic materials. Another advantage of using synthetic materials is their lighter weight. Lighter-weight engines will be made with

more horsepower and improved efficiency. Some experts suggest that the standard 30% engine efficiency could be raised as high as 60% using synthetic materials.

Constant Velocity Transmissions

Another innovation that is promising is the constant velocity transmission (CVT). The CVT is a type of transmission that has no gears for changing torque and speed requirements. Typically, two variable-speed pulleys change the speed ratios as the r/min change. Normally, as the drive pulley speeds up, its running diameter becomes larger. As the driven pulley increases in speed, its running diameter becomes smaller. The combination of these pulleys produces infinite speed ratios between the input and output. The CVT enables the engine to operate at the most efficient r/min for best fuel mileage. Figure 20-16 shows an example of a CVT transmission.

FIGURE 20-16 This constant velocity transmission (CVT) uses a set of pulleys to change speed and torque requirements. *Reprinted from Popular Science with permission © 1988 Times Mirror Magazines, Inc.*

Higher-Performance Engines

Engines of the future will be using various components as standard equipment. The automotive manufacturers are designing small-displacement, high-horsepower engines. Figure 20-17 shows some of these components which include:

■ Turbochargers that extract the heat of the exhaust to turn a turbine. The result is additional forced air in the engine.

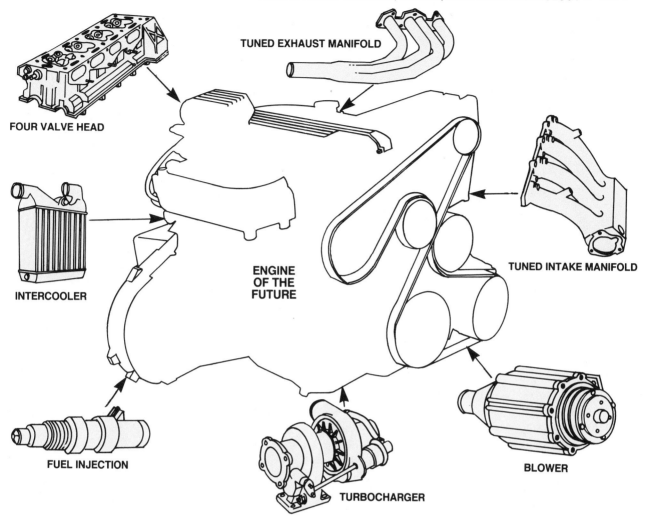

FIGURE 20-17 The engine of the future will include: turbochargers, blowers, intercoolers, fuel injection, tuned intake manifolds, tuned exhaust manifolds and four-valve cylinder heads. Many of these technologies are already being used today.

- Blowers that are driven by belts. Blowers increase the amount of air being sent into the engine. When more fuel is added, increased performance is the result.

- Intercoolers to cool the input air after it is compressed by a turbocharger or blower. When the air is cooled, it becomes more dense. The result is that more air can be forced into the engine.

- Fuel injection controlled by computers. Fuel injection, as used in most cars today, will be improved. The computer will be able to inject more precise amounts of fuel, based upon a greater number of computer input signals.

- Tuned intake manifolds to improve air intake. In a tuned manifold, high-frequency air pulses are set up by the opening and closing of the intake valves. By designing the pulses to occur at the precise time, additional air can be forced into the cylinder.

- Tuned exhaust manifolds to increase exhaust scavenging. With tuned exhaust manifolds, the exhaust pulses from one cylinder empty into the manifold between the pulses of the other cylinders. This has a tendency to clean the exhaust gases more completely from the cylinder. Thus, more air can be added to the cylinder during intake.

- Four-valve cylinder heads to increase the ease at which air and fuel can enter the engine. Volumetric efficiency is thus improved.

The Systems Model and the Future

The future can also be studied by viewing the systems model presented throughout this textbook. Several future predictions can be established by studying this model. In the future:

1. The "inputs" and "outputs" will be directed by the wants and needs of the consumer. Most consumers will continue to desire more choices of technology and conveniences, with less time or effort involved.

2. The "processes" will continue to become more efficient. Mechanical, thermal and volumetric efficiencies will continue to increase in all technologies. In addition, cost and energy as a resource into the process will continue to be of prime importance.

3. The "impacts" of all technology will continue to be monitored closely. Eventually, technology that has too many negative impacts, without positive impacts to offset them, will be discarded and not further developed.

4. The "feedback" systems will continue to infiltrate into all technologies. Control and guidance of transportation, energy, and power technology will take on an ever-increasing role. Because of increased feedback systems, the technology will become improved in its use and efficiency, and will be less wasteful.

Summary

- Forecasting is a method used to predict the future.
- Developing scenarios helps to look at the future by asking the question, "What if......?"
- Major areas of change in the future in transportation, energy, and power include reduced friction, improved engine efficiency, the use of lighter weight materials, the recovery of wasted heat, and improved computer controls.
- Robot transportation for material handling will be used more in the future.
- Navigational systems for automobiles will continue to be developed in the future.
- Automatic braking systems will be designed to alert drivers to potential accidents.
- Magnetic levitation will be developed in the future to support vehicles for improved efficiency.
- Solar power will be used to power vehicles of the future.
- In the future, aerospace planes, (planes that operate in the atmosphere and in space) will be used for travel.
- Space stations will take on important roles in the transportation sector in the future.
- Other advancements in transportation in the future will include computer suspension, four-wheel steering, and improved boat hull and airplane wing designs.
- Cogeneration will become common in many power plants of the future.
- Ground source heat pumps will be increasingly used in the future.
- Waste heat management will become important in most industries of the future.
- One new home innovation of the future will be air-to-air heat exchangers.
- Other advancements in energy will include improved and more efficient batteries, improved wind turbines, new and improved furnaces, and more efficient wood-burning stoves.
- Superconductivity will continue to become a reality in the future. Eventually, materials will be developed that offer very little resistance to electricity.
- Synthetic engines will become a reality in the near future. Eventually, an entire engine may be made of synthetic materials, improving efficiency and reducing heat losses.
- Constant velocity transmission will become a popular transmission device in the future.
- High-performance, 4-cylinder engines will include turbochargers, blowers, tuned intake and exhaust manifolds, increased computer controls, and four-valve cylinder heads.

REVIEW

1. One method used to look into and observe the future is called _____.
2. There will be many changes in the area of transportation, energy, and power. Two such changes include _____ and _____.
3. _____ systems will be added to cars in the future to monitor the vehicle's position and aid in its guidance.
4. When a vehicle is suspended because of the forces between two magnets, it is said to be _____.
5. An _____ plane can take off from conventional airports and fly into and back from space.
6. When wasted heat is captured and reused in a power generation system, it is called _____.
7. It is generally accepted that heat is in any substance down to about _____.
8. The lack of all resistance in a conductor is called _____, and it occurs at about _____ temperature.
9. The purpose of using synthetic engines in the future is to _____ engine temperature.
10. List and describe at least three major changes that will occur in the area of transportation, energy, and power.
11. Define the purpose of developing computer navigational systems for vehicles.
12. Describe how vehicles may be levitated by using magnetism.
13. List and describe at least three probable innovations that will be used on transportation vehicles of the future.
14. Describe the process of cogeneration.
15. How does a ground source heat pump operate?
16. Define waste heat management.
17. Describe several advantages of having superconductive materials at atmospheric temperatures.

CHAPTER ACTIVITIES

 ## MAGNETIC LEVITATION

INTRODUCTION

In the future, vehicles for transportation may use magnetic levitation to hold the vehicle off the ground. This activity is a creative problem-solving activity to experiment with magnetic levitation.

TECHNOLOGICAL LITERACY SKILLS

Problem solving, creativity, design, research, prediction, group analysis, experimentation, and interpersonal skills.

OBJECTIVES

At the completion of this activity, you will be able to:

1. Design an experimental plan for building a magnetic levitation vehicle.
2. Build an experimental magnetic levitation vehicle.
3. Test an experimental magnetic levitation vehicle.

MATERIALS

1. Several 2″ × 4″ and 2″ × 2″ pieces of pine to use for the vehicle bed or track
2. Magnets — a good type to use are bar magnets in rectangular or round shape
3. General woodworking and metalworking tools
4. Metal plates ⅛″ thick and angle iron
5. Pencil and paper for sketching the design
6. Styrofoam blocks to use as the actual vehicle.

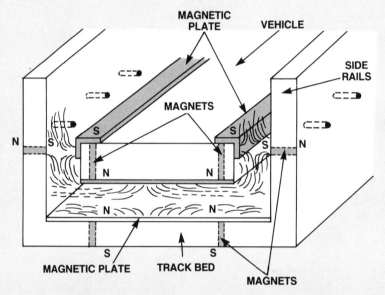

FIGURE 20-18 This is a simplified schematic of how the magnets might be placed on a magnetic levitation vehicle. The magnetic circuits must have a complete path.

PROCEDURE

1. Divide the class into groups of two or three students.
2. The groups are to design a magnetic levitation-type vehicle. Use the following guidelines in your design:
   a. The vehicle must be no longer than six inches.
   b. The vehicle must be no wider than three inches.
   c. The vehicle must be supported both vertically and horizontally by the magnets. The magnets should be placed in three areas. As shown in Figure 20-18, these include:
      ▪ Vehicle
      ▪ Side rails
      ▪ Track bed
   d. The track must be no longer than 5 feet.

e. The best design will use the least number of magnets while being able to carry the most weight.

3. Draw sketches of the design. Include parts identification, dimensions, and magnet locations. Several design considerations include:

   a. Using metal plates to distribute the magnetic fields.

   b. Placing the magnets at angles to produce propulsion forces.

   c. Making sure the magnetic field for all north and south poles have a complete path.

   d. Using electromagnets rather than permanent magnets.

   e. Making the vehicle as light as possible.

4. When the design is completed, build the magnetic levitation vehicle.

   ▶**CAUTION:** Always wear safety glasses when working with tools in the laboratory. Also, make sure you know the correct operation of all tools and machines in the laboratory. If not, check with your instructor.

5. Test the vehicle to see if it works. The vehicle must be able to move from one end of the track to the other without touching the track or sides.

6. Continue working with the design until the vehicle can effectively move through the entire length of the track.

REVIEW QUESTIONS

1. Describe how a magnetic levitation vehicle operates.
2. How could the vehicle be improved?
3. Can the position of the magnets make the vehicle more efficient?
4. How could the vehicle be made to carry more weight?

APPENDIX

Appendix A

Mathematical Appendix

The following mathematical formulas and definitions have been used throughout the textbook.

1. To calculate *miles per gallon per person,* also called "passenger miles":

   Miles per gallon × Average ridership (people) per vehicle

2. To calculate *ton miles:*

   Miles transported × Tons transported

3. To calculate *miles per gallon:*

   $$\frac{\text{Miles driven}}{\text{Number of gallons used}}$$

4. To calculate the *average ridership* in a vehicle:

   $$\frac{\text{Total number of cars being used}}{\text{Number of people being transported}} \times 100$$

5. To calculate *percentage:*
   Percentages can be calculated on any data if the total data are known and the part or (sought after) data are known.

   $$\frac{\text{Part (data)}}{\text{Total (data)}} \times 100$$

   For example, what is the percentage of 28,000 foreign cars in a city that has a total of 100,000 cars?

   28,000 = part data
   100,000 = total data

   $$\frac{28,000}{100,000} \times 100 = 28\%$$

6. One *knot* is equal to 1.15 miles per hour
   One mile per hour is equal to .87 knot
   To calculate knots from miles per hour:

   Knots = Miles per hour × .87
   To calculate miles per hour (mph) from knots:

   mph = knots × 1.15

7. A boat's *propeller pitch* is defined as the number of inches the boat moves forward for each revolution of the propeller (not counting slippage in the water). If a boat propeller is rotating at 3,000 r/min, and the propeller has a pitch of 18, the boat will move 54,000 feet each minute (3,000 × 18).
   To calculate the pitch when the r/min and distance traveled are known:

   $$\frac{\text{distance traveled}}{\text{r/min}} = \text{pitch}$$

8. One way to state *Bernoulli's Principle* is that total pressure (P total) in any gas or liquid system will remain constant. Total pressure can be thought of as both moving or dynamic pressure (P dya) and static pressure (P stat). This can be shown in the formula:

   P total = P dya + P stat

   If the dynamic pressure increases, then the static pressure must decrease to keep the total pressure constant.

9. To convert *thrust* in pounds of force to newtons:

   One pound of force = 4.448 newtons

To convert thrust in newtons to pounds of force:

One newton = .224 pound of force

10. *Efficiency* is calculated by the formula:

$$\text{Efficiency} = \frac{\text{Output energy}}{\text{Input energy}} \times 100$$

11. *Total efficiency* of a system is calculated by:

Total efficiency = Efficiency of each converter multiplied together

12. *Doubling time* is calculated by the formula:

$$\text{Doubling time} = \frac{71}{\text{Percentage of increase}}$$

13. *MB/DOE* is a unit to indicate how much energy is used in millions of barrels of oil per day.

14. Percentage of growth or *growth rate* is calculated by:

Growth rate in % = $\frac{\text{Change — beginning to end}}{\text{Original or starting point}} \times 100$

Example: If, in one month, an energy bill was $22.00, and the next month the bill increased to $24.00, the percentage of increase is calculated by:

Growth rate in % = $\frac{(24 - 22) = 2}{22} \times 100 = 9.09\%$

15. One ccf of natural gas = 100 cubic feet. One ccf is also equal to a *therm*.

16. To convert ccf or *therms to Btu*:

1,030 Btu × ccf or therm = Total Btu

17. *Cost Payback* is calculated by:

$$\text{Cost Payback} = \frac{\text{Initial capital cost}}{\text{Savings per year}}$$

18. To calculate the *amount of Btu* necessary to raise water a certain temperature:

Btu necessary = (gallons of water) × (8 lb) × (change in temperature in degrees)

For example, to raise a 25-gallon tank of water 45 degrees:
25 gal × 8 lb × 45 deg. = 9,000 Btu

19. To calculate the amount of *energy* in Btu that can be taken *from a stack of wood*:
   a. Multiply the size of the wood pile, length × width × height, to get total cubic feet of wood.
   b. Divide the cubic feet of wood by 128 to get the number of cords.
   c. Multiply the number of cords × the energy content in the wood in Btu.
   d. Multiply the energy content in the wood × the wood-burning stove efficiency.

20. To convert between *R and U* values for insulation:

$$R = \frac{1}{U} \quad \text{and} \quad U = \frac{1}{R}$$

21. *Heating Degree Days* are calculated by:

$$\text{Degree days} = 65 - \frac{\text{High + low temperature}}{2}$$

22. *Compression ratio* of an engine is calculated by:

$$\text{Compression ratio} = \frac{\text{Volume above piston at BDC}}{\text{Volume above piston at TDC}}$$

23. *Piston displacement* is calculated by:

Piston displacement = $0.785 \times \text{bore}^2 \times \text{stroke}$

24. *Ohms law* states that:

Voltage is calculated by amperage × resistance

Amperage is calculated by
voltage/resistance

Resistance is calculated by
voltage/amperage

25. *Watts law* states that:

Wattage is calculated by voltage × amperage

26. *Voltage drop* across a load or resistor is calculated by multiplying the amperage through the load by the resistance of the load.

27. *Pascal's law* is calculated by the formula:

$$\text{Pressure} = \frac{\text{Force}}{\text{Area}}$$

Appendix B

Metric Decimal Prefixes

Multiplication factors		Prefix	Symbol
1 000 000 000 000	= 10^{12}	tera	T
1 000 000 000	= 10^9	giga	G
1 000 000	= 10^6	mega	M
1 000	= 10^3	kilo	k
100	= 10^2	hecto	h
10	= 10^1	deka	da
1		(Units)	
0.1	= 10^{-1}	deci	d
0.01	= 10^{-2}	centi	c
0.001	= 10^{-3}	milli	m
0.000 001	= 10^{-6}	micro	μ
0.000 000 001	= 10^{-9}	nano	n
0.000 000 000 001	= 10^{-12}	pico	p
0.000 000 000 000 001	= 10^{-15}	femto	f
0.000 000 000 000 000 001	= 10^{-18}	atto	a

Appendix C

Energy Content of Fuels

Fuel	(Commonly used units)	Values (Btu/ton)
Coal (bituminous and anthracite)		25×10^6
Lignite		10×10^6
Peat		3.5×10^6
Crude oil	5.6×10^6 Btu/barrel	37×10^6
Gasoline	5.2×10^6 Btu/barrel	38×10^6
NGL's (Natural gas liquids)	4.2×10^6 Btu/barrel	37×10^6
Natural gas	1030 Btu/ft^3	47×10^6
Hydrogen gas	333 Btu/ft^3	107×10^6
Methanol (methyl alcohol)	6×10^4 Btu/gal	17×10^6
Charcoal		24×10^6
Wood	20×10^6 Btu/cord	12×10^6
Miscellaneous farm wastes		12×10^6
Dung		15×10^6
Assorted garbage and trash		10×10^6
Bread	1100 kcal/lb	9×10^6
Butter	3600 kcal/lb	29×10^6

Adapted from: Romer, Robert H., *Energy, An Introduction to Physics*, 1976, W.H. Freeman and Company, San Francisco, CA

GLOSSARY

Absolute Zero The temperature at which theoretically there is no thermal energy in a substance. This temperature is usually defined as -273°C or -460°F.

Acid Rain Rain that has an acidic pH level on or below 4.5. Acid rain is produced from sulfur dioxide and nitrogen oxides mixing with the moisture in the air.

Active Suspension A suspension system on a vehicle that is controlled by an onboard computer. The computer monitors the level of the vehicle continually, and makes suspension adjustments when necessary.

Aerial A term used to indicate objects or work that is done in the air.

Aerodynamics The science that deals with the flow of air and other gases.

Aerospace The lower portion of the atmosphere in which both manned and unmanned flights are possible.

Air Box An area in a two-cycle diesel engine into which the blower forces air before it enters the combustion and cylinder area.

Air-fuel Ratio The ratio of air to fuel by volume inside of the combustion chamber of any heat engine.

Air Routes A series of routes from city to city that is established by the airlines. Airplanes travel on these routes each day so that frequent travelers can maintain an established routine.

Aircraft Any air transportation device used or designed for navigation of flight in the air.

Airfoil A surface or body, such as a wing or propeller blade, designed to obtain a reaction, as lift or thrust, from air through which it moves.

Airport A land or water area, including buildings and installations, used for aircraft takeoff, parking, landing and maintenance, among others.

Airspeed The speed of the aircraft in relation to the speed of the air.

Alkaline The term that is defined as the opposite of an acid. An alkaline solution, called a base, is often mixed with an acid to produce a neutral level on the pH scale of 7.

Altimeter An instrument that measures altitude, using air pressure to control a bellows to move a pointer.

Anaerobic Decay Decay without oxygen.

Apogee The highest point of an orbit, or the point of an orbit farthest from the earth's surface.

Associated Well A type of natural gas well that has oil mixed in with the natural gas.

Astronauts Persons who are on-board to operate and control spacecrafts.

Atmosphere A term used to describe the zero point when atmospheric and other pressures are being measured. Normally, we are under 14.7 pounds per square inch of pressure at sea level (psia).

Atom Part of a molecule that has protons, neutrons and electrons. All things are made of atoms.

Attic Ventilators A ventilator or fan used on the ceiling of a building to remove air from the attic area.

Axial Referring to parts about an axis. For example, axial refers to a type of compressor on a jet (reaction) engine that rotates on a center axis with the airflow parallel to the axis of the compressor. In an axial piston pump, the pistons are arranged along or parallel to the axis of a shaft.

Axis A theoretical line extending through the center of gravity of a body. Axes may be longitudinal, lateral or vertical axes.

Azimuth The angle of the sun deviating from the south.

BDC Bottom dead center of the power stroke on a heat engine.

BMEP Break mean effective pressure, or the average pressure during the power stroke from TDC to BDC on a heat engine. *See* TDC.

BRT Bus rapid transit, or a system used in major population areas to increase the speed of buses bringing passengers to the center of the city on special express lanes.

Btu British thermal unit(s) or an amount of energy needed to raise one pound of water one degree Fahrenheit. Also called a measure of thermal energy.

Btu/pound Coal is measured by the pound. A common heating unit of coal is called Btu per pound, or the number of energy units (Btu) in each pound of coal.

Btu/ton/mile A number used to indicate how much energy (Btu) is needed to transport a ton of freight a distance of one mile.

Bimetal Two metals fastened together that have different rates of expansion when heat is applied. A bimetallic coil is used in an automatic flue damper.

Bourdon Pressure Gauge A gauge used to measure fluid pressure by having the fluid pressure straighten a small tube. As the tube straightens, a needle is moved to indicate the pressure.

Breadth A term used to indicate the distance of a ship from side to side.

Breaker Points Two small contact points that act as a switch in the primary circuit of a conventional ignition system.

Breeding The process in a nuclear power plant, whereby the nuclear process actually manufactures fuel from U-238.

Buoyed Floating on water.

Butterfly Valve A circular valve placed in the airflow area of a carburetor used to control the amount of air entering the carburetor.

Calories The amount of energy needed to raise one milliliter one degree Celsius; typically related to the energy in a person's body.

Carbohydrates Chemicals that support the tissue in a plant.

Caulking A soft, rubbery substance that is used to seal cracks in a building to eliminate infiltration.

Chine A ridge or crest designed into the hull of a boat.

Coefficient of Drag A number that automobile manufacturers use to indicate the ease at which a vehicle cuts through the air. Lower coefficient of drag numbers mean better fuel economy.

Cogeneration The process of converting otherwise wasted heat in a power generator system for additional thermal energy needs in the plant.

Compression Gasket The gasket used between the cylinder block and cylinder head on an engine. As the cylinder head is torqued down, the compression gasket is squeezed for correct compression sealing.

Compressor A device on a gas turbine that compresses air for combustion.

Condenser A device used in an ignition system used to store electricity when the breaker points are open. A condenser has a tendency to reduce arching on the breaker points.

Conductor A material used to carry electricity and electrons. A conductor has three or fewer electrons in the outer orbit.

Conical The shape of a boat hull that resembles a cone.

Control Rods Rods used in a nuclear core to absorb neutrons so as to slow down the nuclear reaction.

Controls The devices used by a pilot to operate an airplane.

Conventional Theory A theory stating that electricity flows in a circuit from a positive point to a negative point.

Converter An energy device used to change one form of energy into another.

Cord The unit used to measure an amount of wood. One standard cord is equal to a pile of wood 4 ft × 4 ft × 8 ft, or 128 cubic feet.

Corrosion A process that occurs inside a fluid system when the chemicals in the fluid react with oxygen and form a corrosive chemical in the fluid.

Crankshaft A mechanical device in a heat engine that converts reciprocating motion to rotary motion.

Creosote A chemical by-product from burning wood that condenses and collects on cooler stove pipes.

Cylinder Bore The diameter of the hole in which a piston rides in a gasoline or diesel engine.

Darrieus Wind Turbine A type of vertical wind turbine system using three blades that resemble an eggbeater.

Degree Day The amount of temperature deviation from a standard of 65°F for each day. Degree days are additive throughout a heating or cooling season.

Demand In reference to energy, demand is considered to be the sectors in our society that use or consume energy.

Department of Transportation (DOT) The agency of the federal government that controls the development and growth of the transportation industry.

Depletable A classification of energy that continually becomes less and less. Eventually, depletable resources will be all used up.

Diaphragm Fuel Pump A type of carburetor that uses a small rubber or fiber diaphragm to pump fuel from the fuel tank to the carburetor. The diaphragm is activated by the vacuum and pressure pulses below the piston on a small gas engine.

Differential Pressure A regulator valve used in hydraulic circuits that is sensitive to the pressure difference between the inlet and the outlet points.

Diode A semiconductor device that allows electricity to flow in only one direction.

Dirigible Transportation vehicle (airship). Capable of being steered.

Displacement In reference to boats, the amount or volume of water the boat removes when placed in the water. A boat that sits deep in the water is said to be displacing a greater amount of water.

Distillation The process in a refinery that is used to boil and vaporize all hydrocarbons. The vapors then rise in the distillation column, and condense to form different fractions (portions) or products.

Domains Small sections in a metal bar where atoms line up to produce a magnetic field.

Doubling Time The time in years it takes for a product to double as it grows.

Dynamometer A device used to load an engine so that work can be done.

Efficiency A measure of a machine's ability to convert energy. A ratio of input energy to output energy. Several types of efficiency include mechanical, electrical and volumetric, for example.

Electromagnetic In reference to radiant energy transfer, a scale used to measure frequency of electromagnetic wavelengths.

Electron The negative charge in an atom.

Electron Theory A theory that says electricity flows in a circuit from a negative point to a positive point.

Electronic Fuel Injection A system used on a gasoline engine to monitor and inject fuel at precise amounts to keep an air to fuel ratio of 14.7:1 at all times.

Elliptical The shape of a spacecraft's orbit around the earth. An elliptical shape is much like an elongated circle.

Engine Displacement The volume from TDC to BDC that the piston displaces. Normally, displacement is a measure of the size of a heat engine. See TDC.

Enriched The process of enriching uranium from 0.25% to about 3% U-235.

Entropy The process of making energy more random as it is changed from one form to another. See Rejected Energy.

Exosphere The region of the earth's atmosphere that extends about 200 to 300 miles into outer space.

Federal Aviation Administration A part of the DOT that helps to control and monitor safety in the aviation industry.

Feedback Loop The part of a transportation system that helps to control the input and process.

Fission The process of splitting an atom into two new elements to produce energy.

Fixed Route A route used by transportation modes that is not flexible, such as rail transportation.

Flue The exhaust stack of a furnace or water heater.

Fluidity A term used to describe the thickness or viscosity of a fluid.

Forecasting A method used to predict the future based upon the past.

Fossil The remains of decay from plants and animals over ages of time. Typically, fossil fuels include coal, oil, and natural gas. A type of hydrogen and carbon molecule that has been changed into a fuel over millions of years.

Four-cycle Engine A form of piston engine that has four strokes for each power pulse of the piston. Normally, gasoline (fuel) does not need oil added to it for proper lubrication of the engine parts.

Frictional Horsepower The horsepower consumed in a vehicle for overcoming resistance. This includes wind resistance, tire rolling resistance, gear friction, and so forth.

Fulcrum The center or pivot point, most often used with levers.

Fusion The process of fusing together two atoms to produce energy.

Gear Ratio The speed ratio between two gears of different diameters and number of teeth.

Generators Devices that change mechanical energy into electrical energy.

Geothermal Energy Energy that is in the ground, in the form of thermal energy, produced from radioactive decay of certain elements.

Governor A device placed on a gasoline or diesel engine used to control the amount of fuel or position of the throttle. The governor senses engine speed and, in turn, readjusts for correct throttle setting.

Guidance The part of a transportation device that is used to guide or give direction to a vehicle.

Gypsum A very common mineral, hydrated calcium sulfate, used to make plaster-type products and ornamental material, and is also used as a fertilizer.

Gyroscope A device that has a wheel mounted in a way that it is free to rotate in two axes perpendicular to itself and to each other.

Head The distance on a hydroelectric dam that the water will fall.

Heat Loss The total amount of heat that is lost in a residential dwelling per hour.

Heat Pump A device used to extract heat from water that is above 38°F or air that is above 10°F.

Heating Unit A quantity of heat equal to 100,000 Btu.

Horsepower A term used to indicate the amount of energy produced by an engine. Normally, one horsepower is the energy required to move 33,000 pounds one foot in one minute.

Hydroelectric A form of energy that uses falling water to create power in a turbine.

Hydrofoil A form of water craft that uses a set of winglike foils to cut through the water.

Hydronic A solution of water and antifreeze normally mixed in equal parts.

Hypoid Gear A gear that has curved teeth.

Infiltration The process of cold air entering a home or building through leaks.

Infrared Part of the visible spectrum of light near the red frequency.

Inhibit To prevent a process from occurring.

Input The part of a transportation system that includes the command or objective required.

Insolation Incident solar radiation measured as Btu per square foot per hour.

Insulator A material with five or more electrons in the outer orbit. Prevents electricity from flowing through a conductor.

Integrated Circuit A circuit board with many semiconductors forming a complex circuit.

Intercity Transportation between cities.

Intercity Bus Bus transportation within a city.

Intermodal Using two types of transportation modes to transport freight between two points. For example, train containers can be transported by rail or by truck.

Internal Combustion Combustion of air and fuel inside an engine.

Isotope An atom with an additional number of neutrons in the center or nucleus.

Jib The front sail on a sailboat.

Kilocalorie Equal to 1,000 calories, or 1,000 times the heat necessary to raise one gram one degree Celsius.

Kinetic Pertaining to motion; of or causing motion of an object.

LPG Liquid petroleum gas, or a hydrocarbon that can be either a liquid or a gas, depending upon the pressure placed on the liquid.

Langley A measure of the solar energy used for weather patterns over an average of one year.

Laser *Light amplification by stimulated emission of radiation.* A laser is a highly intense beam of light that produces very high temperatures.

Latent Heat Heat that is present but not visible or noticeable in temperature change.

Lean Mixture Too much air and not enough fuel for combustion in a heat engine.

Levitate To raise or cause to raise on a cushion of air by magnetism.

Locks A system in a river or narrow waterway that is used to raise or lower ships from one level of water to another.

Low-grade Heat Heat produced from solar collectors for residential use, normally between 80 and 250 degrees Fahrenheit.

Magneto Ignition An ignition system that uses a set of magnets in a flywheel to produce the necessary voltage in the primary circuit.

Manned Space Flight A space flight and spacecraft that has a person or persons aboard for control and scientific research. There are also unmanned space flights as well.

Mass Transportation Technology used to transport large numbers of people from one location to another.

Mechanical Converter A machine used to change the energy in fuel into mechanical power. Examples include engines and boilers, among others.

Median The middle number. In terms of degree days, the middle of the high and low temperatures for a day.

Megawatt A unit of electrical power. One megawatt is equal to 1,000,000 watts.

Mesosphere The region of the earth's atmosphere that extends from 22 miles to about 50 miles from the surface of the earth.

Micrometer A small measuring tool used to measure dimensions of various objects in increments of .001 inch.

Microprocessor A series of circuits using semiconductors and integrated circuits for computer applications. Microprocessors are capable of sensing various inputs and feeding information out to control various circuits.

Miles/gallon/person A number to indicate the number of miles per gallon driven on a vehicle, times the average number of people in the vehicle.

Mission In the space program, each spacecraft has a purpose or mission. The mission of a certain type of program may be, for example, to place a person on the moon.

Moderator Any substance in a nuclear power plant used to slow down free neutrons. When the neutrons are slowed down, they have a better chance of hitting a uranium isotope.

Modes A custom or style of transportation.

Module A unit or section of a large part. Several modules are used in the Spacelab vehicle.

Molecular Of or pertaining to a substance that contains molecules.

Nautical Pertaining to ships, seas, and navigation.

Navigational The process of charting a course used to direct a vehicle. Navigational systems will be incorporated into automobiles to help plot and control a course of travel.

Neutron Neutrons are part of the nucleus of an atom, however, they have no charge.

Newton The metric measure of thrust as compared to pounds in the English system of measurement; 4.4 pounds equal 1 newton.

Node A centering point on a bus route where rapid transit buses enter a special express lane or expressway.

Nondepletable A classification of energy that will never run out. It will always renew itself.

Oil Injection A method used to mix the oil and gasoline on two-cycle engines. Oil, kept in a reservoir, is injected into the air and fuel mixture by a small pressure at the proper ratio.

Orbit The path of a spacecraft around the earth.

Output The part of a transportation system that is the final result of the process. *See Process.*

Overburden The dirt, rock and other material between the topsoil and a coal seam.

Parabolic The shape of a concentrating collector having a focal point for collecting intense heat.

Passenger-miles The movement of one passenger for a distance of one mile.

Passenger-miles/gallon A number to indicate the miles driven on a vehicle per gallon, times the average number of people in the vehicle. The same as miles/gallon/person.

Payback The length of time it takes for an initial solar investment to be paid back by the savings. The length of time in heating seasons that a capital improvement will be paid back by the savings.

Penstock A device on a hydroelectric dam that helps to direct the water to the turbine in the most efficient manner.

Perigee The lowest point of an orbit, or the point of an orbit closest to the earth's surface.

Phase-change The temperature point in which a solid changes to a liquid, or a liquid changes to a solid.

Piston A cylindrical object that slides in the cylinder of a heat engine.

Pitch The movement of an aircraft about its lateral axis. Also, the blade angle of a propeller.

Pitot Tube A cylindrical tube with an open end pointed into the airstream. It is used in measuring impact pressures, particularly in an airspeed indicator.

Plutonium A fabricated fuel made by having a free neutron hit a U-238 element, converting immediately to Pu-239.

Pneumatic A term that represents air being used as a fluid in fluid power circuits.

Political Constraints Constraints that are placed on technological developments because of policies, rules, regulations, and other factors.

Pollution Carbon monoxide, nitrogen oxide, sulfur dioxide, and hydrocarbons produced by burning of hydrocarbon fuels. Pollution usually is discharged into the air by manufacturing industries and transportation devices.

Port Induction A method used to allow air and fuel to enter the crankcase in a two-cycle engine. Ports or holes are opened and closed by the position of the piston in the engine.

Potential Related to energy, the ability to accomplish a required procedure.

Power A measure of work that is in the process of being done.

Power Coefficient The unit used to measure a wind turbine system's efficiency. A 100% power coefficient will extract 59% of the total wind energy.

Primary Loop The water loop in a nuclear reactor that is radioactive and comes in contact with the core and control rods.

Process The part of a transportation system that changes various resources to another form, product, or desired result.

Propellant The fuel used in a rocket.

Propeller A device on the back of a boat that has blades used to propel the boat forward or backward. A device on the engine drive shaft used for propelling an aircraft. The propeller has blades that, when rotated, produce a thrust approximately perpendicular to its rotation.

Propulsion The part of a transportation device that is used to produce the power.

Proton The positive charge in the nucleus of an atom.

R Value The resistance to heat flow through a material.

Radiation The emission and diffusion of rays of heat and light from the sun.

Random Energy Energy that has been downgraded in its usefulness. Energy that is less dense.

Reciprocating An up-and-down or back-and-forth motion.

Reed Valve Valves used on a two-cycle engine to allow air and fuel to enter the crankcase area. Reed valves are made of small, thin pieces of spring metal that open and close from small vacuum and pressure pulses.

Reentry The process of a spacecraft as it returns from orbit, back through the atmosphere to the surface of the earth.

Refinery An industry that takes crude oil and natural gas and separates these hydrocarbons into many types of products.

Regenerator A device on a gas turbine used to take the heat of exhaust and direct it into the intake of the engine.

Rejected Energy Total energy lost due to entropy.

Rem A term used to measure the dosages of radiation on a human.

Rich Mixture Too much fuel and not enough air for combustion in a heat engine.

Ridership A term used to indicate the average number of people who ride in a vehicle.

Rocket The propulsion system needed for placing a spacecraft into orbit above the earth.

Rudder A movable control surface usually attached to a vertical stabilizer. The rudder is used to guide the aircraft in a horizontal plane.

SAE The Society of Automotive Engineers, a group that tests and rates different chemicals and so forth.

Satellite A celestial body that revolves around a planet. A man-made object sent into orbit as a weather, communciation, and/or navigational aid.

Scavenging The process of removing gases from the combustion area normally used in a two-cycle engine.

Scenario A picture of a set of events envisioned in the future.

Scrubber The component in a power plant that scrubs out the acid in the exhaust. Quite often, a scrubber forces the exhaust gases to flow through and around an alkaline solution such as lime. This has a tendency to reduce the sulfur from the exhaust.

Sea Kelp A form of plant found in the sea that grows rapidly each day.

Secondary Combustion A combustion chamber in a wood-burning stove used to burn all of the vapors and gases given off during combustion.

Secondary Loop The water loop in a nuclear reactor that is not radioactive and comes in contact with the turbine blades.

Seismograph The result plotted on a graph when a shock wave is sent into the ground and bounced back by nonpermeable rock. A seismograph is used for oil and natural gas exploration.

Semiconductor A material that has exactly four electrons in its outer orbit. A semiconductor can be either a good insulator or a good conductor, depending upon how it is used.

Sensible Heat Heat that is present and observable as a temperature rises.

Setback Thermostat A thermostat that has either mechanical or electrical components to automatic-

ally set back the temperature of the building for a specific length of time.

Sequential A regular sequence of parts. In reference to a boat hull, a series of ribs on the bottom of a hull to aid in its planing and stability characteristics.

Sill The horizontal part that acts as a base for a window or door.

Solar Constant A measure of the solar energy at the outer edge of the atmosphere.

Solenoid A device in a starting system that controls an electrical circuit. Usually, electricity is used to move a plunger back and forth. The action of the plunger opens and closes another circuit for control.

Sonar Of or pertaining to sound. A device used to measure the depth of water by sending out a sound echo and measuring the time it takes to bounce back and return.

Stall A condition of flight caused by an excessive angle of attack. During a stall the air that passes over and under the wings stops, providing insufficient lift to hold the aircraft aloft.

Stator A part in a torque converter that is stationary or not moving.

Strata Referred to as beds of coal; the same as a seam or plate of coal underground.

Stratosphere Part of the earth's atmosphere that is between 7 and 22 miles from the surface of the earth.

Subway A rail or train transit system that runs under the surface of the ground.

Superconductivity All materials typically have resistance to electrical flow. Superconductivity means having no resistance to electrical flow.

Superinsulated Home A home that has extremely high R values in the walls and ceilings and is extremely tight, with half the air changing in the house per hour.

Supply In reference to energy, supply is considered to be the resources that feed energy into our society.

Support Technology The part of a transportation system that is used to process the passengers and goods to and from the vehicle.

Suspension The part of a transportation device that is used to suspend or hold the vehicle.

Swash Plate An angular plate attached to the bottom of the four pistons on a Stirling engine. Its purpose is to change the reciprocating motion of the pistons into rotary motion.

Synthetic Compounds made in a laboratory by combining together several chemicals. A manufactured material that does not occur naturally and is used in engines and other devices to provide improved characteristics of strength, heat transfer, and weight.

Tacking A process when sailing where the boat sails against the wind, while moving in a criss-cross direction.

Taconite A low-grade form of iron ore, found in the Great Lakes regions as a hard rock.

TDC Top dead center of the power stroke on a heat engine.

Technological Impact The social and environmental advantages and disadvantages of using a specific technology as related to its impact on humans.

Technostructure A structure of society that has many technologies that are dependent on and interrelated with one another.

Terrestrial Land forms of transportation.

Theory of Relativity A theory that suggests that mass can be made into energy and energy into mass. In a nuclear power plant, a small amount of uranium is converted into a large amount of energy.

Therm A unit of measure of natural gas. One therm is equal to about 100,000 Btu and 100 cubic feet of natural gas.

Thermal Mass The amount of mass placed in a solar home, used to hold thermal energy for storage.

Thermosphere The region of the earth's atmosphere that extends from about 50 miles to 200 or 300 miles from the surface of the earth.

Threshold The rubber seal on the walk-through part of a door.

Thrust To push with force in a certain direction. Forward thrust is created by the motion of a jet of water being pushed backward or the forward force on an airplane in the air provided by the engine.

Timing The process of identifying when air, fuel and ignition occur in a heat engine in relation to the position of the crankshaft.

Tip Speed Ratio The ratio of the tip of a wind turbine in relation to the wind speed.

Ton-mile/gallon A unit of measure to indicate the amount of energy in one gallon needed to move one ton of weight one mile.

Ton-miles The movement of one ton of freight for a distance of one mile.

Torque A twisting force.

Transbay A tube used under water to transport trains or other rail transportation systems. The BART system in San Francisco uses a transbay.

Transistor A semiconductor device used in circuits to turn on or off a second circuit; also used to amplify an electrical symbol.

Transportation Technology Any technology that is used to transport or move people and goods within a society.

Trophosphere The region of the atmosphere that is closest to the earth.

Trough A channel shaped or long narrow tube used in a concentrating collector.

Turbine A device used in a hydroelectric power station to change falling water energy to torque. A component on a gas turbine that extracts the energy in hot gases to be used for rotational forces. The part in a hydraulic coupling or torque converter that extracts the pressurized fluid to be used as the output.

Turbocharger A device used on many gasoline and diesel engines to increase power. Exhaust gas energy is used to turn a turbine, which forces more air into the intake for increased power.

Two-cycle Engine A form of piston engine that has two strokes for each power pulse of the piston. Normally, oil must be added to the gasoline (fuel) to obtain proper lubrication of the engine parts.

U Value The coefficient of R value or 1/R.

UMTA Urban Mass Transportation Administration.

Unit Train A train that carries only one product, such as coal. Unit trains are much more efficient and cost effective than trains that carry a variety of products.

Uranium A fuel found naturally in the earth used in a nuclear power plant.

Valence Ring The outermost orbit of electrons in an atom.

Vessel A term used to indicate a type of boat or craft afloat on water.

Viscosity A measure of the thickness of a liquid. The higher the viscosity, the thicker the liquid.

VMT Vehicle miles of travel, or a number used to measure the total miles driven by all vehicles in a particular area or population center.

Voltage Drop The voltage that is lost as electricity flows through a load or resistor.

Vortex Fluid flow involving rotation about an axis such as a whirlpool.

Vortices Circular patterns of air created by the movement of an airfoil through the air. As an airfoil moves through the air, the high pressure on the bottom and the lower pressure on top tends to roll up into rapidly rotating circles or vortices. The vortices created depend upon the wind, loading, gross weight, and speed of the aircraft.

Waste Heat Recovery The process of recovering wasted heat in any energy process and using this heat for other needs.

Waste Management The process of managing the wasted and spent fuel and other radiation hazards given off by a nuclear power plant.

Weightlessness A condition in space when the gravitational forces are equal to the centrifugal forces in orbit around the earth.

Wing An airfoil whose major function is to provide lift.

Yaw The motion about a vertical axis on a wind turbine.

Yellow Cake Blocks of uranium that are 70 to 90% uranium.

Zenith The angle the sun makes with the horizon when facing south.

INDEX